18th Conference on Computational Natural Language Learning

(CoNLL 2014)

Held in Conjunction with ACL 2014

Baltimore, Maryland, USA
26 – 27 June 2014

ISBN: 978-1-63439-230-3

Printed from e-media with permission by:

Curran Associates, Inc.
57 Morehouse Lane
Red Hook, NY 12571

proceedings.com

Some format issues inherent in the e-media version may also appear in this print version.

Printed by Curran Associates, Inc. (2014)

Association for Computational Linguistics
209 N. Eighth Street
Stroudsburg, Pennsylvania 18360

Phone: 1-570-476-8006
Fax: 1-570-476-0860

acl@aclweb.org

Additional copies of this publication are available from:

Curran Associates, Inc.
57 Morehouse Lane
Red Hook, NY 12571 USA
Phone: 845-758-0400
Fax: 845-758-2634
Email: curran@proceedings.com
Web: www.proceedings.com

Preface

The Conference on Computational Natural Language Learning (CoNLL) is an annual meeting organized by SIGNLL, the ACL special interest group on natural language learning. CoNLL-2014 is the eighteenth meeting in this series and will be held in Baltimore, Maryland, USA on June 26-27, 2014, in conjunction with ACL-2014.

In the main session of CoNLL, we invited papers on all aspects of computational approaches to natural language learning, as well as on machine reading, the special topic of interest this year. We received 90 submissions, of which 7 were eventually withdrawn, and accepted 20 of the remaining 83 papers. The final version of each accepted paper was allowed nine content pages plus two pages with only bibliographic references.

As in previous years, CoNLL-2014 hosts a high-profile NLP shared task, Grammatical Error Correction, a continuation of the shared task in 2013. Papers of the shared task are collected in a companion volume of the CoNLL-2014 proceedings.

Similar to the arrangement in last year, each accepted paper in CoNLL-2014 will be given an 18 minute oral presentation slot, as well as a poster. There will be a poster session in the afternoon of each day, consisting of papers presented orally earlier on the same day. The shared task posters will also participate in the same poster session on Day 1.

We thank all of the authors who submitted their work to CoNLL-2014, as well as the program committee for helping us select from among the many strong submissions. We are also grateful to our invited speakers, Morten Christiansen and Tom Mitchell, who graciously agreed to give talks at CoNLL. Special thanks to the best paper award committee members, Walter Daelemans, Joakim Nivre and Dan Roth, who helped choose the best paper winner. Also thanks to Xavier Carreras and Alexander Clark, for their valuable advice, to the SIGNLL information officer, Erik Tjong Kim Sang, for publicity and to Ben Verhoeven for maintaining the CoNLL Web site. We also appreciate the additional help we received from the ACL program chairs, workshop chairs, and publication chairs.

Finally, many thanks to Microsoft Research and Google for sponsoring CoNLL-2014.

We hope you enjoy the conference!

Roser Morante and Scott Wen-tau Yih

CoNLL 2014 Conference Chairs

Conference Co-chairs:

Roser Morante (University of Antwerp, Belgium)
Scott Wen-tau Yih (Microsoft Research, United States)

Program Committee:

Steven Abney (Univ of Michigan, United States), Eneko Agirre (University of the Basque Country, Spain), Afra Alishahi (Tilburg University, Netherlands), Yoav Artzi (University of Washington, United States), Marco Baroni (University of Trento, Italy), Chris Brew (Nuance Communications, United States), Sabine Buchholz (SynapseWork Ltd, United Kingdom), Xavier Carreras (Universitat Politecnica de Catalunya, Spain), Asli Celikyilmaz (Microsoft, United States), Daniel Cer (Google, United States), Ming-Wei Chang (Microsoft Research, United States), Kai-Wei Chang (University of Illinois, United States), Colin Cherry (NRC, Canada), Alexander Clark (King's College London, United Kingdom), Shay B. Cohen (University of Edinburgh, United Kingdom), Trevor Cohn (University of Melbourne, Australia), Mark Craven (University of Wisconsin, United States), Aron Culotta (Illinois Institute of Technology, United States), Walter Daelemans (University of Antwerp, CLiPS, Belgium), Dipanjan Das (Google Inc., United States), Doug Downey (Northwestern University, United States), Mark Dras (Macquarie University, Australia), Mark Dredze (Johns Hopkins University, United States), Kevin Duh (Nara Institute of Science and Technology, Japan), Chris Dyer (Carnegie Mellon University, United States), Jacob Eisenstein (Georgia Institute of Technology, United States), Bob Frank (Yale University, United States), Dayne Freitag (SRI International, United States), Michel Galley (Microsoft Research, United States), Michael Gamon (Microsoft Research, United States), Kevin Gimpel (Toyota Technological Institute at Chicago, United States), Joao Graca (Inesc-Id, Portugal), Hannaneh Hajishirzi (University of Washington, United States), Michael Heilman (Educational Testing Service, United States), James Henderson (Xerox Research Centre Europe, France), Iris Hendrickx (Center for Language Studies, Radboud University Nijmegen, Netherlands), Julia Hockenmaier (University of Illinois Urbana-Champaign, United States), Rebecca Hwa (University of Pittsburgh, United States), Richard Johansson (University of Gothenburg, Sweden), Mike Kestemont (University of Antwerp, Belgium), Alexandre Klementiev (Saarland University, Germany), Philipp Koehn (University of Edinburgh, United Kingdom), Alexander Koller (University of Potsdam, Germany), Mirella Lapata (School of Informatics, University of Edinburgh, United Kingdom), Adam Lopez (Johns Hopkins University, United States), Annie Louis (University of Edinburgh, United Kingdom), Erwin Marsi (Norwegian University of Science and Technology (NTNU), Norway), David Martinez (NICTA, Australia), André F. T. Martins (Priberam, Instituto de Telecomunicacoes, Portugal), Yuji Matsumoto (Nara Institute of Science and Technology, Japan), David McClosky (IBM Research, United States), Ryan McDonald (Google, United States), Margaret Mitchell (Microsoft Research, United States), Yusuke Miyao (National Instutite of Informatics, Japan), Robert Moore (Google, United States), Alessandro Moschitti (Qatar Computing Research Institute, Qatar), Lluís Màrquez (Qatar Computing Research Institute, Qatar), Ani Nenkova (University of Pennsylvania, United States), Vincent Ng (University of Texas at Dallas, United States), Joakim Nivre (Uppsala University, Sweden), Naoaki Okazaki (Tohoku University, Japan), Miles Osborne (Edinburgh, United Kingdom), Sebastian Padó (Heidelberg University, Germany), Hoifung Poon (Microsoft Research, United States), Jonathon Read (School of Computing, Teesside University, United Kingdom), Sebastian Riedel (UCL, United Kingdom), Alan Ritter (Carnegie Mellon University, United States), Dan Roth (University of Illinois, United States), Josef Ruppenhofer (Hildesheim University, Germany), Rajhans Samdani (Google Research, United States), Anoop Sarkar (Simon Fraser University, Canada), Nathan Schneider (Carnegie Mellon University, United States), Sabine Schulte im Walde (University of Stuttgart, Germany), Avirup Sil (Temple University, United States), Khalil Sima'an (ILLC, University of Amsterdam, Netherlands), Kevin Small (Amazon, United States), Valentin Spitkovsky (Stanford University and Google Inc., United States), Caroline Sporleder (Trier University, Germany), Vivek Srikumar (Stanford University, United States), Mark Steedman (University of Edinburgh, United Kingdom), Ivan Titov (University of Amsterdam, Netherlands), Peter Turney (National Research Council Canada, Canada), Antal van den Bosch (Radboud University Nijmegen, Netherlands), Erik Velldal (University of Oslo, Norway), Mathias Verbeke (KU Leuven, Belgium), Mengqiu Wang (Stanford University, United States), Michael Wiegand (Saarland University, Germany), Luke Zettlemoyer (University of Washington, United States)

Invited Speakers:

Morten H. Christiansen (Cornell University, USA; Haskins Laboratories, USA; University of Southern Denmark, Denmark)
Tom Mitchell (Carnegie Mellon University, USA)

Table of Contents

Conference Program

Thursday June 26 2014

(9:00 AM - 10:30 AM) Session 1

Opening remarks

What's in a p-value in NLP?
Anders Søgaard, Anders Johannsen, Barbara Plank, Dirk Hovy and Héctor Martínez Alonso

Domain-Specific Image Captioning
Rebecca Mason and Eugene Charniak

Reconstructing Native Language Typology from Foreign Language Usage
Yevgeni Berzak, Roi Reichart and Boris Katz

Automatic Transliteration of Romanized Dialectal Arabic
Mohamed Al-Badrashiny, Ramy Eskander, Nizar Habash and Owen Rambow

(10:30 AM - 11:00 AM) Coffee break

(11:00 PM - 12:30 PM) Session 2: Shared Task

(12:30 AM - 2:00 PM) Lunch break

(2:00 PM - 3:30 PM) Session 3

Learning to Rank Answer Candidates for Automatic Resolution of Crossword Puzzles
Gianni Barlacchi, Massimo Nicosia and Alessandro Moschitti

Inducing Neural Models of Script Knowledge
Ashutosh Modi and Ivan Titov

Grounding Language with Points and Paths in Continuous Spaces
Jacob Andreas and Dan Klein

Looking for hyponyms in vector space
Marek Rei and Ted Briscoe

Lexicon Infused Phrase Embeddings for Named Entity Resolution
Alexandre Passos, Vineet Kumar and Andrew McCallum

(3:30 PM - 5:00 PM) Poster session 1

(5:00 PM - 6:00 PM) Keynote 1: Morten H. Christiansen

Friday June 27 2014

(8:35 AM - 9:35 AM) Keynote 2: Tom Mitchell

(9:35 AM - 10:30 AM) Session 4

Focused Entailment Graphs for Open IE Propositions
Omer Levy, Ido Dagan and Jacob Goldberger

Improved Pattern Learning for Bootstrapped Entity Extraction
Sonal Gupta and Christopher Manning

Towards Temporal Scoping of Relational Facts based on Wikipedia Data
Avirup Sil and Silviu-Petru Cucerzan

(10:30 AM - 11:00 AM) Coffee break

(11:00 AM - 12:30 AM) Session 5

Distributed Word Representation Learning for Cross-Lingual Dependency Parsing
Min Xiao and Yuhong Guo

Treebank Translation for Cross-Lingual Parser Induction
Jörg Tiedemann, Željko Agić and Joakim Nivre

Weakly-Supervised Bayesian Learning of a CCG Supertagger
Dan Garrette, Chris Dyer, Jason Baldridge and Noah A. Smith

Factored Markov Translation with Robust Modeling
Yang Feng, Trevor Cohn and Xinkai Du

Hallucinating Phrase Translations for Low Resource MT
Ann Irvine and Chris Callison-Burch

(12:30 AM - 2:00 PM) Lunch break

(2:00 PM - 3:30 PM) Session 6

Linguistic Regularities in Sparse and Explicit Word Representations
Omer Levy and Yoav Goldberg

Probabilistic Modeling of Joint-context in Distributional Similarity
Oren Melamud, Ido Dagan, Jacob Goldberger, Idan Szpektor and Deniz Yuret

A Rudimentary Lexicon and Semantics Help Bootstrap Phoneme Acquisition
Abdellah Fourtassi and Emmanuel Dupoux

Best Paper Award announcement and bussiness meeting

(3:30 PM - 5:00 PM) Poster session 2

What's in a p-value in NLP?

Anders Søgaard, Anders Johannsen, Barbara Plank, Dirk Hovy and Hector Martinez
Center for Language Technology
University of Copenhagen
soegaard@hum.ku.dk

Abstract

In NLP, we need to document that our proposed methods perform *significantly* better with respect to standard metrics than previous approaches, typically by reporting p-values obtained by rank- or randomization-based tests. We show that significance results following current research standards are unreliable and, in addition, very sensitive to sample size, covariates such as sentence length, as well as to the existence of multiple metrics. We estimate that under the assumption of perfect metrics and unbiased data, we need a significance cut-off at $\sim$0.0025 to reduce the risk of false positive results to $<5\%$. Since in practice we often have considerable selection bias and poor metrics, this, however, will not do alone.

1 Introduction

In NLP, we try to improve upon state of the art language technologies, guided by experience and intuition, as well as error analysis from previous experiments, and research findings often consist in system comparisons showing that System A is better than System B.

Effect size, i.e., one system's improvements over another, can be seen as a random variable. If the random variable follows a known distribution, e.g., a normal distribution, we can use parametric tests to estimate whether System A is better than System B. If it follows a normal distribution, we can use Student's t-test, for example. Effect sizes in NLP are generally not normally distributed or follow any of the other well-studied distributions (Yeh, 2000; Søgaard, 2013). The standard significance testing methods in NLP are therefore rank- or randomization-based non-parametric tests (Yeh, 2000; Riezler and Maxwell, 2005; Berg-Kirkpatrick et al., 2012). Specifically, most system comparisons across words, sentences or documents use bootstrap tests (Efron and Tibshirani, 1993) or approximate randomization (Noreen, 1989), while studies that compare performance across data sets use rank-based tests such as Wilcoxon's test.

The question we wish to address here is: how likely is a research finding in NLP to be *false*? Naively, we would expect all reported findings to be true, but significance tests have their weaknesses, and sometimes researchers are forced to violate test assumptions and basic statistical methodology, e.g., when there is no *one* established metric, when we can't run our models on full-length sentences, or when data is biased. For example, one such well-known bias from the tagging and parsing literature is what we may refer to as the WSJ FALLACY. This is the false belief that performance on the test section of the Wall Street Journal (WSJ) part of the English Penn treebank is representative for performance on other texts in English. In other words, it is the belief that our samples are always representative. However, (the unawareness of) selection bias is not the only reason research findings in NLP may be false.

In this paper, we critically examine significance results in NLP by simulations, as well as running a series of experiments comparing state-of-the-art POS taggers, dependency parsers, and NER systems, focusing on the sensitivity of p-values to various factors.

Specifically, we address three important factors:

Sample size. When system A is reported to be better than system B, this may not hold across domains (cf. WSJ FALLACY). More importantly, though, it may not even hold on a sub-sample of the test data, or if we added more data points to the test set. Below, we show that in 6/10 of our POS tagger evaluations, significant effects become insignificant by (randomly) adding *more* test data.

Proceedings of the Eighteenth Conference on Computational Language Learning, pages 1–10,
Baltimore, Maryland USA, June 26-27 2014.

Covariates. Sometimes we may bin our results by variables that are actually predictive of the outcome (covariates) (Simmons et al., 2011). In some subfields of NLP, such as machine translation or (unsupervised) syntactic parsing, for example, it is common to report results that only hold for sentences up to some length. If a system A is reported to be better than a system B on sentences up to some length, A need not be better than B, neither for a different length nor in general, since sentence length may actually be predictive of A being better than B.

Multiple metrics. In several subfields of NLP, we have various evaluation metrics. However, if a system A is reported to be better than a system B with respect to some metric M_1, it need not be better with respect to some other metric M_2. We show that even in POS tagging it is sometimes the case that results are significant with respect to one metric, but not with respect to others.

While these caveats should ideally be avoided by reporting significance over varying sample sizes and multiple metrics, some of these effects also stem from the p-value cut-off chosen in the NLP literature. In some fields, p-values are required to be much smaller, e.g., in physics, where the 5 σ criterion is used, and maybe we should also be more conservative in NLP?

We address this question by a simulation of the interaction of type 1 and type 2 error in NLP and arrive at an estimate that more than half of research findings in NLP with $p < 0.05$ are likely to be false, even with a valid metric and in the absence of selection bias. From the same simulations, we propose a new cut-off level at 0.0025 or smaller for cases where the metric can be assumed to be valid, and where there is no selection bias.[1] We briefly discuss what to do in case of selection bias or imperfect metrics.

Note that we do not discuss false discovery rate control or family wise error rate procedures here. While testing with different sample sizes could be be considered multiple hypothesis testing, as pointed out by one of our anonymous reviewers, NLP results should be robust across sample sizes. Note that the $p < 0.0025$ cut-off level corresponds to a Bonferroni correction for a family of $m = 20$ hypotheses.

[1]In many fields, including NLP, it has become good practice to report *actual* p-values, but we still need to understand how significance levels relate to the probability that research findings are false, to interpret such values. The fact that we propose a new cut-off level for the ideal case with perfect metrics and no bias does not mean that we do not recommend reporting actual p-values.

Our contributions

Several authors have discussed significance testing in NLP before us (Yeh, 2000; Riezler and Maxwell, 2005; Berg-Kirkpatrick et al., 2012), but while our discussion touches on many of the same topics, this paper is to the best of our knowledge the first to:

a) show experimentally *how* sensitive p-values are to sample size, i.e., that in standard NLP experiments, significant effects may actually disappear by adding *more* data.

b) show experimentally that multiple metrics and the use of covariates in evaluation increase the probability of positive test results.

c) show that even under the assumption of perfect metrics and unbiased data, as well as our estimates of type 1 and 2 error in NLP, you need at least $p < 0.0025$ to reduce the probability of a research finding being false to be $< 5\%$.

2 Significance testing in NLP

Most NLP metric for comparing system outputs can be shown to be non-normally distributed (Søgaard, 2013) and hence, we generally cannot use statistical tests that rely on such an assumption, e.g., Student's t-test. One alternative to such tests are non-parametric rank-based tests such as Wilcoxon's test. Rank-based tests are sometimes used in NLP, and especially when the number of observations is low, e.g., when evaluating performance across data sets, such tests seem to be the right choice (Demsar, 2006; Søgaard, 2013). The draw-back of rank-based tests is their relatively weak statistical power. When we reduce scores to ranks, we throw away information, and rank-based tests are therefore relatively conservative, potentially leading to high type 2 error rate (β, i.e., the number of false negatives over trials). An alternative, however, are randomization-based tests such as the *bootstrap* test (Efron and Tibshirani, 1993) and *approximate randomization* (Noreen, 1989), which are the *de facto* standards in NLP. In this paper, we follow Berg-Kirkpatrick et al. (2012) in focusing on the bootstrap test. The bootstrap test is non-parametric and stronger than rank-based testing, i.e., introduces fewer type 2 errors. For small samples, however, it does so at the expense of a higher type 1 error (α, i.e., the number of false positives). The reason for this is that for the bootstrap test to work, the original sample has to capture most of the variation in the population. If the sample is very small, though, this is likely *not* the case. Consequently, with small sample sizes, there is a risk that the calculated p-value will be artificially low—simply because the bootstrap samples are too similar. In our experiments below, we make sure only to use bootstrap when sample size is > 200, unless otherwise stated. In our experiments, we average across 3 runs for POS and NER and 10 runs for dependency parsing.

DOMAIN	#WORDS	TASKS POS	Dep.	NER
CoNLL 2007				
Bio	4k	•		
Chem	5k	•		
SWITCHBOARD 4				
Spoken	162k	•		
ENGLISH WEB TREEBANK				
Answers	29k	•	•	
Emails	28k	•	•	
Newsgrs	21k	•	•	
Reviews	28k	•	•	
Weblogs	20k	•	•	
WSJ	40k	•	•	
FOSTER				
Twitter	3k	•		
CoNLL 2003				
News	50k			•

Table 1: Evaluation data.

3 Experiments

Throughout the rest of the paper, we use four running examples: a synthetic toy example and three standard experimental NLP tasks, namely POS tagging, dependency parsing and NER. The toy example is supposed to illustrate the logic behind our reasoning and is not specific to NLP. It shows how likely we are to obtain a low p-value for the difference in means when sampling from exactly the same (Gaussian) distributions. For the NLP setups (2-4), we use off-the-shelf models or available runs, as described next.

3.1 Models and data

We use pre-trained models for POS tagging and dependency parsing. For NER, we use the output of the best performing systems from the CoNLL 2003 shared task. In all three NLP setups, we compare the outcome of pairs of systems. The data sets we use for each of the NLP tasks are listed in Table 1 (Nivre et al., 2007a; Foster et al., 2011; Tjong Kim Sang and De Meulder, 2003, LDC99T42; LDC2012T13).

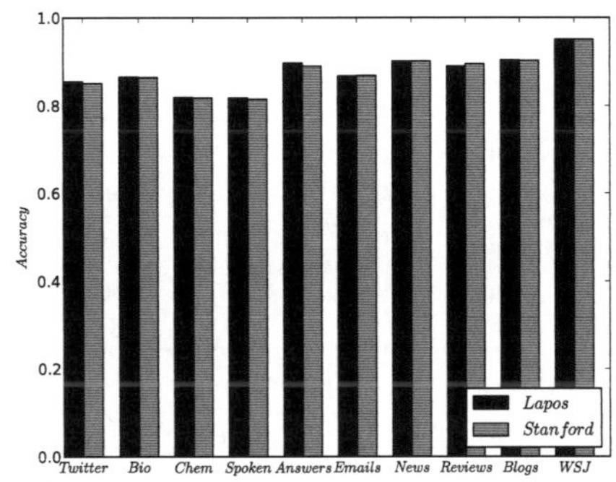

Figure 1: Accuracies of LAPOS VS. STANFORD across 10 data sets.

POS tagging. We compare the performance of two state-of-the-art newswire taggers across 10 evaluation data sets (see Table 1), namely the LAPOS tagger (Tsuruoka et al., 2011) and the STANFORD tagger (Toutanova et al., 2003), both trained on WSJ00–18. We use the publicly available pre-trained models from the associated websites.[2]

Dependency parsing. Here we compare the pre-trained linear SVM MaltParser model for English (Nivre et al., 2007b) to the compositional vector grammar model for the Stanford parser (Socher et al., 2013). For this task, we use the subset of the POS data sets that comes with Stanford-style syntactic dependencies (cf. Table 1), excluding the Twitter data set which we found too small to produce reliable results.

NER. We use the publicly available runs of the two best systems from the CoNLL 2003 shared task, namely FLORIAN (Florian et al., 2003) and CHIEU-NG (Chieu and Ng, 2003).[3]

3.2 Standard comparisons

POS tagging. Figure 1 shows that the LAPOS tagger is marginally better than STANFORD on macro-average, but it is also *significantly* better? If we use the bootstrap test over tagging accuracies, the difference between the two taggers is only significant ($p < 0.05$) in 3/10 cases (see Table 2), namely SPOKEN, ANSWERS and REVIEWS. In two of these cases, LAPOS is significantly better

[2] http://www.logos.ic.i.u-tokyo.ac.jp/~tsuruoka/lapos/ and http://nlp.stanford.edu/software/tagger.shtml

[3] http://www.cnts.ua.ac.be/conll2003/ner/

	TA (b)	UA (b)	SA (b)	SA(w)
Bio	0.3445	0.0430	0.3788	0.9270
Chem	0.3569	0.2566	0.4515	0.9941
Spoken	<0.001	<0.001	<0.001	<0.001
Answers	<0.001	0.0143	<0.001	<0.001
Emails	0.2020	<0.001	0.1622	0.0324
Newsgrs	0.3965	0.0210	0.1238	0.6602
Reviews	0.0020	0.0543	0.0585	0.0562
Weblogs	0.2480	0.0024	0.2435	0.9390
WSJ	0.4497	0.0024	0.2435	0.9390
Twitter	0.4497	0.0924	0.1111	0.7853

Table 2: POS tagging p-values across tagging accuracy (TA), accuracy for unseen words (UA) and sentence-level accuracy (SA) with bootstrap (b) and Wilcoxon (w) ($p < 0.05$ gray-shaded).

	LAS	UAS
Answers	0.020	<0.001
Emails	0.083	<0.001
Newsgroups	0.049	<0.001
Reviews	<0.001	<0.001
Weblogs	<0.001	<0.001
WSJ	<0.001	<0.001

Table 3: Parsing p-values (MALT-LIN VS. STANFORD-RNN) across LAS and UAS ($p < 0.05$ gray-shaded).

than STANFORD, but in one case it is the other way around. If we do a Wilcoxon test over the results on the 10 data sets, following the methodology in Demsar (2006) and Søgaard (2013), the difference, which is $\sim$0.12% on macro-average, is *not* significant ($p \sim 0.1394$). LAPOS is thus not significantly better than STANFORD across data sets, but as we have already seen, it is significantly better on some data sets. So if we allow ourselves to cherry-pick our data sets and report significance over word-level tagging accuracies, we can at least report significant improvements across a few data sets.

Dependency parsing. Using the bootstrap test over sentences, we get the p-values in Table 3. We see that differences are always significant wrt. UAS, and in most cases wrt. LAS.

NER. Here we use the macro-f_1 as our standard metric. FLORIAN is *not* significantly better than CHIEU-NG with $p < 0.05$ as our cut-off ($p \sim 0.15$). The two systems were also reported to have overlapping confidence intervals in the shared task.

3.3 p-values across metrics

In several NLP subfields, multiple metrics are in use. This happens in dependency parsing where multiple metrics (Schwartz et al., 2011; Tsarfaty et al., 2012) have been proposed in addition to unlabeled and labeled attachment scores, as well as exact matches. Perhaps more famously, in machine translation and summarization it is common practice to use multiple metrics, and there exists a considerable literature on that topic (Papineni et al., 2002; Lin, 2004; Banerjee and Lavie, 2005; Clark et al., 2011; Rankel et al., 2011). Even in POS tagging, some report tagging accuracies, tagging accuracies over unseen words, macro-averages over sentence-level accuracies, or number of exact matches.

The existence of several metrics is not in itself a problem, but if researchers can cherry-pick their favorite metric when reporting results, this increases the *a priori* chance of establishing significance. In POS tagging, most papers report significant improvements over tagging accuracy, but some report significant improvements over tagging accuracy of unknown words, e.g., Denis and Sagot (2009) and Umansky-Pesin et al. (2010). This corresponds to the situation in psychology where researchers cherry-pick between several dependent variables (Simmons et al., 2011), which also increases the chance of finding a significant correlation.

Toy example. We draw two times 100 values from identical $(0, 1)$-Gaussians 1000 times and calculate a t-test for two independent samples. This corresponds to testing the effect size between two systems on a 1000 randomly chosen test sets with $N = 100$. Since we are sampling from the same distribution, the chance of $p < \kappa$ should be smaller than κ. In our simulation, the empirical chance of obtaining $p < 0.01$ is .8%, and the chance of obtaining $p < 0.05$ is 4.8%, as expected. If we simulate a free choice between two metrics by introducing choice between a pair of samples and a distorted copy of that pair (inducing random noise at 10%), simulating the scenario where we have a perfect metric and a suboptimal metric, the chance of obtaining $p < 0.05$ is 10.0%. We see a significant correlation ($p < 0.0001$) between Pearson's ρ between the two metrics, and the p-value. The less the two metrics are correlated, the more likely we are to obtain $p < 0.05$. If we allow for a choice between two metrics, the chance of finding a significant difference increases considerably. If the two metrics are identical, but independent (introducing a free choice between two pairs of samples), we have

$P(A \vee B) = P(A) + P(B) - P(A)P(B)$, hence the chance of obtaining $p < 0.01$ is 1.9%, and the chance of obtaining $p < 0.05$ is 9.75%.

POS tagging. In our POS-tagging experiments, we saw a significant improvement in 3/10 cases following the standard evaluation methodology (see Table 2). If we allow for a choice between tagging accuracy and sentence-level accuracy, we see a significant improvement in 4/10 cases, i.e., for 4/10 data sets the effect is significance wrt. at least one metric. If we allow for a free choice between all three metrics (TA, UA, and SA), we observe significance in 9/10 cases. This way the existence of multiple metrics almost guarantees significant differences. Note that there are only two data sets (*Answers* and *Spoken*), where *all* metric differences appear significant.

Dependency parsing. While there are multiple metrics in dependency parsing (Schwartz et al., 2011; Tsarfaty et al., 2012), we focus on the two standard metrics: labeled (LAS) and unlabeled attachment score (UAS) (Buchholz and Marsi, 2006). If we just consider the results in Table 3, i.e., only the comparison of MALT-LIN vs. STANFORD-RNN, we observe significant improvements in all cases, if we allow for a free choice between metrics. Bod (2000) provides a good example of a parsing paper evaluating models using different metrics on different test sets. Chen et al. (2008), similarly, only report UAS.

NER. While macro-f_1 is fairly standard in NER, we do have several available multiple metrics, including the unlabeled f_1 score (collapsing all entity types), as well as the f_1 scores for each of the individual entity types (see Derczynski and Bontcheva (2014) for an example of only reporting f_1 for one entity type). With macro-f_1 and f_1 for the individual entity types, we observe that, while the average p-value for bootstrap tests over five runs is around 0.15, the average p-value with a free choice of metrics is 0.02. Hence, if we allow for a free choice of metrics, FLORIAN comes out significantly better than CHIEU-NG.

3.4 p-values across sample size

We now show that p-values are sensitive to sample size. While it is well-known that studies with low statistical power have a reduced chance of detecting true effects, studies with low statistical power are also more likely to introduce false positives (Button et al., 2013). This, combined with the fact that free choice between different sample sizes also increases the chance of false positives (Simmons et al., 2011), is a potential source of error in NLP.

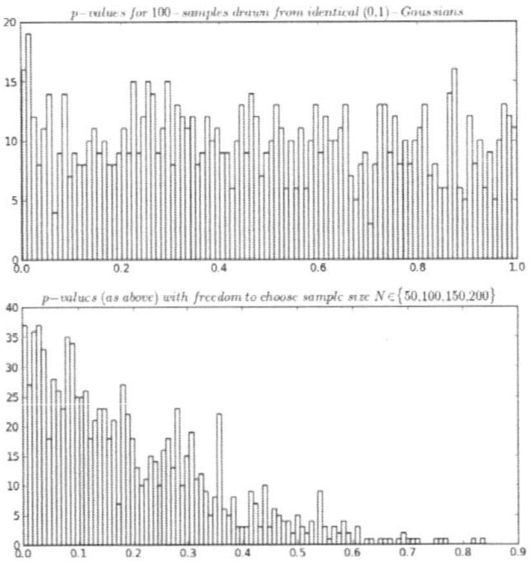

Figure 2: The distribution of p-values with (above) and without (below) multiple metrics.

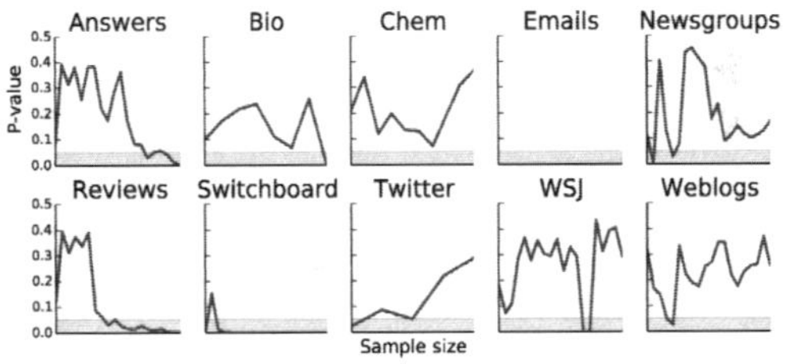

Figure 3: POS tagging p-values varying sample sizes ($p < 0.05$ shaded).

Toy example. The plot in Figure 2 shows the distribution of p-values across 1000 bootstrap tests (above), compared to the distribution of p-values with a free choice of four sample sizes. It is clear that the existence of multiple metrics makes the probability of a positive result much higher.

POS tagging. The same holds for POS tagging. We plot the p-values across various sample sizes in Figure 3. Note that even when we ignore the smallest sample size (500 words), where results may be rather unreliable, it still holds that for *Twitter*, *Answers*, *Newsgrs*, *Reviews*, *Weblogs* and *WSJ*, i.e., more than half of the data sets, a significant result ($p < 0.05$) becomes insignificant by *increasing* the sample size. This shows how unreliable significance results in NLP with cut-off $p < 0.05$ are.

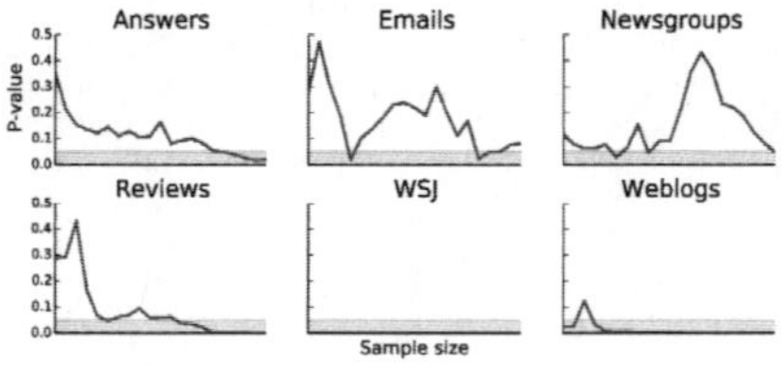

Figure 4: Parsing p-values varying sample sizes ($p < 0.05$ shaded)

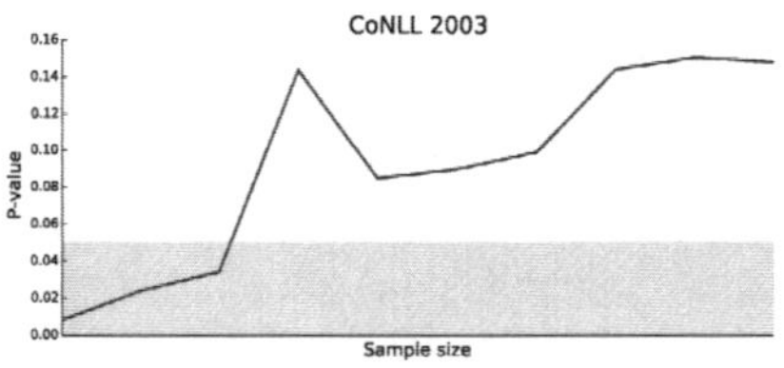

Figure 5: NER p-values varying sample sizes ($p < 0.05$ shaded)

Dependency parsing. We performed similar experiments with dependency parsers, seeing much the same picture. Our plots are presented in Figure 4. We see that while effect sizes are always significant wrt. UAS, LAS differences become significant when adding more data in 4/6 cases. An alternative experiment is to see how often a bootstrap test at a particular sample size comes out significant. The idea is to sample, say, 10% of the test data 100 times and report the ratio of positive results. We only present the results for MALT-LIN VS. STANFORD-RNN in Table 4, but the full set of results (including comparisons of more MaltParser and Stanford parser models) are made available at `http://lowlands.ku.dk`.

For MALT-LIN VS. STANFORD-RNN differences on the full *Emails* data set are consistently insignificant, but on small sample sizes we do get significant test results in more than 1/10 cases. We see the same picture with *Newsgrs* and *Reviews*. On *Weblogs* and *WSJ*, the differences on the full data sets are consistently significant, but here we see that the test is underpowered at small sample sizes. Note that we use bootstrap tests over sentences, so results with small samples may be somewhat unreliable. In sum, these experiments show how small sample sizes not only increase the chance of false negatives, but also the chance of false positives (Button et al., 2013).

NER. Our plots for NER are presented in Figure 5. Here, we see significance at small sample sizes, but the effect disappears with more data. This is an example of how underpowered studies may introduce false positives (Button et al., 2013).

3.5 p-values across covariates

Toy example. If we allow for a choice between two subsamples, using a covariate to single out a subset of the data, the chance of finding a significant difference increases. Even if we let the subset be a random 50-50 split, the chance of obtaining $p < 0.01$ becomes 2.7%, and the chance of obtaining $p < 0.05$ is 9.5%. If we allow for both a choice of dependent variables *and* a random covariate, the chance of obtaining $p < 0.01$ is 3.7%, and the chance of obtaining $p < 0.05$ is 16.2%. So identical Gaussian variables will appear significantly different in 1/6 cases, if our sample size is 100, and if we are allowed a choice between two identical, but independent dependent variables, and a choice between two subsamples provided by a random covariate.

POS We see from Figure 6 that p-values are also very sensitive to sentence length cut-offs. For instance, LAPOS is significantly ($p < 0.05$) better than STANFORD on sentences shorter than 16 words in EMAILS, but not on sentences shorter than 14 words. On the other hand, when longer sentences are included, e.g., up to 22 words, the effect no longer appears significant. On full sentence length, four differences seem significant, but if we allow ourselves to cherry-pick a maximum sentence length, we can observe significant differences in 8/10 cases.

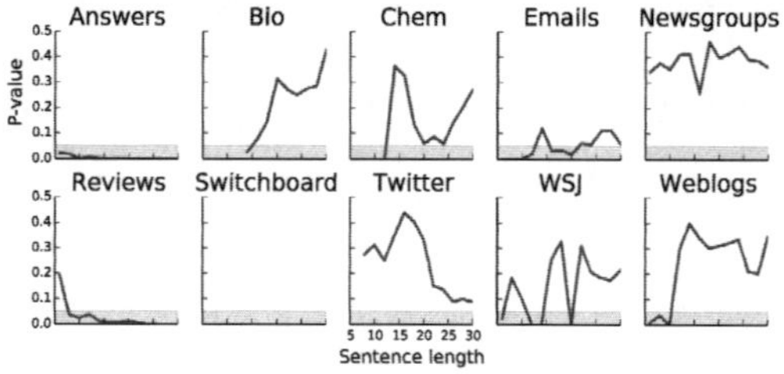

Figure 6: POS tagging p-values varying sentence length ($p < 0.05$ shaded)

We observe similar results in **Dependency parsing** and **NER** when varying sentence length, but do not include them here for space reasons. The results are available at `http://lowlands.ku.dk`. We also found that other covariates are used in evaluations of dependency parsers and NER systems. In dependency parsing, for example, parsers can either be evaluated

N	*Emails*		*Newsgrs*		*Reviews*		*Weblogs*		*WSJ*	
	LAS	UAS	LAS	UAS	LAS	UAS	LAS	UAS	LAS	UAS
10%	14 %	100 %	9 %	100 %	33%	100 %	42 %	99 %	28 %	75 %
25%	15 %	100 %	23 %	100 %	52%	100 %	68 %	100 %	27 %	98 %
50%	19 %	100 %	25 %	100 %	78%	100 %	100 %	100 %	60 %	100 %
75%	22 %	100 %	41 %	100 %	97%	100 %	100 %	100 %	80 %	100 %
100%	0 %	100 %	36 %	100 %	100%	100 %	100 %	100 %	100 %	100 %

Table 4: Ratio of positive results ($p < 0.05$) for MALT-LIN VS. STANFORD-RNN at sample sizes (N)

on naturally occurring text such as in our experiments or at tailored test suites, typically focusing on hard phenomena (Rimell et al., 2009). While such test suites are valuable resources, cf. Manning (2011), they do introduce free choices for researchers, increasing the *a priori* chance of positive results. In NER, it is not uncommon to leave out sentences *without* any entity types from evaluation data. This biases evaluation toward high recall systems, and the choice between including them or not increases chances of positive results.

4 How likely are NLP findings to be false?

The previous sections have demonstrated how many factors can contribute to reporting an erroneously significant result. Given those risks, it is natural to wonder how likely we are as a field to report false positives. This can be quantified by the positive predictive value (PPV), or probability that a research finding is true. PPV is defined as

$$\frac{(1-\beta)R}{R-\beta R+\alpha} \quad (1)$$

The PPV depends on the type 1 and 2 error rates (α and β) and the ratio of true relations over null relations in the field (R) (Ioannidis, 2005).

R. The likelihood that a research finding is true depends on the ratio of true relations over null relations in the field, usually denoted R (Ioannidis, 2005). Out of the systems that researchers in the field would test out (not rejecting them *a priori*), how many of them are better than the current state of the art? The a priori likelihood of a relation being true, i.e., a new system being better than state of the art, is $R/(R+1)$. Note that while the space of reasonably motivated methods may seem big to researchers in the field, there is often more than one method that is better than the current state of the art. Obviously, as the state of the art improves, R drops. On the other hand, if R becomes very low, researchers are likely to move on to new applications where R is higher.

The **type 1 error rate** (α) is also known as the false positive rate, or the likelihood to accept a non-significant result. Since our experiments are fully automated and deterministic, and precision usually high, the type 1 error rate is low in NLP. What is not always appreciated in the field is that this should lead us to expect true effects to be highly significant with very low p-values, much like in physics. The **type 2 error rate** (β) is the false negative rate, i.e., the likelihood that a true relation is never found. This factors into the recall of our experimental set-ups.

So what values should we use to estimate PPV? Our estimate for R (how often reasonable hypotheses lead to improvements over state of the art) is around 0.1. This is based on a sociological rather than an ontological argument. With $\alpha = 0.05$ and $R = 0.1$, researchers get positive results in $R+(1-R)\alpha$ cases, i.e., $\sim 1/7$ cases. If researchers needed to test more than 7 approaches to "hit the nail", they would never get to write papers. With $\alpha = 0.05$, and β set to 0.5, we find that the probability of a research finding being true – given there is *no* selection bias and with perfectly valid metrics – is just 50%:

$$\begin{aligned} PPV &= \frac{(1-\beta)R}{R-\beta R+\alpha} \\ &= \frac{0.5\times 0.1}{0.1-0.05+0.05} = \frac{0.05}{0.1} = 0.5 \end{aligned} \quad (2)$$

In other words, if researchers do a perfect experiment and report $p < 0.05$, the chance of that finding being true is the chance of seeing tail when flipping a coin. With $p < 0.01$, the chance is 5/6, i.e., the chance of not getting a 3 when rolling a die. Of course these parameters are somewhat arbitrary. Figure 7 shows PPV for various values of α.

In the experiments in Section 3, we consistently used the standard p-value cut-off of 0.05. However, our experiments have shown that significance results at this threshold are unreliable and very sensitive to the choice of sample size, covariates, or metrics. Based on the curves in Figure 7, we

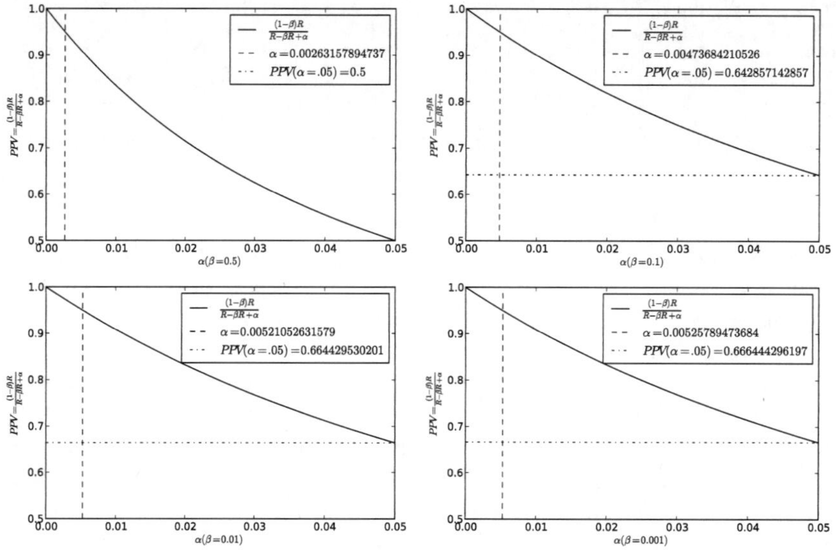

Figure 7: PPV for different α (horizontal line is PPV for $p = 0.05$, vertical line is α for PPV=0.95).

could propose a p-value cut-off at $p < 0.0025$. This is the cut-off that – in the absence of bias and with perfect metrics – gives us the level of confidence we expect as a research community, i.e., $PPV = 0.95$. Significance results would thus be more reliable and reduce type 1 error.

5 Discussion

Incidentally, the $p < 0.0025$ cut-off also leads to a 95% chance of seeing the same effect on held-out test data in Berg-Kirkpatrick et al. (2012) (see their Table 1, first row). The caveat is that this holds only in the absence of bias and with perfect metrics. In reality, though, our data sets are often severely biased (Berg-Kirkpatrick et al., 2012; Søgaard, 2013), and our metrics are far from perfect (Papineni et al., 2002; Lin, 2004; Banerjee and Lavie, 2005; Schwartz et al., 2011; Tsarfaty et al., 2012). Here, we discuss how to address these challenges.

Selection bias. The WSJ FALLACY (Section 1) has been widely discussed in the NLP literature (Blitzer et al., 2006; Daume III, 2007; Jiang and Zhai, 2007; Plank and van Noord, 2011). But if our test data is biased, how do we test whether System A performs better than System B in general? Søgaard (2013) suggests to predict significance across data sets. This only assumes that data sets are randomly chosen, e.g., *not* all from newswire corpora. This is also standard practice in the machine learning community (Demsar, 2006).

Poor metrics. For tasks such as POS tagging and dependency parsing, our metrics are suboptimal (Manning, 2011; Schwartz et al., 2011; Tsarfaty et al., 2012). System A and System B may perform equally well as measured by some metric, but contribute very differently to downstream tasks. Elming et al. (2013) show how parsers trained on different annotation schemes lead to very different downstream results. This suggests that being wrong with respect to a gold standard, e.g., choosing NP analysis over a "correct" DP analysis, may in some cases lead to better downstream performance. See the discussion in Manning (2011) for POS tagging. One simple approach to this problem is to report results across available metrics. If System A improves over System B wrt. most metrics, we obtain significance against the odds. POS taggers and dependency parsers should also be evaluated by their impact on downstream performance, but of course downstream tasks may also introduce multiple metrics.

6 Conclusion

In sum, we have shown that significance results with current research standards are unreliable, and we have provided a more adequate p-value cut-off under the assumption of perfect metrics and unbiased data. In the cases where these assumptions cannot be met, we suggest reporting significance results across datasets wrt. all available metrics.

Acknowledgements

We would like to thank the anonymous reviewers, as well as Jakob Elming, Matthias Gondan, and Natalie Schluter for invaluable comments and feedback. This research is funded by the ERC Starting Grant LOWLANDS No. 313695.

References

Satanjeev Banerjee and Alon Lavie. 2005. METEOR: an automatic metric for MT evaluation with improved correlation with human judgments. In *ACL Workshop on Intrinsic and Extrinsic Evaluation Measures for MT and/or Summarization*.

Taylor Berg-Kirkpatrick, David Burkett, and Dan Klein. 2012. An empirical investigation of statistical significance in nlp. In *EMNLP*.

John Blitzer, Ryan McDonald, and Fernando Pereira. 2006. Domain adaptation with structural correspondence learning. In *EMNLP*.

Rens Bod. 2000. Parsing with the shortest derivation. In *COLING*.

Sabine Buchholz and Erwin Marsi. 2006. CoNLL-X Shared Task on Multilingual Dependency Parsing. In *CoNLL*.

Katherine Button, John Ioannidis, Claire Mokrysz, Brian Nosek, Jonathan Flint, Emma Robinson, and Marcus Munafo. 2013. Power failure: why small sample size undermines the reliability of neuroscience. *Nature Reviews Neuroscience*, 14:365–376.

Wenliang Chen, Youzheng Wu, and Hitoshi Isahara. 2008. Learning Reliable Information for Dependency Parsing Adaptation. In *COLING*.

Hai Leong Chieu and Hwee Tou Ng. 2003. Named entity recognition with a maximum entropy approach. In *CoNLL*.

Jonathan H. Clark, Chris Dyer, Alon Lavie, and Noah A. Smith. 2011. Better hypothesis testing for statistical machine translation: controlling for optimizer instability. In *ACL*.

Hal Daume III. 2007. Frustratingly easy domain adaptation. In *ACL*.

Janez Demsar. 2006. Statistical comparisons of classifiers over multiple data sets. *Journal of Machine Learning Research*, 7:1–30.

Pascal Denis and Benoît Sagot. 2009. Coupling an annotated corpus and a morphosyntactic lexicon for state-of-the-art pos tagging with less human effort. In *PACLIC*.

Leon Derczynski and Kalina Bontcheva. 2014. Passive-aggressive sequence labeling with discriminative post-editing for recognising person entities in tweets. In *EACL*.

Bradley Efron and Robert Tibshirani. 1993. *An introduction to the bootstrap*. Chapman & Hall, Boca Raton, FL.

Jakob Elming, Anders Johannsen, Sigrid Klerke, Emanuele Lapponi, Hector Martinez Alonso, and Anders Søgaard. 2013. Down-stream effects of tree-to-dependency conversions. In *NAACL*.

Radu Florian, Abe Ittycheriah, Hongyan Jing, and Tong Zhang. 2003. Named entity recognition through classifier combination. In *CoNLL*.

Jennifer Foster, Ozlem Cetinoglu, Joachim Wagner, Josef Le Roux, Joakim Nivre, Deirde Hogan, and Josef van Genabith. 2011. From news to comments: Resources and benchmarks for parsing the language of Web 2.0. In *IJCNLP*.

John Ioannidis. 2005. Why most published research findings are false. *PLoS Medicine*, 2(8):696–701.

Jing Jiang and ChengXiang Zhai. 2007. Instance weighting for domain adaptation in NLP. In *ACL*.

Chin-Yew Lin. 2004. ROUGE: a package for automatic evaluation of summaries. In *WAS*.

Chris Manning. 2011. Part-of-speech tagging from 97% to 100%: Is it time for some linguistics? In *CICLing*.

Joakim Nivre, Johan Hall, Sandra Kübler, Ryan McDonald, Jens Nilsson, Sebastian Riedel, and Deniz Yuret. 2007a. The CoNLL 2007 Shared Task on Dependency Parsing. In *EMNLP-CoNLL*.

Joakim Nivre, Johan Hall, Jens Nilsson, Atanas Chanev, Gülsen Eryigit, Sandra Kübler, Svetoslav Marinov, and Erwin Marsi. 2007b. MaltParser: a language-independent system for data-driven dependency parsing. *Natural Language Engineering*, 13(2):95–135.

Eric Noreen. 1989. *Computer intensive methods for testing hypotheses*. Wiley.

Kishore Papineni, Salim Roukus, Todd Ward, and Wei-Jing Zhu. 2002. BLEU: a method for automatic evaluation of machine translation. In *ACL*, pages 311–318, Philadelphia, Pennsylvania.

Barbara Plank and Gertjan van Noord. 2011. Effective measures of domain similarity for parsing. In *ACL*.

Peter Rankel, John Conroy, Eric Slud, and Dianne O'Leary. 2011. Ranking human and machine summarization systems. In *EMNLP*.

Stefan Riezler and John Maxwell. 2005. On some pitfalls in automatic evaluation and significance testing for MT. In *ACL Workshop on Intrinsic and Extrinsic Evaluation Measures for Machine Translation and/or Summarization.*

Laura Rimell, Stephen Clark, and Mark Steedman. 2009. Unbounded dependency recovery for parser evaluation. In *EMNLP.*

Roy Schwartz, and Omri Abend, Roi Reichart, and Ari Rappoport. 2011. Neutralizing linguistically problematic annotations in unsupervised dependency parsing evaluation. In *ACL.*

Joseph Simmons, Leif Nelson, and Uri Simonsohn. 2011. False-positive psychology: undisclosed flexibility in data collection and analysis allows presenting anything as significant. *Psychological Science*, 22(11):1359–1366.

Richard Socher, John Bauer, Chris Manning, and Andrew Ng. 2013. Parsing with compositional vector grammars. In *ACL.*

Anders Søgaard. 2013. Estimating effect size across datasets. In *NAACL.*

Erik F Tjong Kim Sang and Fien De Meulder. 2003. Introduction to the conll-2003 shared task: Language-independent named entity recognition. In *In CoNLL.*

Kristina Toutanova, Dan Klein, Chris Manning, and Yoram Singer. 2003. Feature-rich part-of-speech tagging with a cyclic dependency network. In *NAACL.*

Reut Tsarfaty, Joakim Nivre, and Evelina Andersson. 2012. Cross-framework evaluation for statistical parsing. In *EACL.*

Yoshimasa Tsuruoka, Yusuke Miyao, and Jun'ichi Kazama. 2011. Learning with lookahead: can history-based models rival globally optimized models? In *CoNLL.*

Shulamit Umansky-Pesin, Roi Reichart, and Ari Rappoport. 2010. A multi-domain web-based algorithm for POS tagging of unknown words. In *COLING.*

Alexander Yeh. 2000. More accurate tests for the statistical significance of result differences. In *ACL.*

Domain-Specific Image Captioning

Rebecca Mason and **Eugene Charniak**
Brown Laboratory for Linguistic Information Processing (BLLIP)
Brown University, Providence, RI 02912
{rebecca,ec}@cs.brown.edu

Abstract

We present a data-driven framework for image caption generation which incorporates visual and textual features with varying degrees of spatial structure. We propose the task of domain-specific image captioning, where many relevant visual details cannot be captured by off-the-shelf general-domain entity detectors. We extract previously-written descriptions from a database and adapt them to new query images, using a joint visual and textual bag-of-words model to determine the correctness of individual words. We implement our model using a large, unlabeled dataset of women's shoes images and natural language descriptions (Berg et al., 2010). Using both automatic and human evaluations, we show that our captioning method effectively deletes inaccurate words from extracted captions while maintaining a high level of detail in the generated output.

1. Extract existing human-authored caption according to similarity of coarse visual features.

Query Image — Nearest-Neighbor

Nearest-neighbor caption: *This sporty sneaker clog keeps foot cool and comfortable and fully supported.*

2. Estimate correctness of extracted words using domain-specific joint model of text and visual bag-of-word features.

This sporty sneaker clog keeps foot cool and comfortable and fully supported.

3. Compress extracted caption to adapt its content while maintaining grammatical correctness.

Output: *This clog keeps foot comfortable and supported.*

1 Introduction

Broadly, the task of image captioning is: given a query image, generate a natural language description of the image's visual content. Both the image understanding and language generation components of this task are challenging open problems in their respective fields. A wide variety of approaches have been proposed in the literature, for both the specific task of caption generation as well as related problems in understanding images and text.

Typically, image understanding systems use supervised algorithms to detect visual entities and concepts in images. However, these typically require accurate hand-labeled training data, which is not available in most specific domains. Ideally, a domain-specific image captioning system would learn in a less supervised fashion, using captioned images found on the web.

This paper focuses on image caption generation for a specific domain – images of women's shoes, collected from online shopping websites. Our framework has three main components. We **extract** an existing description from a database of human-captions, by projecting query images into a multi-dimensional space where structurally similar images are near each other. We also train a **joint topic model** to discover the latent topics which generate both captions and images. We combine these two approaches using **sentence compression** to delete modifying details in the extracted caption which are not relevant to the query image.

Our captioning framework is inspired by several recent approaches at the intersection of Natural Language Processing and Computer Vision. Previous work such as Farhadi et al. (2010) and Ordonez et al. (2011) explore extractive methods for image captioning, but these rely on general-domain visual detection systems, and only gener-

Proceedings of the Eighteenth Conference on Computational Language Learning, pages 11–20,
Baltimore, Maryland USA, June 26-27 2014.

ate extractive captions. Other models learn correspondences between domain-specific images and natural language captions (Berg et al., 2010; Feng and Lapata, 2010b) but cannot generate descriptions for new images without the use of auxiliary text. Kuznetsova et al. (2013) propose a sentence compression model for editing image captions, but their compression objective is not conditioned on a query image, and their system also requires general-domain visual detections. This paper proposes an image captioning framework which extends these ideas and culminates in the first domain-specific image caption generation system.

More broadly, our goal for image caption generation is to work toward less supervised captioning methods which could be used to generate detailed and accurate descriptions for a variety of long-tail domains of captioned image data, such as in nature and medicine.

2 Related Work

Our framework for domain-specific image captioning consists of three main components: extractive caption generation, image understanding through topic modeling, and sentence compression. [1] These methods have previously been applied individually to related tasks such as general domain image captioning and annotation. We briefly describe some of the related work:

2.1 Extractive Caption Generation

In previous work on image caption extraction, captions are generated by retrieving human-authored descriptions from visually similar images. Farhadi et al. (2010) and Ordonez et al. (2011) retrieve whole captions to apply to a query image, while Kuznetsova et al. (2012) generate captions using text retrieved from multiple sources. The descriptions are related to visual concepts in the query image, but these models use visual similarity to approximate textual relevance; they do not model image and textual features jointly.

2.2 Image Understanding

Recent improvements in state-of-the-art visual object class detections (Felzenszwalb et al., 2010) have enabled much recent work in image caption generation (Farhadi et al., 2010; Ordonez et al., 2011; Kulkarni et al., 2011; Yang et al., 2011; Mitchell et al., 2012; Yu and Siskind, 2013). However, these systems typically rely on a small number of detection types, e.g. the twenty object categories from the PASCAL VOC challenge.[2] These object categories include entities which are commonly described in general domain images (people, cars, cats, etc) but these require labeled training data which is not typically available for the visually relevant entities in specific domains.

Our caption generation system employs a multimodal topic model from our previous work (Mason and Charniak, 2013) which generates descriptive words, but lacks the spatial structure needed to generate a full sentence caption. Other previous work uses topic models to learn the semantic correspondence between images and labels (e.g. Blei and Jordan (2003)), but learning from natural language descriptions is considerably more difficult because of polysemy, hypernymy, and misalignment between the visual content of an image and the content humans choose to describe. The MixLDA model (Feng and Lapata, 2010b; Feng and Lapata, 2010a) learns from news images and natural language descriptions, but to generate words for a new image it requires both a query image and query text in the form of a news article. Berg et al. (2010) use discriminative models to discover visual attributes from online shopping images and captions, but their models do not generate descriptive words for unseen images.

2.3 Sentence Compression

Typical models for sentence compression (Knight and Marcu, 2002; Furui et al., 2004; Turner and Charniak, 2005; Clarke and Lapata, 2008) have a summarization objective: reduce the length of a source sentence without changing its meaning. In contrast, our objective is to change the meaning of the source sentence, letting its overall correctness relative to the query image determine the length of the output. Our objective differs from that of Kuznetsova et al. (2013), who compress image caption sentences with the objective of creating a corpus of generally transferrable image captions. Their compression objective is to maximize the probability of a caption conditioned on the source

[1] A research proposal for this framework and other image captioning ideas was previously presented at NAACL Student Research Workshop in 2013 (Mason, 2013). This paper presents a completed project including implementation details and experimental results.

[2] `http://pascallin.ecs.soton.ac.uk/challenges/VOC/`

Two adjustable buckle straps top a classic rubber rain boot grounded by a thick lug sole for excellent wet-weather traction.	Available in Plus Size. Faux snake skin flats with a large crossover buckle at the toe. Padded insole for a comfortable all day fit.	Glitter-covered elastic upper in a two-piece dress sandal style with round open toe. Single vamp strap with contrasting trim matching elasticized heel strap crisscrosses at instep.	Explosive! These white leather joggers are sure to make a big impression. Details count, including a toe overlay, millennium trim and lightweight raised sole.

Table 1: Example data from the Attribute Discovery Dataset (Berg et al., 2010). See Section 3.

image, while our objective is conditioned on the query image that we are generating a caption for. Additionally, their model also relies on general-domain trained visual detections.

3 Dataset and Preprocessing

The dataset we use is the women's shoes section of the publicly available Attribute Discovery Dataset[3] from Berg et al. (2010), which consists of product images and captions scraped from the shopping website `Like.com`. We use the women's shoes section of the dataset which has 14764 captioned images. Product descriptions describe many different attributes such as styles, colors, fabrics, patterns, decorations, and affordances (activities that can be performed while wearing the shoe). Some examples are shown in Table 1.

For preprocessing in our framework, we first determine an 80/20% train test split. We define a textual vocabulary of "descriptive words", which are non-function words – adjectives, adverbs, nouns (except proper nouns), and verbs. This gives us a total of 9578 descriptive words in the training set, with an average of 16.33 descriptive words per caption.

4 Image Captioning Framework

4.1 Extraction

To repeat, our overall process is to first find a caption sentence from our database to use as a template, and then correct the template sentences using sentence compresion. We compress by removing details that are probably not correct for the test image. For example, if the sentence describes "a red slipper" but the shoe in the query image is yellow, we want to remove "red" and keep the rest.

As in this simple example, the basic paradigm for compression is to keep the head words of phrases ("slipper") and remove modifiers. Thus we want to extraction stage of our scheme to be more likely to find a candidate sentence with correct head words, figuring that the compression stage can edit the mistakes. Our hypothesis is that headwords tend to describe more spatially structured visual concepts, while modifier words describe those that are more easily represented using local or unstructured features.[4] Table 2 contains additional example captions with parses.

GIST (Oliva and Torralba, 2001) is a commonly used feature in Computer Vision which coarsely localizes perceptual attributes (e.g. rough vs smooth, natural vs manmade). By computing the GIST of the images, we project them into a multi-dimensional Euclidean space where images with semantically similar structures are located near each other. Thus the extraction stage of our caption generation process selects a sentence from the GIST nearest-neighbor to the query image.[5]

4.2 Joint Topic Model

The second component of our framework incorporates visual and textual features using a less structured model. We use a multi-modal topic model

[3] `http://tamaraberg.com/attributesDataset/index.html`

[4] For example, the color "red" can be described using a bag of random pixels, while a "slipper" is a spatial configuration of parts in relationship to each other.

[5] See Section 5.1 for additional implementation details.

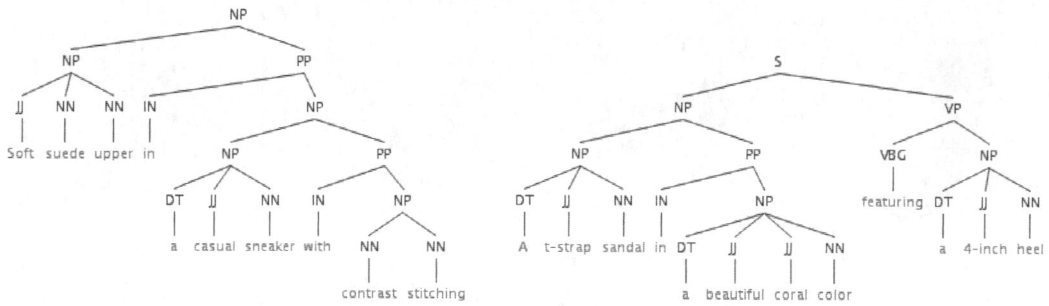

Table 2: Example parses of women's shoes descriptions. Our hypothesis is that the headwords in phrases are more likely to describe visual concepts which rely on spatial locations or relationships, while modifiers words can be represented using less-structured visual bag-of-words features.

to learn the latent topics which generate bag-of-words features for an image and its caption.

The bag-of-words model for Computer Vision represents images as a mixture of topics. Measures of shape, color, texture, and intensity are computed at various points on the image and clustered into discrete "codewords" using the k-means algorithm.[6] Unlike text words, an individual codeword has little meaning on its own, but distributions of codewords can provide a meaningful, though unstructured, representation of an image.

An image and its caption do not express exactly the same information, but they are topically related. We employ the Polylingual Topic Model (Mimno et al., 2009), which is originally used to model corresponding documents in different languages that are topically comparable, but not parallel translations. In particular, we employ our previous work (Mason and Charniak, 2013) which extends this model to topically similar images and natural language captions. The generative process for a captioned image starts with a single topic distribution drawn from concentration parameter α and base measure m:

$$\theta \sim Dir(\theta, \alpha m) \tag{1}$$

Modality-specific latent topic assignments z^{img} and z^{txt} are drawn for each of the text words and codewords:

$$\mathbf{z}^{img} \sim P(\mathbf{z}^{img}|\theta) = \prod_n \theta_{z_n^{img}} \tag{2}$$

[6]While space limits a more detailed explanation of visual bag-of-word features, Section 5.2 provides a brief overview of the specific visual attributes used in this model.

$$\mathbf{z}^{txt} \sim P(\mathbf{z}^{txt}|\theta) = \prod_n \theta_{z_n^{txt}} \tag{3}$$

Observed words are generated according to their probabilities in the modality-specific topics:

$$\mathbf{w}^{img} \sim P(\mathbf{w}^{img}|\mathbf{z}^{img}, \Phi^{img}) = \phi^{img}_{w_n^{img}|z_n^{img}} \tag{4}$$

$$\mathbf{w}^{txt} \sim P(\mathbf{w}^{txt}|\mathbf{z}^{txt}, \Phi^{txt}) = \phi^{txt}_{w_n^{txt}|z_n^{txt}} \tag{5}$$

Given the uncaptioned query image q^{img} and the trained multi-modal topic model, it is now possible to infer the shared topic proportion for q^{img} using Gibbs sampling:

$$\begin{aligned} P(z_n = t|q^{img}, z_{\backslash n}, \Phi^{img}, \alpha m) \\ \propto \phi^{img}_{q_n^{img}|t} \frac{(N_t)_{\backslash n} + \alpha m_t}{\sum_t N_t - 1 + \alpha} \end{aligned} \tag{6}$$

4.3 Sentence Compression

Let $\mathbf{w} = w_1, w_2, ..., w_n$ be the words in the extracted caption for q^{img}. For each word, we define a binary decision variable δ, such that $\delta_i = 1$ if w_i is included in the output compression, and $\delta_i = 0$ otherwise. Our objective is to find values of δ which generate a caption for q^{img} which is both semantically and grammatically correct.

We cast this problem as an Integer Linear Program (ILP), which has previously been used for the standard sentence compression task (Clarke and Lapata, 2008; Martins and Smith, 2009). ILP is a mathematical optimization method for determining the optimal values of integer variables in order to maximize an objective given a set of constraints.

4.3.1 Objective

The ILP objective is a weighted linear combination of two measures which represent the correctness and fluency of the output compression:

Correctness: Recall in Section 3 we defined words as either descriptive words or function words. For each descriptive word, we estimate $P(w_i|q^{img})$, using topic proportions estimated using Equation 6:

$$P(w_i|q^{img}) = \sum_t P(w_i|z_t^{txt})P(z_t|q^{img}) \quad (7)$$

This is used to find $I(w_i)$, a function of the likelihood of each word in the extracted caption:

$$I(w_i) = \begin{cases} P(w_i|q^{img}) - P(w_i), & \text{if descriptive} \\ 0, & \text{function word} \end{cases} \quad (8)$$

This function considers the prior probability of w_i because frequent words often have a high posterior probability even when they are inaccurate. Thus the sum $\sum_{i=1}^{n} \delta_i \cdot I(w_i)$ is the overall measure of the correctness of a proposed caption conditioned on q^{img}.

Fluency: We formulate a trigram language model as an ILP, which requires additional binary decision variables: $\alpha_i = 1$ if w_i begins the output compression, $\beta_{ij} = 1$ if the bigram sequence w_i, w_j ends the compression, $\gamma_{ijk} = 1$ if the trigram sequence w_i, w_j, w_k is in the compression, and a special "start token" $\delta_0 = 1$. This language model favors shorter sentences, which is not necessarily the objective for image captioning, so we introduce a weighting factor, λ, to lessen the effect.

Here is the combined objective, using P to represent $\log P$:

$$\begin{aligned} \max z = & \left(\sum_{i=1}^{n} \alpha_i \cdot P(w_i|\text{start}) \right. \\ & + \sum_{i=1}^{n-2} \sum_{j=i+1}^{n-1} \sum_{k=j+1}^{n} \gamma_{ijk} \cdot P(w_k|w_i, w_j) \\ & \left. + \sum_{i=0}^{n-1} \sum_{j=i+1}^{n} \beta_{ij} \cdot P(\text{end}|w_i, w_j) \right) \cdot \lambda \\ & + \sum_{i=1}^{n} \delta_i \cdot I(w_i) \end{aligned} \quad (9)$$

Sequential	1.) $\sum_i \alpha_i = 1$ 2.) $\delta_k - \alpha_k - \sum_{i=0}^{k-2} \sum_{j=1}^{k-1} \gamma_{ijk} = 0$ $\forall k : k \in 1...n$ 3.) $\delta_j - \sum_{i=0}^{j-1} \sum_{k=j+1}^{n} \gamma_{ijk} - \sum_{i=0}^{j-1} \beta_{ij} = 0$ $\forall j : j \in 1...n$ 4.) $\sum_{j=i+1}^{n-1} \sum_{k=j+1}^{n} \gamma_{ijk} - \sum_{j=i+1}^{n} \beta_{ij} - \sum_{h=0}^{i-1} \beta_{hi} - \delta_i = 0$ $\forall i : i \in 1...n$ 5.) $\sum_{i=0}^{n-1} \sum_{j=i+1}^{n} \beta_{ij} = 1$
Modifier	1. If head of the extracted sentence= w_i, then $\delta_i = 1$ 2. If w_i is head of a noun phrase, then $\delta_i = 1$ 3. Punctuation and coordinating conjunctions follow special rules (below). Otherwise, if $headof(w_i) = w_j$, then $\delta_i \leq \delta_j$
Other	1. $\sum_i \delta_i \geq 3$ 2. Define valid use of puncutation and coordinating conjunctions.

Table 3: Summary of ILP constraints.

4.3.2 ILP Constraints

The ILP constraints ensure both the mathematical validity of the model, and the grammatical correctness of its output. Table 3 summarizes the list of constraints. Sequential constraints are defined as in Clarke (2008) ensure that the ordering of the trigrams is valid, and that the mathematical validity of the model holds.

5 Implementation Details

5.1 Extraction

GIST features are computed using code by Oliva and Torralba (2001)[7]. GIST is computed with images converted to grayscale; since color features tend to act as modifiers in this domain. Nearest-neighbors are selected according to minimum distance from q^{img} to both a regularly-oriented and a horizontally-flipped training image.

Only one sentence from the first nearest-neighbor caption is extracted. In the case of multi-sentence captions, we select the first suitable sentence according to the following criteria 1.) has at least five tokens, 2.) does not contain NNP or NNPS (brand names), 3.) does not fail to parse using Stanford Parser (Klein and Manning, 2003). If the nearest-neighbor caption does not have any sentences meeting these criteria, caption sentences from the next nearest-neighbor(s) are considered.

[7] `http://people.csail.mit.edu/torralba/code/spatialenvelope/`

5.2 Joint Topic Model

We use the Joint Topic Model that we implemented in our previous work; please see Mason and Charniak (2013) for the full model and implementation details. The topic model is trained with 200 topics using the polylingual topic model implementation from MALLET[8]. Briefly, the codewords represent the following attributes:

SHAPE: SIFT (Lowe, 1999) describes the shapes of detected edges in the image, using descriptors which are invariant to changes in rotation and scale.

COLOR: RGB (red, green, blue) and HSV (hue, saturation, value) pixel values are sampled from a central area of the image to represent colors.

TEXTURE: Textons (Leung and Malik, 2001) are computed by convolving images with Gabor filters at multiple orientations and scales, then sampling the outputs at random locations.

INTENSITY: HOG (histogram of gradients) (Dalal and Triggs, 2005) describes the direction and intensity of changes in light. These features are computed on the image over a densely sampled grid.

5.3 Compression

The sentence compression ILP is implemented using the CPLEX optimization toolkit[9]. The language model weighting factor in the objective is $\lambda = 10^{-3}$, which was hand-tuned according to observed output. The trigram language model is trained on training set captions using BerkeleyLM (Pauls and Klein, 2011) with Kneser-Ney smoothing. For the constraints, we use parses from Stanford Parser (Klein and Manning, 2003) and the "semantic head" variation of the Collins headfinder Collins (1999).

6 Evaluation

6.1 Setup

We compare the following systems and baselines:

KL (EXTRACTION): The top performing extractive model from Feng and Lapata (2010a), and the second-best captioning model overall. Using estimated topic distributions from our joint model, we extract the source with minimum KL Divergence from q^{img}.

[8]http://mallet.cs.umass.edu/

[9]http://www-01.ibm.com/software/integration/optimization/cplex-optimization-studio/

ROUGE-2	Average	95% Confidence int.
KL (EXTRACTION)		
P	.06114	(.05690 - .06554)
R	.02499	(.02325 - .02686)
F	.03360	(.03133 - .03600)
GIST (EXTRACTION)		
P	.10894	(.09934 - .11921)
R	.05474	(.04926 - .06045)
F	.06863	(.06207 - .07534)
LM-ONLY (COMPRESSION)		
P	.13782	(.12602 - .14864)
R	.02437	(.02193 - .02700)
F	.03864	(.03512 - .04229)
SYSTEM (COMPRESSION)		
P	**.16752**	(.15679 -.17882)
R	.05060	(.04675 - .05524)
F	.07204	(.06685 - .07802)

Table 4: ROUGE-2 (bigram) scores. The precision of our system compression (bolded) significantly improves over the caption that it compresses (GIST), without a significant decrease in recall.

GIST (EXTRACTION): The sentence extracted using GIST nearest-neighbors, and the uncompressed source for the compression systems.

LM-ONLY (COMPRESSION): We include this baseline to demonstrate that our model is effectively conditioning output compressions on q^{img}, as opposed to simply generalizing captions as in Kuznetsova et al. (2013)[10]. We modify the compression ILP to ignore the content objective and only maximize the trigram language model (still subject to the constraints).

SYSTEM (COMPRESSION): Our full system.

Unfortunately, we cannot compare our system against prior work in general-domain image captioning, because those models use visual detection systems which train on labeled data that is not available in our domain.

6.2 Automatic Evaluation

We perform automatic evaluation using similarity measures between automatically generated and human-authored captions. Note that currently our system and baselines only generate single-sentence captions, but we compare against entire

[10]Technically their model is conditioned on the source image, in order to address alignment issues which are not applicable in our setup.

	BLEU@1
KL (EXTRACTION)	.2098
GIST (EXTRACTION)	.4259
LM-ONLY (COMPRESSION)	.4780
SYSTEM (COMPRESSION)	**.4841**

Table 5: BLEU@1 scores of generated captions against human authored captions. Our model (bolded) has the highest BLEU@1 score with significance.

held-out captions in order to increase the amount of text we have to compare against.

ROUGE (Lin, 2004) is a summarization evaluation metric which has also been used to evaluate image captions (Yang et al., 2011). It is usually a recall-oriented measure, but we also report precision and f-measure because our sentence compressions do not improve recall. Table 4 shows ROUGE-2 (bigram) scores computed without stopwords.

We observe that our system very significantly improves ROUGE-2 precision of the GIST extracted caption, without significantly reducing recall. While LM-Only also improves precision against GIST extraction, it indiscriminately removes some words which are relevant to the query image. We also observe that GIST extraction strongly outperforms the KL model, which demonstrates the importance of visual structure.

We also report BLEU (Papineni et al., 2002) scores, which are the most popularly accepted automatic metric for captioning evaluation (Farhadi et al., 2010; Kulkarni et al., 2011; Ordonez et al., 2011; Kuznetsova et al., 2012; Kuznetsova et al., 2013). Results are very similar to the ROUGE-2 precision scores, except the difference between our system and LM-Only is less pronounced because BLEU counts function words, while ROUGE does not.

6.3 Human Evaluation

We perform human evaluation of compressions generated by our system and LM-Only. Users are shown the query image, the original uncompressed caption, and a compressed caption, and are asked two questions: does the compression improve the accuracy of the caption, and is the compression grammatical.

We collect 553 judgments from six women who are native English-speakers and knowledgeable

Query Image | GIST Nearest-Neighbor

Extraction: Shimmering snake-embossed leather upper in a slingback evening dress sandal style with a round open toe.

Compression: Shimmering upper in a slingback evening dress sandal style with a round open toe.

Query Image | GIST Nearest-Neighbor

Extraction: This sporty sneaker clog keeps foot cool and comfortable and fully supported.

Compression: This clog keeps foot comfortable and supported.

Query Image | GIST Nearest-Neighbor

Extraction: Italian patent leather peep-toe ballet flat with a signature tailored grosgrain bow.

Compression: leather ballet flat with a signature tailored grosgrain bow.

Query Image | GIST Nearest-Neighbor

Extraction: Platform high heel open toe pump with horsebit available in silver guccissima leather with nickel hardware with leather sole.

Compression: Platform high heel open toe pump with horsebit available in leather with nickel hardware with leather sole.

Table 6: Example output from our full system. Red underlined words indicate the words which are deleted by our compression model.

	System		LM-Only	
	Yes	No	Yes	No
Compression improves accuracy	63.2%	36.8%	42.6%	57.4%
Compression is grammatical	73.1%	26.9%	82.2%	17.8%

Table 7: Human evaluation results.

about fashion.[11] Users were recruited via email and did the study over the internet.

Table 7 reports the results of the human evaluation. Users report 63.2% of SYSTEM compressions improve accuracy over the original, while the other 36.8% did not improve accuracy. (Keep in mind that a bad compression does not make the caption less accurate, just less descriptive.) LM-ONLY improves accuracy for less than half of the captions, which is significantly worse than SYSTEM captions (Fisher exact test, two-tailed p less than 0.01).

Users find LM-Only compressions to be slightly more grammatical than System compressions, but the difference is not significant. ($p > 0.05$)

7 Conclusion

We introduce the task of domain-specific image captioning and propose a captioning system which is trained on online shopping images and natural language descriptions. We learn a joint topic model of vision and text to estimate the correctness of extracted captions, and use a sentence compression model to propose a more accurate output caption. Our model exploits the connection between image and sentence structure, and can be used to improve the accuracy of extracted image captions.

The task of domain-specific image caption generation has been overlooked in favor of the general-domain case, but we believe the domain-specific case deserves more attention. While image captioning can be viewed as a complex grounding problem, a good image caption should do more than label the objects in the image. When an expert looks at images in a specific domain, he or she makes inferences that would not be made by a non-expert. Providing this information to non-expert users in the form of an image caption will greatly expand the utility for automatic image captioning.

[11] About 15% of output compressions are the same for both systems, and about 10% have no deleted words in the output compression. We include the former in the human evaluation, but not the latter.

Query Image | GIST Nearest-Neighbor

Extraction: Classic ballet flats with decorative canvas strap and patent leather covered buckle.

Compression: Classic ballet flats covered.

Query Image | GIST Nearest-Neighbor

Extraction: This shoe is the perfect shoe for you , featuring an open toe and a lace up upper with a high heel , and a two tone color .

Compression: This shoe is the shoe , featuring an open toe and upper with a high heel .

Table 8: Examples of bad performance. The top example is a parse error, while the bottom example deletes modifiers that are not part of the image description.

References

Tamara L. Berg, Alexander C. Berg, and Jonathan Shih. 2010. Automatic attribute discovery and characterization from noisy web data. In *Proceedings of the 11th European conference on Computer vision: Part I*, ECCV'10, pages 663–676, Berlin, Heidelberg. Springer-Verlag.

David M. Blei and Michael I. Jordan. 2003. Modeling annotated data. In *Proceedings of the 26th annual international ACM SIGIR conference on Research and development in informaion retrieval*, SIGIR '03, pages 127–134, New York, NY, USA. ACM.

James Clarke and Mirella Lapata. 2008. Global inference for sentence compression an integer linear programming approach. *J. Artif. Int. Res.*, 31(1):399–429, March.

James Clarke. 2008. *Global Inference for Sentence Compression: An Integer Linear Programming Approach*. Dissertation, University of Edinburgh.

Michael John Collins. 1999. *Head-driven statistical models for natural language parsing*. Ph.D. thesis, Philadelphia, PA, USA. AAI9926110.

N. Dalal and B. Triggs. 2005. Histograms of oriented gradients for human detection. In *Computer Vision and Pattern Recognition, 2005. CVPR 2005. IEEE Computer Society Conference on*, volume 1, pages 886 –893 vol. 1, june.

Ali Farhadi, Mohsen Hejrati, Mohammad Amin Sadeghi, Peter Young, Cyrus Rashtchian, Julia Hockenmaier, and David Forsyth. 2010. Every picture tells a story: generating sentences from images. In *Proceedings of the 11th European conference on Computer vision: Part IV*, ECCV'10, pages 15–29, Berlin, Heidelberg. Springer-Verlag.

P. F. Felzenszwalb, R. B. Girshick, D. McAllester, and D. Ramanan. 2010. Object detection with discriminatively trained part based models. *IEEE Transactions on Pattern Analysis and Machine Intelligence*, 32(9):1627–1645.

Yansong Feng and Mirella Lapata. 2010a. How many words is a picture worth? automatic caption generation for news images. In *Proceedings of the 48th Annual Meeting of the Association for Computational Linguistics*, ACL '10, pages 1239–1249, Stroudsburg, PA, USA. Association for Computational Linguistics.

Yansong Feng and Mirella Lapata. 2010b. Topic models for image annotation and text illustration. In *HLT-NAACL*, pages 831–839.

Sadaoki Furui, Tomonori Kikuchi, Yousuke Shinnaka, and Chiori Hori. 2004. Speech-to-text and speech-to-speech summarization of spontaneous speech. *IEEE TRANS. ON SPEECH AND AUDIO PROCESSING*, 12(4):401–408.

Dan Klein and Christopher D. Manning. 2003. Accurate unlexicalized parsing. In *Proceedings of the 41st Annual Meeting on Association for Computational Linguistics - Volume 1*, ACL '03, pages 423–430, Stroudsburg, PA, USA. Association for Computational Linguistics.

Kevin Knight and Daniel Marcu. 2002. Summarization beyond sentence extraction: a probabilistic approach to sentence compression. *Artif. Intell.*, 139(1):91–107, July.

Girish Kulkarni, Visruth Premraj, Sagnik Dhar, Siming Li, Yejin Choi, Alexander C. Berg, and Tamara L. Berg. 2011. Baby talk: Understanding and generating simple image descriptions. In *CVPR*, pages 1601–1608.

Polina Kuznetsova, Vicente Ordonez, Alexander C. Berg, Tamara L. Berg, and Yejin Choi. 2012. Collective generation of natural image descriptions. In *ACL*.

Polina Kuznetsova, Vicente Ordonez, Alexander Berg, Tamara Berg, and Yejin Choi. 2013. Generalizing image captions for image-text parallel corpus. In *ACL*.

T. Leung and J. Malik. 2001. Representing and recognizing the visual appearance of materials using three-dimensional textons. *International Journal of Computer Vision*, 43(1):29–44.

Chin-Yew Lin. 2004. Rouge: A package for automatic evaluation of summaries. In Stan Szpakowicz Marie-Francine Moens, editor, *Text Summarization Branches Out: Proceedings of the ACL-04 Workshop*, pages 74–81, Barcelona, Spain, July. Association for Computational Linguistics.

D.G. Lowe. 1999. Object recognition from local scale-invariant features. In *Computer Vision, 1999. The Proceedings of the Seventh IEEE International Conference on*, volume 2, pages 1150 –1157 vol.2.

André F. T. Martins and Noah A. Smith. 2009. Summarization with a joint model for sentence extraction and compression. In *Proceedings of the Workshop on Integer Linear Programming for Natural Langauge Processing*, ILP '09, pages 1–9, Stroudsburg, PA, USA. Association for Computational Linguistics.

R. Mason and E. Charniak. 2013. Annotation of online shopping images without labeled training examples. Workshop on Vision and Language (WVL).

Rebecca Mason. 2013. Domain-independent captioning of domain-specific images. NAACL Student Research Workshop.

David Mimno, Hanna M. Wallach, Jason Naradowsky, David A. Smith, and Andrew McCallum. 2009. Polylingual topic models. In *Proceedings of the 2009 Conference on Empirical Methods in Natural Language Processing: Volume 2 - Volume 2*, EMNLP '09, pages 880–889, Stroudsburg, PA, USA. Association for Computational Linguistics.

Margaret Mitchell, Jesse Dodge, Amit Goyal, Kota Yamaguchi, Karl Stratos, Xufeng Han, Alyssa Mensch, Alexander C. Berg, Tamara L. Berg, and Hal Daumé III. 2012. Midge: Generating image descriptions from computer vision detections. In *European Chapter of the Association for Computational Linguistics (EACL)*.

Aude Oliva and Antonio Torralba. 2001. Modeling the shape of the scene: A holistic representation of the spatial envelope. *International Journal of Computer Vision*, 42:145–175.

V. Ordonez, G. Kulkarni, and T.L. Berg. 2011. Im2text: Describing images using 1 million captioned photographs. In *NIPS*.

Kishore Papineni, Salim Roukos, Todd Ward, and Wei-Jing Zhu. 2002. Bleu: a method for automatic evaluation of machine translation. In *Proceedings of the 40th Annual Meeting on Association for Computational Linguistics*, ACL '02, pages 311–318, Stroudsburg, PA, USA. Association for Computational Linguistics.

Adam Pauls and Dan Klein. 2011. Faster and smaller n-gram language models. In *Proceedings of ACL*, Portland, Oregon, June. Association for Computational Linguistics.

Jenine Turner and Eugene Charniak. 2005. Supervised and unsupervised learning for sentence compression. In *Proceedings of the 43rd Annual Meeting on Association for Computational Linguistics*, ACL '05, pages 290–297, Stroudsburg, PA, USA. Association for Computational Linguistics.

Yezhou Yang, Ching Lik Teo, Hal Daumé III, and Yiannis Aloimonos. 2011. Corpus-guided sentence generation of natural images. In *Empirical Methods in Natural Language Processing (EMNLP)*, Edinburgh, Scotland.

Haonan Yu and Jeffrey Mark Siskind. 2013. Grounded language learning from video described with sentences. In *Proceedings of the 51st Annual Meeting of the Association for Computational Linguistics (Volume 1: Long Papers)*, volume 1, pages 53–63, Sofia, Bulgaria. Association for Computational Linguistics.

Reconstructing Native Language Typology from Foreign Language Usage

Yevgeni Berzak
CSAIL MIT
berzak@mit.edu

Roi Reichart
Technion IIT
roiri@ie.technion.ac.il

Boris Katz
CSAIL MIT
boris@mit.edu

Abstract

Linguists and psychologists have long been studying cross-linguistic transfer, the influence of native language properties on linguistic performance in a foreign language. In this work we provide empirical evidence for this process in the form of a strong correlation between language similarities derived from structural features in English as Second Language (ESL) texts and equivalent similarities obtained from the typological features of the native languages. We leverage this finding to recover native language typological similarity structure directly from ESL text, and perform prediction of typological features in an unsupervised fashion with respect to the target languages. Our method achieves 72.2% accuracy on the typology prediction task, a result that is highly competitive with equivalent methods that rely on typological resources.

1 Introduction

Cross-linguistic transfer can be broadly described as the application of linguistic structure of a speaker's native language in the context of a new, foreign language. Transfer effects may be expressed on various levels of linguistic performance, including pronunciation, word order, lexical borrowing and others (Jarvis and Pavlenko, 2007). Such traces are prevalent in non-native English, and in some cases are even celebrated in anecdotal hybrid dialect names such as "Frenglish" and "Denglish".

Although cross-linguistic transfer was extensively studied in Psychology, Second Language Acquisition (SLA) and Linguistics, the conditions under which it occurs, its linguistic characteristics as well as its scope remain largely under debate (Jarvis and Pavlenko, 2007; Gass and Selinker, 1992; Odlin, 1989).

In NLP, the topic of linguistic transfer was mainly addressed in relation to the Native Language Identification (NLI) task, which requires to predict the native language of an ESL text's author. The overall high performance on this classification task is considered to be a central piece of evidence for the existence of cross-linguistic transfer (Jarvis and Crossley, 2012). While the success on the NLI task confirms the ability to extract native language signal from second language text, it offers little insight into the linguistic mechanisms that play a role in this process.

In this work, we examine the hypothesis that cross-linguistic structure transfer is governed by the *typological properties of the native language*. We provide empirical evidence for this hypothesis by showing that language similarities derived from structural patterns of ESL usage are strongly correlated with similarities obtained directly from the typological features of the native languages.

This correlation has broad implications on the ability to perform inference from native language structure to second language performance and vice versa. In particular, it paves the way for a novel and powerful framework for *comparing native languages through second language performance*. This framework overcomes many of the inherent difficulties of direct comparison between languages, and the lack of sufficient typological documentation for the vast majority of the world's languages.

Further on, we utilize this transfer enabled framework for the task of reconstructing typological features. Automated prediction of language typology is extremely valuable for both linguistic studies and NLP applications which rely on such information (Naseem et al., 2012; Täckström et al., 2013). Furthermore, this task provides an objective external testbed for the quality of our native

Proceedings of the Eighteenth Conference on Computational Language Learning, pages 21–29,
Baltimore, Maryland USA, June 26-27 2014.

language similarity estimates derived from ESL texts.

Treating native language similarities obtained from ESL as an approximation for typological similarities, we use them to predict typological features without relying on typological annotation for the target languages. Our ESL based method yields 71.4% – 72.2% accuracy on the typology reconstruction task, as compared to 69.1% – 74.2% achieved by typology based methods which depend on pre-existing typological resources for the target languages.

To summarize, this paper offers two main contributions. First, we provide an empirical result that validates the systematic existence of linguistic transfer, tying the typological characteristics of the native language with the structural patterns of foreign language usage. Secondly, we show that ESL based similarities can be directly used for prediction of native language typology. As opposed to previous approaches, our method achieves strong results without access to any a-priori knowledge about the target language typology.

The remainder of the paper is structured as follows. Section 2 surveys the literature and positions our study in relation to previous research on cross-linguistic transfer and language typology. Section 3 describes the ESL corpus and the database of typological features. In section 4, we delineate our method for deriving native language similarities and hierarchical similarity trees from structural features in ESL. In section 5 we use typological features to construct another set of language similarity estimates and trees, which serve as a benchmark for the typological validity of the ESL based similarities. Section 6 provides a correlation analysis between the ESL based and typology based similarities. Finally, in section 7 we report our results on typology reconstruction, a task that also provides an evaluation framework for the similarity structures derived in sections 4 and 5.

2 Related Work

Our work integrates two areas of research, cross-linguistic transfer and linguistic typology.

2.1 Cross-linguistic Transfer

The study of cross-linguistic transfer has thus far evolved in two complementary strands, the linguistic *comparative* approach, and the computational *detection* based approach. While the comparative approach focuses on case study based qualitative analysis of native language influence on second language performance, the detection based approach revolves mainly around the NLI task.

Following the work of Koppel et al. (2005), NLI has been gaining increasing interest in NLP, culminating in a recent shared task with 29 participating systems (Tetreault et al., 2013). Much of the NLI efforts thus far have been focused on exploring various feature sets for optimizing classification performance. While many of these features are linguistically motivated, some of the discriminative power of these approaches stems from cultural and domain artifacts. For example, our preliminary experiments with a typical NLI feature set, show that the strongest features for predicting Chinese are strings such as *China* and *in China*. Similar features dominate the weights of other languages as well. Such content features boost classification performance, but are hardly relevant for modeling linguistic phenomena, thus weakening the argument that NLI classification performance is indicative of cross-linguistic transfer.

Our work incorporates an NLI component, but departs from the performance optimization orientation towards leveraging computational analysis for better understanding of the relations between native language typology and ESL usage. In particular, our choice of NLI features is driven by their relevance to linguistic typology rather than their contribution to classification performance. In this sense, our work aims to take a first step towards closing the gap between the detection and comparative approaches to cross-linguistic transfer.

2.2 Language Typology

The second area of research, language typology, deals with the documentation and comparative study of language structures (Song, 2011). Much of the descriptive work in the field is summarized in the World Atlas of Language Structures (WALS)[1] (Dryer and Haspelmath, 2013) in the form of structural features. We use the WALS features as our source of typological information.

Several previous studies have used WALS features for hierarchical clustering of languages and typological feature prediction. Most notably, Teh et al. (2007) and subsequently Daumé III (2009)

[1] http://wals.info/

predicted typological features from language trees constructed with a Bayesian hierarchical clustering model. In Georgi et al. (2010) additional clustering approaches were compared using the same features and evaluation method. In addition to the feature prediction task, these studies also evaluated their clustering results by comparing them to genetic language clusters.

Our approach differs from this line of work in several aspects. First, similarly to our WALS based baselines, the clustering methods presented in these studies are affected by the sparsity of available typological data. Furthermore, these methods rely on existing typological documentation for the target languages. Both issues are obviated in our English based framework which does not depend on any typological information to construct the native language similarity structures, and does not require any knowledge about the target languages except from the ESL essays of a sample of their speakers. Finally, we do not compare our clustering results to genetic groupings, as to our knowledge, there is no firm theoretical ground for expecting typologically based clustering to reproduce language phylogenies. The empirical results in Georgi et al. (2010), which show that typology based clustering differs substantially from genetic groupings, support this assumption.

3 Datasets

3.1 Cambridge FCE

We use the Cambridge First Certificate in English (FCE) dataset (Yannakoudakis et al., 2011) as our source of ESL data. This corpus is a subset of the Cambridge Learner Corpus (CLC)[2]. It contains English essays written by upper-intermediate level learners of English for the FCE examination.

The essay authors represent 16 native languages. We discarded Dutch and Swedish speakers due to the small number of documents available for these languages (16 documents in total). The remaining documents are associated with the following 14 native languages: Catalan, Chinese, French, German, Greek, Italian, Japanese, Korean, Polish, Portuguese, Russian, Spanish, Thai and Turkish. Overall, our corpus comprises 1228 documents, corresponding to an average of 87.7 documents per native language.

[2] `http://www.cambridge.org/gb/elt/catalogue/subject/custom/item3646603`

3.2 World Atlas of Language Structures

We collect typological information for the FCE native languages from WALS. Currently, the database contains information about 2,679 of the world's 7,105 documented living languages (Lewis, 2014). The typological feature list has 188 features, 175 of which are present in our dataset. The features are associated with 9 linguistic categories: Phonology, Morphology, Nominal Categories, Nominal Syntax, Verbal Categories, Word Order, Simple Clauses, Complex Sentences and Lexicon. Table 1 presents several examples for WALS features and their range of values.

One of the challenging characteristics of WALS is its low coverage, stemming from lack of available linguistic documentation. It was previously estimated that about 84% of the language-feature pairs in WALS are unknown (Daumé III, 2009; Georgi et al., 2010). Even well studied languages, like the ones used in our work, are lacking values for many features. For example, only 32 of the WALS features have known values for all the 14 languages of the FCE corpus. Despite the prevalence of this issue, it is important to bear in mind that some features do not apply to all languages by definition. For instance, feature 81B *Languages with two Dominant Orders of Subject, Object, and Verb* is relevant only to 189 languages (and has documented values for 67 of them).

We perform basic preprocessing, discarding 5 features that have values for only one language. Further on, we omit 19 features belonging to the category Phonology as comparable phonological features are challenging to extract from the ESL textual data. After this filtering, we remain with 151 features, 114.1 features with a known value per language, 10.6 languages with a known value per feature and 2.5 distinct values per feature.

Following previous work, we binarize all the WALS features, expressing each feature in terms of k binary features, where k is the number of values the original feature can take. Note that beyond the well known issues with feature binarization, this strategy is not optimal for some of the features. For example, the feature 111A *Non-periphrastic Causative Constructions* whose possible values are presented in table 1 would have been better encoded with two binary features rather than four. The question of optimal encoding for the WALS feature set requires expert analysis and will be addressed in future research.

ID	Type	Feature Name	Values
26A	Morphology	Prefixing vs. Suffixing in Inflectional Morphology	Little affixation, Strongly suffixing, Weakly suffixing, Equal prefixing and suffixing, Weakly prefixing, Strong prefixing.
30A	Nominal Categories	Number of Genders	None, Two, Three, Four, Five or more.
83A	Word Order	Order of Object and Verb	OV, VO, No dominant order.
111A	Simple Clauses	Non-periphrastic Causative Constructions	Neither, Morphological but no compound, Compound but no morphological, Both.

Table 1: Examples of WALS features. As illustrated in the table examples, WALS features can take different types of values and may be challenging to encode.

4 Inferring Language Similarities from ESL

Our first goal is to derive a notion of similarity between languages with respect to their native speakers' distinctive structural usage patterns of ESL. A simple way to obtain such similarities is to train a probabilistic NLI model on ESL texts, and interpret the uncertainty of this classifier in distinguishing between a pair of native languages as a measure of their similarity.

4.1 NLI Model

The log-linear NLI model is defined as follows:

$$p(y|x;\theta) = \frac{\exp(\theta \cdot f(x,y))}{\sum_{y' \in Y} \exp(\theta \cdot f(x,y'))} \quad (1)$$

where y is the native language, x is the observed English document and θ are the model parameters. The parameters are learned by maximizing the L2 regularized log-likelihood of the training data $D = \{(x_1, y_1), ..., (x_n, y_n)\}$.

$$L(\theta) = \sum_{i=1}^{n} \log p(y_i|x_i;\theta) - \lambda \|\theta\|^2 \quad (2)$$

The model is trained using gradient ascent with L-BFGS-B (Byrd et al., 1995). We use 70% of the FCE data for training and the remaining 30% for development and testing.

As our objective is to relate native language and target language *structures*, we seek to control for biases related to the content of the essays. As previously mentioned, such biases may arise from the essay prompts as well as from various cultural factors. We therefore define the model using only *unlexicalized* morpho-syntactic features, which capture structural properties of English usage.

Our feature set, summarized in table 2, contains features which are strongly related to many of the structural features in WALS. In particular, we use features derived from labeled dependency parses. These features encode properties such as the types of dependency relations, ordering and distance between the head and the dependent. Additional syntactic information is obtained using POS n-grams. Finally, we consider derivational and inflectional morphological affixation. The annotations required for our syntactic features are obtained from the Stanford POS tagger (Toutanova et al., 2003) and the Stanford parser (de Marneffe et al., 2006). The morphological features are extracted heuristically.

4.2 ESL Based Native Language Similarity Estimates

Given a document x and its author's native language y, the conditional probability $p(y'|x;\theta)$ can be viewed as a measure of confusion between languages y and y', arising from their similarity with respect to the document features. Under this interpretation, we derive a language similarity matrix S'_{ESL} whose entries are obtained by averaging these conditional probabilities on the training set documents with the true label y, which we denote as $D_y = \{(x_i, y) \in D\}$.

$$S'_{ESL_{y,y'}} = \begin{cases} \frac{1}{|D_y|} \sum_{(x,y) \in D_y} p(y'|x;\theta) & \text{if } y' \neq y \\ 1 & \text{otherwise} \end{cases} \quad (3)$$

For each pair of languages y and y', the matrix S'_{ESL} contains an entry $S'_{ESL_{y,y'}}$ which captures the average probability of mistaking y for y', and an entry $S'_{ESL_{y',y}}$, which represents the opposite

Feature Type	Examples
Unlexicalized labeled dependencies	Relation = *prep* Head = *VBN* Dependent = *IN*
Ordering of head and dependent	Ordering = *right* Head = *NNS* Dependent = *JJ*
Distance between head and dependent	Distance = 2 Head = *VBG* Dependent = *PRP*
POS sequence between head and dependent	Relation = *det* POS-between = *JJ*
POS n-grams (up to 4-grams)	POS bigram = *NN VBZ*
Inflectional morphology	Suffix = *ing*
Derivational morphology	Suffix = *ity*

Table 2: Examples of syntactic and morphological features of the NLI model. The feature values are set to the number of occurrences of the feature in the document. The syntactic features are derived from the output of the Stanford parser. A comprehensive description of the Stanford parser dependency annotation scheme can be found in the Stanford dependencies manual (de Marneffe and Manning, 2008).

confusion. We average the two confusion scores to receive the matrix of pairwise language similarity estimates S_{ESL}.

$$S_{ESL_{y,y'}} = S_{ESL_{y',y}} = \frac{1}{2}(S'_{ESL_{y,y'}} + S'_{ESL_{y',y}}) \quad (4)$$

Note that comparable similarity estimates can be obtained from the confusion matrix of the classifier, which records the number of misclassifications corresponding to each pair of class labels. The advantage of our probabilistic setup over this method is its robustness with respect to the actual classification performance of the model.

4.3 Language Similarity Tree

A particularly informative way of representing language similarities is in the form of hierarchical trees. This representation is easier to inspect than a similarity matrix, and as such, it can be more instrumental in supporting linguistic inquiry on language relatedness. Additionally, as we show in section 7, hierarchical similarity trees can outperform raw similarities when used for typology reconstruction.

We perform hierarchical clustering using the Ward algorithm (Ward Jr, 1963). Ward is a bottom-up clustering algorithm. Starting with a separate cluster for each language, it successively merges clusters and returns the tree of cluster merges. The objective of the Ward algorithm is to minimize the total within-cluster variance. To this end, at each step it merges the cluster pair that yields the minimum increase in the overall within-cluster variance. The initial distance matrix required for the clustering algorithm is defined as $1 - S_{ESL}$. We use the Scipy implementation[3] of Ward, in which the distance between a newly formed cluster $a \cup b$ and another cluster c is computed with the Lance-Williams distance update formula (Lance and Williams, 1967).

5 WALS Based Language Similarities

In order to determine the extent to which ESL based language similarities reflect the typological similarity between the native languages, we compare them to similarities obtained directly from the typological features in WALS.

The WALS based similarity estimates between languages y and y' are computed by measuring the cosine similarity between the binarized typological feature vectors.

$$S_{WALS_{y,y'}} = \frac{v_y \cdot v_{y'}}{\|v_y\| \|v_{y'}\|} \quad (5)$$

As mentioned in section 3.2, many of the WALS features do not have values for all the FCE languages. To address this issue, we experiment with two different strategies for choosing the WALS features to be used for language similarity computations. The first approach, called *shared-all*, takes into account only the 32 features that have known values in all the 14 languages of our dataset. In the second approach, called *shared-pairwise*, the similarity estimate for a pair of languages is determined based on the features shared between these two languages.

As in the ESL setup, we use the two matrices of similarity estimates to construct WALS based hierarchical similarity trees. Analogously to the ESL case, a WALS based tree is generated by the

[3] `http://docs.scipy.org/.../scipy.cluster.hierarchy.linkage.html`

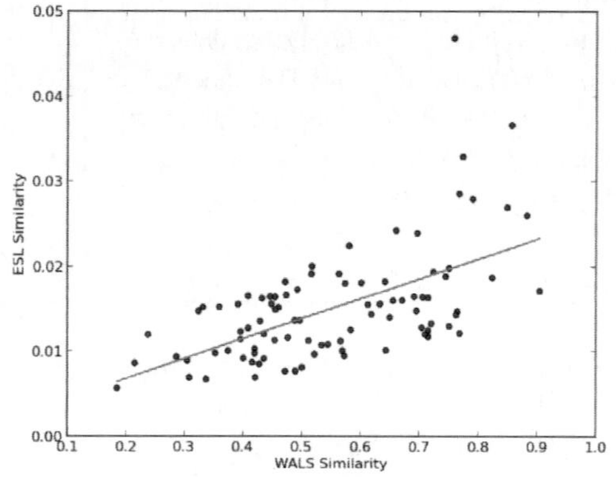

Figure 1: *shared-pairwise* WALS based versus ESL based language similarity scores. Each point represents a language pair, with the vertical axis corresponding to the ESL based similarity and the horizontal axis standing for the typological *shared-pairwise* WALS based similarity. The scores correlate strongly with a Pearson's coefficient of 0.59 for the *shared-pairwise* construction and 0.50 for the *shared-all* feature-set.

Ward algorithm with the input distance matrix $1 - S_{WALS}$.

6 Comparison Results

After independently deriving native language similarity matrices from ESL texts and from typological features in WALS, we compare them to one another. Figure 1 presents a scatter plot of the language similarities obtained using ESL data, against the equivalent WALS based similarities. The scores are strongly correlated, with a Pearson Correlation Coefficient of 0.59 using the *shared-pairwise* WALS distances and 0.50 using the *shared-all* WALS distances.

This correlation provides appealing evidence for the hypothesis that distinctive structural patterns of English usage arise via cross-linguistic transfer, and to a large extent reflect the typological similarities between the respective native languages. The practical consequence of this result is the ability to use one of these similarity structures to approximate the other. Here, we use the ESL based similarities as a proxy for the typological similarities between languages, allowing us to reconstruct typological information without relying on a-priori knowledge about the target language typology.

In figure 2 we present, for illustration purposes, the hierarchical similarity trees obtained with the Ward algorithm based on WALS and ESL similarities. The trees bear strong resemblances to one other. For example, at the top level of the hierarchy, the Indo-European languages are discerned from the non Indo-European languages. Further down, within the Indo-European cluster, the Romance languages are separated from other Indo-European subgroups. Further points of similarity can be observed at the bottom of the hierarchy, where the pairs Russian and Polish, Japanese and Korean, and Chinese and Thai merge in both trees.

In the next section we evaluate the quality of these trees, as well as the similarity matrices used for constructing them with respect to their ability to support accurate nearest neighbors based reconstruction of native language typology.

7 Typology Prediction

Although pairwise language similarities derived from structural features in ESL texts are highly correlated with similarities obtained directly from native language typology, evaluating the absolute quality of such similarity matrices and trees is challenging.

We therefore turn to typology prediction based evaluation, in which we assess the quality of the induced language similarity estimates by their ability to support accurate prediction of unseen typological features. In this evaluation mode we project unknown WALS features to a target language from the languages that are closest to it in the similarity structure. The underlying assumption of this setup is that better similarity structures will lead to better accuracies in the feature prediction task.

Typological feature prediction not only provides an objective measure for the quality of the similarity structures, but also has an intrinsic value as a stand-alone task. The ability to infer typological structure automatically can be used to create linguistic databases for low-resource languages, and is valuable to NLP applications that exploit such resources, most notably multilingual parsing (Naseem et al., 2012; Täckström et al., 2013).

Prediction of typological features for a target language using the language similarity matrix is performed by taking a majority vote for the value of each feature among the K nearest languages of the target language. In case none of the K nearest languages have a value for a feature, or given a tie

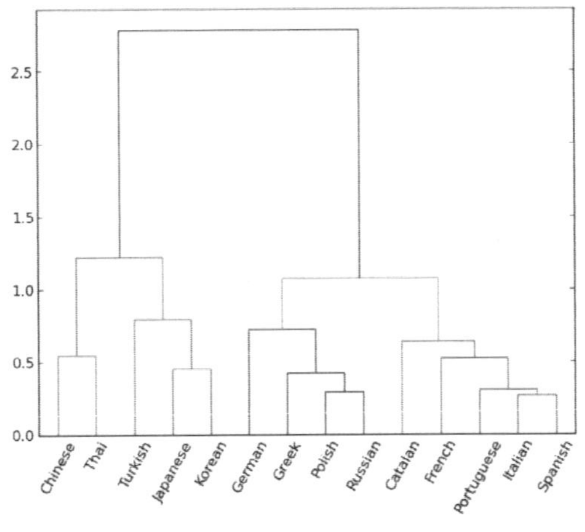

(a) Hierarchical clustering using WALS based *shared-pairwise* distances.

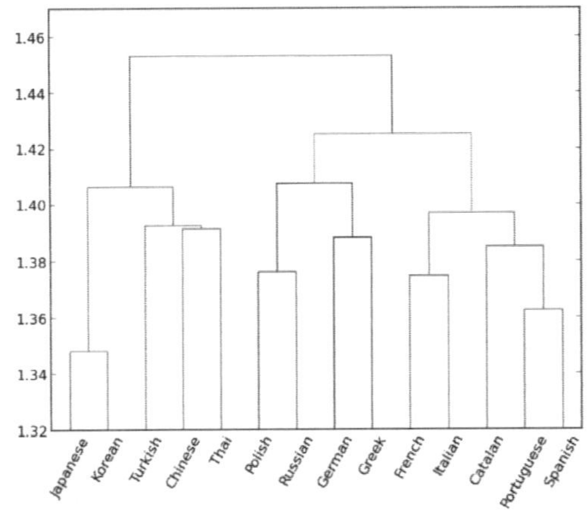

(b) Hierarchical clustering using ESL based distances.

Figure 2: Language Similarity Trees. Both trees are constructed with the Ward agglomerative hierarchical clustering algorithm. Tree (a) uses the WALS based *shared-pairwise* language distances. Tree (b) uses the ESL derived distances.

between several values, we iteratively expand the group of nearest languages until neither of these cases applies.

To predict features using a hierarchical cluster tree, we set the value of each target language feature to its majority value among the members of the parent cluster of the target language, excluding the target language itself. For example, using the tree in figure 2(a), the feature values for the target language French will be obtained by taking majority votes between Portuguese, Italian and Spanish. Similarly to the matrix based prediction, missing values and ties are handled by backing-off to a larger set of languages, in this case by proceeding to subsequent levels of the cluster hierarchy. For the French example in figure 2(a), the first fall-back option will be the Romance cluster.

Following the evaluation setups in Daumé III (2009) and Georgi et al. (2010), we evaluate the WALS based similarity estimates and trees by constructing them using 90% of the WALS features. We report the average accuracy over 100 random folds of the data. In the *shared-all* regime, we provide predictions not only for the remaining 10% of features shared by all languages, but also for all the other features that have values in the target language and are not used for the tree construction.

Importantly, as opposed to the WALS based prediction, our ESL based method does not require any typological features for inferring language similarities and constructing the similarity tree. In particular, no typological information is required for the target languages. Typological features are needed only for the neighbors of the target language, from which the features are projected. This difference is a key advantage of our approach over the WALS based methods, which presuppose substantial typological documentation for all the languages involved.

Table 3 summarizes the feature reconstruction results. The ESL approach is highly competitive with the WALS based results, yielding comparable accuracies for the *shared-all* prediction, and lagging only 1.7% – 3.4% behind the *shared-pairwise* construction. Also note that for both WALS based and ESL based predictions, the highest results are achieved using the hierarchical tree predictions, confirming the suitability of this representation for accurately capturing language similarity structure.

Figure 3 presents the performance of the strongest WALS based typological feature completion method, WALS *shared-pairwise* tree, as a function of the percentage of features used for obtaining the language similarity estimates. The figure also presents the strongest result of the ESL method, using the ESL tree, which does not require any such typological training data for obtaining the language similarities. As can be seen, the WALS based approach would require access to almost 40% of the currently documented WALS features to match the performance of the ESL method.

The competitive performance of our ESL method on the typology prediction task underlines

Method	NN	3NN	Tree
WALS *shared-all*	71.6	71.4	69.1
WALS *shared-pairwise*	73.1	74.1	**74.2**
ESL	71.4	70.7	**72.2**

Table 3: Typology reconstruction results. Three types of predictions are compared, nearest neighbor (NN), 3 nearest neighbors (3NN) and nearest tree neighbors (Tree). WALS *shared-all* are WALS based predictions, where only the 32 features that have known values in all 14 languages are used for computing language similarities. In the WALS *shared-pairwise* predictions the language similarities are computed using the WALS features shared by each language pair. ESL results are obtained by projection of WALS features from the closest languages according to the ESL language similarities.

its ability to extract strong typologically driven signal, while being robust to the partial nature of existing typological annotation which hinders the performance of the baselines. Given the small amount of ESL data at hand, these results are highly encouraging with regard to the prospects of our approach to support typological inference, even in the absence of any typological documentation for the target languages.

8 Conclusion and Outlook

We present a novel framework for utilizing cross-linguistic transfer to infer language similarities from morpho-syntactic features of ESL text. Trading laborious expert annotation of typological features for a modest amount of ESL texts, we are able to reproduce language similarities that strongly correlate with the equivalent typology based similarities, and perform competitively on a typology reconstruction task.

Our study leaves multiple questions for future research. For example, while the current work examines structure transfer, additional investigation is required to better understand lexical and phonological transfer effects.

Furthermore, we currently focuse on native language typology, and assume English as the foreign language. This limits our ability to study the constraints imposed on cross-linguistic transfer by the foreign language. An intriguing research direction would be to explore other foreign languages and compare the outcomes to our results on English.

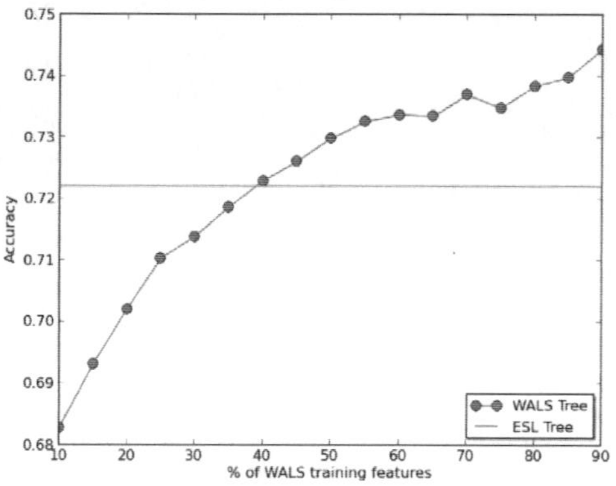

Figure 3: Comparison of the typological feature completion performance obtained using the WALS tree with *shared-pairwise* similarities and the ESL tree based typological feature completion performance. The dotted line represents the WALS based prediction accuracy, while the horizontal line is the ESL based accuracy. The horizontal axis corresponds to the percentage of WALS features used for constructing the WALS based language similarity estimates.

Finally, we plan to formulate explicit models for the relations between specific typological features and ESL usage patterns, and extend our typology induction mechanisms to support NLP applications in the domain of multilingual processing.

Acknowledgments

We would like to thank Yoong Keok Lee, Jesse Harris and the anonymous reviewers for valuable comments on this paper. This material is based upon work supported by the Center for Brains, Minds, and Machines (CBMM), funded by NSF STC award CCF-1231216, and by Google Faculty Research Award.

References

Richard H Byrd, Peihuang Lu, Jorge Nocedal, and Ciyou Zhu. 1995. A limited memory algorithm for bound constrained optimization. *SIAM Journal on Scientific Computing*, 16(5):1190–1208.

Hal Daumé III. 2009. Non-parametric Bayesian areal linguistics. In *Proceedings of human language technologies: The 2009 annual conference of the north american chapter of the association for computational linguistics*, pages 593–601. Association for Computational Linguistics.

Marie-Catherine de Marneffe and Christopher D Manning. 2008. Stanford typed dependencies manual. *URL http://nlp. stanford. edu/software/dependencies manual. pdf.*

Marie-Catherine de Marneffe, Bill MacCartney, Christopher D Manning, et al. 2006. Generating typed dependency parses from phrase structure parses. In *Proceedings of LREC*, volume 6, pages 449–454.

Matthew S. Dryer and Martin Haspelmath, editors. 2013. *WALS Online*. Max Planck Institute for Evolutionary Anthropology, Leipzig.

Susan M Gass and Larry Selinker. 1992. *Language Transfer in Language Learning: Revised edition*, volume 5. John Benjamins Publishing.

Ryan Georgi, Fei Xia, and William Lewis. 2010. Comparing language similarity across genetic and typologically-based groupings. In *Proceedings of the 23rd International Conference on Computational Linguistics*, pages 385–393. Association for Computational Linguistics.

Scott Jarvis and Scott A Crossley. 2012. *Approaching language transfer through text classification: Explorations in the detection-based approach*, volume 64. Multilingual Matters.

Scott Jarvis and Aneta Pavlenko. 2007. *Crosslinguistic influence in language and cognition*. Routledge.

Moshe Koppel, Jonathan Schler, and Kfir Zigdon. 2005. Determining an author's native language by mining a text for errors. In *Proceedings of the eleventh ACM SIGKDD international conference on Knowledge discovery in data mining*, pages 624–628. ACM.

Godfrey N Lance and William Thomas Williams. 1967. A general theory of classificatory sorting strategies ii. clustering systems. *The computer journal*, 10(3):271–277.

M. Paul Lewis. 2014. Ethnologue: Languages of the world. `www.ethnologue.com`.

Tahira Naseem, Regina Barzilay, and Amir Globerson. 2012. Selective sharing for multilingual dependency parsing. In *Proceedings of the 50th Annual Meeting of the Association for Computational Linguistics: Long Papers-Volume 1*, pages 629–637. Association for Computational Linguistics.

Terence Odlin. 1989. *Language transfer: Cross-linguistic influence in language learning*. Cambridge University Press.

J.J. Song. 2011. *The Oxford Handbook of Linguistic Typology*. Oxford Handbooks in Linguistics. OUP Oxford.

Oscar Täckström, Ryan McDonald, and Joakim Nivre. 2013. Target language adaptation of discriminative transfer parsers. *Proceedings of NAACL-HLT*.

Yee Whye Teh, Hal Daumé III, and Daniel M Roy. 2007. Bayesian agglomerative clustering with coalescents. In *NIPS*.

Joel Tetreault, Daniel Blanchard, and Aoife Cahill. 2013. A report on the first native language identification shared task. *NAACL/HLT 2013*, page 48.

Kristina Toutanova, Dan Klein, Christopher D Manning, and Yoram Singer. 2003. Feature-rich part-of-speech tagging with a cyclic dependency network. In *Proceedings of the 2003 Conference of the North American Chapter of the Association for Computational Linguistics on Human Language Technology-Volume 1*, pages 173–180. Association for Computational Linguistics.

Joe H Ward Jr. 1963. Hierarchical grouping to optimize an objective function. *Journal of the American statistical association*, 58(301):236–244.

Helen Yannakoudakis, Ted Briscoe, and Ben Medlock. 2011. A new dataset and method for automatically grading ESOL texts. In *ACL*, pages 180–189.

Automatic Transliteration of Romanized Dialectal Arabic

Mohamed Al-Badrashiny[†], Ramy Eskander, Nizar Habash and Owen Rambow
[†]Department of Computer Science, The George Washington University, Washington, DC
[†]badrashiny@gwu.edu
Center for Computational Learning Systems, Columbia University, NYC, NY
{reskander,habash,rambow}@ccls.columbia.edu

Abstract

In this paper, we address the problem of converting Dialectal Arabic (DA) text that is written in the Latin script (called Arabizi) into Arabic script following the CODA convention for DA orthography. The presented system uses a finite state transducer trained at the character level to generate all possible transliterations for the input Arabizi words. We then filter the generated list using a DA morphological analyzer. After that we pick the best choice for each input word using a language model. We achieve an accuracy of 69.4% on an unseen test set compared to 63.1% using a system which represents a previously proposed approach.

1 Introduction

The Arabic language is a collection of varieties: Modern Standard Arabic (MSA), which is used in formal settings and has a standard orthography, and different forms of Dialectal Arabic (DA), which are commonly used informally and with increasing presence on the web, but which do not have standard orthographies. While both MSA and DA are commonly written in the Arabic script, DA (and less so MSA) is sometimes written in the Latin script. This happens when using an Arabic keyboard is dispreferred or impossible, for example when communicating from a mobile phone that has no Arabic script support. Arabic written in the Latin script is often referred to as "Arabizi". Arabizi is not a letter-based transliteration from the Arabic script as is, for example, the Buckwalter transliteration (Buckwalter, 2004). Instead, roughly speaking, writers use sound-to-letter rules inspired by those of English[1] as well as informally established conventions to render the sounds of the DA sentence. Because the sound-to-letter rules of English are very different from those of Arabic, we obtain complex mappings between the two writing systems. This issue is compounded by the underlying problem that DA itself does not have any standard orthography in the Arabic script. Table 1 shows different plausible ways of writing an Egyptian Arabic (EGY) sentence in Arabizi and in Arabic script.

Arabizi poses a problem for natural language processing (NLP). While some tools have recently become available for processing EGY input, e.g., (Habash et al., 2012b; Habash et al., 2013; Pasha et al., 2014), they expect Arabic script input (or a Buckwalter transliteration). They cannot process Arabizi. We therefore need a tool that converts from Arabizi to Arabic script. However, the lack of standard orthography in EGY compounds the problem: what should we convert Arabizi into? Our answer to this question is to use CODA, a conventional orthography created for the purpose of supporting NLP tools (Habash et al., 2012a). The goal of CODA is to reduce the data sparseness that comes from the same word form appearing in many spontaneous orthographies in data (be it annotated or unannotated). CODA has been defined for EGY as well as Tunisian Arabic (Zribi et al., 2014), and it has been used as part of different approaches for modeling DA morphology (Habash et al., 2012b), tagging (Habash et al., 2013; Pasha et al., 2014) and spelling correction (Eskander et al., 2013; Farra et al., 2014).

This paper makes two main contributions. First, we clearly define the computational problem of transforming Arabizi to CODA. This improves over previous work by unambiguously fixing the

[1]In different parts of the Arab World, the basis for the Latin script rendering of DA may come from different languages that natively uses the Latin script, such as English or French. In this paper, we concentrate on Egyptian Arabic, which uses English as its main source of sound-to-letter rules.

Proceedings of the Eighteenth Conference on Computational Language Learning, pages 30–38,
Baltimore, Maryland USA, June 26-27 2014.

target representation for the transformation. Second, we perform experiments using different components in a transformation pipeline, and show that a combination of character-based transduction, filtering using a morphological analyzer, and using a language model outperforms other architectures, including the state-of-the-art system described in Darwish (2013). Darwish (2013) presented a conversion tool, but did not discuss conversion into a conventionalized orthography, and did not investigate different architectures. We show in this paper that our proposed architecture, which includes an EGY morphological analyzer, improves over Darwish's architecture.

This paper is structured as follows. We start out by presenting relevant linguistic facts (Section 2) and then we discuss related work. We present our approach in Section 4 and our experiments and results in Section 5.

2 Linguistic Facts

2.1 EGY Spontaneous Orthography

An orthography is a specification of how to use a particular writing system (script) to write the words of a particular language. In cases where there is no standard orthography, people use a spontaneous orthography that is based on different criteria. The main criterion is phonology: how to render a word pronunciation in the given writing system. This mainly depends on language-specific assumptions about the grapheme-to-phoneme mapping. Another criterion is to use cognates in a related language (similar language or a language variant), where two words represent a cognate if they are related etymologically and have the same meaning. Additionally, a spontaneous orthography may be affected by speech effects, which are the lengthening of specific syllables to show emphasis or other effects (such as كتييير *ktyyyyr* [2] 'veeeery').

EGY has no standard orthography. Instead, it has a spontaneous orthography that is related to the standard orthography of Modern Standard Arabic. Table 1 shows an example of writing a sentence in EGY spontaneous orthography in different variants.

2.2 Arabizi

Arabizi is a spontaneous orthography used to write DA using the Latin script, the so-called Arabic numerals, and other symbols commonly found on various input devices such as punctuation. Arabizi is commonly used by Arabic speakers to write in social media and SMS and chat applications.

The orthography decisions made for writing in Arabizi mainly depend on a phoneme-to-grapheme mapping between the Arabic pronunciation and the Latin script. This is largely based on the phoneme-to-grapheme mapping used in English. Crucially, Arabizi is *not* a simple transliteration of Arabic, under which each Arabic letter in some orthography is replaced by a Latin letter (as is the case in the Buckwalter transliteration used widely in natural language processing but nowhere else). As a result, it is not straightforward to convert Arabizi to Arabic. We discuss some specific aspects of Arabizi.

Vowels While EGY orthography omits vocalic diacritics representing short vowels, Arabizi uses the Latin script symbols for vowels (a, e, i, o, u, y) to represent EGY's short and long vowels, making them ambiguous. In some cases, Arabizi words omit short vowels altogether as is done in Arabic orthography.

Consonants Another source of ambiguity is the use of a single Latin letter to refer to multiple Arabic phonemes. For example, the Latin letter "d" is used to represent the sounds of the Arabic letters د *d* and ض *D*. Additionally, some pairs of Arabizi letters can ambiguously map to a single Arabic letter or pairs of letters: "sh" can be use to represent ش š or سه *sh*. Arabizi also uses digits to represent some Arabic letters. For example, the digits 2, 3, 5, 6, 7 and 9 are used to represent the Hamza (glottal stop), and the sounds of the letters ع *ς*, خ *x*, ط *T*, ح *H* and ص *S*, respectively. However, when followed by "'", the digits 3, 6, 7 and 9 change their interpretations to the dotted version of the Arabic letter: غ *γ*, ظ *Ď*, خ *x* and ض *D*, respectively. Moreover, "'" (as well as "q") may also refer to the glottal stop.

Foreign Words Arabizi contains a large number of foreign words, that are either borrowings such as *mobile* or instances of code switching such as *I love you*.

Abbreviations Arabizi may also include some abbreviations such as *isa* which means إن شاء الله *Ǎn šA' Allh* 'God willing'.

[2] Arabic transliteration is presented in the Habash-Soudi-Buckwalter scheme (Habash et al., 2007): (in alphabetical order) *AbtθjHxdðrzsšSDTĎςγfqklmnhwy* and the additional symbols: ' ء, Â أ, Ǎ إ, Ā آ, ŵ ؤ, ŷ ئ, ħ ة, ý ى.

Orthography	Example
CODA	ما شفتش صحابي من امبارح *mA šftš SHAby mn AmbArH*
Non-CODA Arabic Script	ماشوفتش صوحابى من امبارح *mAšwftš SwHAbý mn AmbArH* مشفتش صحابى من إنبارح *mšftš SHAbý mn ĂnbArH* ما شفتيش صحابي من إمبارح *mA šftyš SHAby mn ĂmbArH*
Arabizi	*mashoftesh sohaby men embare7* *ma shftesh swhabi mn imbareh* *mshwftish swhaby min ambare7*

Table 1: The different spelling variants in EGY and Arabizi for writing the sentence *"I have not seen my friends since yesterday"* versus its corresponding CODA form.

2.3 CODA

CODA is a conventionalized orthography for Dialectal Arabic (Habash et al., 2012a). In CODA, every word has a single orthographic representation. CODA has five key properties (Eskander et al., 2013). First, CODA is an internally consistent and coherent convention for writing DA. Second, CODA is primarily created for computational purposes, but is easy to learn and recognize by educated Arabic speakers. Third, CODA uses the Arabic script as used for MSA, with no extra symbols from, for example, Persian or Urdu. Fourth, CODA is intended as a unified framework for writing all dialects. CODA has been defined for EGY (Habash et al., 2012a) as well as Tunisian Arabic (Zribi et al., 2014). Finally, CODA aims to maintain a level of dialectal uniqueness while using conventions based on similarities between MSA and the dialects. For a full presentation of CODA and a justification and explanation of its choices, see (Habash et al., 2012a).

CODA has been used as part of different approaches for modeling DA morphology (Habash et al., 2012b), tagging (Habash et al., 2013; Pasha et al., 2014) and spelling correction (Eskander et al., 2013; Farra et al., 2014). Converting Dialectal Arabic (written using a spontaneous Arabic orthography or Arabizi) to CODA is beneficial to NLP applications that better perform on standardized data with less sparsity (Eskander et al., 2013).

Table 1 shows the CODA form corresponding to spontaneously written Arabic.

3 Related Work

Our proposed work has some similarities to Darwish (2013). His work is divided into two sections: language identification and transliteration. He used word and sequence-level features to identify Arabizi that is mixed with English. For Arabic words, he modeled transliteration from Arabizi to Arabic script, and then applied language modeling on the transliterated text. This is similar to our proposed work in terms of transliteration and language modeling. However, Darwish (2013) does not target a conventionalized orthography, while our system targets CODA. Additionally, Darwish (2013) transliterates Arabic words only after filtering out non-Arabic words, while we transliterate the whole input Arabizi. Finally, he does not use any morphological information, while we introduce the use of a morphological analyzer to support the transliteration pipeline.

Chalabi and Gerges (2012) presented a hybrid approach for Arabizi transliteration. Their work relies on the use of character transformation rules that are either handcrafted by a linguist or automatically generated from training data. They also employ word-based and character-based language models for the final transliteration choice. Like Darwish (2013), the work done by Chalabi and Gerges (2012) is similar to ours except that it does not target a conventionalized orthography, and does not use deep morphological information, while our system does.

There are three commercial products that convert Arabizi to Arabic, namely: Microsoft Maren,[3] Google Ta3reeb[4] and Yamli.[5] However, since these products are for commercial purposes, there is not enough information about their approaches. But given their output, it is clear that they do not follow a well-defined standardized orthography like we do. Furthermore, these tools are primarily intended as input method support, not full text transliteration. As a result, their users' goal is to produce Arabic script text not Arabizi text. We expect, for instance, that users of these input method support systems will use less or no code switching to English, and they may employ character sequences that help them arrive at the target Arabic script form, which otherwise they would not write if they are targeting Arabizi.

Eskander et al. (2013) introduced a system to convert spontaneous EGY to CODA, called CODAFY. The difference between CODAFY and our proposed system is that CODAFY works on spontaneous text written in Arabic script, while our system works on Arabizi, which involves a higher degree of ambiguity. However, we use CODAFY as a black-box module in our preprocessing.

Additionally, there is some work on converting from dialectal Arabic to MSA, which is similar to our work in terms of processing a dialectal input. However, our final output is in EGY and not MSA. Shaalan et al. (2007) introduced a rule-based approach to convert EGY to MSA. Al-Gaphari and Al-Yadoumi (2010) also used a rule-based method to transform from Sanaani dialect to MSA. Sawaf (2010), Salloum and Habash (2011) and Salloum and Habash (2013) used morphological analysis and morphosyntactic transformation rules for processing EGY and Levantine Arabic.

There has been some work on machine transliteration by Knight and Graehl (1997). Al-Onaizan and Knight (2002) introduced an approach for machine transliteration of Arabic names. Freeman et al. (2006) also introduced a system for name matching between English and Arabic, which Habash (2008) employed as part of generating English transliterations from Arabic words in the context of machine translation. This work is similar to ours in terms of text transliteration. However, our work is not restricted to names.

[3]http://www.getmaren.com

[4]http://www.google.com/ta3reeb

[5]http://www.yamli.com/

4 Approach

4.1 Defining the Task

Our task is as follows: for each Arabizi word in the input, we choose the Arabic script word which is the correct CODA spelling of the input word and which carries the intended meaning (as determined in the context of the entire available text).

We do not merge two or more input words into a single Arabic script word. If CODA requires two consecutive input Arabizi words to be merged, we indicate this by attaching a plus to the end of the first word. On the other hand, if CODA requires an input Arabizi word to be broken into two or more Arabic script words, we indicate this by inserting a dash between the words. We do this to maintain the bijection between input and output words, i.e., to allow easy tracing of the Arabic script back to the Arabizi input.

4.2 Transliteration Pipeline

The proposed system in this paper is called 3ARRIB.[6] Using the context of an input Arabizi word, 3ARRIB produces the word's best Arabic script CODA transliteration. Figure 1 illustrates the different components of 3ARRIB in both the training and processing phases. We summarize the full transliteration process as follows. Each Arabizi sentence input to 3ARRIB goes through a preprocessing step of lowercasing (de-capitalization), speech effects handling, and punctuation splitting. 3ARRIB then generates a list of all possible transliterations for each word in the input sentence using a finite-state transducer that is trained on character-level alignment from Arabizi to Arabic script. We then experiment with different combinations of the following two components:

Morphological Analyzer We use CALIMA (Habash et al., 2012b), a morphological analyzer for EGY. For each input word, CALIMA provides all possible morphological analyses, including the CODA spelling for each analysis. All generated candidates are passed through CALIMA. If CALIMA has no analysis for a candidate, then that candidate gets filtered out; otherwise, the CODA spellings of the analyses from CALIMA become the new candidates in the rest of the transliteration pipeline. For some words, CALIMA may suggest multiple CODA spellings that reflect different analyses of the word.

[6]3ARRIB (pronounced /ar-rib/) means "Arabize!".

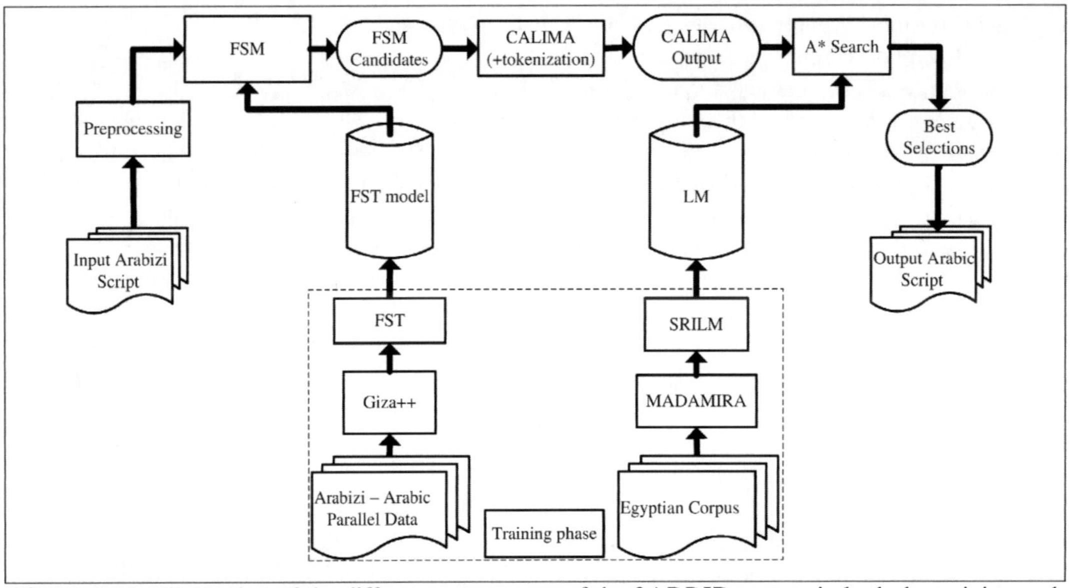

Figure 1: An illustration of the different components of the 3ARRIB system in both the training and processing phases. FST: finite-state Transducer; LM: Language Model; CALIMA: Morphological Analyzer for Dialectal Arabic; MADAMIRA: Morphological Tagger for Arabic.

Language Model We disambiguate among the possibilities for all input words (which constitute a "sausage" lattice) using an n-gram language model.

4.3 Preprocessing

We apply the following preprocessing steps to the input Arabizi text:

- We separate all attached emoticons such as (:D, :p, etc.) and punctuation from the words. We only keep the apostrophe because it is used in Arabizi to distinguish between different sounds. 3ARRIB keeps track of any word offset change, so that it can reconstruct the same number of tokens at the end of the pipeline.
- We tag emoticons and punctuation to protect them from any change through the pipeline.
- We lowercase all letters.
- We handle speech effects by replacing any sequence of the same letter whose length is greater than two by a sequence of exactly length two; for example, *iiiii* becomes *ii*.

4.4 Character-Based Transduction

We use a parallel corpus of Arabizi-Arabic words to learn a character-based transduction model. The parallel data consists of two sources. First, we use 2,200 Arabizi-to-Arabic script pairs from the training data used by (Darwish, 2013). We manually revised the Arabic side to be CODA-compliant. Second, we use about 6,300 pairs of proper names in Arabic and English from the Buckwalter Arabic Morphological Analyzer (Buckwalter, 2004). Since proper names are typically transliterated, we expect them to be a rich source for learning transliteration mappings.

The words in the parallel data are turned into space-separated character tokens, which we align using Giza++ (Och and Ney, 2003). We then use the phrase extraction utility in the Moses statistical machine translation system (Koehn et al., 2007) to extract a *phrase table* which operates over characters. The phrase table is then used to build a finite-state transducer (FST) that maps sequences of Arabizi characters into sequences of Arabic script characters. We use the negative logarithmic conditional probabilities of the Arabizi-to-Arabic pairs in the phrase tables as costs inside the FST. We use the FST to transduce an input Arabizi word to one or more words in Arabic script, where every resulting word in Arabic script is given a probabilistic score.

As part of the preprocessing of the parallel data, we associate all Arabizi letters with their word location information (beginning, middle and ending letters). This is necessary since some Arabizi mapping phenomena happen only at specific locations. For example, the Arabizi letter "o" is likely to be transliterated into أ *Â* in Arabic if it appears at the beginning of the word, but almost never so if it appears in the middle of the word.

For some special Arabizi cases, we directly transliterate input words to their correct Arabic form using a table, without going through the FST. For example, *isa* is mapped to إن شاء الله *Ǎn šA' Allh* 'God willing'. There are currently 32 entries in this table.

4.5 Morphological Analyzer

For every word in the Arabizi input, all the candidates generated by the character-based transduction are passed through the CALIMA morphological analyzer. For every candidate, CALIMA produces a list of all the possible morphological analyses. The CODA for these analyses need not be the same. For example, if the output from the character based transducer is *Aly*, then CALIMA produces the following CODA-compliant spellings: إلى *Ǎlý* 'to', إلي *Ǎlý* 'to me' and آلي *Āly* 'automatic' or 'my family'. All of these CODA spellings are the output of CALIMA for that particular input word. The output from CALIMA then becomes the set of final candidates of the input Arabizi in the rest of the transliteration pipeline. If a word is not recognized by CALIMA, it gets filtered out from the transliteration pipeline. However, if all the candidates of some word are not recognized by CALIMA, then we retain them all since there should be an output for every input word.

We additionally run a tokenization step that makes use of the generated CALIMA morphological analysis. The tokenization scheme we target is D3, which separates all clitics associated with the word (Habash, 2010). For every word, we keep a list of the possible tokenized and untokenized CODA-compliant pairs. We use the tokenized or untokenized forms as inputs to either a tokenized or untokenized language model, respectively, as described in the next subsection. The untokenized form is necessary to retain the surface form at the end of the transliteration process.

Standalone clitics are sometimes found in Arabizi such as *lel ragel* (which corresponds to لل+ راجل *ll+ rAjl* 'for the man'). Since CALIMA does not handle most standalone clitics, we keep a lookup table that associates them with their tokenization information.

4.6 Language Model

We then use an EGY language model that is trained on CODA-compliant text. We investigate two options: a language model that has standard CODA white-space word tokenization conventions ("untokenized"), and a language model that has a D3 tokenized form of CODA in which all clitics are separated ("tokenized"). The output of the morphological analyzer (which is the input to the LM component) is processed to match the tokenization used in the LM.

The language models are built from a large corpus of 392M EGY words.[7] The corpus is first processed using CODAFY (Eskander et al., 2013), a system for spontaneous text conventionalization into CODA. This is necessary so that our system remains CODA-compliant across the whole transliteration pipeline. Eskander et al. (2013) states that the best conventionalization results are obtained by running the MLE component of CODAFY followed by an EGY morphological tagger, MADA-ARZ (Habash et al., 2013). In the work reported here, we use the newer version of MADA-ARZ, named MADAMIRA (Pasha et al., 2014). For the tokenized language model, we run a D3 tokenization step on top of the processed text by MADAMIRA. The processed data is used to build a language model with Kneser-Ney smoothing using the SRILM toolkit (Stolcke, 2002).

We use A* search to pick the best transliteration for each word given its context. The probability of any path in the A* search space combines the FST probability of the words with the probability from the language model. Thus, for any certain path of selected Arabic possibilities $A_{0,i} = \{a_0, a_1, ...a_i\}$ given the corresponding input Arabizi sequence $W_{0,i} = \{w_0, w_1, ...w_i\}$, the transliteration probability can be defined by equation (1).

$$P(A_{0,i}|W_{0,i}) = \prod_{j=0}^{i}(P(a_j|w_j) * P(a_j|a_{j-N+1,j-1})) \quad (1)$$

Where, N is the maximum affordable n-gram length in the LM, $P(a_j|w_j)$ is the FST probability of transliterating the Arabizi word w_j into the Arabic word a_j, and $P(a_j|a_{j-N+1,j-1})$ is the LM probability of the sequence $\{a_{j-N+1}, a_{j-N+2}, ...a_j\}$.

[7] All of the resources we use are available from the Linguistic Data Consortium: www.ldc.upenn.edu.

5 Experiments and Results

5.1 Data

We use two in-house data sets for development (Dev; 502 words) and blind testing (Test; 1004 words). The data contains EGY Arabizi SMS conversations that are mapped to Arabic script in CODA by a CODA-trained EGY native speaker.

5.2 Experiments

We conducted a suite of experiments to evaluate the performance of our approach and identify optimal settings on the Dev set. The optimal result and the baseline are then applied to the blind Test set. During development, the following settings were explored:

- **INV-Selection:** The training data of the finite state transducer is used to generate the list of possibilities for each input Arabizi word. If the input word cannot be found in the FST training data, the word is kept in Arabizi.
- **FST-ONLY:** Pick the top choice from the list generated by the finite state transducer.
- **FST-CALIMA:** Pick the top choice from the list after the CALIMA filtering.
- **FST-CALIMA-Tokenized-LM-5:** Run the full pipeline of 3ARRIB with a 5-gram tokenized LM.[8]
- **FST-CALIMA-Tokenized-LM-5-MLE:** The same as FST-CALIMA-Tokenized-LM-5, but for an Arabizi word that appears in training, force its most frequently seen mapping directly instead of running the transliteration pipeline for that word.
- **FST-CALIMA-Untokenized-LM-5:** Run the full pipeline of 3ARRIB with a 5-gram untokenized LM.
- **FST-Untokenized-LM-5:** Run the full pipeline of 3ARRIB minus the CALIMA filtering with a 5-gram untokenized LM. This setup is analogous to the transliteration approach proposed by (Darwish, 2013). Thus we use it as our baseline.

Each of the above experiments is evaluated with exact match, and with Alif/Ya normalization (El Kholy and Habash, 2010; Habash, 2010).

[8] 3, 5, and 7-gram LMs have been tested. The 3 and 5-gram LMs give the same performance while the 7-gram LM is the worst.

5.3 Results

Table 2 summarizes the results on the Dev set. Our best performing setup is FST-CALIMA-Tokenized-LM-5 which has 77.5% accuracy and 79.1% accuracy with normalization. The baseline system, FST-Untokenized-LM-5, gives 74.1% accuracy and 74.9 % accuracy with normalization. This highlights the value of morphological filtering as well as sparsity-reducing tokenization.

Table 3 shows how we do (best system and best baseline) on a blind Test set. Although the accuracy drops overall, the gap between the best system and the baseline increases.

5.4 Error Analysis

We conducted two error analyses for the best performing transliteration setting on the Dev set. We first analyze in which component the Dev set errors occur. About 29% of the errors are cases where the FST does not generate the correct answer. An additional 15% of the errors happen because the correct answer is not covered by CALIMA. The language model does not include the correct answer in an additional 8% of the errors. The rest of the errors (48%) are cases where the correct answer is available in all components but does not get selected.

Motivated by the value of Arabizi transliteration for machine translation into English, we distinguish between two types of words: words that remain the same when translated into English, such as English words, proper nouns, laughs, emoticons, punctuations and digits (EN-SET) versus EGY-only words (EGY-SET). Examples of words in EN-SET are: *love you very much* (code switching), *Peter* (proper noun), *haha* (laugh), *:D* (emoticon), *!* (punctuation) and *123* (digits).

While the overall performance of our best settings is 77.5%, the accuracy of the EGY-SET by itself is 84.6% as opposed to 46.2% for EN-SET. This large difference reflects the fact that we do not target English word transliteration into Arabic script explicitly.

We now perform a second error analysis only on the errors in the EGY-SET, in which we categorize the errors by their linguistic type. About 25% of the errors are non-CODA-compliant system output, where the answer is a plausible non-CODA form, i.e., a form that may be written or read easily by a native speaker who is not aware of CODA. For example, the system generates the non-CODA

System	Exact-Matching	A/Y-normalization
INV-Selection	37.1	40.6
FST-ONLY (pick top choice)	63.1	65.1
FST-CALIMA (pick top choice)	66.1	68.9
FST-CALIMA-Tokenized-LM-5	**77.5**	**79.1**
FST-CALIMA-Tokenized-LM-5-MLE	68.7	73.5
FST-CALIMA-Untokenized-LM-5	77.3	78.9
FST-Untokenized-LM-5	74.1	74.9

Table 2: Results on the Dev set in terms of accuracy (%).

System	Exact-Matching	A/Y-normalization
FST-CALIMA-Tokenized-LM-5	**69.4**	**73.9**
FST-Untokenized-LM-5	63.1	65.4

Table 3: Results on the blind Test set in terms of accuracy (%).

form مينفعش *mynfςš* instead of the correct CODA form ما ينفعش *mA ynfςš* 'it doesn't work'. Ignoring the CODA-related errors increases the overall accuracy by about 3.0% to become 80.5%. The accuracy of the EGY-SET rises to 88.3% as opposed to 84.6% when considering CODA compliance.

Ambiguous Arabizi input contributes to an additional 27% of the errors, where the system assigns a plausible answer that is incorrect in context. For example, the word *matar* in the input Arabizi *fel matar* 'at the airport' has two plausible out-of-context solutions: مطار *mTAr* 'airport' (contextually correct) and مطر *mTr* 'rain' (contextually incorrect).

In about 2% of the errors, the Arabizi input contains a typo making it impossible to produce the gold reference. For example, the input Arabizi *ba7bet* contains a typo where the final *t* should turn into *k*, so that it means باحبك *bAHbk* 'I love you [2fs]'.

In the rest of the errors (about 46%), the system fails to come up with the correct answer. Instead, it assigns a completely different word or even an impossible word. For example, the correct answer for the input Arabizi *sora* 'picture' is صورة *Swr¯ħ* while the system produces the word سور *swr* 'wall'. Another example is the input Arabizi *talabt* 'I asked for', where the output from the system is طالبة *TAlb¯ħ* 'student', while the correct answer is طلبت *tlbt* 'I asked for, ordered' instead.

6 Conclusion and Future Work

We presented a method for converting dialectal Arabic (specifically, EGY) written in Arabizi to Arabic script following the CODA convention for DA orthography. We achieve a 17% error reduction over our implementation of a previously published work (Darwish, 2013) on a blind test set.

In the future, we plan to improve several aspects of our models, particularly FST character mapping, the morphological analyzer coverage, and language models. We also plan to work on the problem of automatic identification of non-Arabic words. We will extend the system to work on other Arabic dialects. We also plan to make the 3ARRIB system publicly available.

Acknowledgement

This paper is based upon work supported by the Defense Advanced Research Projects Agency (DARPA) under Contract No. HR0011-12-C-0014. Any opinions, findings and conclusions or recommendations expressed in this paper are those of the authors and do not necessarily reflect the views of DARPA.

References

G. Al-Gaphari and M. Al-Yadoumi. 2010. A method to convert Sana'ani accent to Modern Standard Arabic. *International Journal of Information Science and Management*, pages 39–49.

Yaser Al-Onaizan and Kevin Knight. 2002. Machine transliteration of names in arabic text. In *Proceedings of the ACL-02 Workshop on Computational Approaches to Semitic Languages*.

Tim Buckwalter. 2004. Buckwalter Arabic Morphological Analyzer Version 2.0. LDC catalog number LDC2004L02, ISBN 1-58563-324-0.

Achraf Chalabi and Hany Gerges. 2012. Romanized Arabic Transliteration. In *Proceedings of the Second Workshop on Advances in Text Input Methods (WTIM 2012)*.

Kareem Darwish. 2013. Arabizi Detection and Conversion to Arabic. *CoRR*.

Ahmed El Kholy and Nizar Habash. 2010. Techniques for Arabic Morphological Detokenization and Orthographic Denormalization. In *Proceedings of the seventh International Conference on Language Resources and Evaluation (LREC)*, Valletta, Malta.

Ramy Eskander, Nizar Habash, Owen Rambow, and Nadi Tomeh. 2013. Processing Spontaneous Orthography. In *Proceedings of the 2013 Conference of the North American Chapter of the Association for Computational Linguistics: Human Language Technologies (NAACL-HLT)*, Atlanta, GA.

Noura Farra, Nadi Tomeh, Alla Rozovskaya, and Nizar Habash. 2014. Generalized Character-Level Spelling Error Correction. In *Proceedings of the Conference of the Association for Computational Linguistics (ACL)*, Baltimore, Maryland, USA.

Andrew Freeman, Sherri Condon, and Christopher Ackerman. 2006. Cross linguistic name matching in English and Arabic. In *Proceedings of the Human Language Technology Conference of the NAACL, Main Conference*, pages 471–478, New York City, USA.

Nizar Habash, Abdelhadi Soudi, and Tim Buckwalter. 2007. On Arabic Transliteration. In A. van den Bosch and A. Soudi, editors, *Arabic Computational Morphology: Knowledge-based and Empirical Methods*. Springer.

Nizar Habash, Mona Diab, and Owen Rabmow. 2012a. Conventional Orthography for Dialectal Arabic. In *Proceedings of the Language Resources and Evaluation Conference (LREC)*, Istanbul.

Nizar Habash, Ramy Eskander, and Abdelati Hawwari. 2012b. A Morphological Analyzer for Egyptian Arabic. In *Proceedings of the Twelfth Meeting of the Special Interest Group on Computational Morphology and Phonology*, pages 1–9, Montréal, Canada.

Nizar Habash, Ryan Roth, Owen Rambow, Ramy Eskander, and Nadi Tomeh. 2013. Morphological Analysis and Disambiguation for Dialectal Arabic. In *Proceedings of the 2013 Conference of the North American Chapter of the Association for Computational Linguistics: Human Language Technologies (NAACL-HLT)*, Atlanta, GA.

Nizar Habash. 2008. Four Techniques for Online Handling of Out-of-Vocabulary Words in Arabic-English Statistical Machine Translation. In *Proceedings of ACL-08: HLT, Short Papers*, pages 57–60, Columbus, Ohio.

Nizar Habash. 2010. *Introduction to Arabic Natural Language Processing*. Morgan & Claypool Publishers.

Kevin Knight and Jonathan Graehl. 1997. Machine transliteration. In *Proceedings of the European chapter of the Association for Computational Linguistics*.

Philipp Koehn, Hieu Hoang, Alexandra Birch, Chris Callison-Burch, Marcello Federico, Nicola Bertoldi, Brooke Cowan, Wade Shen, Christine Moran, Richard Zens, Chris Dyer, Ondrej Bojar, Alexandra Constantin, and Evan Herbst. 2007. Moses: Open source toolkit for statistical machine translation. In *Proceedings of the Association for Computational Linguistics*, Prague, Czech Republic.

Franz Joseph Och and Hermann Ney. 2003. A systematic comparison of various statistical alignment models. *Computational Linguistics*, 29(1):19–51.

Arfath Pasha, Mohamed Al-Badrashiny, Mona Diab, Ahmed El Kholy, Ramy Eskander, Nizar Habash, Manoj Pooleery, Owen Rambow, and Ryan M. Roth. 2014. MADAMIRA: A Fast, Comprehensive Tool for Morphological Analysis and Disambiguation of Arabic. In *Proceedings of the Language Resources and Evaluation Conference (LREC)*, Reykjavik, Iceland.

Wael Salloum and Nizar Habash. 2011. Dialectal to Standard Arabic Paraphrasing to Improve Arabic-English Statistical Machine Translation. In *Proceedings of the First Workshop on Algorithms and Resources for Modelling of Dialects and Language Varieties*, pages 10–21, Edinburgh, Scotland.

Wael Salloum and Nizar Habash. 2013. Dialectal Arabic to English Machine Translation: Pivoting through Modern Standard Arabic. In *Proceedings of the 2013 Conference of the North American Chapter of the Association for Computational Linguistics: Human Language Technologies (NAACL-HLT)*, Atlanta, GA.

Hassan Sawaf. 2010. Arabic dialect handling in hybrid machine translation. In *Proceedings of the Conference of the Association for Machine Translation in the Americas (AMTA)*, Denver, Colorado.

Khaled Shaalan, Hitham Abo Bakr, and Ibrahim Ziedan. 2007. Transferring Egyptian Colloquial into Modern Standard Arabic. In *International Conference on Recent Advances in Natural Language Processing (RANLP)*, Borovets, Bulgaria.

Andreas Stolcke. 2002. SRILM - an Extensible Language Modeling Toolkit. In *Proceedings of the International Conference on Spoken Language Processing (ICSLP)*, volume 2, pages 901–904, Denver, CO.

Ines Zribi, Rahma Boujelbane, Abir Masmoudi, Mariem Ellouze, Lamia Belguith, and Nizar Habash. 2014. A Conventional Orthography for Tunisian Arabic. In *Proceedings of the Language Resources and Evaluation Conference (LREC)*, Reykjavik, Iceland.

Learning to Rank Answer Candidates for Automatic Resolution of Crossword Puzzles

Gianni Barlacchi
University of Trento
38123 Povo (TN), Italy
gianni.barlacchi@gmail.com

Massimo Nicosia and **Alessandro Moschitti**
Qatar Computing Research Institute
5825 Doha, Qatar
m.nicosia@gmail.com, amoschitti@qf.org.qa

Abstract

In this paper, we study the impact of relational and syntactic representations for an interesting and challenging task: the automatic resolution of crossword puzzles. Automatic solvers are typically based on two answer retrieval modules: (i) a web search engine, e.g., Google, Bing, etc. and (ii) a database (DB) system for accessing previously resolved crossword puzzles. We show that learning to rank models based on relational syntactic structures defined between the clues and the answer can improve both modules above. In particular, our approach accesses the DB using a search engine and reranks its output by modeling paraphrasing. This improves on the MRR of previous system up to 53% in ranking answer candidates and greatly impacts on the resolution accuracy of crossword puzzles up to 15%.

1 Introduction

Crossword puzzles (CPs) are probably the most popular language games played around the world. It is very challenging for human intelligence as it requires high level of general knowledge, logical thinking, intuition and the ability to deal with ambiguities and puns. CPs normally have the form of a square or rectangular grid of white and black shaded squares. The white squares on the border of the grid or adjacent to the black ones are associated with clues. The goal of the game is to fill the sequences of white squares with words answering the clues.

There have been many attempts to build automatic CP solving systems, which have also participated in competitions such as The American Crossword Puzzle Tournament (ACPT). This is the oldest and largest CP tournament for crossword experts held in the United States. The goal of such systems is to outperform human players in solving crosswords more accurately and in less time.

Automatic CP solvers have been mainly targeted by the artificial intelligence (AI) community, who has mostly focused on AI techniques for filling the puzzle grid, given a set of answer candidates for each clue. The basic idea is to optimize the overall probability of correctly filling the entire grid by exploiting the likelihood of each candidate answer, fulfilling at the same time the grid constraints. After several failures in approaching the human expert performance, it has become clear that designing more accurate solvers would not have provided a winning system. In contrast, the Precision and Recall of the answer candidates are obviously a key factor: a very high value for both of them would enable the solver to quickly find the correct solution.

This basically suggests that, similarly to the Jeopardy! challenge case (Ferrucci et al., 2010b), the solution relies on Question Answering (QA) research. However, although some CP clues are rather similar to standard questions, as for example, in the clue/answer pair: ≪What keeps a camera rolling?: *dolly*≫, some specific differences hold: (i) clues can be in interrogative form or not, e.g., ≪Capital of USA: *Washington*≫; (ii) they can contain riddles or be deliberately ambiguous and misleading (e.g., ≪It's green at first: *orange*≫); (iii) the exact length of the answer keyword is known in advance; and (vi) the confidence in the answers is an extremely important input for the CP solver.

In this paper, we study methods for improving the quality of automatic extraction of answer candidate lists for automatic CP resolution. For this purpose, we designed learning to rank models for reordering the answers produced with two different techniques typically used in CP systems: (i) searching the Web with clue representations, e.g.,

Proceedings of the Eighteenth Conference on Computational Language Learning, pages 39–48,
Baltimore, Maryland USA, June 26-27 2014.

exploiting Bing search engine[1]; and (ii) querying the DB of previously resolved CP clues, e.g., using standard SQL techniques.

We rerank the text snippets returned by Bing by means of SVM preference ranking (Herbrich et al., 2000) for improving the first technique. One interesting contribution is that our model exploits a syntactic representation of clues to improve Web search. More in detail, we use structural kernels (e.g., see (Moschitti, 2006; Moschitti, 2008)) in SVMs applied to our syntactic representation of pairs, formed by clues with their candidate snippets. Regarding the DB approach, we provide a completely novel solution by substituting it and the SQL function with a search engine for retrieving clues similar to the target one. Then, we rerank the retrieved clues by applying SVMs and structural kernels to the syntactic representation of clue pairs. This way, SVMs learn to choose the best candidate among similar clues that are available in the DB. The syntactic representation captures clue paraphrasing properties.

In order to carry out our study, we created two different corpora, one for each task: (i) a snippets reranking dataset and (ii) a clue similarity dataset. The first includes 21,000 clues, each associated with 150 candidate snippets whereas the latter comprises 794,190 clues. These datasets constitute interesting resources that we made available to the research community[2].

We compare our methods with one of the best systems for automatic CP resolution, WebCrow (Ernandes et al., 2005). Such system does use the two approaches mentioned before. Regarding snippet reranking, our structural models improve on the basic approach of WebCrow based on Bing by more than 4 absolute percent points in MRR, for a relative improvement of 23%. Concerning the similar clues retrieval, our methods improve on the one used by WebCrow, based on DBs, by 25% absolute, i.e., about 53% of error reduction whereas the answer accuracy at first position improves up to 70%.

Given such promising results, we used our clue reranking method in WebCrow, and obtained an average improvement of 15% in resolving complete CPs. This demonstrates that advanced QA methods such as those based on syntactic structures and learning to rank methods can help to win the CP resolution challenge.

In the reminder of this paper, Sec. 2 introduces the automatic CP resolution task in the context of the related work, Sec. 3 introduces WebCrow, Sec. 4 illustrates our models for snippets reranking and similar clue retrieval using kernel methods, syntactic structures, and traditional feature vectors, Sec. 5 describes our experiments, and finally, Sec. 6 derives the conclusions.

2 Related Work

Proverb (Littman et al., 2002) was the first system for the automatic resolution of CPs. It includes several modules for generating lists of candidate answers. These lists are merged and used to solve a Probabilistic-Constraint Satisfaction Problem. Proverb relies on a very large crossword database as well as several expert modules, each of them mainly based on domain-specific databases (e.g., movies, writers and geography). In addition, it employs generic-word list generators and clue-specific modules to find solutions for particular kinds of clues like ≪Tel ____ (4): *aviv* ≫. Proverb's modules use many knowledge sources: databases of clues, encyclopedias and Web documents. During the 1998 ACPT, Proverb placed 109th out of 251 contestants.

WebCrow (Ernandes et al., 2005) is based on Proverb. It incorporates additional knowledge sources, provides a solver for the Italian language and improves the clues retrieval model from DB. In particular, it enables partial matching to retrieve clues that do not perfectly overlap with the query. WebCrow carries out basic linguistic analysis such as Part-Of-Speech tagging and lemmatization. It takes advantage of semantic relations contained in WordNet, dictionaries and gazetteers. Its Web module is constituted by a search engine, which can retrieve text snippets or documents related to the clue. Answer candidates and their confidence scores are generated from this content. WebCrow uses a WA* algorithm (Pohl, 1970) for Probabilistic-Constraint Satisfaction Problems, adapted for CP resolution. The solver fills the grid entries for which no solution was found by the previous modules. It tries combinations of letters that satisfy the crossword constraints, where the letters are derived from words found in dictionaries or in the generated candidate lists. WebCrow participated in international competitions with good results.

[1]https://www.bing.com/

[2]http://projects.disi.unitn.it/iKernels/projects/webcrow/

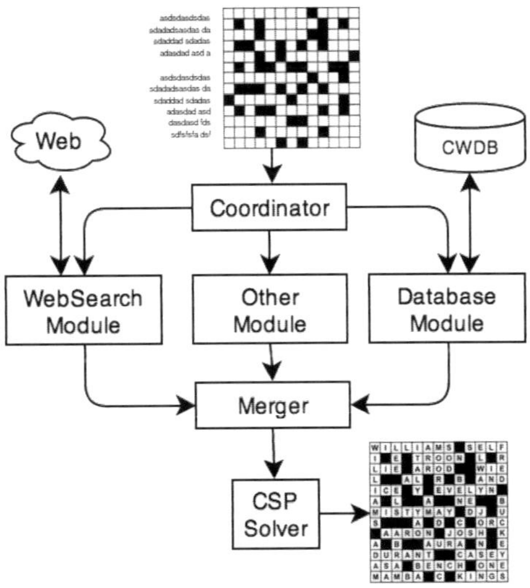

Figure 1: Overview of WebCrow's architecture.

Dr. Fill (Ginsberg, 2011) targets the crossword filling task with a Weighted-Constraint Satisfaction Problem. Constraint violations are weighted and can be tolerated. It heavily relies on huge databases of clues. It was placed 92nd out of more than 600 opponents in the 2013 ACPT.

Specifically for QA using syntactic structures, a referring work for our research is the IBM Watson system (Ferrucci et al., 2010a). This is an advanced QA pipeline based on deep linguistic processing and semantic resources. It demonstrated that automatic methods can be more accurate than human experts in answering complex questions.

More traditional studies on passage reranking, exploiting structural information, were carried out in (Katz and Lin, 2003), whereas other methods explored soft matching (i.e., lexical similarity) based on answer and named entity types (Aktolga et al., 2011). (Radlinski and Joachims, 2006; Jeon et al., 2005) applied question and answer classifiers for passage reranking. In this context, several approaches focused on reranking the answers to definition/description questions, e.g., (Shen and Lapata, 2007; Moschitti et al., 2007; Surdeanu et al., 2008; Severyn and Moschitti, 2012; Severyn et al., 2013b).

3 WebCrow Architecture

Our research focuses on the generation of accurate answer candidate lists, which, when used in a CP resolution systems, can improve the overall solution accuracy. Therefore, the quality of our modules can be assessed by testing them within such systems. For this purpose, we selected WebCrow as it is rather modular, accurate and it was kindly made available by the authors. Its architecture is illustrated in Figure 1.

The solving process is divided in two phases: in the first phase, the coordinator module forwards the clues of an input CP to a set of modules for the generation of several candidate answer lists. Each module returns a list of possible solutions for each clue. Such individual clue lists are then merged by a specific *Merger* component, which uses list confidence values and the probabilities of correctness of each candidate in the lists. Eventually, a single list of candidate-probability pairs is generated for each input clue. During the second phase WebCrow fills the crossword grid by solving a constraint-satisfaction problem. WebCrow selects a single answer from each candidate merged list, trying to satisfy the imposed constraints. The goal of this phase is to find an admissible solution maximizing the number of correct inserted words. In this paper, we focus on two essential modules of WebCrow: the Web and the DB modules, described in the next sections.

3.1 WebSearch Module (WSM)

WSM carries out four different tasks: (i) the retrieval of useful text snippets (TS) and web documents, (ii) the extraction of the answer candidates from such text, (iii) the scoring/filtering of the candidates, and (iv) the estimation of the list confidence. The retrieval of TS is performed by the Bing search engine by simply providing it the clue through its APIs. Then, the latter again are used to access the retrieved TS. The word list generator extracts possible candidate answers from TS or Web documents by picking the terms (also multiwords) of the correct length. The generated lists are merged and sorted using the candidate confidence computed by two filters: the statistical filter and the morphological filter. The score associated with each candidate word w is given by the following heuristic formula:

$$p(w, C) = k(score_{sf}(w, C) \times score_{mf}(w, C)),$$

where (i) C is the target clue, (ii) k is a constant tuned on a validation set such that $\sum_{i=0}^{n} p(w_n, C) = 1$, (iii) $score_{sf}(w, C)$ is computed using statistical information extracted from the text, e.g., the classical TF×IDF, and (iv) $score_{mf}(w, C)$ is computed using morphological features of w.

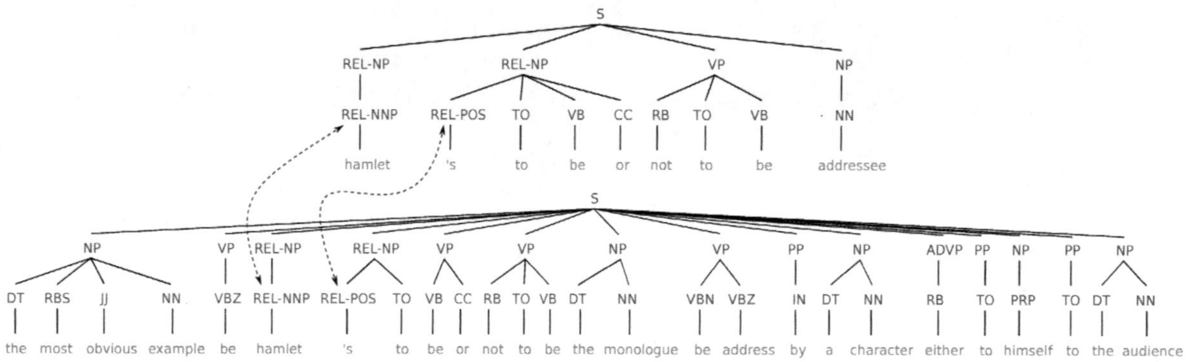

Figure 2: Shallow syntactic trees of clue (upper) and snippet (lower) and their relational links.

3.2 Database module (CWDB)

The knowledge about previous CPs is essential for solving new ones. Indeed, clues often repeat in different CPs, thus the availability of a large DB of clue-answer pairs allows for easily finding the answers to previously used clues. In order to exploit the database of clue-answer pairs, WebCrow uses three different modules:

CWDB-EXACT, which simply checks for an exact matching between the target clue and those in the DB. The score of the match is computed using the number of occurrences of the matched clue.

CWDB-PARTIAL, which employs MySQL's partial matching function, query expansion and positional term distances to compute clue-similarity scores, along with the Full-Text search functions.

CWDB-DICTIO, which simply returns the full list of words of correct length, ranked by their number of occurrences in the initial list.

We improve WSM and CWDB by applying learning-to-rank algorithms based on SVMs and tree kernels applied to structural representations. We describe our models in detail in the next section.

4 Learning to rank with kernels

The basic architecture of our reranking framework is relatively simple: it uses a standard preference kernel reranking approach (e.g., see (Shen and Joshi, 2005; Moschitti et al., 2006)). The structural kernel reranking framework is a specialization of the one we proposed in (Severyn and Moschitti, 2012; Severyn et al., 2013b; Severyn et al., 2013a). However, to tackle the novelty of the task, especially for clue DB retrieval, we modeled innovative kernels. In the following, we first describe the general framework and then we instantiate it for the two reranking tasks studied in this paper.

4.1 Kernel framework

The framework takes a textual query and retrieves a list of related text candidates using a search engine (applied to the Web or a DB), according to some similarity criteria. Then, the query and candidates are processed by an NLP pipeline. The pipeline is based on the UIMA framework (Ferrucci and Lally, 2004) and contains many text analysis components. The latter used for our specific tasks are: the tokenizer[3], sentence detector[1], lemmatizer[1], part-of-speech (POS) tagger[1], chunker[4] and stopword marker[5].

The annotations produced by such processors are used by additional components to produce structural models representing clues and TS. The structure component converts the text fragments into trees. We use both trees and feature vectors to represent pairs of clues and TS, which are employed to train kernel-based rerankers for reordering the candidate lists provided by a search engine. Since the syntactic parsing accuracy can impact the quality of our structure and thus the accuracy of our learning to rank algorithms, we preferred to use shallow syntactic trees over full syntactic representations. In the next section, we first describe the structures we used in our kernels, then the tree kernels used as building blocks for our models. Finally, we show the reranking models for both tasks, TS and clue reranking.

[3] http://nlp.stanford.edu/software/corenlp.shtml

[4] http://cogcomp.cs.illinois.edu/page/software_view/13

[5] Based on a standard stoplist.

Rank	Clue	Answer
1	Kind of support for a computer user	tech
2	Kind of computer connection	wifi
3	Computer connection	port
4	Comb users	bees
5	Traveling bag	grip

Table 1: Clue ranking for the query: *Kind of connection for traveling computer users (wifi)*

4.2 Relational shallow tree representation

The structures we adopt are similar to those defined in (Severyn et al., 2013b). They are essentially shallow syntactic trees built from POS tags grouped into chunks. Each clue and its answer candidate (either a TS or clue) are encoded into a tree having word lemmas at the leaves and POS tags as pre-terminals. The higher tree level organizes POS tags into chunks. For example, the upper tree of Figure 2, shows a shallow tree for the clue: *Hamlet's "To be, or not to be" addressee*, whereas the lower tree represents a retrieved TS containing the answer, *himself*: *The most obvious example is Hamlet's "To be or not to be ... the monologue is addressed by a character either to himself or to the audience.*

Additionally, we use a special REL tag to link the clue/snippet trees above such that structural relations will be captured by tree fragments. The links are established as follows: words from a clue and a snippet sharing a lemma get their parents (POS tags) and grandparents, i.e., chunk labels, marked by a prepending REL tag. We build such structural representations for both snippet and similar clue reranking tasks.

4.3 Tree kernels

We briefly report the different types of kernels (see, e.g., (Moschitti, 2006) for more details).

Syntactic Tree Kernel (STK), also known as a subset tree kernel (Collins and Duffy, 2002), maps objects in the space of all possible tree fragments constrained by the rule that the sibling nodes from their parents cannot be separated. In other words, substructures are composed by atomic building blocks corresponding to nodes along with all of their direct children. These, in case of a syntactic parse tree, are complete production rules of the associated parser grammar.

STK$_b$ extends STK by allowing leaf nodes to be part of the feature space. Leaf in syntactic trees are words, from this the subscript b (bag-of-words).

Subtree Kernel (SbtK) is one of the simplest tree kernels as it only generates complete subtrees, i.e., tree fragments that, given any arbitrary starting node, necessarily include all its descendants.

Partial Tree Kernel (PTK) (Moschitti, 2006) can be effectively applied to both constituency and dependency parse trees. It generates all possible connected tree fragments, e.g., sibling nodes can also be separated and be part of different tree fragments. In other words, a fragment is any possible tree path, from whose nodes other tree paths can depart. Thus, it can generate a very rich feature space resulting in higher generalization ability.

4.4 Snippet reranking

The task of snippet reranking consists in reordering the list of snippets retrieved from the search engine such that those containing the correct answer can be pushed at the top of the list. For this purpose, we transform the target clue in a search query and retrieve candidate text snippets. In our training set, these candidate text snippets are considered as positive examples if they contain the answer to the target clue.

We rerank snippets using preference reranking approach (see, e.g., (Shen and Joshi, 2005)). This means that two snippets are compared to derive which one is the best, i.e., which snippet contains the answer with higher probability. Since we aim at using kernel methods, we apply the following preference kernel:

$$P_K(\langle s_1, s_2\rangle, \langle s_1', s_2'\rangle) = K(s_1, s_1') +$$

$$+K(s_2, s_2') - K(s_1, s_2') - K(s_2, s_1'),$$

where s_r and s_r' refer to two sets of candidates associated with two rankings and K is a kernel applied to pairs of candidates. We represent the latter as pairs of clue and snippet trees. More formally, given two candidates, $s_i = \langle s_i(c), s_i(s)\rangle$ and $s_i' = \langle s_i'(c), s_i'(s)\rangle$, whose members are the clue and snippet trees, we define

$$K(s_i, s_i') = TK(s_i(c), s_i'(c)) + TK(s_i(s), s_i'(s)),$$

where TK can be any tree kernel function, e.g., STK or PTK. Finally, it should be noted that, to add traditional feature vectors to the reranker, it is enough to add the product $(\vec{x}_{s_1} - \vec{x}_{s_2}) \cdot (\vec{x}_{s_1'} - \vec{x}_{s_2'})$ to the structural kernel P_K, where $\vec{x}_s$ is the feature vector associated with the snippet s.

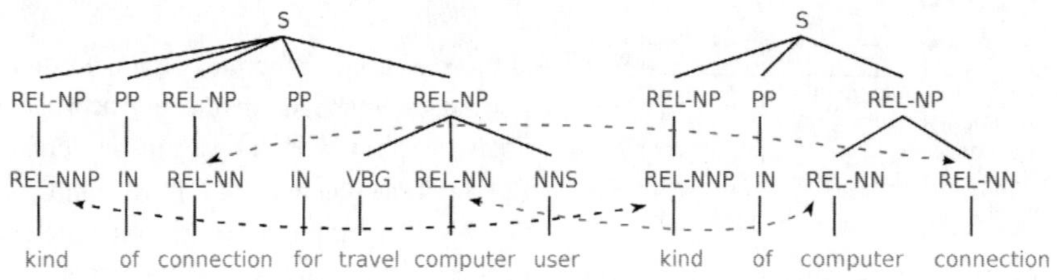

Figure 3: Two similar clues leading to the same answer.

4.5 Similar clue reranking

WebCrow creates answer lists by retrieving clues from the DB of previously solved crosswords. It simply uses the classical SQL operator and full-text search. We instead verified the hypothesis that a search engine could achieve a better result. Thus we opted for indexing the DB clues and their answers with the open source search engine Lucene (McCandless et al., 2010), using the state-of-the-art BM25 retrieval model. This alone significantly improved the quality of the retrieved clue list, which could be further refined by applying reranking. The latter consists in (i) retrieving a list of similar clues using a search engine and (ii) moving those more similar, which more probably contain the same answer to the clue query, at the top. For example, Table 1 shows the first five clues, retrieved for a query built from the clue: *Kind of connection for traveling computer users.* The search engine retrieves the wrong clue, *Kind of connection for traveling computer users*, at the top since it overlaps more with the query.

To solve these kinds of problems by also enhancing the generalization power of our reranking algorithm, we use a structural representation similar to the one for TS that we illustrated in the previous section. The main difference with the previous models is that the reranking pair is only constituted by clues. For example, Fig. 3 shows the representation of the pairs constituted by the query clue and the correct clue ranked in the second position (see Table 1). The relational arrows suggest a syntactic transformation from `connection for * computer` to `computer connection`, which can be used by the reranker to prefer the correct clue to the wrong one. Note that such transformation corresponds to the pair of tree fragments: `[S [REL-NP[REL-NN]][PP][NP[VBG][REL-NN]]]` → `[S [REL-NP[REL-NN][REL-NN]]]`, where the node pairs, ⟨REL-NN, REL-NN⟩ define the arguments of the syntactic transformation. Such fragments can be generated by PTK, which can thus be used for learning clue paraphrasing.

To build the reranking training set, we used the training clues for querying the search engine, which draws candidates from the indexed clues. We stress the fact that this set of clues is disjoint from the clues in the training and test sets. Thus, identical clues are not present across sets. At classification time, the new clue is used as a search query. Similar candidate clues are retrieved and used to form pairs.

4.6 Feature Vectors

In addition to structural representations, we also used features for capturing the degrees of similarity between clues within a pair.

DKPro Similarity. We used similarity features from a top performing system in the Semantic Textual Similarity (STS) task, namely DKPro from the UKP Lab (Bär et al., 2013). These features were effective in predicting the degree of similarity between two sentences. DKPro includes the following syntactic similarity metrics, operating on string sequences, and more advanced semantic similarities:

– *Longest common substring measure* (Gusfield, 1997). It determines the length of the longest substring shared by two text segments.

– *Longest common subsequence measure* (Allison and Dix, 1986). It extends the notion of substrings to word subsequences by applying word insertions or deletions to the original input text pairs.

– *Running-Karp-Rabin Greedy String Tiling* (Wise, 1996). It provides a similarity between two sentences by counting the number of shuffles in their subparts.

– *Resnik similarity* (Resnik, 1995). The WordNet hypernymy hierarchy is used to compute a measure of semantic relatedness between concepts expressed in the text. The aggregation algorithm by Mihalcea et al. (Mihalcea et al., 2006) is applied to extend the measure from words to sentences.

– *Explicit Semantic Analysis* (ESA) similarity

(Gabrilovich and Markovitch, 2007). It represents documents as weighted vectors of concepts learned from Wikipedia, WordNet and Wiktionary.

– *Lexical Substitution* (Biemann, 2013). A supervised word sense disambiguation system is used to substitute a wide selection of high-frequency English nouns with generalizations. Resnik and ESA features are then computed on the transformed text.

New features. Hereafter, we describe new features that we designed for CP reranking tasks.

– *Feasible Candidate*. It is a binary feature signaling the presence or absence of words with the same length of the clue answer (only used for snippet reranking).

– *Term overlap features*. They compute the cosine similarity of text pairs encoded into sets of n-grams extracted from different text features: surface forms of words, lemmas and POS-tags. They are computed keeping and removing stop-words. They complement DKPro features.

– *Kernel similarities*. These are computed using (i) string kernels applied to sentences, or PTK applied to structural representations with and without embedded relational information (REL). This similarity is computed between the members of a $\langle clue, snippet\rangle$ or a $\langle clue, clue\rangle$ pair.

Model	MAP	MRR	AvgRec	REC@1	REC@5
Bing	16.00	18.09	69.00	12.50	24.80
V	18.00	19.88	76.00	14.20	26.10
SbtK	17.00	19.6	75.00	13.80	26.40
STK	18.00	20.44	76.00	15.10	27.00
STK_b	18.00	20.68	76.00	15.30	27.40
PTK	19.00	21.65	77.00	16.10	28.70
V+SbtK	**20.00**	**22.39**	**80.00**	**17.20**	29.10
V+STK	19.00	20.82	78.00	14.90	27.90
STK_b	19.00	21.20	79.00	15.60	28.40
V+PTK	19.00	21.68	79.00	16.00	**29.40**
V+DK	18.00	20.48	77.00	14.60	26.80
V+DK+SbtK	**20.00**	22.29	**80.00**	16.90	28.70
V+DK+STK	19.00	21.47	79.00	15.50	28.30
V+DK+STK_b	19.00	21.58	79.00	15.4	28.60
V+DK+PTK	**20.00**	22.24	**80.00**	16.80	29.30

Table 2: Snippet reranking

Model	MAP	MRR	AvgRec	REC@1	REC@5
MB25	69.00	73.78	80.00	62.11	81.23
WebCrow	-	53.22	58.00	39.60	62.85
SbtK	52.00	54.72	69.00	36.50	64.05
STK	63.00	68.21	77.00	54.57	76.11
STK_b	63.00	67.68	77.00	53.85	75.63
PTK	65.00	70.12	78.00	57.39	77.65
V+SbtK	68.00	73.26	80.00	60.95	81.28
V+STK	71.00	76.01	82.00	64.58	83.95
V+STK_b	70.00	75.68	82.00	63.95	83.77
V+PTK	71.00	76.67	82.00	65.67	84.07
V+DK	71.00	76.76	81.00	65.55	84.29
V+DK+SbtK	72.00	76.91	82.00	65.87	84.51
V+DK+STK	**73.00**	**78.37**	**84.00**	**67.83**	**85.87**
V+DK+STK_b	**73.00**	78.29	**84.00**	67.71	85.77
V+DK+PTK	**73.00**	78.13	83.00	67.39	85.75

Table 3: Reranking of similar clues.

5 Experiments

Our experiments aim at demonstrating the effectiveness of our models on two different tasks: (i) Snippet Reranking and (ii) Similar Clue Retrieval (SCR). Additionally, we measured the impact of our best model for SCR in the WebCrow system by comparing with it. Our referring database of clues is composed by 1,158,202 clues, which belong to eight different crossword editors (downloaded from the Web[6]). We use the latter to create one dataset for snippet reranking and one dataset for clues retrieval.

5.1 Experimental Setup

To train our models, we adopted SVM-light-TK[7], which enables the use of structural kernels (Moschitti, 2006) in SVM-light (Joachims, 2002), with default parameters. We applied a polynomial kernel of degree 3 to the explicit feature vectors, as we believe feature combinations can be valuable. To measure the impact of the rerankers as well as the baselines, we used well known metrics for assessing the accuracy of QA and retrieval systems, i.e.: Recall at rank 1 (R@1 and 5), Mean Reciprocal Rank (MRR), Mean Average Precision (MAP), the average Recall (AvgRec). R@k is the percentage of questions with a correct answer ranked at the first position. MRR is computed as follows: $MRR = \frac{1}{|Q|}\sum_{q=1}^{|Q|}\frac{1}{rank(q)}$, where *rank(q)* is the position of the first correct answer in the candidate list. For a set of queries Q, MAP is the mean over the average precision scores for each query: $\frac{1}{Q}\sum_{q=1}^{Q} AveP(q)$. AvgRec and all the measures are evaluated on the first 10 retrieved snippets/clues. For training and testing the reranker, only the first 10 snippets/clues retrieved by the search engine are used.

5.2 Snippet Reranking

The retrieval from the Web is affected by a significant query processing delay, which prevents us

[6]http://www.crosswordgiant.com

[7]http://disi.unitn.it/moschitti/Tree-Kernel.htm

to use entire documents. Thus, we only considered the text from Bing snippets. Moreover, since our reranking approach does not include the treatment of special clues such as anagrams or linguistic games, e.g., *fill-in-the blank clues*, we have excluded them by our dataset. We crawled the latter from the Web. We converted each clue into a query and downloaded the first 10 snippets as result of a Bing query. In order to reduce noise from the data, we created a black list containing URLs that must not be considered in the download phase, e.g., crossword websites. The training set is composed by 20,000 clues while the test set comprises 1,000 clues.

We implemented and compared many models for reranking the correct snippets higher, i.e., containing the answer to the clue. The compared systems are listed on the first column of Table 2, where: V is the approach using the vector only constituted by the new feature set (see Sec. 4.6); DK is the model using the features made available by DKPro; the systems ending in TK are described in Sec. 4.3; and the plus operator indicates models obtained by summing the related kernels.

Depending on the target measure they suggest slightly different findings. Hereafter, we comment on MRR as it is the most interesting from a ranking viewpoint. We note that: (i) Bing is improved by the reranker based on the new feature vector by 2 absolute points; (ii) DK+V improves on V by just half point; (iii) PTK provides the highest result among individual systems; (iv) combinations improve on the individual systems; and (v) overall, our reranking improves on the ranking of paragraphs of Bing by 4 points in MRR and 5 points in accuracy on the first candidate (REC@1), corresponding to about 20% and 50% of relative improvement and error reduction, respectively.

5.3 Similar clue retrieval

We compiled a crossword database of 794,190 unique pairs of clue-answer. Using the clues contained in this set, we created three different sets: training and test sets and the database of clues. The database of clues can be indexed for retrieving similar clues. It contains 700,000 unique clue-answer pairs. The training set contains 39,504 clues whose answer may be found in database. Using the same approach, we created a test set containing 5,060 clues that (i) are not in the training set and (ii) have at least an answer in the database.

Model	MRR	REC@1	REC@5	REC@10
WebCrow	41.00	33.00	51.00	58.00
Our Model	46.00	39.00	56.00	59.00

Table 4: Performance on the word list candidates averaged over the clues of 10 entire CPs

Model	%Correct words	%Correct letters
WebCrow	34.45	49.72
Our Model	39.69	54.30

Table 5: Performance given in terms of correct words and letters averaged on the 10 CPs

We experimented with all models, as in the previous section, trained for the similar clue retrieval task. However, since WebCrow includes a database module, in Tab. 3, we have an extra row indicating its accuracy. We note that: (i) BM25 shows a very accurate MRR, 73.78%. It largely improves on WebCrow by about 20.5 absolute percent points, demonstrating the superiority of an IR approach over DB methods. (ii) All TK types do not improve alone on BM25, this happens since they do not exploit the initial rank provided by BM25. (iii) All the feature vector and TK combinations achieve high MRR, up to 4.5 absolute percent points of improvement over BM25 and thus 25 points more than WebCrow, corresponding to 53% of error reduction. Finally, (iv) the relative improvement on REC@1 is up to 71% (28.23% absolute). This high result is promising in the light of improving WebCrow for the end task of solving complete CPs.

5.4 Impact on WebCrow

In these experiments, we used our reranking model of similar clues (more specifically, the V+DK+STK model) using 10 complete CPs (for a total of 760 clues) from the New York Times and Washington Post. This way, we could measure the impact of our model on the complete task carried out by WebCrow. More specifically, we give our reranked list of answers to WebCrow in place of the list it would have extracted with the CWDB module. It should be noted that to evaluate the impact of our list, we disabled WebCrow access to other lists, e.g., dictionaries. This means that the absolute resolution accuracy of WebCrow using our and its own lists can be higher (see (Ernandes et al., 2008) for more details).

The first result that we derive is the accuracy of the answer list produced from the new data, i.e., constituted by the 10 entire CPs. The results are reported in Tab. 4. We note that the improvement of our model is lower than before as a non-negligible percentage of clues are not solved using the clue DB. However, when we compute the accuracy in solving the complete CPs, the impact is still remarkable as reported by Tab. 5. Indeed, the results show that when the lists reordered by our reranker are used by WebCrow, the latter improves by more than 5 absolute percent points in both word and character accuracy.

6 Conclusions

In this paper, we improve automatic CP resolution by modeling two innovative reranking tasks for: (i) CP answer list derived from Web search and (ii) CP clue retrieval from clue DBs.

Our rankers are based on SVMs and structural kernels, where the latter are applied to robust shallow syntactic structures. Our model applied to clue reranking is very interesting as it allows us to learn clue paraphrasing by exploiting relational syntactic structures representing pairs of clues.

For our study, we created two different corpora for Snippet Reranking Dataset and Clue Similarity Dataset on which we tested our methods. The latter improve on the lists generated by WebCrow by 25 absolute percent points in MRR (about 53% of relative improvement). When such improved lists are used in WebCrow, its resolution accuracy increases by 15%, demonstrating that there is a large room for improvement in automatic CP resolution. In the future, we would like to add more semantic information to our rerankers and include an answer extraction component in the pipeline.

Acknowledgments

We are deeply in debt with Marco Gori and Marco Ernandes for making available WebCrow, for helping us with their system and for the useful technical discussion regarding research directions. This research has been partially supported by the EC's Seventh Framework Programme (FP7/2007-2013) under the grants #288024: LiMoSINe – Linguistically Motivated Semantic aggregation engiNes. Many thanks to the anonymous reviewers for their valuable work.

References

Elif Aktolga, James Allan, and David A. Smith. 2011. Passage reranking for question answering using syntactic structures and answer types. In *ECIR*.

L Allison and T I Dix. 1986. A bit-string longest-common-subsequence algorithm. *Inf. Process. Lett.*, 23(6):305–310, December.

Daniel Bär, Torsten Zesch, and Iryna Gurevych. 2013. Dkpro similarity: An open source framework for text similarity. In *Proceedings of the 51st Annual Meeting of the Association for Computational Linguistics (System Demonstrations) (ACL 2013)*, pages 121–126, Stroudsburg, PA, USA, August. Association for Computational Linguistics.

Chris Biemann. 2013. Creating a system for lexical substitutions from scratch using crowdsourcing. *Lang. Resour. Eval.*, 47(1):97–122, March.

Michael Collins and Nigel Duffy. 2002. New ranking algorithms for parsing and tagging: Kernels over discrete structures, and the voted perceptron. In *Proceedings of the 40th Annual Meeting on Association for Computational Linguistics*, ACL '02, pages 263–270, Stroudsburg, PA, USA. Association for Computational Linguistics.

Marco Ernandes, Giovanni Angelini, and Marco Gori. 2005. Webcrow: A web-based system for crossword solving. In *In Proc. of AAAI 05*, pages 1412–1417. Menlo Park, Calif., AAAI Press.

Marco Ernandes, Giovanni Angelini, and Marco Gori. 2008. A web-based agent challenges human experts on crosswords. *AI Magazine*, 29(1).

David Ferrucci and Adam Lally. 2004. Uima: An architectural approach to unstructured information processing in the corporate research environment. *Nat. Lang. Eng.*, 10(3-4):327–348, September.

David Ferrucci, Eric Brown, Jennifer Chu-Carroll, James Fan, David Gondek, Aditya Kalyanpur, Adam Lally, J. William Murdock, Eric Nyberg, John Prager, Nico Schlaefer, and Chris Welty. 2010a. Building watson: An overview of the deepqa project. *AI Magazine*, 31(3).

David A. Ferrucci, Eric W. Brown, Jennifer Chu-Carroll, James Fan, David Gondek, Aditya Kalyanpur, Adam Lally, J. William Murdock, Eric Nyberg, John M. Prager, Nico Schlaefer, and Christopher A. Welty. 2010b. Building watson: An overview of the deepqa project. *AI Magazine*, 31(3):59–79.

Evgeniy Gabrilovich and Shaul Markovitch. 2007. Computing semantic relatedness using wikipedia-based explicit semantic analysis. In *Proceedings of the 20th International Joint Conference on Artifical Intelligence*, IJCAI'07, pages 1606–1611, San Francisco, CA, USA. Morgan Kaufmann Publishers Inc.

Matthew L. Ginsberg. 2011. Dr.fill: Crosswords and an implemented solver for singly weighted csps. *J. Artif. Int. Res.*, 42(1):851–886, September.

Dan Gusfield. 1997. *Algorithms on Strings, Trees, and Sequences: Computer Science and Computational Biology*. Cambridge University Press, New York, NY, USA.

R Herbrich, T Graepel, and K Obermayer. 2000. Large margin rank boundaries for ordinal regression. In A.J. Smola, P.L. Bartlett, B. Schölkopf, and D. Schuurmans, editors, *Advances in Large Margin Classifiers*, pages 115–132, Cambridge, MA. MIT Press.

Jiwoon Jeon, W. Bruce Croft, and Joon Ho Lee. 2005. Finding similar questions in large question and answer archives. In *CIKM*.

Thorsten Joachims. 2002. Optimizing search engines using clickthrough data. In *Proceedings of the Eighth ACM SIGKDD International Conference on Knowledge Discovery and Data Mining*, KDD '02, pages 133–142, New York, NY, USA. ACM.

Boris Katz and Jimmy Lin. 2003. Selectively using relations to improve precision in question answering.

Michael L. Littman, Greg A. Keim, and Noam Shazeer. 2002. A probabilistic approach to solving crossword puzzles. *Artificial Intelligence*, 134(12):23 – 55.

Michael McCandless, Erik Hatcher, and Otis Gospodnetic. 2010. *Lucene in Action, Second Edition: Covers Apache Lucene 3.0*. Manning Publications Co., Greenwich, CT, USA.

Rada Mihalcea, Courtney Corley, and Carlo Strapparava. 2006. Corpus-based and knowledge-based measures of text semantic similarity. In *Proceedings of the 21st National Conference on Artificial Intelligence - Volume 1*, AAAI'06, pages 775–780. AAAI Press.

Alessandro Moschitti, Daniele Pighin, and Roberto Basili. 2006. Semantic role labeling via tree kernel joint inference. In *Proceedings of CoNLL-X*, New York City.

Alessandro Moschitti, Silvia Quarteroni, Roberto Basili, and Suresh Manandhar. 2007. Exploiting syntactic and shallow semantic kernels for question/answer classification. In *ACL*.

Alessandro Moschitti. 2006. Efficient convolution kernels for dependency and constituent syntactic trees. In *ECML*, pages 318–329.

Alessandro Moschitti. 2008. Kernel methods, syntax and semantics for relational text categorization. In *CIKM*.

Ira Pohl. 1970. Heuristic search viewed as path finding in a graph. *Artificial Intelligence*, 1(34):193 – 204.

Filip Radlinski and Thorsten Joachims. 2006. Query chains: Learning to rank from implicit feedback. *CoRR*.

Philip Resnik. 1995. Using information content to evaluate semantic similarity in a taxonomy. In *Proceedings of the 14th International Joint Conference on Artificial Intelligence - Volume 1*, IJCAI'95, pages 448–453, San Francisco, CA, USA. Morgan Kaufmann Publishers Inc.

Aliaksei Severyn and Alessandro Moschitti. 2012. Structural relationships for large-scale learning of answer re-ranking. In *Proceedings of the 35th international ACM SIGIR conference on Research and development in information retrieval (SIGIR)*, pages 741–750. ACM.

Aliaksei Severyn, Massimo Nicosia, and Alessandro Moschitti. 2013a. Building structures from classifiers for passage reranking. In *CIKM*, pages 969–978.

Aliaksei Severyn, Massimo Nicosia, and Alessandro Moschitti. 2013b. Learning adaptable patterns for passage reranking. In *Proceedings of the Seventeenth Conference on Computational Natural Language Learning*, pages 75–83, Sofia, Bulgaria, August. Association for Computational Linguistics.

Libin Shen and Aravind K. Joshi. 2005. Ranking and reranking with perceptron. *Machine Learning*, 60(1-3):73–96.

D. Shen and M. Lapata. 2007. Using semantic roles to improve question answering. In *EMNLP-CoNLL*.

M. Surdeanu, M. Ciaramita, and H. Zaragoza. 2008. Learning to rank answers on large online QA collections. In *Proceedings of ACL-HLT*.

Michael J. Wise. 1996. Yap3: Improved detection of similarities in computer program and other texts. In *Proceedings of the Twenty-seventh SIGCSE Technical Symposium on Computer Science Education*, SIGCSE '96, pages 130–134, New York, NY, USA. ACM.

Inducing Neural Models of Script Knowledge

Ashutosh Modi
MMCI,
Saarland University, Germany
amodi@mmci.uni-saarland.de

Ivan Titov
ILLC,
University of Amsterdam, Netherlands
titov@uva.nl

Abstract

Induction of common sense knowledge about prototypical sequence of events has recently received much attention (e.g., Chambers and Jurafsky (2008); Regneri et al. (2010)). Instead of inducing this knowledge in the form of graphs, as in much of the previous work, in our method, distributed representations of event realizations are computed based on distributed representations of predicates and their arguments, and then these representations are used to predict prototypical event orderings. The parameters of the compositional process for computing the event representations and the ranking component of the model are jointly estimated. We show that this approach results in a substantial boost in performance on the event ordering task with respect to the previous approaches, both on natural and crowd-sourced texts.

1 Introduction

It is generally believed that natural language understanding systems would benefit from incorporating common-sense knowledge about prototypical sequences of events and their participants. Early work focused on structured representations of this knowledge (called *scripts* (Schank and Abelson, 1977)) and manual construction of script knowledge bases. However, these approaches do not scale to complex domains (Mueller, 1998; Gordon, 2001). More recently, automatic induction of script knowledge from text have started to attract attention: these methods exploit either natural texts (Chambers and Jurafsky, 2008, 2009) or crowdsourced data (Regneri et al., 2010), and, consequently, do not require expensive expert annotation. Given a text corpus, they extract structured representations (i.e. graphs), for example chains (Chambers and Jurafsky, 2008) or more general directed acyclic graphs (Regneri et al., 2010). These graphs are scenario-specific, nodes in them correspond to events (and associated with sets of potential event mentions) and arcs encode the temporal precedence relation. These graphs can then be used to inform NLP applications (e.g., question answering) by providing information whether one event is likely to precede or succeed another. Note that these graphs encode common-sense knowledge about prototypical ordering of events rather than temporal order of events as described in a given text.

Though representing the script knowledge as graphs is attractive from the human interpretability perspective, it may not be optimal from the application point of view. More specifically, these representations (1) require a model designer to choose an appropriate granularity of event mentions (e.g., whether nodes in the graph should be associated with verbs, or also their arguments); (2) do not provide a mechanism for deciding which scenario applies in a given discourse context and (3) often do not associate confidence levels with information encoded in the graph (e.g., the precedence relation in Regneri et al. (2010)).

Instead of constructing a graph and using it to provide information (e.g., prototypical event ordering) to NLP applications, in this work we advocate for constructing a statistical model which is capable to "answer" at least some of the questions these graphs can be used to answer, but doing this without explicitly representing the knowledge as a graph. In our method, the distributed representations (i.e. vectors of real numbers) of event realizations are computed based on distributed representations of predicates and their arguments, and then the event representations are used in a ranker to predict the prototypical ordering of events. Both the parameters of the compositional process for computing the event representation and the rank-

Proceedings of the Eighteenth Conference on Computational Language Learning, pages 49–57,
Baltimore, Maryland USA, June 26-27 2014.

ing component of the model are estimated from texts (either relying on unambiguous discourse clues or natural ordering in text). In this way we build on recent research on compositional distributional semantics (Baroni and Zamparelli, 2011; Socher et al., 2012), though our approach specifically focuses on embedding predicate-argument structures rather than arbitrary phrases, and learning these representation to be especially informative for prototypical event ordering.

In order to get an intuition why the embedding approach may be attractive, consider a situation where a prototypical ordering of events *the bus disembarked passengers* and *the bus drove away* needs to be predicted. An approach based on frequency of predicate pairs (Chambers and Jurafsky, 2008) (henceforth CJ08), is unlikely to make a right prediction as driving usually precedes disembarking. Similarly, an approach which treats the whole predicate-argument structure as an atomic unit (Regneri et al., 2010) will probably fail as well, as such a sparse model is unlikely to be effectively learnable even from large amounts of unlabeled data. However, our embedding method would be expected to capture relevant features of the verb frames, namely, the transitive use for the predicate *disembark* and the effect of the particle *away*, and these features will then be used by the ranking component to make the correct prediction.

In previous work on learning inference rules (Berant et al., 2011), it has been shown that enforcing transitivity constraints on the inference rules results in significantly improved performance. The same is likely to be true for the event ordering task, as scripts have largely linear structure, and observing that $a \prec b$ and $b \prec c$ is likely to imply $a \prec c$. Interestingly, in our approach we learn the model which satisfies transitivity constraints, without the need for any explicit global optimization on a graph. This results in a significant boost of performance when using embeddings of just predicates (i.e. ignoring arguments) with respect to using frequencies of ordered verb pairs, as in CJ08 (76% vs. 61% on the natural data).

Our model is solely focusing on the ordering task, and admittedly does not represent all the information encoded by a script graph structure. For example, it cannot be directly used to predict a missing event given a set of events (the narrative cloze task (Chambers and Jurafsky, 2009)). Nevertheless, we believe that the framework (a probabilistic model using event embeddings as its component) can be extended to represent other aspects of script knowledge by modifying the learning objective, but we leave this for future work. In this paper, we show how our model can be used to predict if two event mentions are likely paraphrases of the same event.

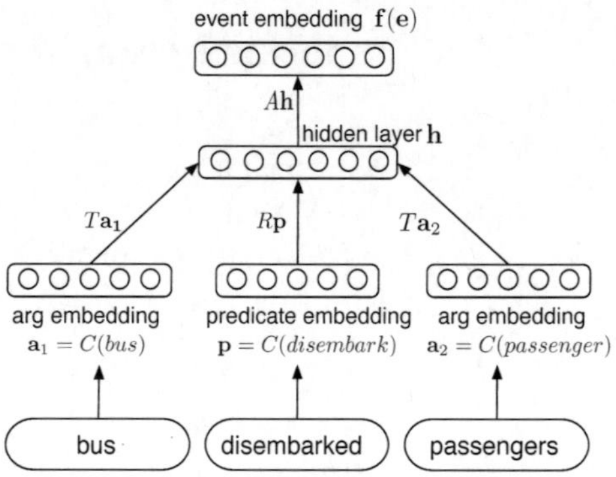

Figure 1: Computation of an event representation for a predicate with two arguments (*the bus disembarked passengers*), an arbitrary number of arguments is supported by our approach.

The approach is evaluated in two set-ups. First, we consider the crowdsourced dataset of Regneri et al. (2010) and demonstrate that using our model results in the 13.5% absolute improvement in $F1$ on event ordering with respect to their graph induction method (84.1% vs. 70.6%). Secondly, we derive an event ordering dataset from the Gigaword corpus, where we also show that the embedding method beats the frequency-based baseline (i.e. reimplementation of the scoring component of CJ08) by 22.8% in accuracy (83.5% vs. 60.7%).

2 Model

In this section we describe the model we use for computing event representations as well as the ranking component of our model.

2.1 Event Representation

Learning and exploiting distributed word representations (i.e. vectors of real values, also known as *embeddings*) have been shown to be beneficial in many NLP applications (Bengio et al., 2001; Turian et al., 2010; Collobert et al., 2011). These representations encode semantic and syntactic properties of a word, and are normally learned in the language modeling setting (i.e. learned to be predictive of local word context), though they can also be specialized by learning in the context of other NLP applications such as PoS tagging or semantic role labeling (Collobert et al., 2011). More recently, the area of distributional compositional semantics have started to emerge (Baroni and Zamparelli, 2011; Socher et al., 2012), they focus on inducing representations of phrases by learning a compositional model. Such a model would compute a representation of a phrase by starting with embeddings of individual words in the phrase, often this composition process is recursive and guided by some form of syntactic structure.

In our work, we use a simple compositional model for representing semantics of a verb frame e (i.e. the predicate and its arguments). We will refer to such verb frames as events. The model is shown in Figure 1. Each word c_i in the vocabulary is mapped to a real vector based on the corresponding lemma (the embedding function C). The hidden layer is computed by summing linearly transformed predicate and argument[1] embeddings and passing it through the logistic sigmoid function. We use different transformation matrices for arguments and predicates, T and R, respectively. The event representation $\boldsymbol{f}(e)$ is then obtained by applying another linear transform (matrix A) followed by another application of the sigmoid function. Another point to note in here is that, as in previous work on script induction, we use lemmas for predicates and specifically filter out any tense markers as our goal is to induce common-sense knowledge about an event rather than properties predictive of temporal order in a specific discourse context.

We leave exploration of more complex and linguistically-motivated models for future work.[2] These event representations are learned in the context of event ranking: the transformation parameters as well as representations of words are forced to be predictive of the temporal order of events. In our experiments, we also consider initialization of predicate and arguments with the SENNA word embeddings (Collobert et al., 2011).

[1]Only syntactic heads of arguments are used in this work. If an argument is *a coffee maker*, we will use only the word *maker*.

[2]In this study, we apply our model in two very different settings, learning from crowdsourced and natural texts. Crowdsourced collections are relatively small and require not over-expressive models.

2.2 Learning to Order

The task of learning stereotyped order of events naturally corresponds to the standard ranking setting. We assume that we are provided with sequences of events, and our goal is to capture this order. We discuss how we obtain this learning material in the next section. We learn a linear ranker (characterized by a vector $\boldsymbol{w}$) which takes an event representation and returns a ranking score. Events are then ordered according to the score to yield the model prediction. Note that during the learning stage we estimate not only $\boldsymbol{w}$ but also the event representation parameters, i.e. matrices T, R and A, and the word embedding C. Note that by casting the event ordering task as a global ranking problem we ensure that the model implicitly exploits transitivity of the relation, the property which is crucial for successful learning from finite amount of data, as we argued in the introduction and will confirm in our experiments.

At training time, we assume that each training example k is a list of events $e_1^{(k)}, \ldots, e_{n^{(k)}}^{(k)}$ provided in the stereotypical order (i.e. $e_i^{(k)} \prec e_j^{(k)}$ if $i < j$), $n^{(k)}$ is the length of the list k. We minimize the L_2-regularized ranking hinge loss:

$$\sum_k \sum_{i<j\leq n^{(k)}} \max(0, 1-\mathbf{w}^T\boldsymbol{f}(e_i^{(k)};\Theta)+\mathbf{w}^T\boldsymbol{f}(e_j^{(k)};\Theta)) + \alpha(\|\mathbf{w}\|_2 + \|\Theta\|_2),$$

where $\boldsymbol{f}(e;\Theta)$ is the embedding computed for event e, Θ are all embedding parameters corresponding to elements of the matrices $\{R, C, T, A\}$. We use stochastic gradient descent, gradients w.r.t. Θ are computed using back propagation.

3 Experiments

We evaluate our approach in two different set-ups. First, we induce the model from the crowdsourced data specifically collected for script induction by Regneri et al. (2010), secondly, we consider an arguably more challenging set-up of learning the model from news data (Gigaword (Parker et al., 2011)), in the latter case we use a learning scenario inspired by Chambers and Jurafsky (2008).[3]

[3]Details about downloading the data and models are at: http://www.coli.uni-saarland.de/projects/smile/docs/nmReadme.txt

	Precision (%)					Recall (%)					F1 (%)				
	BL	EE_{verb}	MSA	BS	EE	BL	EE_{verb}	MSA	BS	EE	BL	EE_{verb}	MSA	BS	EE
Bus	70.1	81.9	80.0	76.0	85.1	71.3	75.8	80.0	76.0	91.9	70.7	78.8	80.0	76.0	88.4
Coffee	70.1	73.7	70.0	68.0	69.5	72.6	75.1	78.0	57.0	71.0	71.3	74.4	74.0	62.0	70.2
Fastfood	69.9	81.0	53.0	97.0	90.0	65.1	79.1	81.0	65.0	87.9	67.4	80.0	64.0	78.0	88.9
Return	74.0	94.1	48.0	87.0	92.4	68.6	91.4	75.0	72.0	89.7	71.0	92.8	58.0	79.0	91.0
Iron	73.4	80.1	78.0	87.0	86.9	67.3	69.8	72.0	69.0	80.2	70.2	69.8	75.0	77.0	83.4
Microw.	72.6	79.2	47.0	91.0	82.9	63.4	62.8	83.0	74.0	90.3	67.7	70.0	60.0	82.0	86.4
Eggs	72.7	71.4	67.0	77.0	80.7	68.0	67.7	64.0	59.0	76.9	70.3	69.5	66.0	67.0	78.7
Shower	62.2	76.2	48.0	85.0	80.0	62.5	80.0	82.0	84.0	84.3	62.3	78.1	61.0	85.0	82.1
Phone	67.6	87.8	83.0	92.0	87.5	62.8	87.9	86.0	87.0	89.0	65.1	87.8	84.0	89.0	88.2
Vending	66.4	87.3	84.0	90.0	84.2	60.6	87.6	85.0	74.0	81.9	63.3	84.9	84.0	81.0	88.2
Average	69.9	81.3	65.8	85.0	**83.9**	66.2	77.2	78.6	71.7	**84.3**	68.0	79.1	70.6	77.6	**84.1**

Table 1: Results on the crowdsourced data for the verb-frequency baseline (BL), the verb-only embedding model (EE_{verb}), Regneri et al. (2010) (MSA), Frermann et al. (2014)(BS) and the full model (EE).

3.1 Learning from Crowdsourced Data

3.1.1 Data and task

Regneri et al. (2010) collected descriptions (called *event sequence descriptions, ESDs*) of various types of human activities (e.g., going to a restaurant, ironing clothes) using crowdsourcing (Amazon Mechanical Turk), this dataset was also complemented by descriptions provided in the OMICS corpus (Gupta and Kochenderfer, 2004). The datasets are fairly small, containing 30 ESDs per activity type in average (we will refer to different activities as *scenarios*), but in principle the collection can easily be extended given the low cost of crowdsourcing. The ESDs list events forming the scenario and are written in a bullet-point style. The annotators were asked to follow the prototypical event order in writing. As an example, consider a ESD for the scenario *prepare coffee* :

$\{$*go to coffee maker*$\} \rightarrow \{$*fill water in coffee maker*$\} \rightarrow \{$*place the filter in holder*$\} \rightarrow \{$*place coffee in filter*$\} \rightarrow \{$*place holder in coffee maker*$\} \rightarrow \{$*turn on coffee maker*$\}$

Regneri et al. also automatically extracted predicates and heads of arguments for each event, as needed for their MSA system and our compositional model.

Though individual ESDs may seem simple, the learning task is challenging because of the limited amount of training data, variability in the used vocabulary, optionality of events (e.g., going to the coffee machine may not be mentioned in a ESD), different granularity of events and variability in the ordering (e.g., coffee may be put in the filter before placing it in the coffee maker). Unlike our work, Regneri et al. (2010) relies on WordNet to provide extra signal when using the Multiple Sequence Alignment (MSA) algorithm. As in their work, each description was preprocessed to extract a predicate and heads of argument noun phrases to be used in the model.

The methods are evaluated on human annotated scenario-specific tests: the goal is to classify event pairs as appearing in a stereotypical order or not (Regneri et al., 2010).[4]

The model was estimated as explained in Section 2.2 with the order of events in ESDs treated as gold standard. We used 4 held-out scenarios to choose model parameters, no scenario-specific tuning was performed, and the 10 test scripts were not used to perform model selection. The selected model used the dimensionality of 10 for event and word embeddings. The initial learning rate and the regularization parameter were set to 0.005 and 1.0, respectively and both parameters were reduced by the factor of 1.2 every epoch the error function went up. We used 2000 epochs of stochastic gradient descent. Dropout (Hinton et al., 2012) with the rate of 20% was used for the hidden layers in all our experiments. When testing, we predicted that the event pair (e_1,e_2) is in the stereotypical order $(e_1 \prec e_2)$ if the ranking score for e_1 exceeded the ranking score for e_2.

3.1.2 Results and discussion

We evaluated our event embedding model (*EE*) against baseline systems (*BL* , *MSA* and *BS*). MSA is the system of Regneri et al. (2010). BS is a hierarchical Bayesian model by Frermann et al. (2014). BL chooses the order of events based on the preferred order of the corresponding verbs in the training set: (e_1, e_2) is predicted to be in the

[4]The event pairs are not coming from the same ESDs making the task harder as the events may not be in any temporal relation.

stereotypical order if the number of times the corresponding verbs v_1 and v_2 appear in this order in the training ESDs exceeds the number of times they appear in the opposite order (not necessary at adjacent positions); a coin is tossed to break ties (or if v_1 and v_2 are the same verb). This frequency counting method was previously used in CJ08.[5]

We also compare to the version of our model which uses only verbs (EE_{verbs}). Note that EE_{verbs} is conceptually very similar to BL, as it essentially induces an ordering over verbs. However, this ordering can benefit from the implicit transitivity assumption used in EE_{verbs} (and EE), as we discussed in the introduction. The results are presented in Table 1.

The first observation is that the full model improves substantially over the baseline and the previous method (MSA) in F1 (13.5% improvement over MSA and 6.5% improvement over BS). Note also that this improvement is consistent across scenarios: EE outperforms MSA and BS on 9 scenarios out of 10 and 8 out of 10 scenarios in case of BS. Unlike MSA and BS, no external knowledge (i.e. WordNet) was exploited in our method.

We also observe a substantial improvement in all metrics from using transitivity, as seen by comparing the results of BL and EE_{verb} (11% improvement in F1). This simple approach already substantially outperforms the pipelined MSA system. These results seem to support our hypothesis in the introduction that inducing graph representations from scripts may not be an optimal strategy from the practical perspective.

We performed additional experiments using the SENNA embeddings (Collobert et al., 2011). Instead of randomly initializing arguments and predicate embeddings (vectors), we initialized them with pre-trained SENNA embeddings. We have not observed any significant boost in performance from using the initialization (average F1 of 84.0% for EE). We attribute the lack of significant improvement to the following three factors. First of all, the SENNA embeddings tend to place antonyms / opposites near each other (e.g., come and go, or end and start). However, 'opposite' predicates appear in very different positions in scripts. Additionally, the SENNA embeddings have dimensionality of 50 which appears to be too high for small crowd-sourced datasets, as it forces us to use larger matrices T and R. Moreover, the SENNA embeddings are estimated from Wikipedia, and the activities in our crowdsourced domain are perhaps underrepresented there.

[5]They scored permutations of several events by summing the logarithmed differences of the frequencies of ordered verb pairs. However, when applied to event pairs, their approach would yield exactly the same prediction rule as BL.

3.1.3 Paraphrasing

Regneri et al. (2010) additionally measure paraphrasing performance of the MSA system by comparing it to human annotation they obtained: a system needs to predict if a pair of event mentions are paraphrases or not. The dataset contains 527 event pairs for the 10 test scenarios. Each pair consists of events from the same scenario. The dataset is fairly balanced containing from 47 to 60 examples per scenario.

This task does not directly map to any statistical inference problem with our model. Instead we use an approach inspired by the interval algebra of Allen (1983).

Our ranking model maps event mentions to positions on the time line (see Figure 2). However, it would be more natural to assume that events are intervals rather than points. In principle, these intervals can be overlapping to encode a rich set of temporal relations (see (Allen, 1983)). However, we make a simplifying assumption that the intervals do not overlap and every real number belongs to an interval. In other words, our goal is to induce a segmentation of the line: event mentions corresponding to the same interval are then regarded as paraphrases.

One natural constraint on this segmentation is the following: if two event mentions are from the same training ESD, they cannot be assigned to the same interval (as events in ESD are not supposed to be paraphrases). In Figure 2 arcs link event mentions from the same ESD. We look for a segmentation which produces the minimal number of segments and satisfy the above constraint for event mentions appearing in training data.

Though inducing intervals given a set of temporal constraints is known to be NP-hard in general (see, e.g., (Golumbic and Shamir, 1993)), for our constraints a simple greedy algorithm finds an optimal solution. We trace the line from the left maintaining a set of event mentions in the current unfinished interval and create a boundary when the constraint is violated; we repeat the process until we processed all mentions. In Figure 2, we would create the first boundary between *arrive in a restaurant* and *order beverages*: *order bev-*

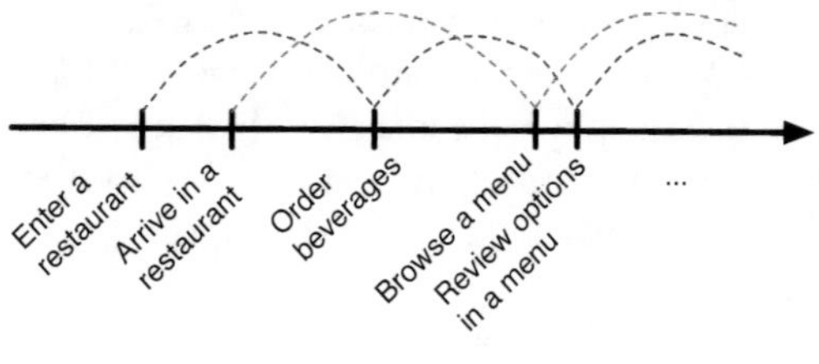

Figure 2: Events on the time line, dotted arcs link events from the same ESD.

Scenario	F1 (%)			
	APBL	MSA	BS	EE
Take bus	53.7	74.0	47.0	63.5
Make coffee	42.1	65.0	52.0	63.5
Order fastfood	37.0	59.0	80.0	62.6
Return food back	64.8	71.0	67.0	81.1
Iron clothes	43.3	67.0	60.0	56.7
Microwave cooking	43.2	75.0	82.0	57.8
Scrambled eggs	57.6	69.0	76.0	53.0
Take shower	42.1	78.0	67.0	55.7
Answer telephone	71.0	89.0	81.0	79.4
Vending machine	56.1	69.0	77.0	69.3
Average	51.1	**71.6**	68.9	64.5

Table 2: Paraphrasing results on the crowdsourced data for Regneri et al. (2010) (MSA), Fremmann et al. (2014)(BS) and the all-paraphrase baseline (APBL) and using intervals induced from our model (EE).

erages and *enter a restaurant* are from the same ESD and continuing the interval would violate the constraint. It is not hard to see that this results in an optimal segmentation. First, the segmentation satisfies the constraint by construction. Secondly, the number of segments is minimal as the arcs which caused boundary creation are non-overlapping, each of these arcs needs to be cut and our algorithm cuts each arc exactly once.

This algorithm prefers to introduce a boundary as late as possible. For example, it would introduce a boundary between *browse a menu* and *review options in a menu* even though the corresponding points are very close on the line. We modify the algorithm by moving the boundaries left as long as this move does not result in new constraint violations and increases margin at boundaries. In our example, the boundary would be moved to be between *order beverages* and *browse a menu*, as desired.

The resulting performance is reported in Table 2. We report results of our method, as well as results for MSA, BS and a simple all-paraphrase baseline which predict that all mention pairs in a test set are paraphrases (APBL).[6] We can see that interval induction technique results in a lower F1 than that of MSA or BS. This might be partially due to not using external knowledge (WordNet) in our method.

We performed extra analyses on the development scenario *doorbell*. The analyses revealed that the interval induction approach is not very robust to noise: removing a single noisy ESD results in a dramatic change in the interval structure induced and in a significant increase of F1. Consequently, soft versions of the constraint would be beneficial. Alternatively, event embeddings (i.e. continuous vectors) can be clustered directly. We leave this investigation for future work.

[6]The results for the random baseline are lower: F1 of 40.6% in average.

3.2 Learning from Natural Text

In the second set of experiments we consider a more challenging problem, inducing knowledge about the stereotyped ordering of events from natural texts. In this work, we are largely inspired by the scenario of CJ08. The overall strategy is the following: we process the Gigaword corpus with a high precision rule-based temporal classifier relying on explicit clues (e.g., "then", "after") to get ordered pairs of events and then we train our model on these pairs (note that clues used by the classifier are removed from the examples, so the model has to rely on verbs and their arguments). Conceptually, the difference between our approach and CJ08 is in using a different temporal classifier, not enforcing that event pairs have the same protagonist, and learning an event embedding model instead of scoring event sequences based on verb-pair frequencies.

We also evaluate our system on examples extracted using the same temporal classifier (but validated manually) which allows us to use much larger tests set, and, consequently, provide more detailed and reliable error analysis.

3.2.1 Data and task

The Gigaword corpus consists of news data from different news agencies and newspapers. For testing and development we took the AFP (Agence France-Presse) section, as it appeared most different from the rest when comparing sets of extracted event pairs (other sections correspond mostly to US agencies). The AFP section was not used for

	Accuracy (%)
BL	60.7
CJ08	60.1
EE_{verb}	75.9
EE	**83.5**

Table 3: Results on the Gigaword data for the verb-frequency baseline (BL), the verb-only embedding model (EE_{verb}), the full model (EE) and CJ08 rules.

training. This selection strategy was chosen to create a negative bias for our model which is more expressive than the baseline methods and, consequently, better at memorizing examples.

As a rule-based temporal classifier, we used high precision "happens-before" rules from the VerbOcean system (Chklovski and Pantel, 2004). Consider "*to* ⟨*verb-x*⟩ *and then* ⟨*verb-y*⟩" as one example of such rule. We used predicted collapsed Stanford dependencies (de Marneffe et al., 2006) to extract arguments of the verbs, and used only a subset of dependents of a verb.[7] This preprocessing ensured that (1) clues which form part of a pattern are not observable by our model both at train and test time; (2) there is no systematic difference between both events (e.g., for collapsed dependencies, the noun subject is attached to both verbs even if the verbs are conjoined); (3) no information about the order of events in text is available to the models. Applying these rules resulted in 22,446 event pairs for training, and we split additional 1,015 pairs from the AFP section into 812 for final testing and 203 for development. We manually validated random 50 examples and all 50 of them followed the correct temporal order, so we chose not to hand correct the test set.

We largely followed the same training and evaluation regime as for the crowdsourced data. We set the regularization parameter and the learning rate to 0.01 and $5.e-4$ respectively. The model was trained for 600 epochs. The embedding sizes were 30 and 50 dimensions for words and events, respectively.

3.2.2 Results and discussion

In our experiments, as before, we use BL as a baseline, and EE_{verb} as a verb-only simplified version of our approach. We used another baseline consisting of the verb pair ordering counts provided by Chambers and Jurafsky (2008).[8] We refer this baseline as CJ08. Note also that BL can be regarded as a reimplementation of CJ08 but with a different temporal classifier. We report results in Table 3.

The observations are largely the same as before: (1) the full model substantially outperforms all other approaches (p-level < 0.001 with the permutation test); (2) enforcing transitivity is very helpful (75.9 % for EE_{verb} vs. 60.1% for BL). Surprisingly CJ08 rules produce as good results as BL, suggesting that maybe our learning set-ups are not that different.

However, an interesting question is in which situations using a more expressive model, EE, is beneficial. If these accuracy gains have to do with memorizing the data, it may not generalize well to other domains or datasets. In order to test this hypothesis we divided the test examples in three frequency bands according to the frequency of the corresponding verb pairs in the training set (total, in both orders). There are 513, 249 and 50 event pairs in the bands corresponding to unseen pairs of verbs, frequency ≤ 10 and frequency $>$ 10, respectively. These counts emphasize that correct predictions on unseen pairs are crucial and these are exactly where BL would be equivalent to a random guess. Also, this suggest, even before looking into the results, that memorization is irrelevant. The results for BL, CJ08, EE_{verb} and EE are shown in Figure 3.

One observation is that most gains for EE and EE_{verb} are due to an improvement on unseen pairs. This is fairly natural, as both transitivity and information about arguments are the only sources of information available. In this context it is important to note that some of the verbs are *light*, in the sense that they have little semantic content of their own (e.g., *take*, *get*) and the event semantics can only be derived from analyzing their arguments (e.g., *take an exam* vs. *take a detour*). On the high frequency verb pairs all systems perform equally well, except for CJ08 as it was estimated from somewhat different data.

In order to understand how transitivity works, we considered a few unseen predicate pairs where the EE_{verb} model was correctly predicting their order. For many of these pairs there were no infer-

[7] The list of dependencies not considered: *aux*, *auxpass*, *attr*, *appos*, *cc*, *conj*, *complm*, *cop*, *dep*, *det*, *punct*, *mwe*.

[8] These verb pair frequency counts are available at www.usna.edu/Users/cs/nchamber/data/schemas/acl09/verb-pair-orders.gz

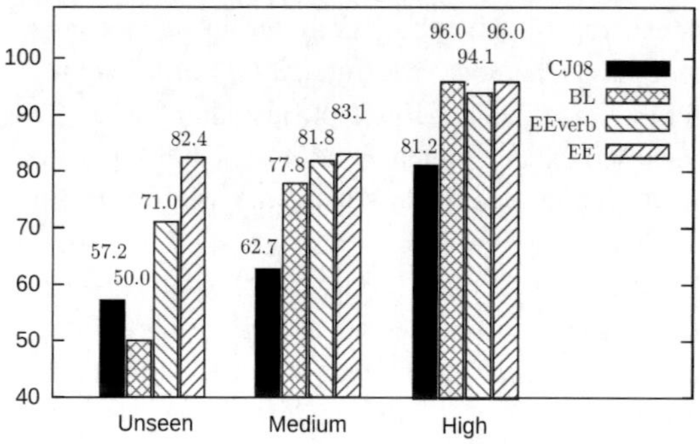

Figure 3: Results for different frequency bands: unseen, medium frequency (between 1 and 10) and high frequency (> 10) verb pairs.

ence chains of length 2 (e.g., chain of length 2 was found for the pair *accept* $\prec$ *carry*: *accept* $\prec$ *get* and *get* $\prec$ *carry* but not many other pairs). This observation suggest that our model captures some non-trivial transitivity rules.

4 Related Work

Additionally to the work on script induction discussed above (Chambers and Jurafsky, 2008, 2009; Regneri et al., 2010), other methods for unsupervised learning of event semantics have been proposed. These methods include unsupervised *frame* induction techniques (O'Connor, 2012; Modi et al., 2012). Frames encode situations (or objects) along with their participants and properties (Fillmore, 1976). Events in these unsupervised approaches are represented with categorical latent variables, and they are induced relying primarily on the selectional preferences' signal. The very recent work of Cheung et al. (2013) can be regarded as their extension but Cheung et al. also model transitions between events with Markov models. However, neither of these approaches considers (or directly optimizes) the discriminative objective of learning to order events, and neither of them uses distributed representations to encode semantic properties of events.

As we pointed out before, our embedding approach is similar (or, in fact, a simplification of) the phrase embedding methods studied in the recent work on distributional compositional semantics (Baroni and Zamparelli, 2011; Socher et al., 2012). However, they have not specifically looked into representing script information. Approaches which study embeddings of relations in knowledge bases (e.g., Riedel et al. (2013)) bear some similarity to the methods proposed in this work but they are mostly limited to binary relations and deal with predicting missing relations rather than with temporal reasoning of any kind.

Identification of temporal relations within a text is a challenging problem and an active area of research (see, e.g., the TempEval task (UzZaman et al., 2013)). Many rule-based and supervised approaches have been proposed in the past. However, integration of common sense knowledge induced from large-scale unannotated resources still remains a challenge. We believe that our approach will provide a powerful signal complementary to information exploited by most existing methods.

5 Conclusions

We have developed a statistical model for representing common sense knowledge about prototypical event orderings. Our model induces distributed representations of events by composing predicate and argument representations. These representations capture properties relevant to predicting stereotyped orderings of events. We learn these representations and the ordering component from unannotated data. We evaluated our model in two different settings: from crowdsourced data and natural news texts. In both set-ups our method outperformed baselines and previously proposed systems by a large margin. This boost in performance is primarily caused by exploiting transitivity of temporal relations and capturing information encoded by predicate arguments.

The primary area of future work is to exploit our method in applications such as question answering. Another obvious applications is discovery of temporal relations within documents (UzZaman et al., 2013) where common sense knowledge implicit in script information, induced from large unannotated corpora, should be highly beneficial. Our current model uses a fairly naive semantic composition component, we plan to extend it with more powerful recursive embedding methods which should be especially beneficial when considering very large text collections.

6 Acknowledgements

Thanks to Lea Frermann, Michaela Regneri and Manfred Pinkal for suggestions and help with the data. This work is partially supported by the MMCI Cluster of Excellence at the Saarland University.

References

James F Allen. 1983. Maintaining knowledge about temporal intervals. *Communications of the ACM*, 26(11):832–843.

Marco Baroni and Robert Zamparelli. 2011. Nouns are vectors, adjectives are matrices: Representing adjective-noun constructions in semantic space. In *Proceedings of EMNLP*.

Yoshua Bengio, Réjean Ducharme, and Pascal Vincent. 2001. A neural probabilistic language model. In *Proceedings of NIPS*.

Jonathan Berant, Ido Dagan, and Jacob Goldberger. 2011. Global learning of typed entailment rules. In *Proceedings of ACL*.

Nathanael Chambers and Dan Jurafsky. 2009. Unsupervised learning of narrative schemas and their participants. In *Proceedings of ACL*.

Nathanael Chambers and Daniel Jurafsky. 2008. Unsupervised learning of narrative event chains. In *Proceedings of ACL*.

Jackie Chi Kit Cheung, Hoifung Poon, and Lucy Vanderwende. 2013. Probabilistic frame induction. In *Proceedings of NAACL*.

Timothy Chklovski and Patrick Pantel. 2004. Verbocean: Mining the web for fine-grained semantic verb relations. In *Proceedings of EMNLP*.

R. Collobert, J. Weston, L. Bottou, M. Karlen, K. Kavukcuoglu, and P. Kuksa. 2011. Natural language processing (almost) from scratch. *Journal of Machine Learning Research*, 12:2493–2537.

Marie-Catherine de Marneffe, Bill MacCartney, and Christopher D. Manning. 2006. Generating typed dependency parses from phrase structure parses. In *Proceedings of LREC*.

Charles Fillmore. 1976. Frame semantics and the nature of language. *Annals of the New York Academy of Sciences*, 280(1):20–32.

Lea Frermann, Ivan Titov, and Manfred Pinkal. 2014. A hierarchical bayesian model for unsupervised induction of script knowledge. In *EACL, Gothenberg, Sweden*.

Martin Charles Golumbic and Ron Shamir. 1993. Complexity and algorithms for reasoning about time: A graph-theoretic approach. *Journal of ACM*, 40(5):1108–1133.

Andrew Gordon. 2001. Browsing image collections with representations of common-sense activities. *JAIST*, 52(11).

Rakesh Gupta and Mykel J. Kochenderfer. 2004. Common sense data acquisition for indoor mobile robots. In *Proceedings of AAAI*.

Geoffrey E. Hinton, Nitish Srivastava, Alex Krizhevsky, Ilya Sutskever, and Ruslan Salakhutdinov. 2012. Improving neural networks by preventing co-adaptation of feature detectors. *arXiv: CoRR, abs/1207.0580*.

Ashutosh Modi, Ivan Titov, and Alexandre Klementiev. 2012. Unsupervised induction of frame-semantic representations. In *Proceedings of the NAACL-HLT Workshop on Inducing Linguistic Structure*. Montreal, Canada.

Erik T. Mueller. 1998. *Natural Language Processing with Thought Treasure*. Signiform.

Brendan O'Connor. 2012. Learning frames from text with an unsupervised latent variable model. *CMU Technical Report*.

Robert Parker, David Graff, Junbo Kong, Ke Chen, and Kazuaki Maeda. 2011. English gigaword fifth edition. *Linguistic Data Consortium*.

Michaela Regneri, Alexander Koller, and Manfred Pinkal. 2010. Learning script knowledge with web experiments. In *Proceedings of ACL*.

Sebastian Riedel, Limin Yao, Andrew McCallum, and Benjamin Marlin. 2013. Relation extraction with matrix factorization and universal schemas. *TACL*.

R. C Schank and R. P Abelson. 1977. *Scripts, Plans, Goals, and Understanding*. Lawrence Erlbaum Associates, Potomac, Maryland.

Richard Socher, Brody Huval, Christopher D. Manning, and Andrew Y. Ng. 2012. Semantic compositionality through recursive matrix-vector spaces. In *Proceedings of EMNLP*.

Joseph Turian, Lev Ratinov, and Yoshua Bengio. 2010. Word representations: A simple and general method for semi-supervised learning. In *Proceedings of ACL*.

Naushad UzZaman, Hector Llorens, Leon Derczynski, James Allen, Marc Verhagen, and James Pustejovsky. 2013. Semeval-2013 task 1: Tempeval-3: Evaluating time expressions, events, and temporal relations. In *Proceedings of SemEval*.

Grounding Language with Points and Paths in Continuous Spaces

Jacob Andreas and **Dan Klein**
Computer Science Division
University of California, Berkeley
{jda,klein}@cs.berkeley.edu

Abstract

We present a model for generating path-valued interpretations of natural language text. Our model encodes a map from natural language descriptions to paths, mediated by segmentation variables which break the language into a discrete set of events, and alignment variables which reorder those events. Within an event, lexical weights capture the contribution of each word to the aligned path segment. We demonstrate the applicability of our model on three diverse tasks: a new color description task, a new financial news task and an established direction-following task. On all three, the model outperforms strong baselines, and on a hard variant of the direction-following task it achieves results close to the state-of-the-art system described in Vogel and Jurafsky (2010).

1 Introduction

This paper introduces a probabilistic model for predicting grounded, real-valued trajectories from natural language text. A long tradition of research in compositional semantics has focused on discrete representations of meaning. The original focus of such work was on logical translation: mapping statements of natural language to a formal language like first-order logic (Zettlemoyer and Collins, 2005) or database queries (Zelle and Mooney, 1996). Subsequent work has integrated this logical translation with interpretation against a symbolic database (Liang et al., 2013).

There has been a recent increase in interest in perceptual grounding, where lexical semantics anchor in perceptual variables (points, distances, etc.) derived from images or video. Bruni et al. (2014) describe a procedure for constructing word representations using text- and image-based distributional information. Yu and Siskind (2013) describe a model for identifying scenes given descriptions, and Golland et al. (2010), Kollar et al. (2010), and Krishnamurthy and Kollar (2013) describe models for identifying individual components of scenes described by text. These all have the form of matching problems between text and observed groundings—what has been missing so far is the ability to *generate* grounded interpretations from scratch, given only text.

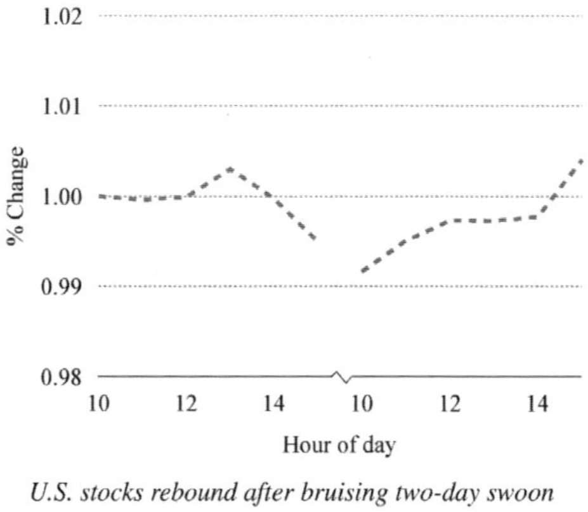

Figure 1: Example stock data. The chart displays index value over a two-day period (divided by the dotted line), while the accompanying headline describes the observed behavior.

Our work continues in the tradition of this perceptual grounding work, but makes two contributions. First, our approach is able to predict simple world states (and their evolution): for a general class of continuous domains, we produce a representation of $p(\text{world} \mid \text{text})$ that admits easy sampling and maximization. This makes it possible to produce grounded interpretations of text without reference to a pre-existing scene. Simultaneously, we extend the range of temporal phenomena that can be modeled—unlike the aforementioned spatial semantics work, we consider language that de-

Proceedings of the Eighteenth Conference on Computational Language Learning, pages 58–67,
Baltimore, Maryland USA, June 26-27 2014. ©2014 Association for Computational Linguistics

scribes time-evolving trajectories, and unlike Yu and Siskind (2013), we allow these trajectories to have event substructure, and model temporal ordering. Our class of models generalizes to a variety of different domains: a new color-picking task, a new financial news task, and a more challenging variant of the direction-following task established by Vogel and Jurafsky (2010).

As an example of the kinds of phenomena we want to model, consider Figure 1, which shows the value of the Dow Jones Industrial Average over June 3rd and 4th 2008, along with a financial news headline from June 4th. There are several effects of interest here. One phenomenon we want to capture is that the lexical semantics of individual words must be combined: *swoon* roughly describes a drop while *bruising* indicates that the drop was severe. We isolate this lexical combination in Section 4, where we consider a limited model of color descriptions (Figure 2). A second phenomenon is that the description is composed of two separate events, a *swoon* and a *rebound*; moreover, those events do not occur in their textual order, as revealed by *after*. In Section 5, we extend the model to include segmentation and ordering variables and apply it to this stock data.

The situation where language describes a path through some continuous space—literal or metaphorical—is more general than stock headlines. Our claim is that a variety of problems in language share these same characteristics. To demonstrate generality of the model, we also apply it in Section 6 to a challenging variant of the direction-following task described by Vogel and Jurafsky (2010) (Figure 3), where we achieve results close to a state-of-the-art system that makes stronger assumptions about the task.

2 Three tasks in grounded semantics

The problem of inferring a structured state representation from sensory input is a hard one, but we can begin to tackle grounded semantics by restricting ourselves to cases where we have sequences of real-valued observations directly described by text. In this paper we'll consider the problems of recognizing colors, describing time series, and following navigational instructions. While these tasks have been independently studied, we believe that this is the first work which presents them in a unified framework, and carries them out with a single family of models.

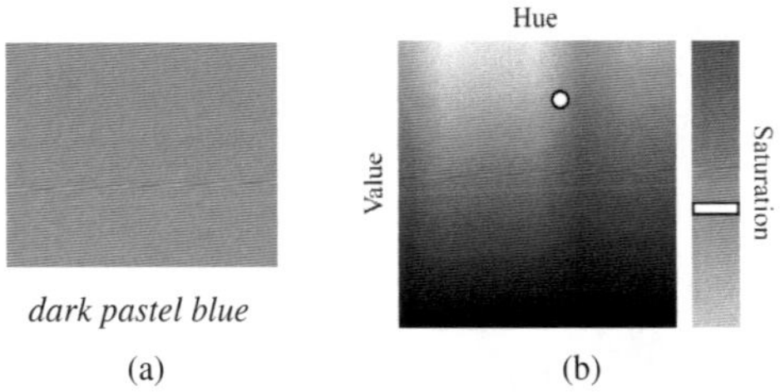

Figure 2: Example color data: (a) a named color; (b) its coordinates in color space.

Colors Figure 2 shows a color called *dark pastel blue*. English speakers, even if unfamiliar with the specific color, can identify roughly what the name signifies because of prior knowledge of the meanings of the individual words.

Because the color domain exhibits lexical compositionality but not event structure, we present it here to isolate the non-temporal compositional effects in our model. Any color visible to the human eye can be identified with three coordinates, which we'll take to be hue, saturation and value (HSV). As can be seen in Figure 2 the "hue" axis corresponds to the differentiation made by basic color names in most languages. Other modifiers act on the saturation and value axes: either simple ones like *dark* (which decreases value), or more complicated ones like *pastel* (which increases value and decreases saturation). Given a set of named colors and their HSV coordinates, a learning algorithm should be able to identify the effects of each word in the vocabulary and predict the appearance of new colors with previously-unseen combinations of modifiers.

Compositional interpretations of color have received attention in linguistics and philosophy of language (Kennedy and McNally, 2010), but while work in grounded computational semantics like that of Krishnamurthy and Kollar (2013) has succeeded in learning simple color predicates, our model is the first to capture the machine learning of color in a fine-grained, compositional way.

Time series As a first step into temporal structure, we'll consider language describing the behavior of stock market indices. Here, again, there is a simple parameterization—in this case just a single number describing the total value of the index—but as shown by the headline example in Figure 1, the language used to describe changes in the stock market can be quite complex. Head-

right round the white water [...] but stay quite close 'cause you don't otherwise you're going to be in that stone creek

Figure 3: Example map data: a portion of a map, and a single line from a dialog which describes navigation relative to the two visible landmarks.

lines may describe multiple events, or multi-part events like *rebound* or *extend*; stocks do not simply *rise* or *fall*, but *stagger*, *stumble*, *swoon*, and so on. There are compositional effects here as well: distinction is made between *falling* and *falling sharply*; gradual trends are distinguished from those which occur suddenly, at the beginning or end of the trading day. Along with temporal structure, the problem requires a more sophisticated treatment of *syntax* than the colors case—now we have to identify which subspans of the sentence are associated with each event observed, and determine the correspondence between surface order and actual order in time.

The learning of correspondences between text and time series has attracted more interest in natural language generation than in semantics (Yu et al., 2007). Research on natural language processing and stock data, meanwhile, has largely focused on prediction of future events (Kogan et al., 2009).

Direction following We'll conclude by applying our model to the well-studied problem of following navigational directions. A variety of reinforcement-learning approaches for following directions on a map were previously investigated by Vogel and Jurafsky (2010) using a corpus assembled by Anderson et al. (1991). An example portion of a path and its accompanying instruction is shown in Figure 3. While also representable as a set of real valued coordinates, here 2-d, this data set looks very different—a typical example consists of more than a hundred sentences of the kind shown in Figure 3, accompanying a long path. The language, a transcript of a spoken dialog, is also considerably less formal than the language found in the *Wall Street Journal* examples, involving disfluency, redundancy and occasionally errors. Nevertheless the underlying structure of this problem and the stock problem are fundamentally similar.

In addition to Vogel and Jurafsky, Tellex et al. (2011) give a weakly-supervised model for mapping single sentences to commands, and Branavan et al. (2009) give an alternative reinforcement-learning approach for following long command sequences. An intermediate between this approach and ours is the work of Chen and Mooney (2011) and Artzi and Zettlemoyer (2013), which bootstrap a semantic parser to generate logical forms specifying the output path, rather than predicting the path directly.

Between them, these tasks span a wide range of linguistic phenomena relevant to grounded semantics, and provide a demonstration of the usefulness and general applicability of our model. While development of the perceptual groundwork necessary to generalize these results to more complex state spaces remains a major problem, our three examples provide a starting point for studying the relationship between perception, time and the semantics of natural language.

3 Preliminaries

In the experiments that follow, each training example will consist of:

- Natural language text, consisting of a constituency parse tree or trees. For a given example, we will denote the associated trees $(\mathcal{T}_1, \mathcal{T}_2, \ldots)$. These are also observed at test time, and used to predict new groundings.
- A vector-valued, grounded observation, or a sequence of observations (a path), which we will denote $\mathcal{V}$ for a given example. We will further assume that each of these paths has been pre-segmented (discussed in detail in Section 5) into a sequence $(\mathcal{V}_1, \mathcal{V}_2, \ldots)$. These are only observed during training.

The probabilistic backbone of our model is a collection of linear and log-linear predictors. Thus it will be useful to work with vector-valued representations of both the language and the path, which we accomplish with a pair of feature functions ϕ_t and ϕ_v. As the model is defined only in terms of these linear representations, we can

$\phi_t(T)$	▪ Label at root of T ▪ Lemmatized leaves of T
$\phi_v(V)$	▪ Last element of V ▪ Curvature of quadratic approx. to V (stocks only)
$\phi_a(T, A_i, A_{i-1})$	Cartesian prod. of $\phi_t(T)$ with: ▪ $\mathbb{I}[A_i$ is aligned$]$ ▪ $\mathbb{I}[A_{i-1}$ is aligned$]$ ▪ $A_1 - A_{i-1}$ (if both aligned)

Table 1: Features used for linear parameterization of the grounding model.

simplify notation by writing $T_i = \phi_t(\mathcal{T}_i)$ and $V_i = \phi_v(\mathcal{V}_i)$. As the ultimate prediction task is to produce paths, and not their featurized representations, we will assume that it is also straightforward to compute ϕ_v^{-1}, which projects path features back into the original grounding domain.

All parse trees are predicted from input text using the Berkeley Parser (Petrov and Klein, 2007). Feature representations for both trees and paths are simple and largely domain-independent; they are explicitly enumerated in Table 1.

The general framework presented here leaves one significant problem unaddressed: given a large state vector encoding properties of multiple objects, how do we resolve an utterance about a single object to the correct subset of indices in the vector? While none of the tasks considered in this paper require an argument resolution step of this kind, interpretation of noun phrases is one of the better-studied problems in compositional semantics (Zelle and Mooney (1996), inter alia), and we expect generalization of this approach to be straightforward using these tools.

We will consider the color, stock, and navigation tasks in turn. It is possible to view the models we give for all three as instantiations of the same graphical model, but for ease of presentation we will introduce this model incrementally.

4 Predicting vectors

Prediction of a color variable from text has the form of a regression problem: given a vector of lexical features extracted from the name, we wish to predict the entries of a vector in color space. It seems linguistically plausible that this regression is *sparse* and *linear*: that most words, if they provide any constraints at all, tend to express preferences about a subset of the available dimensions; and that composition within the domain of a single event largely consists of words additively predicting that event's parameters, without complex nonlinear interactions. This is motivated by the observation that pragmatic concerns force linguistic descriptors to orient themselves along a small set of perceptual bases: once we have words for *north* and *east*, we tend to describe intermediates as *northeast* rather than inventing an additional word which means "a little of both".

As discussed above, we can represent a color as a point in a three-dimensional HSV space. Let T denote features on the parse tree of the color name, and V its representation in color space (consistent with the definition of ϕ_v given in Table 1). Linearity suggests the following model:

$$p(T, V) \propto e^{-\|\theta_t^\top T - V\|_2^2} \quad (1)$$

The learning problem is then:

$$\operatorname*{argmin}_{\theta_t} \sum_{T,V} \left\|\theta_t^\top T - V\right\|_2^2 \quad (2)$$

which, with a sparse prior on θ_t, is the probabilistic formulation of Lasso regression (Tibshirani, 1996), for which standard tools are available in the optimization literature.

To predict color space values from a new (featurized) name T, we output:

$$\operatorname*{argmax}_{V} p(T, V) = \theta_t^\top T$$

4.1 Evaluation

We collect a set of color names and their corresponding HSV triples from the English Wikipedia's *List of Colors*, retaining only those color names in which every word appears at least three times in the training corpus. This leaves a set of 419 colors, which we randomly divide into a 377-item training set and 42-item test set. The model's goal will be to learn to identify new colors given only their names.

We consider two evaluations: one which measures the model's ability to distinguish the named color from a random alternative—analogous to the evaluation in Yu and Siskind (2013)—and one which measures the absolute difference between predicted and true color values. In particular, in the first evaluation the model is presented with the name of a color and a pair of candidates, one

Method	Sel. ↑	H ↓	S ↓	V ↓
Random	0.50	0.30	0.38	0.39
Last word	0.78	**0.05**	0.26	0.17
Full model	**0.81**	0.07	**0.21**	**0.13**
Human	0.86	-	-	-

Table 2: Results for the color selection task. Sel(ection accuracy) is frequency with which the system was able to correctly identify the color described when paired with a random alternative. Other columns are the magnitude of the average prediction error along the axes of the color space. Full model selection accuracy is a statistically significant ($p < 0.05$) improvement over the baseline using a paired sign test.

the color corresponding to the name and another drawn randomly from the test set, and report the fraction of times the true color is assigned a higher probability than the random alternative. In the second, we report the absolute value of the difference between true and predicted hue, saturation, and luminosity.

We compare against two baselines: one which looks only at the last word in the color name (almost always a hue category), and so captures no compositional effects, and another which outputs random values for all three coordinates. Results are shown in Table 2. The model with all lexical features outperforms both baselines on selection and all but one absolute error metric.

4.2 Error analysis

An informal experiment in which the color selection task was repeated on one of the authors' colleagues (the "Human" row in Table 2) yielded an accuracy of 86%, only 5% better than the system. While not intended as a rigorous upper bound on performance, this suggests that the model capacity and training data are sufficient to capture most interesting color behavior. The errors that do occur appear to mostly be of two kinds. In one case, a base color is seen only with a small (or related) set of modifiers, from which the system is unable to infer the meaning of the base color (e.g. from *Japanese indigo*, *lavender indigo*, and *electric indigo*, the learning algorithm infers that indigo is bright purple). In the other, no part of the color word is seen in training, and the system outputs an unrelated "default" color (*teal* is predicted to be bright red).

5 Predicting paths

The idea that a sentence's meaning is fundamentally described by a set of *events*, each associated with a set of predicates, is well-developed in neo-Davidsonian formal semantics (Parsons, 1990). We adopt the skeleton of this formal approach by tying our model to (latent) partitions of the input sentence into disjoint events. Rather than attempting to pass through a symbolic meaning representation, however, this event structure will be used to map text directly into the grounding domain. We assume that this domain has pre-existing structure—in particular, that in our input paths $\mathcal{V}$, the boundaries of events have already been identified, and that the problem of aligning text to portions of the segment only requires aligning to segment indices rather than fine-grained time indices. This is a strong assumption, and one that future work may wish to revisit, but there exist both computational tools from the changepoint detection literature (Basseville and Nikiforov, 1995) and pieces of evidence from cognitive science (Zacks and Swallow, 2007) which suggest that assuming a pre-linguistic structuring of events is a reasonable starting point.

In the text domain, we make the corresponding assumption that each of these events is *syntactically local*—that a given span of the input sentence provides information about at most one of these segmented events.

The main structural difference between the color example in Figure 2 and the stock market example in Figure 1 is the introduction of a time dimension orthogonal to the dimensions of the state space. To accommodate this change, we extend the model described in the previous subsection in the following way: Instead of a single vector, each tree representation T is paired with a *sequence* of path features $\mathbf{V} = (V_1, V_2, \ldots, V_M)$. For the time being we continue to assume that there is only one input tree per training example. As before, we wish to model the probability $p(T, \mathbf{V})$, but the problem becomes harder: a single sentence might describe multiple events, but we don't know what the correspondence is between regions of the sentence and segments $\mathbf{V}$.

Though the ultimate goal is still prediction of V vectors from novel T instances, we cannot do this without also inferring a set of latent *alignments* between portions of the path and input sentence during training. To allow a sentence to explain mul-

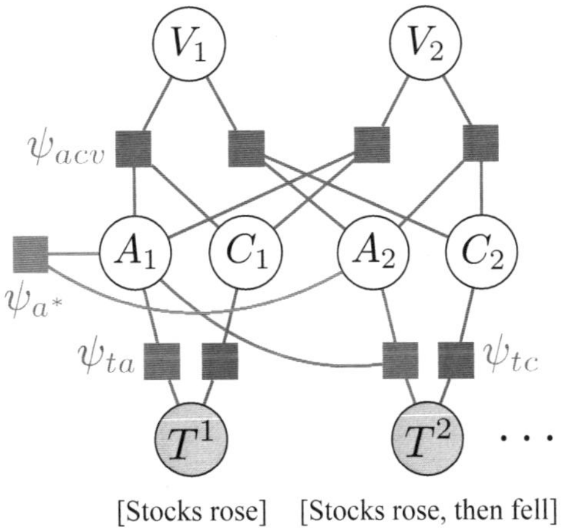

Figure 4: Factor graph for stocks grounding model. Only a subset of the alignment candidates are shown. ψ_{tc} maps text to constraints, ψ_{acv} maps constraints to grounded segments, and ψ_{ta} determines which constraints act on which segments.

tiple events, we'll break each T apart into a set of *alignment candidates* T^i. We'll allow as an alignment candidate any subtree of T, and additionally any subtree from which a single constituent has been deleted.

We then introduce two groups of latent variables: alignment variables $\mathbf{A} = (A_1, A_2, \ldots)$, which together describe a mapping from pieces of the input sentence to segments of the observed path, and what we'll call "constraint" variables $\mathbf{C} = (C_1, C_2, \ldots)$, which express each aligned tree segment's prediction about what its corresponding path should look like (so that the possibly-numerous parts of the tree aligned to a single segment can independently express preferences about the segment's path features).

In addition to ensuring that the alignment is consistent with the bracketing of the tree, it might be desirable to impose additional global constraints on the alignment. There are various ways to do this in a graphical modeling framework; the most straightforward is to add a combinatorial factor touching all alignment variables which checks for satisfaction of the global constraint. In general this makes alignment intractable. If the total number of alignments licensed by this combinatorial factor is small (i.e. if acceptable alignments are sparse within the exponentially-large set of all possible assignments to $\mathbf{A}$), it is possible to directly sum them out during inference. Otherwise approximate techniques (as discussed in the following section) will be necessary.

As discussed in Section 2, our financial timelines cover two-day periods, and it seems natural to treat each day as a separate event. Then the simple regression model described in the preceding section, extended to include alignment and constraint variables, has the form of the factor graph shown in Figure 4. In particular, the joint distribution $p(T, \mathbf{V})$ is the product of four groups of factors:

Alignment factors ψ_{ta}, which use a log-linear model to score neighboring pairs of factors with a feature function ϕ_a:

$$\psi_{ta}(T^i, A_i, A_{i-1}) = \frac{e^{\theta_a^\top \phi_a(T_i, A_i, A_{i-1})}}{\sum_{A_i', A_{i-1}'} e^{\theta_a^\top \phi_a(T^i, A_i', A_{i-1}')}} \tag{3}$$

Constraint factors ψ_{tc}, which map text features onto constraint values:

$$\psi_{tc}(T^i, C_i) = e^{-||\theta_t^\top T_i - C_i||_2^2} \tag{4}$$

Prediction factors ψ_{acv} which encourage predicted constraints and path features to agree:

$$\psi_{acv}(A_i, C_i, V_j) = \begin{cases} 1 & \text{if } A_i \neq j \\ e^{-||C_i - V_j||_2^2} & \text{o.w.} \end{cases} \tag{5}$$

A **global factor** $\psi_{a^*}(A_1, A_2, \cdots)$ which places an arbitrary combinatorial constraint on the alignment.

Note the essential similarity between Equations 1 and 4—in general, it can be shown that this factor model reduces to the regression model we gave for colors when there is only one of each T^i and V_j.

5.1 Learning

In order to make learning in the stocks domain tractable, we introduce the following global constraints on alignment: every terminal must be aligned, and two constituents cannot be aligned to the same segment. Together, these simplify learning by ensuring that the number of terms in the sum over $\mathbf{A}$ and $\mathbf{C}$ is polynomial (in fact $\mathcal{O}(n^2)$) in the length of the input sentence. We wish to find the maximum *a posteriori* estimate $p(\theta_t, \theta_a | T, \mathbf{V})$ for θ_t and θ_a, which we can do using the Expectation–Maximization algorithm. To find regression scoring weights θ_t, we have:

E step:

$$M = \mathbb{E}\left[\sum_i T^i (T^i)^\top\right]; \; N = \mathbb{E}\left[\sum_i T^i V_{A_i}^\top\right] \quad (6)$$

M step:

$$\theta_t = M^{-1} N \quad (7)$$

To find alignment scoring weights θ_a, we must maximize:

$$\sum_i \mathbb{E}\left[\log\left(\frac{e^{\theta_a^\top \phi_a(A_i, A_{i-1}, T^i)}}{\sum_{A_i', A_{i-1}'} e^{\theta_a^\top \phi_a(A_i', A_{i-1}', T^i)}}\right)\right] \quad (8)$$

which can be done using a variety of convex optimization tools; we used L-BFGS (Liu and Nocedal, 1989).

The predictive distribution $p(\mathbf{V}|T)$ can also be straightforwardly computed using the standard inference procedures for graphical models.

5.2 Evaluation

Our stocks dataset consists of a set of headlines from the "Market Snapshot" column of the *Wall Street Journal*'s MarketWatch website,[1] paired with hourly stock charts for each day described in a headline. Data is collected over a roughly decade-long period between 2001 and 2012; after removing weekends and days with incomplete stock data, we have a total of 2218 headline/time series pairs. As headlines most often discuss a single day or a short multi-day period, each training example consists of two days' worth of stock data concatenated together. We use a 90%/10% train/test split, with all test examples following all training examples chronologically.

We compare against two baselines: one which uses no text (and so learns only the overall market trend during the training period), and another which uses a fixed alignment instead of summing, aligning the entire tree to the second day's time series. Prediction error is the sum of squared errors between the predicted and gold time series.

We report both the magnitude of the prediction error, and the model's ability to distinguish between the described path and a randomly-selected alternative. The system scores poorly on squared

[1] http://www.marketwatch.com/Search?m=Column&mp=Market%20Snapshot

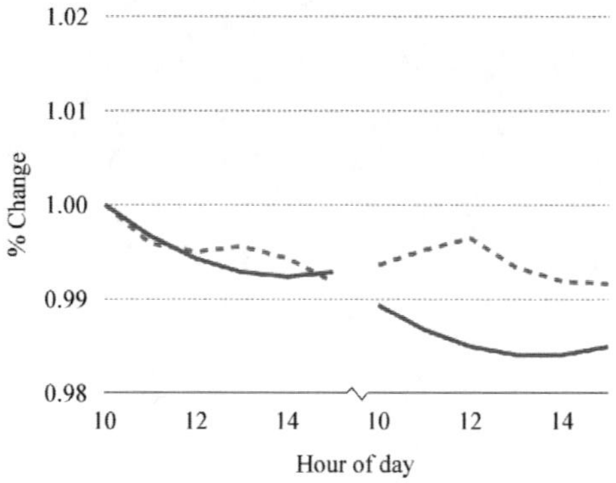

[*U.S. stocks end lower*]$_2$ [*as economic worries persist*]$_1$

Figure 5: Example output from the stocks task. The model prediction is given in blue (solid), and the reference time series in green (dashed). Brackets indicate the predicted boundaries of event-introducing spans, and subscripts their order in the sentence. The model correctly identifies that *end lower* refers to the current day, and *persist* provides information about the previous day.

Method	Sel. acc. ↑	Pred. err. ↓
No text	0.51	0.0012
Fixed alignment	0.59	**0.0011**
Full model	**0.61**	0.0018
Human	0.72	–

Table 3: Results for the stocks task. Sel(ection accuracy) measures the frequency with which the system correctly identifies the stock described in the headline when paired with a random alternative. Pred(iction error) is the mean sum of squared errors between the real and predicted paths. Full model selection accuracy is a statistically significant improvement ($p < 0.05$) over the baseline using a paired sign test.

error (which disproportionately penalizes large deviations from the correct answer, preferring conservative models), but outperforms both baselines on the task of choosing the described stock history—when it is wrong, its errors are often large in magnitude, but its predictions more frequently resemble the correct time series than the other systems.

Figure 5 shows example system output for an example sentence. The model correctly identifies the two events, orders them in time and gets their approximate trend correct. Table 4 shows some

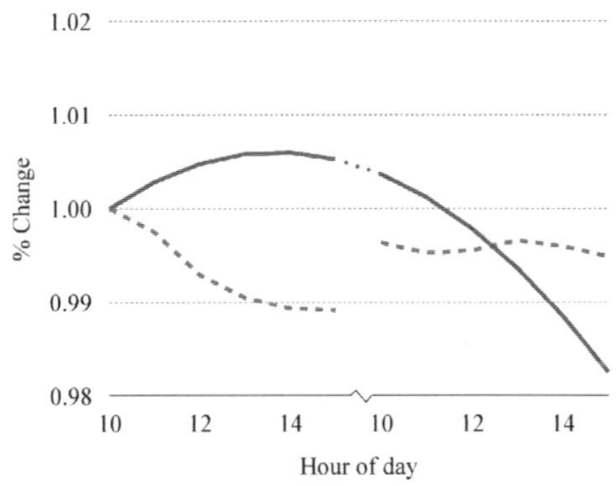

[*U.S. stocks extend losing stretch*]$_1$

Figure 6: Example error from the stocks task. The system's prediction, in blue (solid), fails to segment the input into two events, and thus incorrectly extends the *losing* trend to the entire output time span.

features learned by the model—as desired, it correctly interprets a variety of different expressions used to describe stock behavior.

5.3 Error analysis

As suggested by Table 4, learned weights for the trajectory-grounded features θ_t are largely correct. Thus, most incorrect outputs from the system involve alignment to time. Many multipart events (like *rebound*) can be reasonably explained using the curvature feature without splitting the text into two segments; as a result, the system tends to be fairly conservative about segmentation and often under-segments. This results in examples like Figure 6, in which the downward trend suggested by *losing* is incorrectly extended to the entire output curve. Here, another informal experiment using humans as the predictors indicates that predictions are farther from human-level performance

Word	Sign	Magnitude $\cdot 10^3$
rise	0.27	-0.78
swoon	-0.57	0
sharply	-0.22	0.28
slammed	-0.36	0
lifted	0.66	0

Table 4: Learned parameter settings for overall daily change, which the path featurization decomposes into a sign and a magnitude.

than they are on the colors task.

6 Generalizing the model

Last we consider the problem of following navigational directions. The difference between this and the previous task is largely one of scale: rather than attempting to predict the values of only two segments, we have a long string of them. The text, rather than a single tree, consists of a sequence of tens or hundreds of pre-segmented utterances.

There is one additional complication—rather than being defined in an absolute space, as they are in the case of stocks, constraints in the maps domain are provided relative to a set of known landmarks (like the *white water* and *stone creek* in Figure 3). We resolve landmarks automatically based on string matching, in a manner similar to Vogel and Jurafsky (2010), and assign each sentence in the discourse with a single referred-to landmark l_i. If no landmark is explicitly named, it inherits from the previous utterance. We continue to score constraints as before, but update the prediction factor:

$$\psi_{acv}(A_i, C_i, V_j) = \begin{cases} 1 & \text{if } A_i \neq j \\ e^{-\|l_i + C_i - V_j\|_2^2} & \text{o.w.} \end{cases} \quad (9)$$

The factor graph is shown in Figure 7; observe that this is simply an unrolled version of Figure 4—the basic structure of the model is unchanged. While pre-segmentation of the discourse means we can avoid aligning internal constituents of trees, we still need to treat every utterance as an alignment candidate, without a sparse combinatorial constraint. As a result, the sum over $\mathbf{A}$ and $\mathbf{C}$ is no longer tractable to compute explicitly, and approximate inference will be necessary.

For the experiments described in this paper, we do this with a sequence of Monte Carlo approximations. We run a Gibbs sampler, iteratively resampling each A_i and C_i as well as the parameter vectors θ_t and θ_a to obtain estimates of $\mathbb{E}\theta_t$ and $\mathbb{E}\theta_a$. The resampling steps for θ_t and θ_a are themselves difficult to perform exactly, so we perform an internal Metropolis-Hastings run (with a Gaussian proposal distribution) to obtain samples from the marginal distributions over θ_t and θ_a.

We approximate the mode of the posterior distribution by its mean. To follow a new set of directions in the prediction phase, we fix the parameter vectors and instead sample over $\mathbf{A}$, $\mathbf{C}$ and $\mathbf{V}$, and output $\mathbb{E}\mathbf{V}$. To complete the prediction process

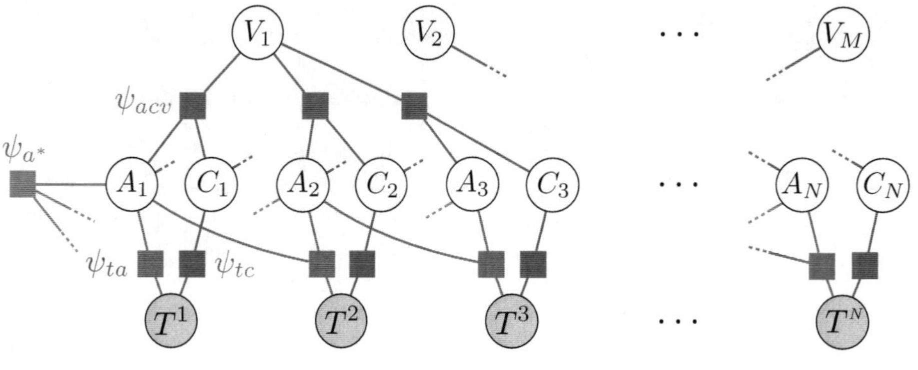

Figure 7: Factor graph for the general grounding model. Note that Figure 4 is a subgraph.

we must invert ϕ_v, which we do by producing the shortest path licensed by the features.

6.1 Evaluation

The Map Task Corpus consists of 128 dialogues describing paths on 16 maps, accompanied by transcriptions of spoken instructions, presegmented using prosodic cues. See Vogel and Jurafsky (2010) for a more detailed description of the corpus in a language learning setting. For comparability, we'll use the same evaluation as Vogel and Jurafsky, which rewards the system for moving between pairs of landmarks that also appear in the reference path, and penalizes it for additional superfluous movement. Note that we are solving a significantly harder problem: the version addressed by Vogel and Jurafsky is a discrete search problem, and the system has hard-coded knowledge that all paths pass along one of the four sides of each landmark. Our system, by contrast, can navigate to any point in $\mathbb{R}^2$, and must *learn* that most paths stay close to a named landmark.

At test time, the system is given a new sequence of text instructions, and must output the corresponding path. It is scored on the fraction of correct transitions in its output path (precision), and the fraction of transitions in the gold path recovered (recall). Vogel and Jurafsky compare their system to a policy-gradient algorithm for using language to follow natural language instructions described by Branavan et al. (2009), and we present both systems for comparison.

Results are shown in Table 5. Our system substantially outperforms the policy gradient baseline of Branavan et al., and performs close (particularly with respect to transition recall) to the system of Vogel and Jurafsky, with fewer assumptions.

System	Prec.	Recall	F_1
Branavan et al. (09)	0.31	0.44	0.36
Vogel & Jurafsky (10)	0.46	0.51	0.48
This work	0.43	0.51	0.45

Table 5: Results for the navigation task. Higher is better for all of precision, recall and F_1.

6.2 Error analysis

As in the case of stocks, most of the prediction errors on this task are a result of misalignment. In particular, many of the dialogues make passing reference to already-visited landmarks, or define destinations in empty regions of the map in terms of multiple landmarks simultaneously. In each of these cases, the system is prone to directly visiting the named landmark or landmarks instead of ignoring or interpolating as necessary.

7 Conclusion

We have presented a probabilistic model for grounding natural language text in vector-valued state sequences. The model is capable of segmenting text into a series of events, ordering these events in time, and compositionally determining their internal structure. We have evaluated on a variety of new and established applications involving colors, time series and navigation, demonstrating improvements over strong baselines in all cases.

Acknowledgments

This work was partially supported by BBN under DARPA contract HR0011-12-C-0014. The first author is supported by a National Science Foundation Graduate Research Fellowship.

References

Anne H Anderson, Miles Bader, Ellen Gurman Bard, Elizabeth Boyle, Gwyneth Doherty, Simon Garrod, Stephen Isard, Jacqueline Kowtko, Jan McAllister, Jim Miller, et al. 1991. The HCRC map task corpus. *Language and speech*, 34(4):351–366.

Yoav Artzi and Luke Zettlemoyer. 2013. Weakly supervised learning of semantic parsers for mapping instructions to actions. *Transactions of the Association for Computational Linguistics*, 1(1):49–62.

Michele Basseville and Igor V Nikiforov. 1995. Detection of abrupt changes: theory and applications. *Journal of the Royal Statistical Society-Series A Statistics in Society*, 158(1):185.

SRK Branavan, Harr Chen, Luke S Zettlemoyer, and Regina Barzilay. 2009. Reinforcement learning for mapping instructions to actions. In *Proceedings of the Joint Conference of the 47th Annual Meeting of the ACL and the 4th International Joint Conference on Natural Language Processing of the AFNLP: Volume 1-Volume 1*, pages 82–90. Association for Computational Linguistics.

Elia Bruni, Nam Khanh Tran, and Marco Baroni. 2014. Multimodal distributional semantics. *Journal of Artificial Intelligence Research*, 49:1–47.

David L Chen and Raymond J Mooney. 2011. Learning to interpret natural language navigation instructions from observations. In *AAAI*, volume 2.

Dave Golland, Percy Liang, and Dan Klein. 2010. A game-theoretic approach to generating spatial descriptions. In *Proceedings of the 2010 conference on Empirical Methods in Natural Language Processing*, pages 410–419. Association for Computational Linguistics.

Christopher Kennedy and Louise McNally. 2010. Color, context, and compositionality. *Synthese*, 174(1):79–98.

Shimon Kogan, Dimitry Levin, Bryan R Routledge, Jacob S Sagi, and Noah A Smith. 2009. Predicting risk from financial reports with regression. In *Proceedings of Human Language Technologies: The 2009 Annual Conference of the North American Chapter of the Association for Computational Linguistics*, pages 272–280. Association for Computational Linguistics.

Thomas Kollar, Stefanie Tellex, Deb Roy, and Nicholas Roy. 2010. Grounding verbs of motion in natural language commands to robots. In *International Symposium on Experimental Robotics*.

Jayant Krishnamurthy and Thomas Kollar. 2013. Jointly learning to parse and perceive: connecting natural language to the physical world. *Transactions of the Association for Computational Linguistics*.

Percy Liang, Michael I Jordan, and Dan Klein. 2013. Learning dependency-based compositional semantics. *Computational Linguistics*, 39(2):389–446.

Dong C Liu and Jorge Nocedal. 1989. On the limited memory BFGS method for large scale optimization. *Mathematical programming*, 45(1-3):503–528.

Terence Parsons. 1990. *Events in the semantics of English*. MIT Press.

Slav Petrov and Dan Klein. 2007. Improved inference for unlexicalized parsing. In *Proceedings of Human Language Technologies: The 2007 Annual Conference of the North American Chapter of the Association for Computational Linguistics*. Assocation for Computational Linguistics.

Stefanie Tellex, Thomas Kollar, Steven Dickerson, Matthew R. Walter, Ashis Gopal Banerjee, Seth Teller, and Nicholas Roy. 2011. Understanding natural language commands for robotic navigation and mobile manipulation. In *In Proceedings of the National Conference on Artificial Intelligence*.

Robert Tibshirani. 1996. Regression shrinkage and selection via the lasso. *Journal of the Royal Statistical Society. Series B (Methodological)*, pages 267–288.

Adam Vogel and Dan Jurafsky. 2010. Learning to follow navigational directions. In *Proceedings of the 48th Annual Meeting of the Association for Computational Linguistics*, pages 806–814. Association for Computational Linguistics.

Haonan Yu and Jeffrey Mark Siskind. 2013. Grounded language learning from videos described with sentences. In *Proceedings of the 51st Annual Meeting of the Association for Computational Linguistics*. Association for Computational Linguistics.

Jin Yu, Ehud Reiter, Jim Hunter, and Chris Mellish. 2007. Choosing the content of textual summaries of large time-series data sets. *Natural Language Engineering*, 13(1):25–49.

Jeffrey M Zacks and Khena M Swallow. 2007. Event segmentation. *Current Directions in Psychological Science*, 16(2):80–84.

John M Zelle and Raymond J Mooney. 1996. Learning to parse database queries using inductive logic programming. In *Proceedings of the National Conference on Artificial Intelligence*, pages 1050–1055.

Luke S. Zettlemoyer and Michael Collins. 2005. Learning to map sentences to logical form: Structured classification with probabilistic categorial grammars. In *Proceedings of the 21st Conference on Uncertainty in Artificial Intelligence*, pages 658–666.

Looking for Hyponyms in Vector Space

Marek Rei
SwiftKey
95 Southwark Bridge Rd
London, UK
marek@swiftkey.net

Ted Briscoe
Computer Laboratory
University of Cambridge
Cambridge, UK
ted.briscoe@cl.cam.ac.uk

Abstract

The task of detecting and generating hyponyms is at the core of semantic understanding of language, and has numerous practical applications. We investigate how neural network embeddings perform on this task, compared to dependency-based vector space models, and evaluate a range of similarity measures on hyponym generation. A new asymmetric similarity measure and a combination approach are described, both of which significantly improve precision. We release three new datasets of lexical vector representations trained on the BNC and our evaluation dataset for hyponym generation.

1 Introduction

Hyponymy is a relation between two word senses, indicating that the meaning of one word is also contained in the other. It can be thought of as a *type-of* relation; for example *car*, *ship* and *train* are all hyponyms of *vehicle*. We denote a hyponymy relation between words a and b as $(a \rightarrow b)$, showing that a is a hyponym of b, and b is a hypernym of a. Hyponymy relations are closely related to the concept of entailment, and this notation is consistent with indicating the direction of inference – if a is true, b must be true as well.

Automatic detection and generation of hyponyms has many practical applications in nearly all natural language processing tasks. Information retrieval, information extraction and question answering can be improved by performing appropriate query expansions. For example, a user searching for *arthritis treatment* is most likely also interested in results containing the hyponyms of *treatment*, such as *arthritis therapy*, *arthritis medication*, and *arthritis rehabilitation*. Summarisation systems can increase coherence and reduce repetition by correctly handling hyponymous words in the input text. Entailment and inference systems can improve sentence-level entailment resolution by detecting the presence and direction of word-level hyponymy relations. Distributionally similar words have been used for smoothing language models and word co-occurrence probabilities (Dagan et al., 1999; Weeds and Weir, 2005), and hyponyms can be more suitable for this application.

We distinguish between three different tasks related to hyponyms. Given a directional word pair, the goal of **hyponym detection** is to determine whether one word is a hyponym of the other (Zhitomirsky-Geffet and Dagan, 2009; Kotlerman et al., 2010; Baroni and Lenci, 2011). In contrast, **hyponym acquisition** is the task of extracting all possible hyponym relations from a given text (Hearst, 1992; Caraballo, 1999; Pantel and Ravichandran, 2004; Snow et al., 2005). Such systems often make use of heuristic rules and patterns for extracting relations from surface text, and populate a database with hyponymous word pairs. Finally, the task of **hyponym generation** is to return a list of all possible hyponyms, given only a single word as input. This is most relevant to practical applications, as many systems require a set of appropriate substitutes for a specific term. Automated ontology creation (Biemann, 2005) is a related field that also makes use of distributional similarity measures. However, it is mostly focused on building prototype-based ontologies through clustering (Ushioda, 1996; Bisson et al., 2000; Wagner, 2000; Paaß et al., 2004; Cimiano and Staab, 2005), and is not directly applicable to hyponym generation.

While most work has been done on hyponym detection (and the related task of lexical substitution), barely any evaluation has been done for hyponym generation. We have found that systems for hyponym detection often perform poorly on hyponym generation, as the latter requires returning results from a much less restricted candidate set,

Proceedings of the Eighteenth Conference on Computational Language Learning, pages 68–77,
Baltimore, Maryland USA, June 26-27 2014.

and therefore a task-specific evaluation is required.

In this paper we focus on hyponym generation and approach it by scoring a very large candidate set of potential hyponyms. Distributional similarity methods are especially interesting for this task, as they can be easily applied to different domains, genres and languages without requiring annotated training data or manual pattern construction. We perform a systematic comparison of different vector space models and similarity measures, in order to better understand the properties of a successful method for hyponym generation.

The main contributions of this paper are:

1. Systematic evaluation of different vector space models and similarity measures on the task of hyponym generation.

2. Proposal of new properties for modelling the directional hyponymy relation.

3. Release of three lexical vector datasets, trained using neural network, window-based, and dependency-based features.

2 Vector space models

In order to use similarity measures for hyponym detection, every word needs to be mapped to a point in vector space. The method of choosing appropriate features for these vectors is crucial to achieving the optimal performance. We compare five different approaches:

Window: As a simple baseline, we created vectors by counting word co-occurrences in a fixed context window. Every word that occurs within a window of three words before or after is counted as a feature for the target word. Pointwise mutual information is then used for weighting.

CW: Collobert and Weston (2008) constructed a neural network language model that is trained to predict the next word in the sequence, and simultaneously learns vector representations for each word. The vectors for context words are concatenated and used as input for the neural network, which uses a sample of possible outputs for gradient calculation to speed up the training process. Turian et al. (2010) recreated their experiments and made the vectors available online.[1]

HLBL: Mnih and Hinton (2007) created word representations using the hierarchical log-bilinear model – a neural network that takes the concatenated vectors of context words as input, and is trained to predict the vector representation of the next word, which is then transformed into a probability distribution over possible words. To speed up training and testing, they use a hierarchical data structure for filtering down the list of candidates. Both CW and HLBL vectors were trained using 37M words from RCV1.

Word2vec: We created word representations using the word2vec[2] toolkit. The tool is based on a feedforward neural network language model, with modifications to make representation learning more efficient (Mikolov et al., 2013a). We make use of the skip-gram model, which takes each word in a sequence as an input to a log-linear classifier with a continuous projection layer, and predicts words within a certain range before and after the input word. The window size was set to 5 and vectors were trained with both 100 and 500 dimensions.

Dependencies: Finally, we created vector representations for words by using dependency relations from a parser as features. Every incoming and outgoing dependency relation is counted as a feature, together with the connected term. For example, given the dependency relation *(play, dobj, guitar)*, the tuple *(>dobj, guitar)* is extracted as a feature for *play*, and *(<dobj, play)* as a feature for *guitar*. We use only features that occur more than once in the dataset, and weight them using pointwise mutual information to construct feature vectors for every term. Features with negative weights were retained, as they proved to be beneficial for some similarity measures.

The window-based, dependency-based and word2vec vector sets were all trained on 112M words from the British National Corpus, with preprocessing steps for lowercasing and lemmatising. Any numbers were grouped and substituted by more generic tokens. For constructing the dependency-based vector representations, we used the parsed version of the BNC created by Andersen et al. (2008) with the RASP toolkit (Briscoe et al., 2006). When saved as plain text, the 500-dimensional word2vec vectors and dependency-based vectors are comparable in size (602MB and 549MB), whereas the window-based vectors are twice as large (1,004MB). We make these vector

[1]http://metaoptimize.com/projects/wordreprs/

[2]https://code.google.com/p/word2vec/

sets publically available for download.[3]

Recently, Mikolov et al. (2013b) published interesting results about linguistic regularities in vector space models. They proposed that the relationship between two words can be characterised by their **vector offset**, for example, we could find the vector for word "queen" by performing the operation "king - man + woman" on corresponding vectors. They also applied this approach to hyponym relations such as $(shirt \rightarrow clothing)$ and $(bowl \rightarrow dish)$. We evaluate how well this method applies to hyponym generation with each of the vector space models mentioned above. Using the training data, we learn a vector for the hyponymy relation by averaging over all the offset vectors for hyponym-hypernym pairs. This vector is then added to the hypernym during query time, and the result is compared to hyponym candidates using cosine similarity. For sparse high-dimensional vector space models it was not feasible to use the full offset vector during experiments, therefore we retain only the top 1,000 highest-weighted features.

3 Similarity measures

We compare the performance of a range of similarity measures, both directional and symmetrical, on the task of hyponym generation.

Cosine similarity is defined as the angle between two feature vectors and has become a standard measure of similarity between weighted vectors in information retrieval (IR).

Lin similarity, created by Lin (1998), uses the ratio of shared feature weights compared to all feature weights. It measures the weighted proportion of features that are shared by both words.

DiceGen2 is one possible method for generalising the Dice measure to real-valued weights (Curran, 2003; Grefenstette, 1994). The dot product of the weight vectors is normalised by the total sum of all weights. The same formula can also be considered as a possible generalisation for the Jaccard measure.

WeedsPrec and **WeedsRec** were proposed by Weeds et al. (2004) who suggested using precision and recall as directional measures of word similarity. In this framework, the features are treated similarly to retrieved documents in information retrieval – the vector of the broader term b is used as the gold standard, and the vector of the narrower term a is in the role of retrieval results. Precision is then calculated by comparing the intersection (*items correctly returned*) to the values of the narrower term only (*all items returned*). In contrast, WeedsRec quantifies how well the features of the breader term are covered by the narrower term.

Balprec is a measure created by Szpektor and Dagan (2008). They proposed combining WeedsPrec together with the Lin measure by taking their geometric average. This aims to balance the WeedsPrec score, as the Lin measure will penalise cases where one vector contains very few features.

ClarkeDE, proposed by Clarke (2009), is an asymmetric *degree of entailment* measure, based on the concept of distributional generality (Weeds et al., 2004). It quantifies the weighted coverage of the features of the narrower term a by the features of the broader term b.

BalAPInc, a measure described by Kotlerman et al. (2010), combines the APInc score with Lin similarity by taking their geometric average. The APInc measure finds the proportion of shared features relative to the features for the narrower term, but this can lead to unreliable results when the number of features is very small. The motivation behind combining these measures is that the symmetric Lin measure will decrease the final score for such word pairs, thereby balancing the results.

4 Properties of a directional measure

Finding similar words in a vector space, given a symmetric similarity measure, is a relatively straightforward task. However finding hyponyms is arguably more difficult, as the relation is asymmetric, and looking at the distance or angle between the two words may not be enough.

Kotlerman et al. (2010) investigate the related problem of detecting directional lexical entailment, and they propose three desirable properties that a directional distributional similarity measure should capture:

1. The relevance of the shared features to the narrower term.
2. The relevance of the shared features to the broader term.
3. That relevance is less reliable if the number of features of either the narrower or the broader term is small.

[3] http://www.marekrei.com/projects/vectorsets/

Given a term pair ($a \rightarrow b$) we refer to a as the narrower term and b as the broader term. The features of a that are also found in b (have non-zero weights for both a and b) are referred to as *shared features*.

They show that existing measures which correspond to these criteria perform better and construct the BalAPInc measure based on the principles. However, it is interesting to note that these properties do not explicitly specify any directional aspects of the measure, and symmetric similarity scores can also fulfil the requirements.

Based on investigating hyponym distributions in our training data, we suggest two additions to this list of desired properties, one of which specifically targets the asymmetric properties of the desired similarity measures:

4. The shared features are more important to the directional score calculation, compared to non-shared features.

5. Highly weighted features of the broader term are more important to the score calculation, compared to features of the narrower term.

Most existing directional similarity scores measure how many features of the narrower term are present for the broader term. If a entails b, then it is assumed that the possible contexts of a are a subset of contexts for b, but b occurs in a wider range of contexts compared to a. This intuition is used by directional measures such as $ClarkeDE$, $WeedsPrec$ and $BalAPInc$. In contrast, we found that many features of the narrower term are often highly specific to that term and do not generalise even to hypernyms. Since these features have a very high weight for the narrower term, their absence with the broader term will have a big negative impact on the similarity score.

We hypothesise that many terms have certain individual features that are common to them but not to other related words. Since most weighting schemes reward high relative co-occurrence, these features are also likely to receive high weights. Therefore, we suggest that features which are not found for both terms should have a decreased impact on the score calculation, as many of them are not expected to be shared between hyponyms and hypernyms. However, removing them completely is also not advisable, as they allow the measure to estimate the overall relative importance of the shared features to the specific term.

We also propose that among the shared features, those ranked higher for the broader term are more important to the directional measure. In the hyponymy relation ($a \rightarrow b$), the term b is more general and covers a wider range of semantic concepts. This also means it is more likely to be used in contexts that apply to different hyponyms of b. For example, some of the high-ranking features for *food* are *blandly-flavoured*, *high-calorie* and *uneaten*. These are properties that co-occur often with the term $food$, but can also be applied to most hyponyms of *food*. Therefore, we hypothesise that the presence of these features for the narrower term is a good indication of a hyponymy relation. This is somewhat in contrast to most previous work, where the weights of the narrower term have been used as the main guideline for similarity calculation.

5 Weighted cosine

We now aim to construct a similarity measure that follows all five of the properties mentioned above. Cosine similarity is one of the symmetric similarity measures which corresponds to the first three desired properties, and our experiments showed that it performs remarkably well at the task of hyponym generation. Therefore, we decided to modify cosine similarity to also reflect the final two properties and produce a more appropriate asymmetric score.

The standard feature vectors for each word contain weights indicating how important this feature is to the word. We specify additional weights that measure how important the feature is to that specific directional relation between the two terms. Weighted cosine similarity, shown in Table 1, can then be used to calculate a modified similarity score. F_a denotes the set of weighted features for word a, $w_a(f)$ is the weight of feature f for word a, and $z(f)$ is the additional weight for feature f, given the directional word pair (a, b).

Based on the new desired properties we want to downweight the importance of features that are not present for both terms. For this, we choose the simple solution of scaling them with a small constant $C \in [0, 1]$. Next, we also want to assign higher $z(f)$ values to the shared features that have high weights for the broader term b. We use the relative rank of feature f in F_b, $r_b(f)$, as the indicator of its importance and scale this value to the range from C to 1. This results in the importance

$$WeightedCosine(F_a, F_b) = \frac{\sum_{f \in F_a \cap F_b} (z(f) \times w_a(f)) \times (z(f) \times w_b(f))}{\sqrt{\sum_{f \in F_a} (z(f) \times w_a(f))^2} \times \sqrt{\sum_{f \in F_b} (z(f) \times w_b(f))^2}}$$

$$z(f) = \begin{cases} (1 - \frac{r_b(f)}{|F_b|+1}) \times (1 - C) + C & \text{if } f \in F_a \cap F_b \\ C & \text{otherwise} \end{cases}$$

Table 1: Weighted cosine similarity measure

function decreasing linearly as the rank number increases, but the weights for the shared features always remain higher compared to the non-shared features. Tied feature values are handled by assigning them the average rank value. Adding 1 to the denominator of the relative rank calculation avoids exceptions with empty vectors, and also ensures that the value will always be strictly greater than C. While the basic function is still the symmetric cosine, the $z(f)$ values will be different depending on the order of the arguments.

The parameter C controls the relative importance of the 'unimportant' features to the directional relation. Setting it to 0 will ignore these features completely, while setting it to 1 will result in the traditional cosine measure. Experiments on the development data showed that the exact value of this parameter is not very important, as long as it is not too close to the extreme values of 0 or 1. We use the value $C = 0.5$ for reporting our results, meaning that the non-shared features are half as important, compared to the shared features.

6 Dataset

As WordNet (Miller, 1995) contains numerous manually annotated hyponymy relations, we can use it to construct suitable datasets for evaluating hyponym generation. While WordNet terms are annotated with only the closest hyponyms, we are considering all indirect/inherited hyponyms to be relevant – for example, given relations ($genomics \rightarrow genetics$) and ($genetics \rightarrow biology$), then $genomics$ is also regarded as a hyponym of $biology$. WordNet relations are defined between synsets, but we refrain from the task of word sense disambiguation and count word a as a valid hyponym for word b if it is valid for any sense of b.

Synonymy can be thought of as a symmetric *is-a* relation, and most real-world applications would require synonyms to also be returned, together with hyponyms. Therefore, in our dataset we consider synonyms as hyponyms in both directions. We also performed experiments without synonyms and found that this had limited effect on the results – while the accuracy of all similarity measures slightly decreased (due to fewer numbers of correct answers), the relative ranking remained the same. As shown in the next section, the number of synonyms is typically small compared to the number of all inherited hyponyms.

To construct the dataset, we first found all single-word nouns in WordNet that are contained at least 10 times in the British National Corpus (BNC). Next, we retained only words that have at least 10 hyponyms, such that they occur 10 or more times in the BNC. This selection process aims to discard WordNet hypernyms that are very rare in practical use, and would not have enough examples for learning informative vector representations. The final dataset contains the remaining terms, together with all of their hyponyms, including the rare/unseen hyponyms. As expected, some general terms, such as *group* or *location*, have a large number of inherited hyponyms. On average, each hypernym in the dataset has 233 hyponyms, but the distribution is roughly exponential, and the median is only 36.

In order to better facilitate future experiments with supervised methods, such as described by Baroni et al. (2012), we randomly separated the data into training (1230 hypernyms), validation (922), and test (922) sets, and we make these datasets publically available online.[4]

7 Experiments

We evaluate how well different vector space models and similarity measures perform on the task of hyponym generation. Given a single word as input, the system needs to return a ranked list of words with correct hyponyms at the top. As the list of candidates for scoring we use all words in the BNC that occur at least 10 times (a total of 86,496 words). All the experiments are performed using tokenised and lemmatised words.

As the main evaluation measure, we report

[4]http://www.marekrei.com/projects/hypgen/

	Cosine			Cosine+offset		
	MAP	**P@1**	**P@5**	**MAP**	**P@1**	**P@5**
Window	2.18	19.76	12.20	2.19	19.76	12.25
CW-100	0.66	3.80	3.21	0.59	3.91	2.89
HLBL-100	1.01	10.31	6.04	1.01	10.31	6.06
Word2vec-100	1.78	15.96	10.12	1.50	12.38	8.71
Word2vec-500	2.06	19.76	11.92	1.77	17.05	10.71
Dependencies	**2.73**	**25.41**	**14.90**	**2.73**	**25.52**	**14.92**

Table 2: Experiments using different vector space models for hyponym generation on the test set. We report results using regular cosine similarity and the vector offset method described in Section 2.

Mean Average Precision (MAP), which averages precision values at various recall points in the returned list. It combines both precision and recall, as well as the quality of the ranking, into a single measure, and is therefore well-suited for comparing different methods. The reported MAP values are very low – this is due to many rare WordNet hyponyms not occurring in the candidate set, for which all systems are automatically penalised. However, this allows us to evaluate recall, making the results comparable between different systems and background datasets. We also report precision at top-1 and top-5 returned hyponyms.

As a baseline we report the results of a traditional hyponym acquisition system. For this, we implemented the pattern-based matching process described by Hearst (1992), and also used by Snow et al. (2005). These patterns look for explicit examples of hyponym relations mentioned in the text, for example:

$$X \; such \; as \; \{Y_1, \; Y_2, \; ... \; , \; (and|or)\} \; Y_n$$

where X will be extracted as the hypernym, and Y_1 to Y_n as hyponyms. We ran the patterns over the BNC and extracted 21,704 hyponym pairs, which were then ranked according to the number of times they were found.

7.1 Evaluation of vector spaces

Table 2 contains experiments with different vector space models. We report here results using cosine, as it is an established measure and a competitive baseline. For our task, the HLBL vectors perform better than CW vectors, even though they were trained on the same data. Both of them are outperformed by word2vec-100 vectors, which have the same dimensionality but are trained on much more text. Increasing the dimensionality with word2vec-500 gives a further improvement. Interestingly, the simple window-based vectors perform just as well as the ones trained with neural networks. However, the advantage of word2vec-500 is that the representations are more compact and require only about half the space. Finally, the dependency-based vectors outperform all other vector types, giving 2.73% MAP and 25.41% precision at the top-ranked result. While the other models are built by using neighbouring words as context, this model looks at dependency relations, thereby taking both semantic and syntactic roles into account. The results indicate that word2vec and window-based models are more suitable when the general topic of words needs to be captured, whereas dependency-based vectors are preferred when the task requires both topical and functional similarity between words. Our experiments also included the evaluation of other similarity measures on different vector space models, and we we found these results to be representative.

Contrary to previous work, the vector offset method, described in Section 2, did not provide substantial improvements on the hyponym generation task. For the neural network-based vectors this approach generally decreased performance, compared to using direct cosine similarity. There are some marginal improvements for window and dependency-based models. Unfortunately, the original work did not include baseline performance using cosine similarity, without applying vector modifications. It is possible that this method does not generalise to all word relations equally well. As part of future work, it is worth exploring if a hypernym-specific strategy of selecting training examples could improve the performance.

	Validation			Test		
	MAP	**P@1**	**P@5**	**MAP**	**P@1**	**P@5**
Pattern-based	0.53	7.06	4.58	0.51	8.14	4.45
Cosine	2.48	21.06	12.96	2.73	25.41	14.90
Lin	1.87	16.50	10.75	2.01	21.17	12.23
DiceGen2	2.27	18.57	12.62	2.44	21.82	14.55
WeedsPrec	0.13	0.00	0.09	0.12	0.11	0.04
WeedsRec	0.72	0.33	2.45	0.69	0.54	2.41
BalPrec	1.78	15.31	10.55	1.88	17.48	11.34
ClarkeDE	0.23	0.00	0.02	0.24	0.00	0.09
BalAPInc	1.64	14.22	9.12	1.68	15.85	9.66
WeightedCosine	2.59	21.39	13.59	2.85	25.84	15.46
Combined	**3.27**	**23.02**	**16.09**	**3.51**	**27.69**	**18.02**

Table 3: Evaluation of different vector similarity measures on the validation and test set of hyponym generation. We report Mean Average Precision (MAP), precision at rank 1 (P@1), and precision at rank 5 (P@5).

7.2 Evaluation of similarity measures

Table 3 contains experiments with different similarity measures, using the dependency-based model, and Table 4 contains sample output from the best system. The results show that the pattern-based baseline does rather poorly on this task. MAP is low due to the system having very limited recall, but higher precision at top ranks would have been expected. Analysis showed that this system was unable to find any hyponyms for more than half (513/922) of the hypernyms in the validation set, leading to such poor recall that it also affects Precision@1. While the pattern-based system did extract a relatively large number of hyponyms from the corpus (21,704 pairs), these are largely concentrated on a small number of hypernyms (e.g., *area*, *company*, *material*, *country*) that are more likely to be mentioned in matching contexts.

Cosine, DiceGen2 and Lin – all symmetric similarity measures – perform relatively well on this task, whereas established directional measures perform unexpectedly poorly. This can perhaps be explained by considering the distribution of hyponyms. Given a word, the most likely candidates for a high cosine similarity are synonyms, antonyms, hypernyms and hyponyms of that word – these are words that are likely to be used in similar topics, contexts, and syntactic roles. By definition, there are an equal number of hyponym and hypernym relations in WordNet, but this ratio changes rapidly as we remove lower-frequency words. Figure 1 shows the number of relations extracted from WordNet, as we restrict the minimum frequency of the main word. It can be seen that the number of hyponyms increases much faster compared to the other three relations. This also applies to real-world data – when averaging over word instances found in the BNC, hyponyms cover 85% of these relations. Therefore, the high performance of cosine can be explained by distributionally similar words having a relatively high likelihood of being hyponyms.

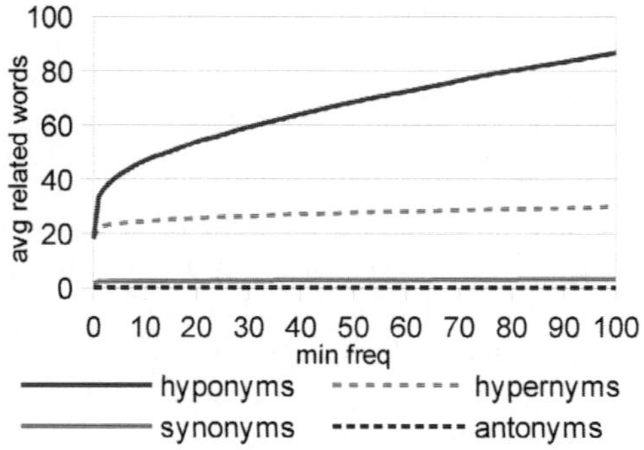

Figure 1: Average number of different relations per word in WordNet, as we restrict the minimum word frequency.

One possible reason for the poor performance of directional measures is that most of them quantify how well the features of the narrower term are included in the broader term. In contrast, we found that for hyponym generation it is more important to measure how well the features of the broader term are included in the narrower term. This

scientist	**researcher**, **biologist**, **psychologist**, **economist**, observer, **physicist**, **sociologist**
sport	**football**, **golf**, club, **tennis**, **athletics**, **rugby**, **cricket**, game, recreation, entertainment
treatment	**therapy**, **medication**, patient, procedure, surgery, remedy, regimen, medicine

Table 4: Examples of top results using the combined system. WordNet hyponyms are marked in bold.

is supported by WeedsRec outperforming WeedsPrec, although the opposite was intended by their design.

Another explanation for the low performance is that these directional measures are often developed in an artificial context. For example, Kotlerman et al. (2010) evaluated lexical entailment detection on a dataset where the symmetric Lin similarity measure was used to select word pairs for manual annotation. This creates a different task, as correct terms that do not have a high symmetric similarity will be excluded from evaluation. The BalAPInc measure performed best in that setting, but does not do as well for hyponym generation, where candidates are filtered only based on minimum frequency.

The weighted cosine measure, proposed in Section 5, outperformed all other similarity measures on both hyponym generation datasets. The improvement over cosine is relatively small; however, it is consistent and the improvement in MAP is statistically significant on both datasets ($p < 0.05$), using the Approximate Randomisation Test (Noreen, 1989; Cohen, 1995) with 10^6 iterations. This further supports the properties of a directional similarity measure described in Section 4.

Finally, we created a new system by combining together two separate approaches: the weighted cosine measure using the dependency-based vector space, and the normal cosine similarity using word2vec-500 vectors. We found that the former is good at modelling the grammatical roles and directional containment, whereas the latter can provide useful information about the topic and semantics of the word. Turney (2012) also demonstrated the importance of both topical (domain) and functional vector space models when working with semantic relations. We combined these approaches by calculating both scores for each word pair and taking their geometric average, or 0 if it could not be calculated. This final system gives considerable improvements across all evaluation metrics, and is significantly ($p < 0.05$) better compared to cosine or weighted cosine methods individually. Table 4 contains some example output from this system.

8 Conclusion

Hyponym generation has a wide range of possible applications in NLP, such as query expansion, entailment detection, and language model smoothing. Pattern-based hyponym acquisition can be used to find relevant hyponyms, but these approaches rely on both words being mentioned together in a specific context, leading to very low recall. Vector similarity methods are interesting for this task, as they can be easily applied to different domains and languages without any supervised learning or manual pattern construction. We created a dataset for evaluating hyponym generation systems and experimented with a range of vector space models and similarity measures.

Our results show that choosing an appropriate vector space model is equally important to using a suitable similarity measure. We achieved the highest performance using dependency-based vector representations, which outperformed neural network and window-based models. Symmetric similarity measures, especially cosine similarity, performed surprisingly well on this task. This can be attributed to an unbalanced distribution of hyponyms, compared to other high-similarity words. The choice of vector space can be highly dependent on the specific task, and we have made available our vector datasets created from the same source using three different methods.

We proposed two new properties for detecting hyponyms, and used them to construct a new directional similarity measure. This weighted cosine measure significantly outperformed all others, showing that a theoretically-motivated directional measure is still the most accurate method for modelling hyponymy relations. Finally, we combined together two different methods, achieving further substantial improvements on all evaluation metrics.

References

Øistein E. Andersen, Julien Nioche, Edward J. Briscoe, and John Carroll. 2008. The BNC parsed with RASP4UIMA. In *Proceedings of the Sixth Interna-*

tional Language Resources and Evaluation Conference (LREC08), Marrakech, Morocco.

Marco Baroni and Alessandro Lenci. 2011. How we BLESSed distributional semantic evaluation. In *Proceedings of the GEMS 2011 Workshop on GEometrical Models of Natural Language Semantics*, Edinburgh.

Marco Baroni, Raffaella Bernardi, Ngoc-Quynh Do, and Chung-chieh Shan. 2012. Entailment above the word level in distributional semantics. In *Proceedings of the 13th Conference of the European Chapter of the Association for Computational Linguistics*, pages 23–32.

Chris Biemann. 2005. Ontology learning from text: A survey of methods. *LDV Forum*, 20(2002):75–93.

Gilles Bisson, Claire Nédellec, and Dolores Cañamero. 2000. Designing clustering methods for ontology building-The Mo'K workbench. In *ECAI Ontology Learning Workshop*.

Ted Briscoe, John Carroll, and Rebecca Watson. 2006. The second release of the RASP system. In *Proceedings of the COLING/ACL 2006 Interactive Presentation Sessions*, number July, pages 77–80, Sydney, Australia. Association for Computational Linguistics.

Sharon A. Caraballo. 1999. Automatic construction of a hypernym-labeled noun hierarchy from text. *Proceedings of the 37th annual meeting of the Association for Computational Linguistics on Computational Linguistics*, pages 120–126.

Philipp Cimiano and Steffen Staab. 2005. Learning concept hierarchies from text with a guided hierarchical clustering algorithm. In *ICML-Workshop on Learning and Extending Lexical Ontologies by using Machine Learning Methods*.

Daoud Clarke. 2009. Context-theoretic semantics for natural language: an overview. In *Proceedings of the Workshop on Geometrical Models of Natural Language Semantics*, number March, pages 112–119. Association for Computational Linguistics.

Paul R Cohen. 1995. *Empirical Methods for Artificial Intelligence*. The MIT Press, Cambridge, MA.

Ronan Collobert and Jason Weston. 2008. A unified architecture for natural language processing: Deep neural networks with multitask learning. *Proceedings of the 25th international conference on Machine learning*.

James R. Curran. 2003. *From distributional to semantic similarity*. Ph.D. thesis, University of Edinburgh.

Ido Dagan, Lillian Lee, and Fernando C. N. Pereira. 1999. Similarity-based models of word cooccurrence probabilities. *Machine Learning*, 31:1–31.

Gregory Grefenstette. 1994. *Explorations in Automatic Thesaurus Discovery*. Kluwer Academic Publishers, Norwell, MA, USA.

Marti A. Hearst. 1992. Automatic acquisition of hyponyms from large text corpora. In *Proceedings of the 14th conference on Computational linguistics (COLING '92)*, number July, page 539, Morristown, NJ, USA. Association for Computational Linguistics.

Lili Kotlerman, Ido Dagan, Idan Szpektor, and Maayan Zhitomirsky-Geffet. 2010. Directional distributional similarity for lexical inference. *Natural Language Engineering*, 16(04):359–389.

Dekang Lin. 1998. Automatic retrieval and clustering of similar words. In *Proceedings of the 17th international conference on Computational linguistics-Volume 2*, pages 768–774. Association for Computational Linguistics.

Tomas Mikolov, Kai Chen, Greg Corrado, and Jeffrey Dean. 2013a. Efficient Estimation of Word Representations in Vector Space. *ICLR Workshop*, pages 1–12.

Tomas Mikolov, Wen-tau Yih, and Geoffrey Zweig. 2013b. Linguistic Regularities in Continuous Space Word Representations. (June):746–751.

George A. Miller. 1995. WordNet: a lexical database for English. *Communications of the ACM*, 38(11):39–41.

Andriy Mnih and Geoffrey Hinton. 2007. Three new graphical models for statistical language modelling. *Proceedings of the 24th international conference on Machine learning - ICML '07*, pages 641–648.

Eric W. Noreen. 1989. *Computer Intensive Methods for Testing Hypotheses: An Introduction*. Wiley, New York.

Gerhard Paaß, Jörg Kindermann, and Edda Leopold. 2004. Learning prototype ontologies by hierachical latent semantic analysis.

Patrick Pantel and Deepak Ravichandran. 2004. Automatically labeling semantic classes. In *Proceedings of HLT/NAACL*.

Rion Snow, Daniel Jurafsky, and Andrew Y. Ng. 2005. Learning syntactic patterns for automatic hypernym discovery. In *Advances in Neural Information Processing Systems*.

Idan Szpektor and Ido Dagan. 2008. Learning entailment rules for unary templates. In *Proceedings of the 22nd International Conference on Computational Linguistics (COLING '08)*, pages 849–856, Morristown, NJ, USA. Association for Computational Linguistics.

Joseph Turian, Lev Ratinov, and Y Bengio. 2010. Word representations: a simple and general method for semi-supervised learning. In *Proceedings of the 48th Annual Meeting of the Association for Computational Linguistics.*

Peter D. Turney. 2012. Domain and function: A dual-space model of semantic relations and compositions. *Journal of Artificial Intelligence Research*, 44:533–585.

Akira Ushioda. 1996. Hierarchical clustering of words and application to NLP tasks. In *Fourth Workshop on Very Large Corpora*, pages 28–41.

Andreas Wagner. 2000. Enriching a lexical semantic net with selectional preferences by means of statistical corpus analysis. In *ECAI Workshop on Ontology Learning*.

Julie Weeds and David Weir. 2005. Co-occurrence retrieval: A flexible framework for lexical distributional similarity. *Computational Linguistics*.

Julie Weeds, David Weir, and Diana McCarthy. 2004. Characterising measures of lexical distributional similarity. *Proceedings of the 20th international conference on Computational Linguistics - COLING '04*.

Maayan Zhitomirsky-Geffet and Ido Dagan. 2009. Bootstrapping Distributional Feature Vector Quality. *Computational Linguistics*, 35(3):435–461, September.

Lexicon Infused Phrase Embeddings for Named Entity Resolution

Alexandre Passos, Vineet Kumar, Andrew McCallum
School of Computer Science
University of Massachusetts, Amherst
{apassos,vineet,mccallum}@cs.umass.edu

Abstract

Most state-of-the-art approaches for named-entity recognition (NER) use semi supervised information in the form of word clusters and lexicons. Recently neural network-based language models have been explored, as they as a byproduct generate highly informative vector representations for words, known as word embeddings. In this paper we present two contributions: a new form of learning word embeddings that can leverage information from relevant lexicons to improve the representations, and the first system to use neural word embeddings to achieve state-of-the-art results on named-entity recognition in both CoNLL and Ontonotes NER. Our system achieves an F1 score of 90.90 on the test set for CoNLL 2003—significantly better than any previous system trained on public data, and matching a system employing massive private industrial query-log data.

1 Introduction

In many natural language processing tasks, such as named-entity recognition or coreference resolution, syntax alone is not enough to build a high performance system; some external source of information is required. In most state-of-the-art systems for named-entity recognition (NER) this knowledge comes in two forms: domain-specific lexicons (lists of word types related to the desired named entity types) and word representations (either clusterings or vectorial representations of word types which capture some of their syntactic and semantic behavior and allow generalizing to unseen word types).

Current state-of-the-art named entity recognition systems use Brown clusters as the form of word representation (Ratinov and Roth, 2009; Turian et al., 2010; Miller et al., 2004; Brown et al., 1992), or other cluster-based representations computed from private data (Lin and Wu, 2009). While very attractive due to their simplicity, generality, and hierarchical structure, Brown clusters are limited because the computational complexity of fitting a model scales quadratically with the number of words in the corpus, or the number of "base clusters" in some efficient implementations, making it infeasible to train it on large corpora or with millions of word types.

Although some attempts have been made to train named-entity recognition systems with other forms of word representations, most notably those obtained from training neural language models (Turian et al., 2010; Collobert and Weston, 2008), these systems have historically underperformed simple applications of Brown clusters. A disadvantage of neural language models is that, while they are inherently more scalable than Brown clusters, training large neural networks is still often expensive; for example, Turian et al (2010) report that some models took multiple days or weeks to produce acceptable representations. Moreover, language embeddings learned from neural networks tend to behave in a "nonlinear" fashion, as they are trained to encourage a many-layered neural network to assign high probability to the data. These neural networks can detect nonlinear relationships between the embeddings, which is not possible in a log-linear model such as a conditional random field, and therefore limiting how much information from the embeddings can be actually leveraged.

Recently Mikolov et al (Mikolov et al., 2013a;

Proceedings of the Eighteenth Conference on Computational Language Learning, pages 78–86,
Baltimore, Maryland USA, June 26-27 2014.

Mikolov et al., 2013b) proposed two simple log-linear language models, the CBOW model and the Skip-Gram model, that are simplifications of neural language models, and which can be very efficiently trained on large amounts of data. For example it is possible to train a Skip-gram model over more than a billion tokens with a single machine in less than half a day. These embeddings can also be trained on phrases instead of individual word types, allowing for fine granularity of meaning.

In this paper we make the following contributions. (1) We show how to extend the Skip-Gram language model by injecting supervisory training signal from a collection of curated lexicons—effectively encouraging training to learn similar embeddings for phrases which occur in the same lexicons. (2) We demonstrate that this method outperforms a simple application of the Skip-Gram model on the semantic similarity task on which it was originally tested. (3) We show that a linear-chain CRF is able to successfully use these log-linearly-trained embeddings better than the other neural-network-trained embeddings. (4) We show that lexicon-infused embeddings let us easily build a new highest-performing named entity recognition system on CoNLL 2003 data (Tjong Kim Sang and De Meulder, 2003) which is trained using only publicly available data. (5) We also present results on the relatively understudied Ontonotes NER task (Weischedel et al., 2011), where we show that our embeddings outperform Brown clusters.

2 Background and Related Work

2.1 Language models and word embeddings

A statistical language model is a way to assign probabilities to all possible documents in a given language. Most such models can be classified in one of two categories: they can directly assign probabilities to sequences of word types, such as is done in n-gram models, or they can operate in a lower-dimensional latent space, to which word types are mapped. While most state-of-the-art language models are n-gram models, the representations used in models of the latter category, henceforth referred to as "embeddings," have been found to be useful in many NLP applications which don't actually need a language model. The underlying intuition is that when language models compress the information about the word types in a latent space they capture much of the commonalities and differences between word types. Hence features extracted from these models then can generalize better than features derived from the word types themselves.

One simple language model that discovers useful embeddings is known as *Brown clustering* (Brown et al., 1992). A Brown clustering is a class-based bigram model in which (1) the probability of a document is the product of the probabilities of its bigrams, (2) the probability of each bigram is the product of the probability of a bigram model over latent classes and the probability of each class generating the actual word types in the bigram, and (3) each word type has non-zero probability only on a single class. Given a one-to-one assignment of word types to classes, then, and a corpus of text, it is easy to estimate these probabilities with maximum likelihood by counting the frequencies of the different class bigrams and the frequencies of word tokens of each type in the corpus. The Brown clustering algorithm works by starting with an initial assignment of word types to classes (which is usually either one unique class per type or a small number of seed classes corresponding to the most frequent types in the corpus), and then iteratively selecting the pair of classes to merge that would lead to the highest post-merge log-likelihood, doing so until all classes have been merged. This process produces a hierarchical clustering of the word types in the corpus, and these clusterings have been found useful in many applications (Ratinov and Roth, 2009; Koo et al., 2008; Miller et al., 2004). There are other similar models of distributional clustering of English words which can be similarly effective (Pereira et al., 1993).

One limitation of Brown clusters is their computational complexity, as training takes $O(kV^2 + N)$x time to train, where k is the number of base clusters, V size of vocabulary, and N number of tokens. This is infeasible for large corpora with millions of word types.

Another family of language models that produces embeddings is the *neural language models*. Neural language models generally work by mapping each word type to a vector in a low-dimensional vector space and assigning probabilities to n-grams by processing their embeddings in a neural network. Many different neural language models have been proposed (Bengio et al., 2003; Morin and Bengio, 2005; Bengio, 2008;

Mnih and Hinton, 2008; Collobert and Weston, 2008; Mikolov et al., 2010). While they can capture the semantics of word types, and often generalize better than n-gram models in terms of perplexity, applying them to NLP tasks has generally been less successful than Brown clusters (Turian et al., 2010).

Finally, there are algorithms for computing word embeddings which do not use language models at all. A popular example is the CCA family of word embeddings (Dhillon et al., 2012; Dhillon et al., 2011), which work by choosing embeddings for a word type that capture the correlations between the embeddings of word types which occur before and after this type.

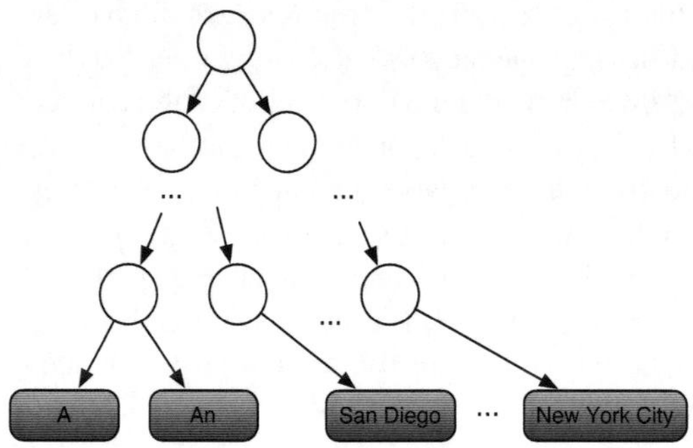

Figure 1: A binary Huffman tree. Circles represent binary classifiers. Rectangles represent tokens, which can be multi-word.

2.2 The Skip-gram Model

A main limitation of neural language models is that they often have many parameters and slow training times. To mitigate this, Mikolov et al. (2013a; 2013b) recently proposed a family of log-linear language models inspired by neural language models but designed for efficiency. These models operate on the assumption that, even though they are trained as language models, users will only look at their embeddings, and hence all they need is to produce good embeddings, and not high-accuracy language models.

The most successful of these models is the *skip-gram model*, which computes the probability of each n-gram as the product of the conditional probabilities of each context word in the n-gram conditioned on its central word. For example, the probability for the n-gram "the cat ate my homework" is represented as $P(the|ate)P(cat|ate)P(my|ate)P(homework|ate)$.

To compute these conditional probabilities the model assigns an embedding to each word type and defines a binary tree of logistic regression classifiers with each word type as a leaf. Each classifier takes a word embedding as input and produces a probability for a binary decision corresponding to a branch in the tree. Each leaf in the tree has a unique path from the root, which can be interpreted as a set of (classifier,label) pairs. The skip-gram model then computes a probability of a context word given a target word as the product of the probabilities, given the target word's embeddings, of all decisions on a path from the root to the leaf corresponding to the context word. Figure 1 shows such a tree structured model.

The likelihood of the data, then, given a set N of n-grams, with m_n being n-gram n's middle-word, c_n each context word, $w_i^{c_n}$ the parameters of the i-th classifier in the path from the root to c_n in the tree, $l_i^{c_n}$ its label (either 1 or -1), e_f the embedding of word type f, and σ is the logistic sigmoid function, is

$$\prod_{n \in N} \prod_{c_n \in n} \prod_{i} \sigma(l_i^{c_n} {w_i^{c_n}}^T e_{m_n}). \qquad (1)$$

Given a tree, then, choosing embeddings e_{m_n} and classifier parameters $w_i^{c_n}$ to maximize equation (1) is a non-convex optimization problem which can be solved with stochastic gradient descent.

The binary tree used in the model is commonly estimated by computing a Huffman coding tree (Huffman, 1952) of the word types and their frequencies. We experimented with other tree estimation schemes but found no perceptible improvement in the quality of the embeddings.

It is possible to extend these embeddings to model phrases as well as tokens. To do so, Mikolov et al (2013b) use a phrase-building criterion based on the pointwise mutual information of bigrams. They perform multiple passes over a corpus to estimate trigrams and higher-order phrases. We instead consider candidate trigrams for all pairs of bigrams which have a high PMI and share a token.

2.3 Named Entity Recognition

Named Entity Recognition (NER) is the task of finding all instances of explicitly named entities and their types in a given document. While detecting named entities is superficially simple, since most sequences of capitalized words are named entities (excluding headlines, sentence beginnings, and a few other exceptions), finding all entities is non trivial, and determining the correct named entity type can sometimes be surprisingly hard. Performing the task well often requires external knowledge of some form.

In this paper we evaluate our system on two labeled datasets for NER: CoNLL 2003 (Tjong Kim Sang and De Meulder, 2003) and Ontonotes (Weischedel et al., 2011). The CoNLL dataset has approximately 320k tokens, divided into 220k tokens for training, 55k tokens for development, and 50k tokens for testing. While the training and development sets are quite similar, the test set is substantially different, and performance on it depends strongly on how much external knowledge the systems have. The CoNLL dataset has four entity types: PERSON, LOCATION, ORGANIZATION, AND MISCELLANEOUS. The Ontonotes dataset is substantially larger: it has 1.6M tokens total, with 1.4M for training, 100K for development, and 130k for testing. It also has eighteen entity types, a much larger set than the CoNLL dataset, including works of art, dates, cardinal numbers, languages, and events.

The performance of NER systems is commonly measured in terms of precision, recall, and F1 on the sets of entities in the ground truth and returned by the system.

2.3.1 Baseline System

In this section we describe in detail the baseline NER system we use. It is inspired by the system described in Ratinov and Roth (2009).

Because NER annotations are commonly not nested (for example, in the text "the US Army", "US Army" is treated as a single entity, instead of the location "US" and the organization "US Army") it is possible to treat NER as a sequence labeling problem, where each token in the sentence receives a label which depends on which entity type it belongs to and its position in the entity. Following Ratinov and Roth (2009) we use the BILOU encoding, where each token can either BEGIN an entity, be INSIDE an entity, be the LAST token in an entity, be OUTSIDE an entity, or be the single UNIQUE token in an entity.

Our baseline architecture is a stacked linear-chain CRF (Lafferty et al., 2001) system: we train two CRFs, where the second CRF can condition on the predictions made by the first CRF as well as features of the data. Both CRFs, following Zhang and Johnson (2003), have roughly similar features.

While local features capture a lot of the clues used in text to highlight named entities, they cannot necessarily disambiguate entity types or detect named entities in special positions, such as the first tokens in a sentence. To solve these problems most NER systems incorporate some form of external knowledge. In our baseline system we use lexicons of months, days, person names, companies, job titles, places, events, organizations, books, films, and some minor others. These lexicons were gathered from US Census data, Wikipedia category pages, and Wikipedia redirects (and will be made publicly available upon publication).

Following Ratinov and Roth (2009), we also compare the performance of our system with a system using features based on the Brown clusters of the word types in a document. Since, as seen in section 2.1, Brown clusters are hierarchical, we use features corresponding to prefixes of the path from the root to the leaf for each word type.

More specifically, the feature templates of the baseline system are as follows. First for each token we compute:

- its word type;
- word type, after excluding digits and lower-casing it;
- its capitalization pattern;
- whether it is punctuation;
- 4-character prefixes and suffixes;
- character n-grams from length 2 to 5;
- whether it is in a wikipedia-extracted lexicon of person names (first, last, and honorifics), dates (months, years), place names (country, US state, city, place suffixes, general location words), organizations, and man-made things;
- whether it is a demonym.

For each token's label we have feature templates considering all token's features, all neighboring token's features (up to distance 2), and bags of words of features of tokens in a window of size 8 around each token. We also add a feature marking whether a token is the first occurrence of its word type in a document.

When using Brown clusters we add as token features all prefixes of lengths 4, 6, 10, and 20, of its brown cluster.

For the second-layer model we use all these features, as well as the label predicted for each token

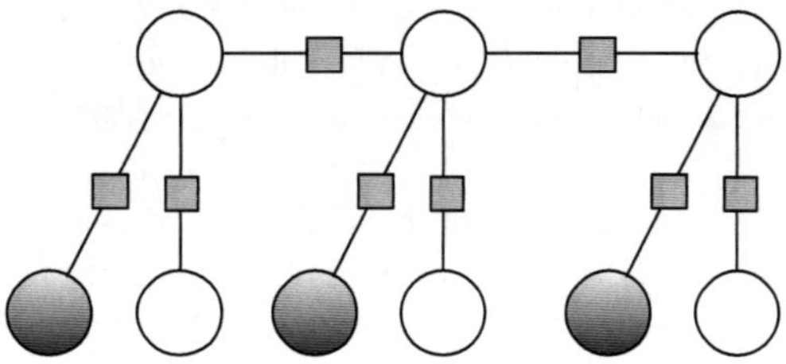

Figure 2: Chain CRF model for a NER system with three tokens. Filled rectangles represent factors. Circles at top represent labels, circles at bottom represent binary token based features. Filled circles indicate the phrase embeddings for each token.

by the first-layer model.

As seen in the Experiments Section, our baseline system is competitive with state-of-the-art systems which use similar forms of information.

We train this system with stochastic gradient ascent, using the AdaGrad RDA algorithm (Duchi et al., 2011), with both ℓ_1 and ℓ_2 regularization, automatically tuned for each experimental setting by measuring performance on the development set.

2.4 NER with Phrase Embeddings

In this section we describe how to extend our baseline NER system to use word embeddings as features.

First we group the tokens into phrases, assigning to each token a single phrase greedily. We prefer shorter phrases over longer ones, sinceour embeddings are often more reliable for the shorter phrases, and since the longer phrases in our dictionary are mostly extracted from Wikipedia page titles, which are not always semantically meaningful when seen in free text. We then add factors connecting each token's label with the embedding for its phrase.

Figure 2 shows how phrase embeddings are plugged into a chain-CRF based NER system. Following Turian (2010), we scale the embedding vector by a real number, which is a hyperparameter tuned on the development data. Connecting tokens to phrase embeddings of their neighboring tokens did not improve performance for phrase embeddings, but it was mildly beneficial for token embeddings.

3 Lexicon-infused Skip-gram Models

The Skip-gram model as defined in Section 2.2 is fundamentally trained in unsupervised fashion using simply words and their n-gram contexts. Injecting some NER-specific supervision into the embeddings can make them more relevant to the NER task.

Lexicons are a simple yet powerful way to provide task-specific supervisory information to the model without the burden of labeling additional data. However, while lexicons have proven useful in various NLP tasks, a small amount of noise in a lexicon can severely impair the its usefulness as a feature in log-linear models. For example, even legitimate data, such as the Chinese last name "He" occurring in a lexicon of person last names, can cause the lexicon feature to fire spuriously for many training tokens that are labeled PERSON, and then this lexicon feature may be given low or even negative weight.

We propose to address both these problems by employing lexicons as part of the word embedding training. The skip-gram model can be trained to predict not only neighboring words but also lexicon membership of the central word (or phrase). The resulting embedding training will thus be somewhat supervised by tending to bring together the vectors of words sharing a lexicon membership. Furthermore, this type of training can effectively "clean" the influence of noisy lexicons because even if "He" appears in the PERSON lexicon, it will have a sufficiently different context distribution than labeled named person entities (*e.g.* a lack of preceding honorifics, etc) that the presence of this noise in the lexicon will not be as problematic as it was previously.

Furthermore, while Skip-gram models can be trained on billions of tokens to learn word embeddings for over a million word types in a single day, this might not be enough data to capture reliable embeddings of all relevant named entity phrases. Certain sets of word types, such as names of famous scientists, can occur infrequently enough that the Skip-gram model will not have enough contextual examples to learn embeddings that highlight their relevant similarities.

In this section we describe how to extend the Skip-gram model to incorporate auxiliary information from lexicons, or lists of related words, encouraging the model to assign similar embeddings to word types in similar lexicons.

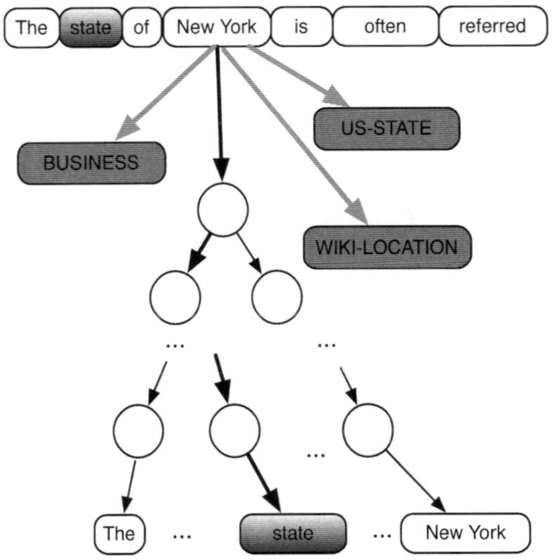

Figure 3: A Semi supervised Skip-gram Model. "New York" predicts the word "state". With lexicon-infusion, "New York" also predicts its lexicon classes: US-State, Wiki-location

In the basic Skip-gram model, as seen in Section 2.2, the likelihood is, for each n-gram, a product of the probability of the embedding associated with the middle word conditioned on each context word. We can inject supervision in this model by also predicting, given the embedding of the middle word, whether it is a member of each lexicon. Figure 3 shows an example, where the word "New York" predicts "state", and also its lexicon classes: Business, US-State and Wiki-Location.

Hence, with subscript s iterating over each lexicon (or set of related words), and $l_s^{m_n}$ being a label for whether each word is in the set, and w_s indicating the parameters of its classifier, the full likelihood of the model is

$$\prod_{n \in N} \left(\prod_{c_n \in n} \prod_{i} \sigma(l_i^{c_n} {w_i^{c_n}}^T e_{m_n}) \right) \left(\prod_{s} \sigma(l_s^{m_n} w_s^T e_{m_n}) \right). \tag{2}$$

This is a simple modification to equation (1) that also predicts the lexicon memberships. Note that the parameters w_s of the auxiliary per-lexicon classifiers are also learned. The lexicons are not inserted in the binary tree with the words; instead, each lexicon gets its own binary classifier.

Algorithm 1 Generating the training examples for lexicon-infused embeddings

```
for all n-gram n with middle word m_n do
    for all Context-word c_n do
        for all Classifier, label pair (w_i^{c_n}, l_i^{c_n}) in the tree do
            Add training example e_{m_n}, w_i^{c_n}, l^{c_n}
        end for
    end for
    for all Lexicon s, with label l_s^{m_n} do
        Add training example e_{m_n}, w_s, l_s^{m_n}
    end for
end for
```

In practice, a very small fraction of words are present in a lexicon-class and this creates skewed training data, with overwhelmingly many negative examples. We address this issue by aggressively sub-sampling negative training data for each lexicon class. We do so by randomly selecting only 1% of the possible negative lexicons for each token.

A Skip-gram model has V binary classifiers. A lexicon-infused Skip-gram model predicts an additional K classes, and thus has $V + K$ binary classifiers. If number of classes K is large, we can induce a tree over the classes, similarly to what is done over words in the vocabulary. In our trained models, however, we have one million words in the vocabulary and twenty-two lexicons, so this is not necessary.

4 Experiments

Our phrase embeddings are learned on the combination of English Wikipedia and the RCV1 Corpus (Lewis et al., 2004). Wikipedia contains 8M articles, and RCV1 contains 946K. To get candidate phrases we first select bigrams which have a pointwise mutual information score larger than 1000. We discard bigrams with stopwords from a manually selected list. If two bigrams share a token we add its corresponding trigram to our phrase list. We further add page titles from the English Wikipedia to the list of candidate phrases, as well as all word types. We get a total of about 10M phrases. We restrict the vocabulary to the most frequent 1M phrases. All our reported experiments are on 50-dimensional embeddings. Longer embeddings, while performing better on the semantic similarity task, as seen in Mikolov et al (2013a;

Model	Accuracy
Skip-Gram	29.89
Lex-0.05	30.37
Lex-0.01	**30.72**

Table 1: Accuracy for Semantic-Syntactic task, when restricted to Top 30K words. Lex-0.01 refers to a model trained with lexicons, where 0.01% of negative examples were used for training.

2013b), did not perform as well on NER.

To train phrase embeddings, we use a context of length 21. We use lexicons derived from Wikipedia categories and data from the US Census, totaling $K = 22$ lexicon classes. We use a randomly selected 0.01% of negative training examples for lexicons.

We perform two sets of experiments. First, we validate our lexicon-infused phrase embeddings on a semantic similarity task, similar to Mikolov et al (Mikolov et al., 2013a). Then we evaluate their utility on two named-entity recognition tasks.

For the NER Experiments, we use the baseline system as described in Section 2.3.1. NER systems marked as "Skip-gram" consider phrase embeddings; "LexEmb" consider lexicon-infused embeddings; "Brown" use Brown clusters, and "Gaz" use our lexicons as features.

4.1 Syntactic and Semantic Similarity

Mikolov et al. (2013a) introduce a test set to measure syntactic and semantic regularities for words. This set contains 8869 semantic and 10675 syntactic questions. Each question consists of four words, such as big, biggest, small, smallest. It asks questions of the form "What is the word that is similar to *small* in the same sense as *biggest* is similar to *big*". To test this, we compute the vector $X = vector(\text{``}biggest\text{''}) - vector(\text{``}big\text{''}) + vector(\text{``}small\text{''})$. Next, we search for the word closest to X in terms of cosine distance (excluding "biggest", "small", and "big"). This question is considered correctly answered only if the closest word found is "smallest". As in Mikolov et al (Mikolov et al., 2013a), we only search over words which are among the 30K most frequent words in the vocabulary.

Table 1 depicts the accuracy on Semantic Syntactic Task for models trained with 50 dimensions. We find that lexicon-infused embeddings perform better than Skip-gram. Further, lex-0.01 performs the best, and we use this model for further NER experiments. There was no perceptible difference in computation cost from learning lexicon-infused embeddings versus learning standard Skip-gram embeddings.

System	Dev	Test
Baseline	92.22	87.93
Baseline + Brown	93.39	90.05
Baseline + Skip-gram	93.68	89.68
Baseline + LexEmb	93.81	89.56
Baseline + Gaz	93.69	89.27
Baseline + Gaz + Brown	93.88	90.67
Baseline + Gaz + Skip-gram	94.23	90.33
Baseline + Gaz + LexEmb	**94.46**	**90.90**
Ando and Zhang (2005)	93.15	89.31
Suzuki and Isozaki (2008)	**94.48**	89.92
Ratinov and Roth (2009)	93.50	90.57
Lin and Wu (2009)	-	**90.90**

Table 2: Final NER F1 scores for the CoNLL 2003 shared task. On the top are the systems presented in this paper, and on the bottom we have baseline systems. The best results within each area are highlighted in bold. Lin and Wu 2009 use massive private industrial query-log data in training.

4.2 CoNLL 2003 NER

We applied our models on CoNLL 2003 NER data set. All hyperparameters were tuned by training on training set, and evaluating on the development set. Then the best hyperparameter values were trained on the combination of training and development data and applied on the test set, to obtain the final results.

Table 2 shows the phrase F1 scores of all systems we implemented, as well as state-of-the-art results from the literature. Note that using traditional unsupervised Skip-gram embeddings is worse than Brown clusters. In contrast, our lexicon-infused phrase embeddings **Lex-0.01** achieves 90.90—a state-of-the-art F1 score for the test set. This result matches the highest F1 previously reported, in Lin and Wu (2009), but is the first system to do so without using massive private data. Our result is signficantly better than the previous best using public data.

4.3 Ontonotes 5.0 NER

Similarly to the CoNLL NER setup, we tuned the hyperparameters on the development set. We use

System	Dev	Test
Baseline	79.04	79.85
Baseline + Brown	79.95	81.38
Baseline + Skip-gram	80.59	81.91
Baseline + LexEmbd	80.65	81.82
Baseline + Gaz	79.85	81.31
Baseline + Gaz + Brown	80.53	82.05
Baseline + Gaz + Skip-gram	80.70	**82.30**
Baseline + Gaz + LexEmb	**80.81**	82.24

Table 3: Final NER F1 scores for Ontonotes 5.0 dataset. The results in bold face are the best on each evaluation set.

the same list of lexicons as for CoNLL NER.

Table 3 summarize our results. We found that both Skip-gram and Lexicon infused embeddings give better results than using Brown Clusters as features. However, in this case Skip-gram embeddings give marginally better results. (So as not to jeopardize our ability to fairly do further research on this task, we did not analyze the test set errors that may explain this.) These are, to the best of our knowledge, the first published performance numbers on the Ontonotes NER task.

5 Conclusions

We have shown how to inject external supervision to a Skip-gram model to learn better phrase embeddings. We demonstrate the quality of phrase embeddings on three tasks: Syntactic-semantic similarity, CoNLL 2003 NER, and Ontonotes 5.0 NER. In the process, we provide a new public state-of-the-art NER system for the widely contested CoNLL 2003 shared task.

We demonstrate how we can plug phrase embeddings into an existing log-linear CRF System.

This work demonstrates that it is possible to learn high-quality phrase embeddings and fine-tune them with external supervision from billions of tokens within one day computation time. We further demonstrate that learning embeddings is important and key to improve NLP Tasks such as NER.

In future, we want to explore employing embeddings to other NLP tasks such as dependency parsing and coreference resolution. We also want to explore improving embeddings using error gradients from NER.

References

Rie Kubota Ando and Tong Zhang. 2005. A high-performance semi-supervised learning method for text chunking. In *Proceedings of the 43rd Annual Meeting on Association for Computational Linguistics*, pages 1–9. Association for Computational Linguistics.

Yoshua Bengio, Rejean Ducharme, and Pascal Vincent. 2003. A neural probabilistic language model. *Journal of Machine Learning Research*, 3:1137–1155.

Yoshua Bengio. 2008. Neural net language models. *Scholarpedia*, 3(1):3881.

Peter F Brown, Peter V Desouza, Robert L Mercer, Vincent J Della Pietra, and Jenifer C Lai. 1992. Class-based n-gram models of natural language. *Computational linguistics*, 18(4):467–479.

Ronan Collobert and Jason Weston. 2008. A unified architecture for natural language processing: Deep neural networks with multitask learning. In *Proceedings of the 25th international conference on Machine learning*, pages 160–167. ACM.

Paramveer Dhillon, Dean P Foster, and Lyle H Ungar. 2011. Multi-view learning of word embeddings via cca. In *Advances in Neural Information Processing Systems*, pages 199–207.

Paramveer Dhillon, Jordan Rodu, Dean Foster, and Lyle Ungar. 2012. Two step cca: A new spectral method for estimating vector models of words. *arXiv preprint arXiv:1206.6403*.

John Duchi, Elad Hazan, and Yoram Singer. 2011. Adaptive subgradient methods for online learning and stochastic optimization. *The Journal of Machine Learning Research*, 999999:2121–2159.

David A Huffman. 1952. A method for the construction of minimum-redundancy codes. *Proceedings of the IRE*, 40(9):1098–1101.

Terry Koo, Xavier Carreras, and Michael Collins. 2008. Simple semi-supervised dependency parsing.

John Lafferty, Andrew McCallum, and Fernando CN Pereira. 2001. Conditional random fields: Probabilistic models for segmenting and labeling sequence data.

David D Lewis, Yiming Yang, Tony G Rose, and Fan Li. 2004. Rcv1: A new benchmark collection for text categorization research. *The Journal of Machine Learning Research*, 5:361–397.

Dekang Lin and Xiaoyun Wu. 2009. Phrase clustering for discriminative learning. In *Proceedings of the Joint Conference of the 47th Annual Meeting of the ACL and the 4th International Joint Conference on Natural Language Processing of the AFNLP: Volume 2-Volume 2*, pages 1030–1038. Association for Computational Linguistics.

Tomas Mikolov, Martin Karafiát, Lukas Burget, Jan Cernockỳ, and Sanjeev Khudanpur. 2010. Recurrent neural network based language model. In *INTERSPEECH*, pages 1045–1048.

Tomas Mikolov, Kai Chen, Greg Corrado, and Jeffrey Dean. 2013a. Efficient estimation of word representations in vector space. *arXiv preprint arXiv:1301.3781*.

Tomas Mikolov, Ilya Sutskever, Kai Chen, Greg Corrado, and Jeffrey Dean. 2013b. Distributed representations of words and phrases and their compositionality. *arXiv preprint arXiv:1310.4546*.

Scott Miller, Jethran Guinness, and Alex Zamanian. 2004. Name tagging with word clusters and discriminative training. In *HLT-NAACL*, volume 4, pages 337–342. Citeseer.

Andriy Mnih and Geoffrey E Hinton. 2008. A scalable hierarchical distributed language model. In *Advances in neural information processing systems*, pages 1081–1088.

Frederic Morin and Yoshua Bengio. 2005. Hierarchical probabilistic neural network language model. In *Proceedings of the international workshop on artificial intelligence and statistics*, pages 246–252.

Fernando Pereira, Naftali Tishby, and Lillian Lee. 1993. Distributional clustering of english words. In *Proceedings of the 31st annual meeting on Association for Computational Linguistics*, pages 183–190. Association for Computational Linguistics.

Lev Ratinov and Dan Roth. 2009. Design challenges and misconceptions in named entity recognition. In *Proceedings of the Thirteenth Conference on Computational Natural Language Learning*, pages 147–155. Association for Computational Linguistics.

Jun Suzuki and Hideki Isozaki. 2008. Semi-supervised sequential labeling and segmentation using giga-word scale unlabeled data. In *ACL*, pages 665–673. Citeseer.

Erik F Tjong Kim Sang and Fien De Meulder. 2003. Introduction to the conll-2003 shared task: Language-independent named entity recognition. In *Proceedings of the seventh conference on Natural language learning at HLT-NAACL 2003-Volume 4*, pages 142–147. Association for Computational Linguistics.

Joseph Turian, Lev Ratinov, and Yoshua Bengio. 2010. Word representations: a simple and general method for semi-supervised learning. In *Proceedings of the 48th Annual Meeting of the Association for Computational Linguistics*, pages 384–394. Association for Computational Linguistics.

Ralph Weischedel, Martha Palmer, Mitchell Marcus, Eduard Hovy, Sameer Pradhan, Lance Ramshaw, Nianwen Xue, Ann Taylor, Jeff Kaufman, Michelle Franchini, et al. 2011. *OntoNotes Release 4.0*. Linguistic Data Consortium.

Tong Zhang and David Johnson. 2003. A robust risk minimization based named entity recognition system. In *Proceedings of the seventh conference on Natural language learning at HLT-NAACL 2003-Volume 4*, pages 204–207. Association for Computational Linguistics.

Focused Entailment Graphs for Open IE Propositions

Omer Levy[†] **Ido Dagan**[†] **Jacob Goldberger**[§]
† Computer Science Department § Faculty of Engineering
Bar-Ilan University
Ramat-Gan, Israel
{omerlevy,dagan,goldbej}@{cs,cs,eng}.biu.ac.il

Abstract

Open IE methods extract structured propositions from text. However, these propositions are neither consolidated nor generalized, and querying them may lead to insufficient or redundant information. This work suggests an approach to organize open IE propositions using entailment graphs. The entailment relation unifies equivalent propositions and induces a specific-to-general structure. We create a large dataset of gold-standard proposition entailment graphs, and provide a novel algorithm for automatically constructing them. Our analysis shows that predicate entailment is extremely context-sensitive, and that current lexical-semantic resources do not capture many of the lexical inferences induced by proposition entailment.

1 Introduction

Open information extraction (open IE) extracts natural language propositions from text without pre-defined schemas as in supervised relation extraction (Etzioni et al., 2008). These propositions represent predicate-argument structures as tuples of natural language strings. Open IE enables knowledge search by aggregating billions of propositions from the web[1]. It may also be perceived as capturing an unsupervised knowledge representation schema, complementing supervised knowledge bases such as Freebase (Bollacker et al., 2008), as suggested by Riedel et al (2013).

However, language variability obstructs open IE from becoming a viable knowledge representation framework. As it does not consolidate natural language expressions, querying a database of open IE propositions may lead to either insufficient or redundant information. As an illustrative example, querying the demo (footnote 1) for the generally equivalent *relieves headache* or *treats headache* returns two different lists of entities; out of the top few results, the only answers these queries seem to agree on are *caffeine* and *sex*. This is a major drawback relative to supervised knowledge representations, which map natural language expressions to structured formal representations, such as *treatments* in Freebase.

In this work, we investigate an approach for organizing and consolidating open IE propositions using the novel notion of *proposition entailment graphs* (see Figure 1) – graphs in which each node represents a proposition and each directed edge reflects an entailment relation, in the spirit of textual entailment (Dagan et al., 2013). Entailment provides an effective structure for aggregating natural-language based information; it merges semantically equivalent propositions into cliques, and induces specification-generalization edges between them. For example, *(aspirin, eliminate, headache)* entails, and is more specific than, *(headache, respond to, painkiller)*.

We thus propose the task of constructing an entailment graph over a set of open IE propositions (Section 3), which is closely related to Berant et al's work (2012) who introduced *predicate* entailment graphs. In contrast, our work explores *propositions*, which are essentially predicates instantiated with arguments, and thus semantically richer. We provide a dataset of 30 such graphs, which represent *1.5 million* pairwise entailment decisions between propositions (Section 4).

To approach this task, we extend the state-of-the-art method for building entailment graphs (Berant et al., 2012) from predicates to complete propositions. Both Snow et al (2006) and Berant et al used WordNet as distant supervision when training a local pairwise model of lexical entailment. However, analyzing our data revealed that the lexical inferences captured in WordNet are quite dif-

[1] See demo: openie.cs.washington.edu

Proceedings of the Eighteenth Conference on Computational Language Learning, pages 87–97,
Baltimore, Maryland USA, June 26-27 2014.

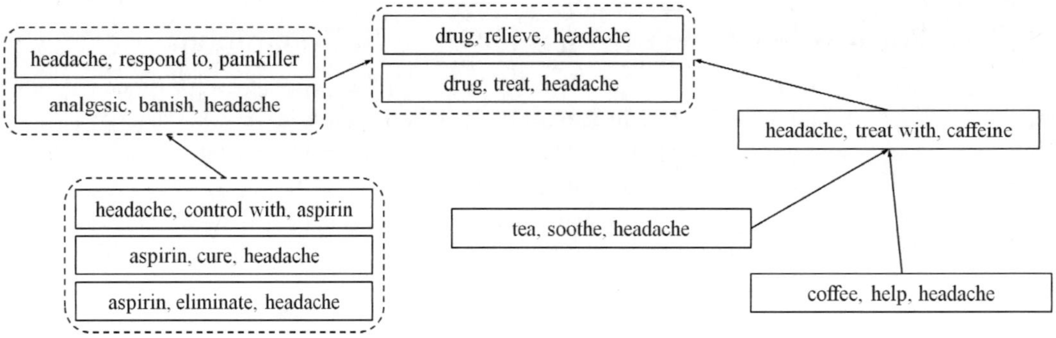

Figure 1: An excerpt from a proposition entailment graph focused on the topic *headache*. The dashed boundaries in the figure denote cliques, meaning that all propositions within them are equivalent.

ferent from the *real* lexical inferences induced by proposition entailment, making WordNet a misleading form of supervision. We therefore employ *direct* proposition-level supervision, and design a probabilistic model that captures the underlying lexical-component inferences (Section 5). We explore a variety of natural extensions to prior art as baselines (Section 6) and show that our model outperforms them (Section 7).

While our model increases performance on this task, there is still much room for improvement. A deeper analysis (Section 8) shows that common lexical-semantic resources, on which we rely as well, are either too noisy or provide inadequate recall regarding lexical entailment. In particular, we find that predicate inference within propositions often goes beyond inference between the predicates' linguistic meanings. While *pneumonia requires antibiotics* and *pneumonia is treated by antibiotics* mean the same, the inherent meanings of *require* and *treat* are different. These inferences pertain to specific world knowledge, and warrant future research.

Our work also contributes to textual entailment research. First, we extend entailment graphs to complete propositions. Secondly, we investigate an intermediate problem of recognizing entailment between language-based predicate-argument tuples. Though this problem is simpler than sentence-level entailment, it does capture entailment of complete statements, which proves to be quite challenging indeed.

2 Background

Our work builds upon two major research threads: open IE, and entailment graphs.

2.1 Open Information Extraction

Research in open IE (Etzioni et al., 2008) has focused on transforming text to predicate-argument tuples (propositions). The general approach is to learn proposition extraction patterns, and use them to create tuples while denoting extraction confidence. Various methods differ in the type of patterns they acquire. For instance, (Banko et al., 2007) and (Fader et al., 2011) used surface patterns, while (Mausam et al., 2012) and (Xu et al., 2013) used syntactic dependencies.

Yates and Etzioni (2009) tried to mitigate the issue of language variability (as exemplified in the introduction) by clustering synonymous predicates and arguments. While these clusters do contain semantically *related* items, they do not necessarily reflect *equivalence* or *implication*. For example, *coffee*, *tea*, and *caffeine* may all appear in one cluster, but *coffee* does not imply *tea*; on the other hand, separating any element from this cluster removes a valid implication. Entailment, however, can capture the fact that both beverages imply caffeine, but not one another. Also related, Riedel et al (2013) try to generalize over open IE extractions by combining knowledge from Freebase and globally predicting which unobserved propositions are true. In contrast, our work identifies inference relations between concrete *pairs* of *observed* propositions.

2.2 Entailment Graphs of Words and Phrases

Previous work focused on entailment graphs or similar structures at the sub-propositional level. In these graphs, each node represents a natural language word or phrase, and each directed edge an entailment (or generalization) relation. Snow et al (2006) created a taxonomy of sensedisambiguated nouns and their hyponymy relations. Berant et al (2012) constructed entailment graphs of predicate templates. Recently, Mehdad et al (2013) built an entailment graph of noun phrases and partial sentences for topic labeling. The notion of *proposition* entailment graphs, however, is novel. This distinction is critical, because apparently, entailment in the context of specific propositions does not behave like context-oblivious lexical entailment (see Section 8).

Berant et al's work was implemented in Adler et al's (2012) text exploration demo, which instantiated manually-annotated predicate entailment graphs with arguments, and used an additional lexical resource to determine argument entailment. The combined graphs of predicate and argument entailments induced a proposition entailment graph, which could then be explored in a faceted-search scheme. Our work goes beyond, and attempts to build entailment graphs of propositions automatically.

2.2.1 Berant et al's Algorithm for Predicate Entailment Graph Construction

We present Berant et al's algorithm in detail, as we rely on it later on. Given a set of predicates $\{i\}_{1..n}$ as input (constituting the graph nodes), it returns a set of entailment decisions (i, j), which become the directed edges of the entailment graph. The method works in two phases: (1) *local estimation*, and (2) *global optimization*.

The **local estimation** model considers every potential edge (i, j) and estimates the probability p_{ij} that this edge indeed exists, i.e. that i entails j. Each predicate pair is represented with distributional similarity features, providing some indication of whether i entails j. The estimator then uses logistic regression (or a linear SVM) over those features to predict the probability of entailment. It is trained with distant supervision from WordNet, employing synonyms, hypernyms, and (WordNet) entailments as positive examples, and antonyms, hyponyms, and cohyponyms as negative.

The **global optimization** phase then searches for the most probable *transitive* entailment graph, given the local probability estimations. It does so with an integer linear program (ILP), where each pair of predicates is represented by a binary variable x_{ij}, denoting whether there is an entailment edge from i to j. The objective function corresponds to the log likelihood of the assignment: $\sum_{i \neq j} x_{ij} \left(\log \left(\frac{p_{ij}}{1-p_{ij}} \right) + \log \left(\frac{\pi}{1-\pi} \right) \right)$. The prior term π is the probability of a random pair of predicates to be in an entailment relation, and can be estimated in advance. The ILP solver searches for the optimal assignment that maximizes the objective function under transitivity constraints, expressed as linear constraints $\forall_{i,j,k} \;\; x_{ij} + x_{jk} - x_{ik} \leq 1$.

3 Task Definition

A *proposition entailment graph* is a directed graph where each node is a proposition s_i (s for *sentence*) and each edge (s_i, s_j) represents an entailment relation from s_i to s_j. A proposition s_i is a predicate-argument structure $s_i = (p_i, a_i^1, a_i^2, ..., a_i^{m_i})$ with one predicate p_i and its arguments. A proposition-level entailment (s_i, s_j) holds if the verbalization of s_i implies s_j, according to the definition of textual entailment (Dagan et al., 2013); i.e. if humans reading s_i would typically infer that s_j is most likely true. Given a set of propositions (graph nodes), the task of constructing a proposition entailment graph is to recognize all the entailments among the propositions, i.e. deciding which directional edges connect which pairs of nodes.

In this paper, we consider the narrower task of constructing *focused* proposition entailment graphs, following Berant et al's methodology in creating focused predicate entailment graphs. First, all predicates are binary (have two arguments) and are denoted $s_i = (a_i^1, p_i, a_i^2)$. Secondly, we assume that the propositions were retrieved by querying for a particular concept; out of the two arguments, one argument t (topic) is common to all the propositions in a single graph. We denote the non-topic argument as a_i. Figure 1 presents an example of an informative entailment graph focused on the topic *headache*.

Though confined, this setting still challenges the state-of-the-art in textual entailment (see Section 7). Moreover, these restrictions facilitate piece-wise investigation of the entailment problem (see Section 8).

4 Dataset

To construct our dataset of open IE extractions, we found Google's syntactic ngrams (Goldberg and Orwant, 2013) as a useful source of high-quality propositions. Based on a corpus of 3.5 million English books, it aggregates every *syntactic ngram*

– subtree of a dependency parse – with at most 4 dependency arcs. The resource contains only tree fragments that appeared at least 10 times in the corpus, filtering out many low-quality syntactic ngrams.

We extracted the syntactic ngrams that reflect propositions, i.e. *subject-verb-object* fragments where *object* modifies the verb with either *dobj* or *pobj*. Prepositions in *pobj* were concatenated to the verb (e.g. *use with*). In addition, both *subject* and *object* must each be a noun phrase containing two tokens at most, which are either nouns or adjectives. Each token in the extracted fragments was then lemmatized using WordNet. After lemmatization, we grouped all identical propositions and aggregated their counts. Approximately 68 million propositions were collected.

We chose 30 topics from the healthcare domain (such as *influenza*, *hiv*, and *penicillin*). For each topic, we collected the set of propositions containing it, and manually filtered noisy extractions. This yielded 30 high-quality sets of 5,714 propositions in total, where each set becomes the set of nodes in a separate focused entailment graph. The graphs range from 55 propositions (*scurvy*) to 562 (*headache*), with an average of over 190 propositions per graph. Summing the number of proposition pairs within each graph amounts to a total of *1.5 million potential entailment edges*, which makes it by far the largest annotated textual entailment dataset to date.

We used a semi-automatic annotation process, which dramatically narrows down the number of manual decisions, and hence, the required annotation time. In short, the annotators are given a series of small clustering tasks before annotating entailment between those clusters.[2]

The annotation process was carried out by two native English speakers, with the aid of encyclopedic knowledge for unfamiliar medical terms. The agreement on a subset of five randomly sampled graphs was $\kappa = 0.77$. Annotating a single graph took about an hour and a half on average.

Positive entailment judgements constituted only 8.4% of potential edges, and were found to be 100% transitive. We observe that in nearly all of those cases, a natural alignment between entailing components occurs: predicates align with each other, the topic is shared, and the remaining non-topic argument aligns with its counterpart. Consider the topic *arthritis* and the entailing proposition pair *(arthritis, cause, pain)→(symptom, associate with, arthritis)*; *cause→associate with*, while *pain→symptom*. Rarely, some misalignments do occur; for instance *(vaccine, protects, body)→(vaccine, provides, protection)*. However, it is almost always the case that propositions entail if and only if their aligned lexical components entail as well.

5 Algorithm

In this section, we extend Berant et al's algorithm (2012) to construct entailment graphs of *propositions*. As described in Section 2.2.1, their method first performs local estimation of predicate entailment and then global optimization. We modify the local estimation phase to estimate *proposition* entailment instead, and then apply the same global optimization in the second phase.

In Section 4, we observed the alignment-based relationship between proposition and lexical entailment. We leverage this observation to predict proposition entailment with lexical entailment features (as Berant et al), using the Component Entailment Conjunction (CEC) model in Section 5.1.

Following Snow et al (2006) and Berant et al, we could train CEC using distant supervision from WordNet. In fact, we did try this approach (presented as baseline methods, Section 6) and found that it performed poorly. Furthermore, our analysis (Section 8) suggests that WordNet relations do not adequately capture the lexical inferences induced by proposition-level entailment. Instead, we use a more realistic signal to train CEC – direct supervision from the annotated dataset. Section 5.2 describes how we propagate proposition-level entailment annotations to the latent lexical components.

5.1 Component Entailment Conjunction

CEC assumes that proposition-level entailment is the result of entailment within each pair of aligned components, i.e. a pair of propositions entail if and only if both their predicate and argument pairs entail. This assumption stems from our observation of alignment in Section 4. Furthermore, CEC leverages this interdependence to learn separate predicate-entailment and argument-entailment features through proposition-level supervision.

[2]The annotated dataset is publicly available on the first author's website.

Formally, for every ordered pair of propositions (i, j) we denote proposition entailment as a binary random variable x_{ij}^s and predicate and argument entailments as x_{ij}^p and x_{ij}^a, respectively. In our setting, proposition entailment (x_{ij}^s) is observed, but component entailments (x_{ij}^p, x_{ij}^a) are hidden. We use logistic regression, with features ϕ_{ij}^p and parameter w^p, as a probabilistic model of predicate entailment (and so for arguments with ϕ_{ij}^a and w^a):

$$p_{ij} = P\left(x_{ij}^p = 1 \middle| \phi_{ij}^p; w^p\right) = \sigma\left(\phi_{ij}^p \cdot w^p\right)$$

$$a_{ij} = P\left(x_{ij}^a = 1 \middle| \phi_{ij}^a; w^a\right) = \sigma\left(\phi_{ij}^a \cdot w^a\right) \quad (1)$$

where σ is the sigmoid $\sigma(z) = \frac{1}{1+e^{-z}}$. We then define proposition entailment as the conjunction of its binary components: $x_{ij}^s = x_{ij}^p \wedge x_{ij}^a$. Therefore, the probability of proposition entailment given the component features is:

$$s_{ij} = P\left(x_{ij}^s = 1 \middle| \phi_{ij}^p, \phi_{ij}^a; w^p, w^a\right)$$

$$= P\left(x_{ij}^p = 1, x_{ij}^a = 1 \middle| \phi_{ij}^p, \phi_{ij}^a; w^p, w^a\right)$$

$$= P\left(x_{ij}^p = 1 \middle| \phi_{ij}^p; w^p\right) \cdot P\left(x_{ij}^a = 1 \middle| \phi_{ij}^a; w^a\right)$$

$$= p_{ij} \cdot a_{ij}$$

The proposition entailment probability is thus the product of component entailment probabilities.

Given the proposition-level information $\left\{x_{ij}^s\right\}$, the log-likelihood is:

$$\ell(w^p, w^a) = \sum_{i \neq j} \log P\left(x_{ij}^s \middle| \phi_{ij}^p, \phi_{ij}^a; w^p, w^a\right) =$$

$$\sum_{i \neq j} \left(x_{ij}^s \log(p_{ij} a_{ij}) + \left(1 - x_{ij}^s\right) \log(1 - p_{ij} a_{ij})\right)$$

5.2 Learning Component Models

We wish to learn the model's parameters (w^p, w^a). Our approach uses direct proposition-level supervision from our annotated dataset to train the component logistic regression models. Since component entailment (x_{ij}^p, x_{ij}^a) is not observed in the data, we apply the iterative EM algorithm (Dempster et al., 1977). In the E-step we estimate their probabilities from proposition-level labels (x_{ij}^s), and in the M-step we use those estimates as "soft" labels to learn the component-level model parameters (w^p, w^a).

E-Step During the E-step in iteration $t + 1$, we compute the probability of component entailments given the proposition entailment information, based on the parameters at iteration t (w_t^p, w_t^a). The predicate probabilities are given by:

$$c_{ij}^p = P\left(x_{ij}^p = 1 \middle| x_{ij}^s, \phi_{ij}^p, \phi_{ij}^a; w_t^p, w_t^a\right) \quad (2)$$

and are computed with Bayes' law:

$$c_{ij}^p = \begin{cases} 1 & \text{if } x_{ij}^s = 1 \\ \frac{p_{ij}^t (1 - a_{ij}^t)}{1 - p_{ij}^t a_{ij}^t} & \text{if } x_{ij}^s = 0 \end{cases} \quad (3)$$

where p_{ij}^t is computed as in Equations 1, with the parameters at iteration t (w_t^p). Argument entailment probabilities (c_{ij}^a) are computed analogously.

M-Step In the M-step, we compute new values for the parameters (w_{t+1}^p, w_{t+1}^a). In our case, there is no closed-form formula for updating the parameters. Instead, at each iteration, we solve a separate logistic regression for each component. While we have each component model's features (ϕ_{ij}^p, assuming predicates for notation), we do not observe the component-level entailment labels (x_{ij}^p); instead, we obtain their probabilities (c_{ij}^p) from the expectation step.

To learn the parameters (w_{t+1}^p, w_{t+1}^a) from the component entailment probabilities (c_{ij}^p), we employ a weighted variant of logistic regression, that can utilize "soft" class labels (i.e. a probability distribution over $\{0, 1\}$). To solve such a logistic regression (e.g. for w_{t+1}^p), we maximize the log-likelihood:

$$\ell\left(w_{t+1}^p\right) =$$

$$\sum_{ij} \left(c_{ij}^p \log\left(P\left(x_{ij}^p = 1 \middle| \phi_{ij}^p; w_{t+1}^p\right)\right) + \left(1 - c_{ij}^p\right) \log\left(P\left(x_{ij}^p = 0 \middle| \phi_{ij}^p; w_{t+1}^p\right)\right)\right)$$

For optimization, we calculate the derivative, and use gradient ascent to update w_{t+1}^p:

$$\Delta w_{t+1}^p = \frac{\partial \ell(w_{t+1}^p)}{\partial w_{t+1}^p} =$$

$$\sum_{ij} \left(c_{ij}^p - P\left(x_{ij}^p = 1 \middle| \phi_{ij}^p; w_{t+1}^p\right)\right) \phi_{ij}^p$$

This optimization is concave, and therefore the unique global maximum can be efficiently obtained.

5.3 Features

Similar to Berant et al, we used three types of features to describe both predicate pairs (ϕ_{ij}^p) and argument pairs (ϕ_{ij}^a): distributional similarities, lexical resources, and string distances.

We used the entire database of 68 million extracted propositions (see Section 4) to create a word-context matrix; context was defined as other words that appeared in the same proposition, and each word was represented as $(string, role)$, $role$ being the location within the proposition, either a_1, p, or a_2. The matrix was then normalized with pointwise mutual information (Church and Hanks, 1990). We used various metrics to measure different types of similarities between each component pair, including: cosine similarity, Lin's similarity (1998), inclusion (Weeds and Weir, 2003), average precision, and balanced average precision (Kotlerman et al., 2010). Weed's and Kotlerman's metrics are directional (asymmetric) and indicate the direction of a potential entailment relation. These features were used for both predicates and arguments. In addition, we used Melamud et al's (2013) method to learn a context-sensitive model of predicate entailment, which estimates predicate similarity in the context of the given arguments.

We leveraged the Unified Medical Language System (UMLS) to check argument entailment, using the *parent* and *synonym* relations. A single feature indicated whether such a connection exists. We also used WordNet relations as features, specifically: synonyms, hypernyms, entailments, hyponyms, cohyponyms, antonyms. Each WordNet relation constituted a different feature for both predicates and arguments.

Finally, we added a string equality feature and a Levenshtein distance feature (Levenshtein, 1966) for different spellings of the same word to both predicate and argument feature vectors.

6 Baseline Methods

We consider four algorithms that naturally extend the state-of-the-art to propositions, while using distant supervision (from WordNet). Since CEC uses direct supervision, we also examined another (simpler) directly-supervised algorithm. As a naive unsupervised baseline, we use *Argument Equality*, which returns "entailing" if the argument pair is identical. *Predicate Equality* is defined similarly for predicates.

Component-Level Distant Supervision The following methods use distant supervision from WordNet (as in Berant et al's work, Section 2.2.1) to explicitly train component-level entailment estimators. Specifically, we train a logistic regression model for each component as specified in Equations 1 in Section 5.1. We present four methods, which differ in the way they obtain global graph-level entailment decisions for propositions, based on the local component entailment estimates (p_{ij}, a_{ij} in Section 5.1).

The first method, $Opt(Arg \wedge Pred)$, uses the product of both component models to estimate local proposition-level entailment: $s_{ij} = p_{ij} \cdot a_{ij}$. The global set of proposition entailments is then determined using Berant et al's global optimization, according to the proposition-level scores s_{ij}. Note that this method is identical to CEC during inference, but differs in the way the local estimators are learned (with component-level supervision from WordNet).

An alternative is $Opt(Arg) \wedge Opt(Pred)$. It first obtains local probabilities (p_{ij}, a_{ij}) for each component as in $Opt(Arg \wedge Pred)$, but then employs component-level global optimization (transitivity enforcement), yielding two sets of entailment decisions, x^p_{ij} and x^a_{ij}. Proposition entailment is then determined by the conjunction $x^s_{ij} = x^p_{ij} \wedge x^a_{ij}$, as in (Adler et al., 2012).

Finally, $Opt(Arg)$ ignores the predicate component. Instead, it uses only the argument entailment graph (as produced by $Opt(Arg) \wedge Opt(Pred)$) to decide on proposition entailment; i.e. a pair of propositions entail if and only if their arguments entail. $Opt(Pred)$ is defined analogously.

Proposition-Level Direct Supervision A simpler alternative to CEC that also employs proposition-level supervision is *Joint Features*, which concatenates the component level features into a unified feature vector: $\phi^s_{ij} = \phi^p_{ij} \oplus \phi^a_{ij}$. We then couple them with the gold-standard annotations x^s_{ij} to create a training set for a single logistic regression. We use the trained logistic regression to estimate the local probability of proposition entailment, and then perform global optimization to construct the entailment graph.

7 Empirical Evaluation

We evaluate the models in Sections 5 & 6 on the 30 annotated entailment graphs presented in Section 4. During testing, each graph was evaluated separately. The results presented in this section are all micro-averages, though macro-averages were also computed and found to reflect the same trends. Models trained with distant supervision were evaluated on all graphs. For directly supervised methods, we used 2 × 6-fold cross validation (25 training graphs per fold). In this scenario, each graph induced a set of labeled examples – its edges being positive examples, and the missing potential edges being negative ones – and the union of these sets was used as the training set of that cross-validation fold.

7.1 Results

Table 1 compares the performance of CEC with that of the baseline methods.

While *Joint Features* and CEC share exactly the same features, CEC exploits the inherent conjunction between predicate and argument entailments (as observed in Section 4 and modeled in Section 5.1), and forces both components to decide on entailment *separately*. This differs from the simpler log-linear model (*Joint Features*) where, for example, a very strong predicate entailment feature might override the overall proposition-level decision, even if there was no strong indication of argument entailment. As a result, CEC dominates *Joint Features* in both precision and recall. The F_1 difference between these methods is statistically significant with McNemar's test (1947) with $p \ll 0.01$. Specifically, CEC corrected *Joint Features* 7621 times, while the opposite occurred only 4048 times.

CEC also yields relatively high precision and recall. While it has 2% less recall than $Opt(Arg)$ (the highest-recall baseline), it surpasses $Opt(Arg)$'s precision by 14%. Along with a similar comparison to *Argument Equality* (the highest precision baseline), CEC notably outperforms all baselines.

It is also evident that both directly supervised methods outperform the distantly supervised methods. Our analysis (Section 8.1) shows that WordNet lacks significant coverage, and may therefore be a problematic source of supervision.

Perhaps the most surprising result is the complete failure of WordNet-supervised methods that consider predicate information. A deeper analysis (Section 8.2) shows that predicate inference is highly context-sensitive, and deviates beyond the lexical inferences provided by WordNet.

7.2 Learning Curve

We measure the supervision needed to train the directly supervised models by their learning curves (Figure 2). Each point is the average F_1 score across 12 cross-validation folds; e.g. for 10 training graphs, we used 4 × 3-fold cross validation. Even 5 training graphs (a day's worth of annotation) are enough for CEC to perform on-par with the best distantly supervised method, and with 15 training graphs it outperforms every baseline, including *Joint Features* trained with 25 graphs.

Supervision	Method	Prec.	Rec.	F1
None	*Argument Equality*	**81.6%**	42.2%	55.6%
	Predicate Equality	9.3%	1.5%	2.6%
Component (WordNet)	$Opt(Arg \wedge Pred)$	73.8%	3.8%	7.2%
	$Opt(Arg) \wedge Opt(Pred)$	72.3%	3.2%	6.0%
	$Opt(Arg)$	64.6%	**55.4%**	59.7%
	$Opt(Pred)$	11.0%	6.2%	8.0%
Proposition (Annotated)	*Joint Features*	76.3%	51.7%	61.6%
	CEC	78.7%	53.5%	**63.7%**

Table 1: Performance on gold-standard (micro averaged).

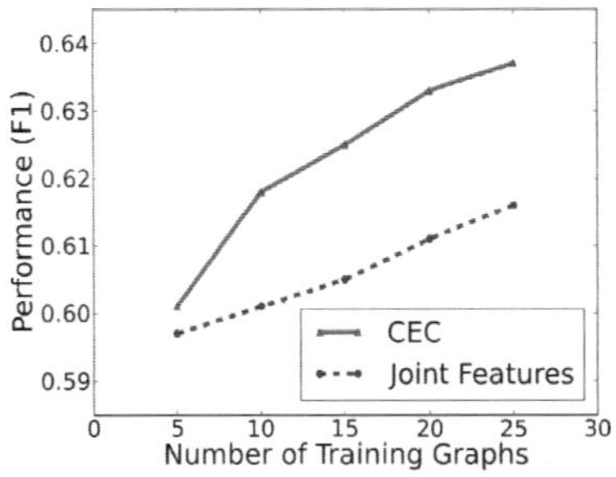

Figure 2: Learning curve of directly supervised methods.

7.3 Effects of Global Optimization

We evaluate the effects of enforcing transitivity by considering CEC with and without the global optimization phase. Table 2 shows how many entailment edges were added (and removed) by enforcing transitivity, and measures how many of those modifications were correct. Apparently, transitivity's greatest effect is the removal of incorrect entailment edges. The same phenomenon was also observed in the work on predicate entailment graphs (Berant et al., 2012). Overall, transitivity made 4,848 correct modifications out of 6,734 in total. A χ^2 test reveals that the positive contribution of enforcing transitivity is indeed statistically significant ($p \ll 0.01$).

Gold Standard	Global Opt Added Edge	Global Opt Removed Edge
Edge Exists	1150	482
No Edge	1404	3698

Table 2: The modifications made by enforcing transitivity w.r.t. the gold standard. 55% of the edges added by enforcing transitivity are incorrect, but it removed even more incorrect edges, improving the overall performance.

8 Analysis of Lexical Inference

Although CEC had a statistically-significant improvement upon the baselines, its absolute performance leaves much room for improvement. We hypothesize that the lexical entailment features we used, following state-of-the-art lexical entailment modeling, do *not* capture many of the actual lexical inferences induced by proposition entailment. We demonstrate that this is indeed the case.

8.1 Argument Entailment

To isolate the effect of different features on predicting argument entailment, we collected all proposition pairs that shared exactly the same predicate and topic, and thus differed in only their "free" argument. This yielded 20,336 aligned argument pairs, whose entailment annotations are equal to the corresponding proposition-entailment annotation in the dataset.

Using WordNet synonyms and hypernyms to predict entailment yielded a precision of about 88%, at 40% recall. Though relatively precise, WordNet's coverage is limited, and misses many inferences. We describe three typical types of inferences that were absent from WordNet.

The first type constitutes of widely-used paraphrases such as *people↔persons*, *woman↔female*, and *pain↔ache*. These may be seen as weaker types of synonyms, which may have nuances, but are typically interchangeable.

Another type is metonymy, in which a concept is not referred to by its own name, but by that of an associated concept. This is very common in our healthcare dataset, where a disease is often referred to by its underlying pathogen and vice-versa (e.g. *pneumonia↔pneumococcus*).

The third type of missing inferences is causality. Many instances of metonymy (such as the disease-pathogen example) may be seen as causality as well. Other examples can be drug and effect (*laxative→diarrhea*) or condition and symptom (*influenza→fever*).

WordNet's lack of such common-sense inferences, which are abundant in our proposition entailment dataset, might make WordNet a problematic source of distant supervision. The fact that 60% of the entailing examples in our dataset are labeled by WordNet as non-entailing, means that for each truly positive training example, there is a higher chance that it will have a negative label.

Distributional similarity is commonly used to capture such missing inferences and complement WordNet-like resources. On this dataset, however, it failed to do so. One of the more indicative similarity measures, inclusion (Weeds and Weir, 2003), yielded only 27% precision at 40% recall when tuning a threshold to optimize F_1. Increasing precision caused a dramatic drop in recall: 50% precision limited recall to 3.2%. Other similarity measures performed similarly or worse. It seems that current methods of distributional word similarity also capture relations quite different from inference, such as cohyponyms and domain relatedness, and might be less suitable for modeling lexical entailment on their own.

8.2 Context-Sensitive Predicate Entailment

The proposition-level entailment annotation induces an entailment relation between the predicates, which holds in the *particular context* of the proposition pair. We wish to understand the nature of this predicate-level entailment, and how it compares to classic lexical inference as portrayed in the lexical semantics literature. To that end, we collected all the entailing proposition pairs with equal arguments, and extracted the corresponding predicate pairs (which, assuming alignment, are necessarily entailing in that context). This list contains 52,560 predicate pairs.

In our first analysis, we explored which WordNet relations correlate with predicate entailment, by checking how well each relation covers the set of entailed predicate pairs. Synonyms and hypernyms, which are considered positive entailment indicators, covered only about 8% each. Surprisingly, the hyponym and cohyponym relations (which are considered negative entailment indicators) covered over 9% and 14%, respectively. Table 3 shows the exact details.

It seems that WordNet relations are hardly correlated with the context-sensitive predicate-level entailments in our dataset, and that the classic interpretation of WordNet relations with respect to entailment does not hold in practice, where en-

Interpretation	WordNet Relation	Coverage
Positive	Synonyms	7.85%
	Direct Hypernyms	5.62%
	Indirect Hypernyms	3.14%
	Entailment	0.33%
Negative	Antonyms	0.31%
	Direct Hyponyms	5.74%
	Indirect Hyponyms	3.51%
	Cohyponyms	14.30%

Table 3: The portion of positive predicate entailments covered by each WordNet relation. WordNet relations are divided according to their common interpretations with respect to lexical entailment.

tailments are judged in the context of concrete propositions. In fact, negative indicators in WordNet seem to cover more predicate entailments than positive ones. This explains the failure of WordNet-supervised methods with predicate entailment features (Section 7.1).

Since we do not expect WordNet to cover all shades of entailment, we conducted a manual analysis as well. 100 entailing predicate pairs were randomly sampled, and manually annotated for lexical-level entailment, without seeing their arguments. To compensate for the lack of context, we guided the annotators to assume a general healthcare scenario, and use a more lenient interpretation of textual entailment (biased towards positive entailment decisions). Nevertheless, only 56% of the predicate pairs were labeled as entailing, indicating that the context-sensitive predicate inferences captured in our dataset can be quite different from generic predicate inferences.

We suggest that this phenomenon goes one step beyond what the current literature considers as context-sensitive entailment, and that it is more specific than determining an appropriate lexical sense. To demonstrate, we present four such predicate-entailment phenomena.

First, there are cases in which an appropriate lexical sense could exist in principle, but it is too specific to be practically covered by a manual resource. For example, *cures cancer→kills cancer*, but the appropriate sense for *kill* (cause to cease existing) does not exist, and in turn, neither does the hypernymy relation from *cure* to *kill*. It is hard to expect these kinds of obscure senses or relationships to comprehensively appear in a manually-constructed resource.

In many cases, such a specific sense *does not* exist. For example, *(pneumonia, require, antibiotic)→(pneumonia, treated by, antibiotics)*, but *require* does not have a general sense which means *treat by*. The inference in this example does not stem from the linguistic meaning of each predicate, but rather from the real-world situation their encapsulating propositions describe.

Another aspect of predicate entailment that may change when considering propositional context is the direction of inference. For instance, *cause↛trigger*. While it may be the case that *trigger* entails *cause*, the converse is not necessarily true since *cause* is far more general. However, when considering *(caffeine, cause, headache)* and *(caffeine, trigger, headache)*, both propositions describe the same real-world situation, and thus both propositions are mutually entailing. In this context, *cause* does indeed entail *trigger* as well.

Finally, figures of speech (such as metaphors) are abundant and diverse. Though it may not be so common to read about a drug that "banishes" headaches, most readers would understand the underlying meaning. These phenomena exceed the current scope of lexical-semantic resources such as WordNet, and require world knowledge.

9 Conclusion

This paper proposes a novel approach, based on entailment graphs, for consolidating information extracted from large corpora. We define the problem of building proposition entailment graphs, and provide a large annotated dataset. We also present the CEC model, which models the connection between proposition entailment and lexical entailment. Although it outperforms the state-of-the-art, its performance is not ideal because it relies on inadequate lexical-semantic resources that do not capture the common-sense and context-sensitive inferences which are inherent in proposition entailment. In future work, we intend to further investigate lexical entailment as induced by proposition entailment, and hope to develop richer methods of lexical inference that address the phenomena exhibited in this setting.

Acknowledgements

This work has been supported by the Israeli Ministry of Science and Technology grant 3-8705, the Israel Science Foundation grant 880/12, and the European Communitys Seventh Framework Programme (FP7/2007-2013) under grant agreement no. 287923 (EXCITEMENT). We would like to thank our reviewers for their insightful comments.

References

Meni Adler, Jonathan Berant, and Ido Dagan. 2012. Entailment-based text exploration with application to the health-care domain. In *Proceedings of the System Demonstrations of the 50th Annual Meeting of the Association for Computational Linguistics (ACL 2012)*, pages 79–84.

Michele Banko, Michael J. Cafarella, Stephen Soderland, Matthew Broadhead, and Oren Etzioni. 2007. Open information extraction from the web. In *IJCAI*, volume 7, pages 2670–2676.

Jonathan Berant, Ido Dagan, and Jacob Goldberger. 2012. Learning entailment relations by global graph structure optimization. *Computational Linguistics*, 38(1):73–111.

Kurt Bollacker, Colin Evans, Praveen Paritosh, Tim Sturge, and Jamie Taylor. 2008. Freebase: a collaboratively created graph database for structuring human knowledge. In *Proceedings of the 2008 ACM SIGMOD international conference on Management of data*, pages 1247–1250. ACM.

Kenneth Ward Church and Patrick Hanks. 1990. Word association norms, mutual information, and lexicography. *Computational Linguistics*, 16(1):22–29.

Ido Dagan, Dan Roth, Mark Sammons, and Fabio Massimo Zanzotto. 2013. Recognizing textual entailment: Models and applications. *Synthesis Lectures on Human Language Technologies*, 6(4):1–220.

Arthur P. Dempster, Nan M. Laird, and Donald B. Rubin. 1977. Maximum likelihood from incomplete data via the em algorithm. *Journal of the Royal Statistical Society. Series B (Methodological)*, pages 1–38.

Oren Etzioni, Michele Banko, Stephen Soderland, and Daniel S Weld. 2008. Open information extraction from the Web. *Communications of the ACM*, 51(12):68–74.

Anthony Fader, Stephen Soderland, and Oren Etzioni. 2011. Identifying relations for open information extraction. In *Proceedings of the 2011 Conference on Empirical Methods in Natural Language Processing*, pages 1535–1545, Edinburgh, Scotland, UK., July. Association for Computational Linguistics.

Yoav Goldberg and Jon Orwant. 2013. A dataset of syntactic-ngrams over time from a very large corpus of english books. In *Second Joint Conference on Lexical and Computational Semantics (*SEM), Volume 1: Proceedings of the Main Conference and the Shared Task: Semantic Textual Similarity*, pages 241–247, Atlanta, Georgia, USA, June. Association for Computational Linguistics.

Lili Kotlerman, Ido Dagan, Idan Szpektor, and Maayan Zhitomirsky-Geffet. 2010. Directional distributional similarity for lexical inference. *Natural Language Engineering*, 16(4):359–389.

Vladimir I. Levenshtein. 1966. Binary codes capable of correcting deletions, insertions and reversals. In *Soviet Physics Doklady*, volume 10, page 707.

Dekang Lin. 1998. Automatic retrieval and clustering of similar words. In *Proceedings of the 36th Annual Meeting of the Association for Computational Linguistics and 17th International Conference on Computational Linguistics, Volume 2*, pages 768–774, Montreal, Quebec, Canada, August. Association for Computational Linguistics.

Mausam, Michael Schmitz, Stephen Soderland, Robert Bart, and Oren Etzioni. 2012. Open language learning for information extraction. In *Proceedings of the 2012 Joint Conference on Empirical Methods in Natural Language Processing and Computational Natural Language Learning*, pages 523–534, Jeju Island, Korea, July. Association for Computational Linguistics.

Quinn McNemar. 1947. Note on the sampling error of the difference between correlated proportions or percentages. *Psychometrika*, 12(2):153–157.

Yashar Mehdad, Giuseppe Carenini, Raymond T. Ng, and Shafiq Joty. 2013. Towards topic labeling with phrase entailment and aggregation. In *Proceedings of the 2013 Conference of the North American Chapter of the Association for Computational Linguistics: Human Language Technologies*, pages 179–189, Atlanta, Georgia, June. Association for Computational Linguistics.

Oren Melamud, Jonathan Berant, Ido Dagan, Jacob Goldberger, and Idan Szpektor. 2013. A two level model for context sensitive inference rules. In *Proceedings of the 51st Annual Meeting of the Association for Computational Linguistics (Volume 1: Long Papers)*, pages 1331–1340, Sofia, Bulgaria, August. Association for Computational Linguistics.

Sebastian Riedel, Limin Yao, Andrew McCallum, and Benjamin M. Marlin. 2013. Relation extraction with matrix factorization and universal schemas. In *Proceedings of the 2013 Conference of the North American Chapter of the Association for Computational Linguistics: Human Language Technologies*, pages 74–84, Atlanta, Georgia, June. Association for Computational Linguistics.

Rion Snow, Dan Jurafsky, and Andrew Y. Ng. 2006. Semantic taxonomy induction from heterogenous evidence. In *Proceedings of the 21st International Conference on Computational Linguistics and the 44th Annual Meeting of the Association for Computational Linguistics (ACL-COLING 2006)*, pages 801–808.

Julie Weeds and David Weir. 2003. A general framework for distributional similarity. In Michael Collins and Mark Steedman, editors, *Proceedings of the 2003 Conference on Empirical Methods in Natural Language Processing*, pages 81–88.

Ying Xu, Mi-Young Kim, Kevin Quinn, Randy Goebel, and Denilson Barbosa. 2013. Open information extraction with tree kernels. In *Proceedings of the 2013 Conference of the North American Chapter of the Association for Computational Linguistics: Human Language Technologies*, pages 868–877, Atlanta, Georgia, June. Association for Computational Linguistics.

Alexander Yates and Oren Etzioni. 2009. Unsupervised methods for determining object and relation synonyms on the web. *Journal of Artificial Intelligence Research*, 34(1):255.

Improved Pattern Learning for Bootstrapped Entity Extraction

Sonal Gupta **Christopher D. Manning**
Department of Computer Science
Stanford University
{sonal, manning}@cs.stanford.edu

Abstract

Bootstrapped pattern learning for entity extraction usually starts with seed entities and iteratively learns patterns and entities from unlabeled text. Patterns are scored by their ability to extract more positive entities and less negative entities. A problem is that due to the lack of labeled data, unlabeled entities are either assumed to be negative or are ignored by the existing pattern scoring measures. In this paper, we improve pattern scoring by predicting the labels of unlabeled entities. We use various unsupervised features based on contrasting domain-specific and general text, and exploiting distributional similarity and edit distances to learned entities. Our system outperforms existing pattern scoring algorithms for extracting drug-and-treatment entities from four medical forums.

Seed dictionary for class 'animals': {dog}

Text:
I *own a* ***cat*** named Fluffy. I run with *my pet* ***dog***. I also nap with *my pet* ***cat***. I *own a* ***car***.

Pattern 1: my pet **X**
Extractions = positive : {dog}, unlabeled : {cat}

Pattern 2: own a **X**
Extractions = positive : {dog}, unlabeled : {car}

Figure 1: An example pattern learning system for the class 'animals' from the text. Pattern 1 and 2 are candidate patterns. Text matched with the patterns is shown in italics and the extracted entities are shown in bold.

1 Introduction

This paper considers the problem of building effective entity extractors for custom entity types from specialized domain corpora. We approach the problem by learning rules bootstrapped using seed sets of entities. Though entity extraction using machine learning is common in academic research, rule-based systems dominate in commercial use (Chiticariu et al., 2013), mainly because rules are effective, interpretable, and are easy to customize by non-experts to cope with errors. They also have been shown to perform better than state-of-the-art machine learning methods on some specialized domains (Nallapati and Manning, 2008; Gupta and Manning, 2014a). In addition, building supervised machine learning systems for a reasonably large domain-specific corpus would require hand-labeling sufficient data to train a model, which can be costly and time consuming. Bootstrapped machine-learned rules can make extraction easier and more efficient on such a corpus.

In a bootstrapped rule-based entity learning system, seed dictionaries and/or patterns provide weak supervision to label data. The system iteratively learns new entities belonging to a specific class from unlabeled text (Riloff, 1996; Collins and Singer, 1999). Rules are typically defined by creating patterns around the entities, such as lexico-syntactic surface word patterns (Hearst, 1992) and dependency tree patterns (Yangarber et al., 2000). Patterns are scored by their ability to extract more positive entities and less negative entities. Top ranked patterns are used to extract candidate entities from text. High scoring candidate entities are added to the dictionaries and are used to generate more candidate patterns around them. In a supervised setting, the efficacy of patterns can be judged by their performance on a fully labeled dataset (Califf and Mooney, 1999; Ciravegna, 2001). In a bootstrapped system, where the data is not fully labeled, existing systems score patterns by either ignoring the un-

Proceedings of the Eighteenth Conference on Computational Language Learning, pages 98–108,
Baltimore, Maryland USA, June 26-27 2014.

labeled entities or assuming them to be negative. However, these scoring schemes cannot differentiate between patterns that extract good versus bad unlabeled entities. The problem is similar to the closed world assumption in distantly supervised information extraction systems, when all propositions missing from a knowledge base are considered false (Ritter et al., 2013; Xu et al., 2013).

Predicting labels of unlabeled entities can improve scoring patterns. Consider the example shown in Figure 1. Current pattern learning systems would score both patterns equally. However, features like distributional similarity can predict 'cat' to be closer to {dog} than 'car', and a pattern learning system can use that information to rank 'Pattern 1' higher than 'Pattern 2'.

In this paper, we work on bootstrapping entity extraction using seed sets of entities and an unlabeled text corpus. We improve the scoring of patterns for an entity class by defining a pattern's score by the number of positive entities it extracts and the ratio of number of positive entities to *expected* number of negative entities it extracts. Our main contribution is introducing the expected number of negative entities in pattern scoring – we predict probabilities of unlabeled entities belonging to the negative class. We estimate an unlabeled entity's negative class probability by averaging probabilities from various unsupervised class predictors, such as distributional similarity, string edit distances from learned entities, and TF-IDF scores. Our system performs significantly better than existing pattern scoring measures for extracting drug-and-treatment entities from four medical forums on MedHelp[1], a user health discussion website.

We release the code for the systems described in this paper at `http://nlp.stanford.edu/software/patternslearning.shtml`. We also release a visualization tool, described in Gupta and Manning (2014b), that visualizes and compares output of multiple pattern-based entity extraction systems. It can be downloaded at `http://nlp.stanford.edu/software/patternviz.shtml`.

2 Related Work

Rule based learning has been a topic of interest for many years. Patwardhan (2010) gives a good overview of the research in the field. Rule learning systems differ in how they create rules, score them, and score the entities they extract. Here, we mainly discuss the rule scoring part of the previous entity extraction research.

The pioneering work by Hearst (1992) used hand written rules to automatically generate more rules that were manually evaluated to extract hypernym-hyponym pairs from text. Other supervised systems like SRV (Freitag, 1998), SLIPPER (Cohen and Singer, 1999), $(LP)^2$ (Ciravegna, 2001), and RAPIER (Califf and Mooney, 1999) used a fully labeled corpus to either create or score rules.

Riloff (1996) used a set of seed entities to bootstrap learning of rules for entity extraction from unlabeled text. She scored a rule by a weighted conditional probability measure estimated by counting the number of positive entities among all the entities extracted by the rule. Thelen and Riloff (2002) extended the above bootstrapping algorithm for multi-class learning. Yangarber et al. (2002) and Lin et al. (2003) used a combination of accuracy and confidence of a pattern for multiclass entity learning, where the accuracy measure ignored unlabeled entities and the confidence measure treated them as negative. Gupta and Manning (2014a) used the ratio of scaled frequencies of positive entities among all extracted entities. None of the above measures predict labels of unlabeled entities to score patterns. Our system outperforms them in our experiments. Stevenson and Greenwood (2005) used Wordnet to assess patterns, which is not feasible for domains that have low coverage in Wordnet, such as medical data.

More recently, open information extraction systems have garnered attention. They focus on extracting entities and relations from the web. KnowItAll's entity extraction from the web (Downey et al., 2004; Etzioni et al., 2005) used components such as list extractors, generic and domain specific pattern learning, and subclass learning. They learned domain-specific patterns using a seed set and scored them by ignoring unlabeled entities. One of our baselines is similar to their domain-specific pattern learning component. Carlson et al. (2010) learned multiple semantic types using coupled semi-supervised training from web-scale data, which is not feasible for all datasets and entity learning tasks. They assessed patterns by their precision, assuming unla-

[1] `www.medhelp.org`

beled entities to be negative; one of our baselines is similar to their pattern assessment method.

Other open information extraction systems like ReVerb (Fader et al., 2011) and OLLIE (Mausam et al., 2012) are mainly geared towards generic, domain-independent relation extractors for web data. We tested learning an entity extractor for a given class using ReVerb. We labeled the binary and unary ReVerb extractions using the class seed entities and retrained its confidence function, with poor results. Poon and Domingos (2010) found a similar result for inducing a probabilistic ontology: an open information extraction system extracted low accuracy relational triples on a small corpus.

In this paper, we use features such as distributional similarity and edit distances from learned entities to score patterns. Similar measures have been used before but for learning entities, labeling semantic classes, or for reducing noise in seed sets (Pantel and Ravichandran, 2004; McIntosh and Curran, 2009). Measures for improving entity learning can be used alongside ours since we focus on scoring candidate patterns.

3 Approach

We use lexico-syntactic surface word patterns to extract entities from unlabeled text starting with seed dictionaries of entities for multiple classes. For ease of exposition, we present the approach below for learning entities for one class C. It can easily be generalized to multiple classes. We refer to entities belonging to C as positive and entities belonging to all other classes as negative. The bootstrapping process involves the following steps, iteratively performed until no more patterns or entities can be learned.

1. Labeling data and creating patterns: The text is labeled using the class dictionaries, starting with the seed dictionaries in the first iteration. A phrase matching a dictionary phrase is labeled with the dictionary's class. Patterns are then created using the context around the positively labeled entities to create candidate patterns for C.

2. Scoring Patterns: Candidate patterns are scored using a pattern scoring measure and the top ones are added to the list of learned patterns for C.

3. Learning entities: Learned patterns for the class are applied to the text to extract candidate entities. An entity scorer ranks the candidate entities and adds the top entities to C's dictionary.

The success of bootstrapped pattern learning methods crucially depends on the effectiveness of the pattern scorer and the entity scorer. Here we focus on improving the pattern scoring measure (Step 2 above).

3.1 Creating Patterns

Candidate patterns are created using contexts of words or their lemmas in a window of two to four words before and after a positively labeled token. Context words that are labeled with one of the classes are generalized with that class. The target term has a part-of-speech (POS) restriction, which is the POS tag of the labeled token. We create flexible patterns by ignoring the words {'a', 'an', 'the'} and quotation marks when matching patterns to the text. Some examples of the patterns are shown in Table 4.

3.2 Scoring Patterns

Judging the efficacy of patterns without using a fully labeled dataset can be challenging because of two types of failures: 1. penalizing good patterns that extract good (that is, positive) unlabeled entities, and 2. giving high scores to bad patterns that extract bad (that is, negative) unlabeled entities. Existing systems that assume unlabeled entities as negative are too conservative in scoring patterns and suffer from the first problem. Systems that ignore unlabeled entities can suffer from both the problems. In this paper, we propose to estimate the labels of unlabeled entities to more accurately score the patterns.

For a pattern r, sets P_r, N_r, and U_r denote the positive, negative, and unlabeled entities extracted by r, respectively. The pattern score, $ps(r)$ is calculated as

$$ps(r) = \frac{|P_r|}{|N_r| + \sum_{e \in U_r}(1 - score(e))} \log(|P_r|)$$

where $|.|$ denotes size of a set. The function $score(e)$ gives the probability of an entity e belonging to C. If e is a common word, $score(e)$ is 0. Otherwise, $score(e)$ is calculated as the average of five feature scores (explained below), each of which give a score between 0 and 1. The feature scores are calculated using the seed dictionaries, learned entities for all labels, Google N-grams[2], and clustering of domain words using distributional similarity. The $\log |P_r|$ term, inspired from (Riloff, 1996), gives higher scores to patterns that extract more positive entities. Candidate patterns are ranked by $ps(r)$ and the top patterns are added to the list of learned patterns.

To calculate $score(e)$, we use features that assess unlabeled entities to be either closer to positive or negative entities in an unsupervised way. We motivate our choice of the five features below with the following insights. If the dataset consists of informally written text, many unlabeled entities are spelling mistakes and morphological variations of labeled entities. We use two edit distance based features to predict labels for these unlabeled entities. Second, some unlabeled entities are substrings of multi-word dictionary phrases but do not necessarily belong to the dictionary's class. For example, for learning drug names, the positive dictionary might contain 'asthma meds', but 'asthma' is negative and might occur in a negative dictionary as 'asthma disease'. To predict the labels of entities that are a substring of dictionary phrases, we use SemOdd, which was used in Gupta and Manning (2014a) to learn entities. Third, for a specialized domain, unlabeled entities that commonly occur in generic text are more likely to be negative. We use Google Ngrams (called GN) to get a fast, non-sparse estimate of the frequency of entities over a broad range of domains. The above features do not consider the context in which the entities occur in text. We use the fifth feature, DistSim, to exploit contextual information of the labeled entities using distributional similarity. The features are defined as:

Edit distance from positive entities (EDP): This feature gives a score of 1 if e has low edit distance to the positive entities. It is computed as $max_{p \in P_r} \mathbb{1}(\frac{editDist(p,e)}{|p|} < 0.2)$, where $\mathbb{1}(c)$ returns 1 if the condition c is true and 0 otherwise, $|p|$ is the length of p, and $editDist(p, e)$ is the Damerau-Levenshtein string edit distance between p and e.

Edit distance from negative entities (EDN): It is similar to EDP and gives a score of 1 if e has high edit distance to the negative entities. It is computed as $1 - \max_{n \in N_r} \mathbb{1}(\frac{editDist(n,e)}{|n|} < 0.2)$.

Semantic odds ratio (SemOdd): First, we calculate the ratio of frequency of the entity term in the positive entities to its frequency in the negative entities with Laplace smoothing. The ratio is then normalized using a softmax function. The feature values for the unlabeled entities extracted by all the candidate patterns are then normalized using the min-max function to scale the values between 0 and 1.[3]

Google Ngram (GN): We calculate the ratio of scaled frequency of e in the dataset to the frequency in Google Ngrams. The scaling factor is to balance the two frequencies and is computed as the ratio of total number of phrases in the dataset to the total of phrases in Google Ngrams. The feature values are normalized in the same way as SemOdd.

Distributional similarity score (DistSim): Words that occur in similar contexts, such as 'asthma' and 'depression', are clustered using distributional similarity. Unlabeled entities that get clustered with positive entities are given higher score than the ones clustered with negative entities. To score the clusters, we learn a logistic regression classifier using cluster ID as features, and use their weights as scores for all the entities in those clusters. The dataset for logistic regression is created by considering all positively labeled words as positive and sampling negative and unlabeled words as negative. The scores for entities are normalized in the same way as SemOdd and GN.

Out of feature vocabulary entities for SemOdd, GN, and DistSim are given a score of 0. We use a simple way of combining the feature values: we give equal weights to all features and average their scores. Features can be combined using a weighted average by manually tuning the weights on a development set; we leave it to the future work. Another way of weighting the features is to learn the weights using machine learning. We experimented with learning weights for

[2]http://storage.googleapis.com/books/ngrams/books/datasetsv2.html. Accessed January 2008.

[3]We do min-max normalization on top of the softmax normalization because the maximum and minimum value by softmax might not be close to 1 and 0, respectively. And, treating the out-of-feature-vocabulary entities same as the worst scored entities by the feature, that is giving them a score of 0, performed best on the development dataset.

the features by training a logistic regression classifier. We considered all positive words as positive and randomly sampled negative and unlabeled entities as negative to predict $score(e)$, but it performed worse compared to averaging the scores on the development dataset. Preliminary investigation suggests that since the classifier was trained on a dataset heuristically labeled using the seed dictionaries, it was too noisy for the classifier to learn accurate weights. Presumably, the classifier also suffered from the closed world assumption of treating unlabeled examples as negative.

3.3 Learning Entities

We apply the learned patterns to the text and extract candidate entities. We discard common words, negative entities, and those containing non-alphanumeric characters from the set. The rest are scored by averaging the scores of DistSim, SemOdd, EDO, and EDN features from Section 3.2 and the following features.

Pattern TF-IDF scoring (PTF): For an entity e, it is calculated as $\frac{1}{\log freq_e} \sum_{r \in R} ps(r)$, where R is the set of learned patterns that extract e and $freq_e$ is the frequency of e in the corpus. Entities that are extracted by many high weighted patterns get higher weight. To mitigate the effect of many commonly occurring entities also getting extracted by several patterns, we normalize the feature value with the log of the entity's frequency. The values are normalized in the same way as DistSim and SemOdd.

Domain N-gram TF-IDF (DN): This feature gives higher scores to entities that are more prevalent in the corpus compared to the general domain. For example, to learn entities about a specific disease from a disease-related corpus, the feature favors entities related to the disease over generic medical entities. It is calculated in the same way as GN except the frequency is computed in the n-grams of the generic domain text.

Including GN in the phrase scoring features or including DN in the pattern scoring features did not perform well on the development set in our pilot experiments.

4 Experiments

4.1 Dataset

We evaluate our system on extracting drug-and-treatment (DT) entities in sentences from four forums on the MedHelp user health discussion website: 1. Acne, 2. Adult Type II Diabetes (called Diabetes), 3. Ear Nose & Throat (called ENT), and 4. Asthma. The forums have discussion threads by users concerning health related problems and treatments. The number of sentences in each forum are: 215,623 in ENT, 39,637 in Asthma, 63,355 in Diabetes, and 65,595 in Acne. We used Asthma as the development forum for feature engineering and parameter tuning. Similar to Gupta and Manning (2014a), a DT entity is defined as a pharmaceutical drug, or any treatment or intervention mentioned that may help a symptom or a condition. It includes surgeries, lifestyle changes, alternative treatments, home remedies, and components of daily care and management of a disease, but does not include diagnostic tests and devices. More information is in the supplemental material. A few example sentences from the dataset are below.

> I plan to start **cinnamon** and **holy basil** - known to lower glucose in many people.
>
> She gave me **albuteral** and **symbicort** (plus some hayfever **meds** and asked me to use the peak flow meter.
>
> My sinus infections were treated electrically, with **high voltage million volt electricity**, which solved the problem, but the **treatment** is not FDA approved and generally unavailable, except under experimental **treatment** protocols.

In these sentences, 'cinanmon', 'holy basil', 'albuteral', 'symbicort', 'meds', 'high voltage million volt electricity', and 'treatment' are DT entities.

We used entities from the following classes as negative: symptoms and conditions (SC), medical specialists, body parts, and common temporal nouns to remove dates and dosage information. We used the DT and SC seed dictionaries from Gupta and Manning (2014a).[4] The lists of

[4]The DT seed dictionary (36,091 phrases) and SC seed dictionary (97,211 phrases) were automatically constructed from various sources on the Internet and expanded using the OAC Consumer Health Vocabulary (http://www.consumerhealthvocab.org), which maps medical jargon to everyday phrases and their variants. Both dictionaries are large because they contain many variants of entities. For each system, the SC dictionary was further expanded by running the system with the SC class as positive (considering DT

body parts and temporal nouns were obtained from Wordnet (Fellbaum, 1998). The common words list was created using most common words on the web and Twitter.[5]

For evaluation, the first author hand labeled the learned entities pooled from all systems. A word was evaluated by querying the word and the forum name on Google and manually inspecting the results. More details on the labeling guidelines are in the Supplement section. Inter annotator agreement between the annotator and another researcher was computed on 200 randomly sampled learned entities from each of the Asthma and ENT forum. The agreement for the entities from the Asthma forum was 96% and from the ENT forum was 92.46%. The Cohen's kappa scores were 0.91 and 0.83, respectively. Most disagreements were on food items like 'yogurt', which are hard to label. Note that we use the hand labeled entities only as a test set for evaluation.

4.2 Baselines

As in Section 3, the sets P_r, N_r, and U_r are defined as the positive, negative, and unlabeled entities extracted by a pattern r, respectively. The set A_r is defined as union of all the three sets. We compare our system with the following pattern scoring algorithms. Candidate entities are scored in the same way as described in Section 3.3. It is important to note that previous works also differ in how they create patterns, apply patterns, and score entities. Since we focus on only the pattern scoring aspect, we run experiments that differ in only that component.

PNOdd: Defined as $|P_r|/|N_r|$, this measure ignores unlabeled entities and is similar to the domain specific pattern learning component of Etzioni et al. (2005) since all patterns with $|P_r| < 2$ were discarded (more details in the next section).

PUNOdd: Defined as $|P_r|/(|U_r| + |N_r|)$, this measure treats unlabeled entities as negative entities.

RlogF: Measure used by Riloff (1996) and Thelen and Riloff (2002), and calculated as $R_r \log |P_r|$, where R_r was defined as $|P_r|/|A_r|$ (labeled RlogF-PUN). It assumed unlabeled entities as negative entities. We also compare with a variant that ignores the unlabeled entities, that is by defining R_r as $|P_r|/(|P_r + |N_r|)$ (labeled RlogF-PN).

Yangarber02: This measure from Yangarber et al. (2002) calculated two scores, $acc_r = |P_r|/|N_r|$ and $conf_r = (|P_r|/|A_r|) \log |P_r|$. Patterns with acc_r less than a threshold were discarded and the rest were ranked using $conf_r$. We empirically determined that a threshold of 0.8 performed best on the development forum.

Lin03: A measure proposed in Lin et al. (2003), it was similar to Yangarber02, except $conf_r$ was defined as $\log |P_r|(|P_r| - |N_r|)/|A_r|$. In essence, it discards a pattern if it extracts more negative entities than positive entities.

SqrtRatioAll: This pattern scoring method was used in Gupta and Manning (2014a) and defined as $\sum_{k \in P_r} \sqrt{freq_k} / \sum_{j \in A_r} \sqrt{freq_j}$, where $freq_i$ is the number of times entity i is extracted by r. Sublinear scaling of the term-frequency prevents high frequency words from overshadowing the contribution of low frequency words.

4.3 Experimental Setup

We used the same experimental setup for our system and the baselines. When matching phrases from a seed dictionary to text, a phrase is labeled with the dictionary's class if the sequence of phrase words or their lemmas match with the sequence of words of a dictionary phrase. Since our corpora are from online discussion forums, they have many spelling mistakes and morphological variations of entities. To deal with the variations, we do fuzzy matching of words – if two words are one edit distance away and are more than 6 characters long, then they are considered a match.

We used Stanford TokensRegex (Chang and Manning, 2014) to create and apply surface word patterns to text, and used the Stanford Part-of-Speech (POS) tagger (Toutanova et al., 2003) to find POS tags of tokens and lemmatize them. When creating patterns, we discarded patterns whose left or right context was 1 or 2 stop words to avoid generating low precision patterns.[6] In each iteration, we learned a maximum 20 patterns with $ps(r) \geq \theta_r$ and maximum 10 words with score $\geq$

and other classes as negative) and adding the top 50 words extracted by the top 300 patterns to the SC class dictionary. This helps in adding corpus specific SC words to the dictionary.

[5]We used top 10,000 words from Google N-grams and top 5,000 words from Twitter (`www.twitter.com`), accessed from May 19 to 25, 2012.

[6]Three or more stop words resulted in some good patterns like 'I am on **X**'. Our stop words list consists of punctuation marks and around 200 very common English words.

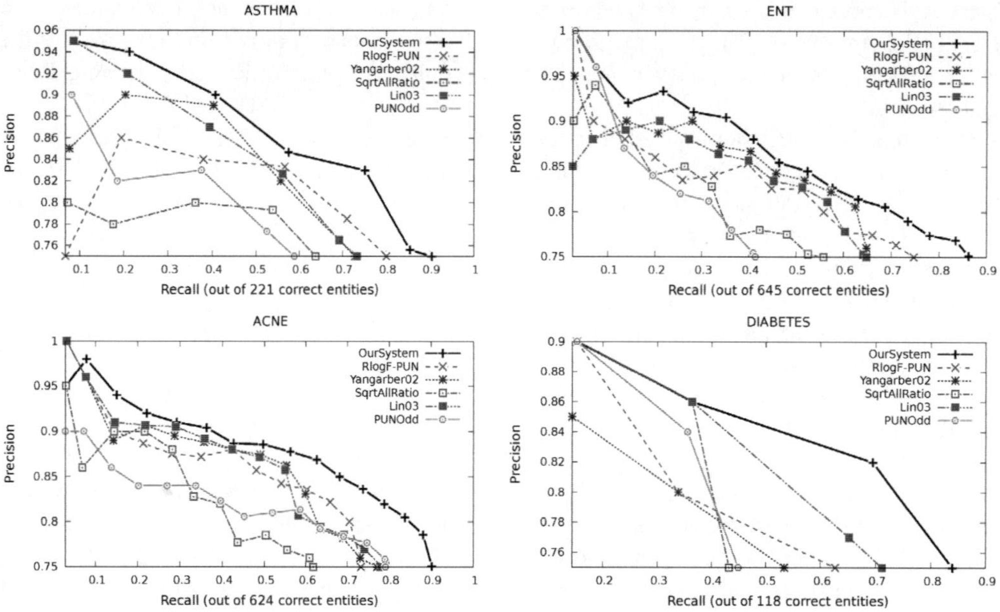

Figure 2: Precision vs. Recall curves of our system and the baselines for the four forums. Rlog-PN and PNOdd are not shown to improve clarity.

0.2. The initial value of θ_r was 1.0, which was reduced to $0.8 \times \theta_r$ whenever the system did not extract any more patterns and words. We discarded patterns that extracted less than 2 positive entities. We selected these parameters by their performance on the development forum.

For calculating the DistSim feature used for scoring patterns and entities, we clustered all of MedHelp's forum data into 1000 clusters using the Brown clustering algorithm (Brown et al., 1992; Liang, 2005).[7] For calculating the Domain Ngram feature for scoring entities, we used n-grams from all user forums in MedHelp as the domain n-grams.

We evaluate systems by their precision and recall in each iteration. Precision is defined as the fraction of correct entities among the entities extracted. We stopped learning entities for a system if the precision dropped below 75% to extract entities with reasonably high precision. Recall is defined as the fraction of correct entities among the total unique correct entities pooled from all systems while maintaining the precision $\geq 75\%$. Note that true recall is very hard to compute since our dataset is unlabeled. To compare the systems overall, we calculate the area under the precision-recall curves (AUC-PR).

System	Asthma	ENT	Diabetes	Acne
OurSystem	**68.36**	**60.71**	**67.62**	**68.01**
PNOdd	51.62	50.31	05.91	58.45
PUNOdd	42.42	30.44	36.11	58.38
RlogF-PUN	56.13	54.11	48.70	57.04
RlogF-PN	53.46	52.84	16.59	62.35
SqrtRatioAll	41.49	40.44	35.47	46.46
Yangarber02	53.76	48.46	41.45	59.85
Lin03	54.58	47.98	56.15	60.79

Table 1: Area under Precision-Recall curves of the systems.

4.4 Results

Figure 2 plots the precision and recall of systems.[8] Table 1 shows AUC-PR scores for all systems. RlogF-PN and PNOdd have low value for Diabetes because they learned generic patterns in initial iteration, which led them to learn incorrect entities. Overall our system performed significantly better than existing systems. All systems extract more entities for Acne and ENT because different drugs and treatments are more prevalent in these forums. Diabetes and Asthma have more interventions and lifestyle changes that are harder to

[7]The data consisted of around 4 million tokens. Words that occurred less than 50 times were discarded, which resulted in 50353 unique words.

[8]We do not show plots of PNOdd and RlogF-PN to improve clarity. They performed similarly to other baselines.

Feature	Asthma	ENT	Diabetes	Acne
All Features	68.36	**60.71**	67.62	68.01
EDP	**68.66**	59.07	60.03	65.15
EDN	59.39	59.21	16.75	65.96
SemOdd	67.07	58.41	60.51	65.04
GN	57.52	59.53	48.76	68.61
DistSim	64.87	59.05	**71.11**	**69.48**

Table 2: Individual feature effectiveness: Area under Precision-Recall curves when our system uses individual features during pattern scoring. Other features are still used for entity scoring.

Feature	Asthma	ENT	Diabetes	Acne
All Features	**68.36**	60.71	67.62	68.01
*minus*EDP	66.29	60.45	69.84	**69.46**
*minus*EDN	67.19	60.39	69.89	67.57
*minus*GN	65.53	60.33	66.07	67.28
*minus*SemOdd	66.66	**60.76**	**70.79**	68.25
*minus*DistSim	66.10	60.58	66.59	67.85

Table 3: Feature ablation study: Area under Precision-Recall curves when individual features are removed from our system during pattern scoring. The feature is still used for entity scoring.

extract.

To compare the effectiveness of each feature in our system, Table 2 shows the AUC-PR values when each feature was individually used for pattern scoring (other features were still used to learn entities). EDP and DistSim were strong predictors of labels of unlabeled entities because many good unlabeled entities were spelling mistakes of DT entities and occurred in similar context as them. Table 3 shows the AUC-PR values when each feature was removed from the set of features used to score patterns (the feature was still used for learning entities). Removing GN and DistSim reduced the AUC-PR scores for all forums.

Table 4 shows some examples of patterns and the entities they extracted along with their labels when the pattern was learned. We learned the first pattern because 'pinacillin' has low edit distance from the positive entity 'penicillin'. Similarly, we scored the second pattern higher than the baseline because 'desoidne' is a typo of the positive entity 'desonide'. Note that the seed dictionaries are noisy – the entity 'metro', part of the positive entity 'metrogel', was falsely considered a negative entity because it was in the common web words list. Our system learned the third pattern for two reasons: 'inhaler', 'inhalers', and 'hfa' occurred frequently as sub-phrases in the DT dictionary, and they were clustered with positive entities by distributional similarity. Since RlogF-PUN does not distinguish between unlabeled and negative entities, it is does not learn the pattern. Table 5 shows top 10 patterns learned for the ENT forum by our system and RlogF-PUN, the best performing baseline for the forum. Our system preferred to learn patterns with longer contexts, which are usually higher precision, first.

Our System	RlogF-PUN
low dose of **X***	mg of **X**
mg of **X**	treat with **X**
X 10 mg	take *DT* and **X**
she prescribe **X**	be take **X**
X 500 mg	she prescribe **X**
be take *DT* and **X***	put on **X**
ent put I on **X***	stop take **X**
DT (like X:NN	i be prescribe **X**
like *DT* and **X**	have be take **X**
then prescribe **X***	tell I to take **X**

Table 5: Top 10 (simplified) patterns learned by our system and RlogF-PUN from the ENT forum. An asterisk denotes that the pattern was never learned by the other system. **X** is the target word.

5 Discussion and Conclusion

Our system extracted entities with higher precision and recall than other existing systems. However, learning entities from an informal text corpus that is partially labeled from seed entities presents some challenges. Our system made mistakes primarily due to three reasons. One, it sometimes extracted typos of negative entities that were not easily predictable by the edit distance measures, such as 'knowwhere'. Second, patterns that extracted many good but some bad unlabeled entities got high scores because of the good unlabeled entities. However, the bad unlabeled entities extracted by the highly weighted patterns were scored high by the PTF feature during the entity scoring phase, leading to extraction of the bad entities. Better features to predict negative entities and robust text normalization would help mitigate both the problems. Third, we used automatically constructed seed dictionaries that were not dataset specific, which led to incorrectly labeling of some entities (for example, 'metro' as negative in Table 4). Reducing noise in the dictionaries would increase precision and recall.

In this paper, the features are weighted equally

Forum	Pattern	Positive entities	Negative	Unlabeled	Our System	Baseline
ENT	he give I more **X**	antibiotics, steroid, antibiotic		pinacillin	68	NA (RlogF-PUN)
Acne	topical *DT* (**X**	prednisone, clindamycin, differin, benzoyl peroxide, tretinoin, metrogel	metro	desoidne	149	231 (RlogF-PN)
Asthma	i be put on **X**	cortisone, prednisone, asmanex, advair, augmentin, bypass, nebulizer, xolair, steroids, prilosec		inhaler, inhalers, hfa	8	NA (RlogF-PUN)

Table 4: Example patterns and the entities extracted by them, along with the rank at which the pattern was added to the list of learned patterns. NA means that the system never learned the pattern. Baseline refers to the best performing baseline system on the forum. The patterns have been simplified to show just the sequence of lemmas. **X** refers to the target entity; all of them in these examples had noun POS restriction. Terms that have already been identified as the positive class were generalized to their class DT.

by taking the average of the feature scores. One area of future work is to learn weights using more sophisticated techniques; in pilot experiments, learning a logistic regression classifier on heuristically labeled data did not work well for either pattern scoring or entity scoring.

One limitation of our system and evaluation is that we learned single word entities, since calculating some features for multi-word phrases is not straightforward. For example, word clusters using distributional similarity were constructed for single words. Our future work includes expanding the features to evaluate multi-word phrases. Another avenue for future work is to use our pattern scoring method for learning other kinds of rules, such as dependency patterns, and in different kinds of systems, such as hybrid entity learning systems (Etzioni et al., 2005; Carlson et al., 2010). In addition, we did not explicitly address the problem of semantic drift (Curran et al., 2007) in this paper. In theory, learning better patterns would help lessen the problem; we plan to investigate this further.

In conclusion, we show that predicting the labels of unlabeled entities in the pattern scorer of a bootstrapped entity extraction system significantly improves precision and recall of learned entities. Our experiments demonstrate the importance of having models that contrast domain-specific and general domain text, and the usefulness of features that allow spelling variations when dealing with informal texts. Our pattern scorer outperforms existing pattern scoring methods for learning drug-and-treatment entities from four medical web forums.

Acknowledgments

We thank Diana MacLean for labeling the test data for calculating the inter-annotator agreement. We are also grateful to Gabor Angeli, Angel Chang, Manolis Savva, and the anonymous reviewers for their useful feedback. We thank MedHelp for sharing their anonymized data with us.

References

Peter F. Brown, Peter V. deSouza, Robert L. Mercer, Vincent J. Della Pietra, and Jenifer C. Lai. 1992. Class-based n-gram models of natural language. *Computational Linguistics*, 18:467–479.

Mary Elaine Califf and Raymond J. Mooney. 1999. Relational learning of pattern-match rules for information extraction. In *Proceedings of the 16th National Conference on Artificial Intelligence and the 11th Innovative Applications of Artificial Intelligence Conference*, AAAI-IAAI '99, pages 328–334.

Andrew Carlson, Justin Betteridge, Richard C. Wang, Estevam R. Hruschka, Jr., and Tom M. Mitchell. 2010. Coupled semi-supervised learning for information extraction. In *Proceedings of the 3rd ACM International Conference on Web Search and Data Mining*, WSDM '10, pages 101–110.

Angel X. Chang and Christopher D. Manning. 2014. TokensRegex: Defining cascaded regular expressions over tokens. Technical Report CSTR 2014-02, Department of Computer Science, Stanford University.

Laura Chiticariu, Yunyao Li, and Frederick R. Reiss. 2013. Rule-based information extraction is dead! Long live rule-based information extraction systems! In *Proceedings of the Conference on Empirical Methods in Natural Language Processing*, EMNLP '13, pages 827–832.

Fabio Ciravegna. 2001. Adaptive information extraction from text by rule induction and generalisation. In *Proceedings of the 17th International Joint Conference on Artificial Intelligence*, IJCAI'01, pages 1251–1256.

William W. Cohen and Yoram Singer. 1999. A simple, fast, and effective rule learner. In *Proceedings of the 16th National Conference on Artificial Intelligence and the 11th Innovative Applications of Artificial Intelligence Conference*, pages 335–342.

Michael Collins and Yoram Singer. 1999. Unsupervised models for named entity classification. In *Proceedings of the Joint SIGDAT Conference on Empirical Methods in Natural Language Processing and Very Large Corpora*, pages 100–110.

J. R. Curran, T. Murphy, and B. Scholz. 2007. Minimising semantic drift with mutual exclusion bootstrapping. *Proceedings of the Conference of the Pacific Association for Computational Linguistics*, pages 172–180.

D. Downey, O. Etzioni, S. Soderland, and D. S. Weld. 2004. Learning Text Patterns for Web Information Extraction and Assessment. In *Proceedings of AAAI 2004 Workshop on Adaptive Text Extraction and Mining*, ATEM '04.

Oren Etzioni, Michael Cafarella, Doug Downey, Ana-Maria Popescu, Tal Shaked, Stephen Soderland, Daniel S. Weld, and Alexander Yates. 2005. Unsupervised named-entity extraction from the web: An experimental study. *Artificial Intelligence*, 165(1):91 - 134.

Anthony Fader, Stephen Soderland, and Oren Etzioni. 2011. Identifying relations for open information extraction. In *Proceedings of the Conference on Empirical Methods in Natural Language Processing*, EMNLP '11, pages 1535–1545.

Christiane Fellbaum. 1998. *WordNet: An Electronic Lexical Database*. Bradford Books.

Dayne Freitag. 1998. Toward general-purpose learning for information extraction. In *Proceedings of the 36th Annual Meeting of the Association for Computational Linguistics and 17th International Conference on Computational Linguistics*, COLING-ACL '98, pages 404–408.

Sonal Gupta and Christopher D. Manning. 2014a. Induced lexico-syntactic patterns improve information extraction from online medical forums. *Under Submission*.

Sonal Gupta and Christopher D. Manning. 2014b. Spied: Stanford pattern-based information extraction and diagnostics. In *Proceedings of the ACL 2014 Workshop on Interactive Language Learning, Visualization, and Interfaces (ACL-ILLVI)*.

Marti A Hearst. 1992. Automatic acquisition of hyponyms from large text corpora. In *Proceedings of the 14th International Conference on Computational linguistics*, COLING '92, pages 539–545.

Percy Liang. 2005. Semi-supervised learning for natural language. Master's thesis, MIT EECS.

Winston Lin, Roman Yangarber, and Ralph Grishman. 2003. Bootstrapped learning of semantic classes from positive and negative examples. In *Proceedings of the ICML 2003 Workshop on The Continuum from Labeled to Unlabeled Data in Machine Learning and Data Mining*.

Mausam, Michael Schmitz, Stephen Soderland, Robert Bart, and Oren Etzioni. 2012. Open language learning for information extraction. In *Proceedings of the 2012 Joint Conference on Empirical Methods in Natural Language Processing and Computational Natural Language Learning*, EMNLP-CoNLL '12, pages 523–534.

Tara McIntosh and James R. Curran. 2009. Reducing semantic drift with bagging and distributional similarity. In *Proceedings of the Joint Conference of the 47th Annual Meeting of the ACL and the 4th International Joint Conference on Natural Language Processing of the AFNLP*, ACL-IJCNLP '09, pages 396–404.

Ramesh Nallapati and Christopher D. Manning. 2008. Legal docket-entry classification: Where machine learning stumbles. In *Proceedings of the Conference on Empirical Methods in Natural Language Processing*, EMNLP '08, pages 438–446.

Patrick Pantel and Deepak Ravichandran. 2004. Automatically labeling semantic classes. In *Proceedings of the Conference of the North American Chapter of the Association for Computational Linguistics on Human Language Technologies*, HLT-NAACL '04, pages 321–328.

S. Patwardhan. 2010. *Widening the Field of View of Information Extraction through Sentential Event Recognition*. Ph.D. thesis, University of Utah, May.

Hoifung Poon and Pedro Domingos. 2010. Unsupervised ontology induction from text. In *Proceedings of the 48th Annual Meeting of the Association for Computational Linguistics*, ACL '10, pages 296–305.

Ellen Riloff. 1996. Automatically generating extraction patterns from untagged text. In *Proceedings of the 13th National Conference on Artificial Intelligence*, AAAI'96, pages 1044–1049.

Alan Ritter, Luke Zettlemoyer, Mausam, and Oren Etzioni. 2013. Modeling missing data in distant supervision for information extraction. *Transactions of the Association for Computational Linguistics*, 1:367–378.

Mark Stevenson and Mark A. Greenwood. 2005. A semantic approach to IE pattern induction. In *Proceedings of the 43rd Annual Meeting on Association for Computational Linguistics*, ACL '05, pages 379–386.

Michael Thelen and Ellen Riloff. 2002. A bootstrapping method for learning semantic lexicons using extraction pattern contexts. In *Proceedings of the Conference on Empirical Methods in Natural Language Processing*, EMNLP '02, pages 214–221.

Kristina Toutanova, Dan Klein, Christopher D. Manning, and Yoram Singer. 2003. Feature-rich part-of-speech tagging with a cyclic dependency network. In *Proceedings of the 2003 Conference of the North American Chapter of the Association for Computational Linguistics on Human Language Technology*, HLT-NAACL '03, pages 173–180.

Wei Xu, Raphael Hoffmann, Le Zhao, and Ralph Grishman. 2013. Filling knowledge base gaps for distant supervision of relation extraction. In *Proceedings of the Association for Computational Linguistics (ACL)*, pages 665–670.

Roman Yangarber, Ralph Grishman, and Pasi Tapanainen. 2000. Automatic acquisition of domain knowledge for information extraction. In *Proceedings of the 18th International Conference on Computational Linguistics*, COLING '00, pages 940–946.

Roman Yangarber, Winston Lin, and Ralph Grishman. 2002. Unsupervised learning of generalized names. In *Proceedings of the 19th International Conference on Computational Linguistics*, COLING '02.

Temporal Scoping of Relational Facts based on Wikipedia Data

Avirup Sil *
Computer and Information Sciences
Temple University
Philadelphia, PA 19122
avi@temple.edu

Silviu Cucerzan
Microsoft Research
One Microsoft Way
Redmond, WA 98052
silviu@microsoft.com

Abstract

Most previous work in information extraction from text has focused on named-entity recognition, entity linking, and relation extraction. Less attention has been paid given to extracting the temporal scope for relations between named entities; for example, the relation `president-Of`(John F. Kennedy, USA) is true only in the time-frame (January 20, 1961 - November 22, 1963). In this paper we present a system for temporal scoping of relational facts, which is trained on distant supervision based on the largest semi-structured resource available: Wikipedia. The system employs language models consisting of patterns automatically bootstrapped from Wikipedia sentences that contain the main entity of a page and slot-fillers extracted from the corresponding infoboxes. This proposed system achieves state-of-the-art results on 6 out of 7 relations on the benchmark Text Analysis Conference 2013 dataset for temporal slot filling (TSF), and outperforms the next best system in the TAC 2013 evaluation by more than 10 points.

1 Introduction

Previous work on relation extraction (Agichtein and Gravano, 2000; Etzioni et al., 2004) by systems such as NELL (Carlson et al., 2010), KnowItAll (Etzioni et al., 2004) and YAGO (Suchanek et al., 2007) have targeted the extraction of entity tuples, such as `president-Of`(George W. Bush, USA), in order to build large knowledge bases of facts. These systems assume that relational facts are time-invariant. However, this assumption is not always true, for example `president-Of`(George W. Bush, USA) holds within the time-frame (2001-2009) only. In this paper, we focus on the relatively less explored problem of attaching temporal scope to relation between entities. The Text Analysis Conference (TAC) introduced temporal slot filling (TSF) as one of the knowledge base population (KBP) tasks in 2013 (Dang and Surdeanu, 2013). The input to a TAC-TSF system is a binary relation *e.g.* `per:spouse`(Brad Pitt, Jennifer Aniston) and a document assumed to contain supporting evidence for the relation. The required output is a 4-tuple timestamp [T1, T2, T3, T4], where T1 and T2 are normalized dates that provide a range for the start date of the relation, and T3 and T4 provide the range for the end of the relationship. Systems must also output the offsets of the text mentions that support the temporal information extracted. For example, from a text such as *"Pitt married Jennifer Aniston on July 29, 2000 [...] the couple divorced five years later in 2005."*, a system must extract the normalized timestamp [2000-07-29, 2000-07-29, 2005-01-01, 2005-12-31], together with the entity and date offsets that support the timestamp.

In this paper, we describe TSRF, a system for **t**emporal **s**coping of **r**elational **f**acts. For every relation type, TSRF uses distant supervision from Wikipedia infobox tuples to learn a language model consisting of patterns of entity types, categories, and word n-grams. Then it uses this trained relation-specific language model to extract the top k sentences that support the given relation between the query entity and the slot filler. In a second stage, TSRF performs timestamp classification by employing models which learn "Start", "End" and "In" predictors of entities in a relationship; it computes the best 4-tuple timestamp [T1, T2, T3, T4] based on the confidence values associated to the top sentences extracted. Following the TAC-TSF task for 2013, TSRF is trained and evaluated for seven relation types, as shown in Table 1.

* This research was carried out during an internship at Microsoft Research.

Proceedings of the Eighteenth Conference on Computational Language Learning, pages 109–118,
Baltimore, Maryland USA, June 26-27 2014.

per:spouse
per:title
per:employee_or_member_of
org:top_employees/members
per:cities_of_residence
per:statesorprovinces_of_residence
per:countries_of_residence

Table 1: Types of relations in the TAC-TSF.

The remainder of the paper is organized as follows: The next section describes related work. Section 3 introduces the TAC-TSF input and output formats. Section 4 discusses the main challenges, and Section 5 details our method for temporal scoping of relations. Section 6 describes our experiments and results, and it is followed by concluding remarks.

2 Related Work

To our knowledge, there are only a small number of systems that have tackled the temporal scoping of relations task. YAGO (Wang et al., 2010) extracts temporal facts using regular expressions from Wikipedia infoboxes, while PRAVDA (Wang et al., 2011) uses a combination of textual patterns and graph-based re-ranking techniques to extract facts and their temporal scopes simultaneously. Both systems augment an existing KB with temporal facts similarly to the CoTS system by Talukdar et al. (2012a; 2012b). However, their underlying techniques are not applicable to arbitrary text. In contrast, TSRF automatically bootstraps patterns to learn relation-specific language models, which can be used then for processing any text. CoTS, a recent system that is part of CMU's NELL (Carlson et al., 2010) project, performs temporal scoping of relational facts by using manually edited temporal order constraints. While manual ordering is appealing and can lead to high accuracy, it is impractical from a scalability perspective. Moreover, the main goal of CoTS is to predict temporal ordering of relations rather than to scope temporally individual facts. Conversely, our system automatically extracts text patterns, and then uses them to perform temporal classification based on gradient boosted decision trees (Friedman, 2001).

The TempEval task (Pustejovsky and Verhagen, 2009) focused mainly on temporal event ordering. Systems such as (Chambers et al., 2007) and (Bethard and Martin, 2007) have been successful in extracting temporally related events. Sil et al. (2011a) automatically extract STRIPS representations (Fikes and Nilsson, 1971) from web text, which are defined as states of the world before and after an event takes place. However, all these efforts focus on temporal ordering of either events or states of the world and do not extract timestamps for events. By contrast, the proposed system extracts temporal expressions and also produces an ordering of the timestamps of relational facts between entities.

The current state-of-the-art systems for TSF have been the RPI-Blender system by Artiles et al. (2011) and the UNED system by Garrido et al. (2011; 2012). These systems obtained the top scores in the 2011 TAC TSF evaluation by outperforming the other participants such as the Stanford Distant Supervision system (Surdeanu et al., 2011). Similar to our work, these systems use distant supervision to assign temporal labels to relations extracted from text. While we employ Wikipedia infoboxes in conjunction with Wikipedia text, the RPI-Blender and UNED systems use tuples from structured repositories like Freebase. There are major differences in terms of learning strategies of these systems: the UNED system uses a rich graph-based document-level representation to generate novel features whereas RPI-Blender uses an ensemble of classifiers combining flat features based on surface text and dependency paths with tree kernels. Our system employs language models based on Wikipedia that are annotated automatically with entity tags in a boosted-trees learning framework. A less important difference between TSRF and RPI-Blender is that the latter makes use of an additional temporal label (Start-And-End) for facts within a time range; TSRF employs Start, End, and In labels.

Col.1: TEMP72211	Col.7: 1492
Col.2: per:spouse	Col.8: 1311
Col.3: Brad Pitt	Col.9: 1.0
Col.4: AFP_ENG_20081208.0592	Col.10: E0566375
Col.5: Jennifer Aniston	Col.11: E0082980
Col.6: 1098	

Table 2: Input to a TSF System.

3 The Temporal Slot Filling Task

3.1 Input

The input format for a TSF system as instantiated for the relation `per:spouse`(Brad Pitt, Jennifer

Aniston) is shown in Table 2. The field Column 1 contains a unique query ID for the relation. Column 2 is the name of the relationship, which also encodes the type of the target entity. Column 3 contains the name of the query entity, i.e., the subject of the relation. Column 4 contains a valid document ID and Column 5 indicates the slot-filler entity. Columns 6 through 8 are offsets of the slot-filler, query entity and the relationship justification in the given text. Column 9 contains a confidence score set to 1 to indicate that the relation is correct. Columns 10 and 11 contain the IDs in the KBP knowledge base of the entity and filler, respectively. All of the above are provided by TAC. For the query in this example, a TSF system has to scope temporally the `per:spouse` relation between Brad Pitt and Jennifer Aniston.

3.2 Output

Similar to the regular slot filling task in TAC, the TSF output includes the offsets for at least one entity mention and up to two temporal mentions used for the extraction and normalization of hypothesized answer. For instance, assume that a system extracts the relative timestamp "Monday" and normalizes it to "2010-10-04" for the relation `org:top_employee`(Twitter, Williams) using the document date from the following document:

```
<DOCID> AFP_ENG_20101004.0053.LDC2010T13 </DOCID>
<DATETIME> 2010-10-04 </DATETIME>
<HEADLINE>
Twitter co-founder steps down as CEO
</HEADLINE>
<TEXT>
<P>
Twitter co-founder Evan Williams announced on Monday
that he was stepping down as chief executive [...]
```

The system must report the offsets for both "Monday" in the text body and "2010-10-04" in the DATETIME block for the justification.

The TAC-TSF task uses the following representation for the temporal information extracted: For each relation provided in the input, TSF systems must produce a 4-tuple of dates: [T1, T2, T3, T4], which indicates that the relation is true for a period beginning at some point in time between T1 and T2 and ending at some time between T3 and T4. By convention, a hyphen in one of the positions implies a lack of a constraint. Thus, [-, 20120101, 20120101, -] implies that the relation was true starting on or before January 1, 2012 and ending on or after January 1, 2012. As discussed in the TAC 2011 pilot study by Ji et al. (2011), there are situations that cannot be covered by this representation, such as recurring events, for example repeated marriages between two persons. However, the most common situations for the relations covered in this task are captured correctly by this 4-tuple representation.

4 Challenges

We discuss here some of the main challenges encountered in building a temporal scoping system.

4.1 Lack of Annotated Data

Annotation of data for this task is expensive, as the human annotators must have extensive background knowledge and need to analyze the evidence in text and reliable knowledge resources. As per (Ji et al., 2013), a large team of human annotators were able to generate only 1,172 training instances for 8 slots for KBP 2011. The authors of the study concluded that such amount of data is not enough for training a supervised temporal scoping system. They also noted that only 32% of `employee_Of` queries were found to have potential temporal arguments, and only one third of the queries could have reliable start or end dates.

4.2 Date Normalization

Sometimes temporal knowledge is not stated explicitly in terms of dates or timestamps. For example, from the text "they got married on Valentine's Day" a system can extract Valentine's Day as the surface form of the start of the `per:spouse` relation. However, for a temporal scoping system it needs to normalize the temporal string to the date of February 14 and the year to which the document refers to explicitly in text or implicitly, such as the year in which the document was published.

4.3 Lexico-Syntactic Variety

A relation can be specified in text by employing numerous syntactic and lexical constructions; *e.g.* for the `per:spouse` relation the patterns "got married on [DATE]" and "vowed to spend eternity on [DATE]" have the same meaning. Additionally, entities can appear mentioned in text in various forms, different from the canonical form given as input. For instance, Figure 1 shows an example in which the input entity Bernardo Hees, which is not in Wikipedia, is mentioned three times, with two of the mentions using a shorter form (the last name of the person).

```
org:top_members_employees     America Latina Logistica / NIL     Bernardo Hees / NIL

<HEADLINE> Burger King buyer names future CEO </HEADLINE>
<DATELINE> NEW YORK 2010-09-09 13:00:29 UTC </DATELINE>
<TEXT>
<P> The investment firm buying Burger King has named Bernardo Hees, a Latin
American railroad executive, to be CEO of the company after it completes its
$3.26 billion buyout of the fast-food chain. </P>
<P> 3G Capital is naming Hees to replace John Chidsey, who will become co-
chairman after the deal closes. </P>
<P> Hees was most recently CEO of America Latina Logistica, Latin America's
largest railroad company. Alexandre Behring, managing partner at 3G Capital, was
also a prior CEO of the railroad. </P>
<P> 3G Capital is expected to begin its effort to acquire the outstanding shares
of Burger King for $24 per share by Sept. 17. </P>
</TEXT>
```

Figure 1: Example data point from the TAC TSF 2013 training set, with the annotations hypothesized by our system. The entity mentions identified by the entity linking (EL) component are shown in bold blue; those that were linked to Wikipedia are also underlined. The highlighting (blue and green) is used to show the mentions in the coreference chains identified for the two input entities, "America Latina Logistica" and "Bernardo Hees".

4.4 Inferred Meaning

A temporal scoping system also needs to learn the inter-dependence of relations, and how one event affects another. For instance, in our automatically generated training data, we learn that a `death` event specified by n-grams like "was assassinated" affects the `per:title` relation, and it indicates that the relationship ended at that point. In Figure 1, while the CEO relationships for Bernardo Hees with America Latina Logistica and Burger King are indicated by clear patterns ("was most recently CEO of" and "to be CEO of"), the temporal stamping is difficult to achieve in both cases, as there is no standard normalization for "recently" in the former, and it is relative to the completion of the `buyout` event in the latter.

4.5 Pattern Trustworthiness

A temporal scoping system should also be able to model the trustworthiness of text patterns, and even the evolution of patterns that indicate a relationship over time. For example, in current news, the birth of a child does not imply that a couple is married, although it does carry a strong signal about the marriage relationship.

5 Learning to Attach Temporal Scope

5.1 Automatically Generating Training Data

As outlined in Section 4, one of the biggest challenges of a temporal scoping system is the lack of annotated data to create a strong information extraction system. Previous work on relation extraction such as (Mintz et al., 2009) has shown that distant supervision can be highly effective in building a classifier for this purpose. Similar to supervised classification techniques, some advantages of using distant supervision are:

- It allows building classifiers with a large number of features;
- The supervision is provided intrinsically by the detailed user-contributed knowledge;
- There is no need to expand patterns iteratively.

Mintz et al. also point out that similar to unsupervised systems, distant supervision also allows:

- Using large amounts of unlabeled data such as the Web and social media;
- Employing techniques that are not sensitive to the genre of training data.

We follow the same premise as (Cucerzan, 2007; Weld et al., 2009) that the richness of the Wikipedia collection, whether semantic, lexical, syntactic, or structural, is a key enabler in redefining the state-of-the-art for many NLP and IR task. Our target is to use distant supervision from Wikipedia data to build an automatic temporal scoping system. However, for most relations, we find that Wikipedia does not indicate specific start or end dates in a structured form. In addition to this, we need our system to be able to predict whether two entities are currently in a relationship or not based on the document date as well.

Hence, in our first step, we build an automatic system which takes as input a binary relation between two entities *e.g.* `per:spouse`(Brad Pitt, Jennifer Aniston) and a number of documents. The system needs to extract highly ranked/relevant sentences, which indicate that the two entities are in the targeted relationship. The next component takes as input the top k sentences generated in the previous step and extracts temporal labels for the input relation. Note that our target is to develop algorithms that are not relation-specific but rather can work well for a multitude of relations. We elaborate on these two system components further.

5.1.1 Using Wikipedia as a Resource for Distant Supervision

Wikipedia is the largest freely available encyclopedic collection, which is built and organized as a user-contributed knowledge base (KB) of entities. The current version of the English Wikipedia contains information about 4.2 million entities. In addition to the plain text about these entities, Wikipedia also contains structured components. One of these is the *infobox*. Infoboxes contain information about a large number of relations for the target entity of the Wikipedia page, *e.g.* names of spouses, birth and death dates, residence *etc.*. Similar to structured databases, the infoboxes contain the most important/useful relations in which entities take part, while the text of Wikipedia pages contains mentions and descriptions of these relations. Because of this, Wikipedia can be seen as a knowledge repository that contains parallel structured and unstructured information about entities, and therefore, can be employed more easily than Freebase or other structured databases for building a relation extraction system. Figure 2 shows how sentences from Wikipedia can be used to train a system for the temporal slot filling task.

5.1.2 Extracting Relevant Sentences

For every relation, we extract slot-filler names from infoboxes of each Wikipedia article. We also leverage Wikipedia's rich interlinking model to automatically retrieve labeled entity mentions in text. Because the format of the text values provided by different users for the infobox attributes can vary greatly, we rely on regular expressions to extract slot-filler names from the infoboxes. For every relation targeted, we build a large set of regular expressions to extract entity names and filter out noise *e.g.* html tags, redundant text *etc.*.

To extract all occurrences of named-entities in the Wikipedia text, we relabel each Wikipedia article with Wikipedia interlinks by employing the entity linking (EL) system by Cucerzan (2012), which obtained the top scores for the EL task in successive TAC evaluations. This implementation takes into account and preserves the interlinks created by the Wikipedia contributors, and extracts all other entity mentions and links them to Wikipedia pages if possible or hypothesizes coreference chains for the mentions of entities that are not in Wikipedia. The latter are extremely important when the slot-filler for a relation is an entity that does not have a Wikipedia page, as often is the case with spouses or other family members of famous people (as shown in Figure 1 for the slot-filler Bernardo Hees).

As stated in Section 4, temporal information in text is specified in various forms. To resolve temporal mentions, we use the Stanford SUTime (Chang and Manning, 2012) *temporal tagger*. The system exhibits strong performance outperforming state-of-the-art systems like HeidelTime (Strötgen and Gertz, 2010) on the TempEval-2 Task A (Verhagen et al., 2010) in English. SUTime is a rule-based temporal tagger that employs regular expression. Its input is English text in tokenized format; its output contains annotations in the form of TIMEX3 tags. TIMEX3 is a part of the TimeML annotation language as introduced by (Pustejovsky et al., 2003) and is used to markup date and time, events, and their temporal relations in text. When processing Web text, we often encounter date expressions that contain a relative time *e.g.* "last Thursday". To resolve them to actual dates/time is a non-trivial task. However, the heuristic of employing the document's publication date as the reference works very well in practice *e.g.* for a document published on 2011-07-05, SUTime resolves "last Thursday" to 2011-06-30. It provides temporal tags in the following labels: Time, Duration, Set and Interval. For our experiments we used Time and Duration.

After running the Stanford SUTime, which automatically converts date expressions to their normalized form, we collect sets of contiguous sentences from the page that contain one mention of the targeted entity and one mention of the slot-filler, as extracted by the entity linking system. We then build a large language model by bootstrapping textual patterns supporting the relations, similar to (Agichtein and Gravano, 2000). The general intuition is that a set of sentences that mention the two entities are likely to state something about relationships in which they are.

For assigning sentences a relevance score with respect to a targeted relation, we represent the sentences in an input document (i.e., Wikipedia page) as d dimensional feature vectors, which incorporate statistics about how relevant sentences are to the relation between a query_entity q and the slot_filler z. For example, for the `per:spouse` relation, one binary feature is "does the input sentence contain the n-gram "QUERY_ENTITY got married"". Note that the various surface forms/mentions of q and z are resolved to their canonical target at this stage.

We were able to extract 61,872 tuples of query entity and slot filler relations from Wikipedia for the `per:spouse` relation. Figure 2 shows how we extract relevant sentences using slot-filler names from Wikipedia. Consider the following text (already processed by our EL system and Stanford SUTime) taken from the Wikipedia page of Tom Cruise:

> On [November 18, 2006$|_{2006-11-18}$], [Holmes$|_{Katie_Holmes}$] and [Cruise$|_{Tom_Cruise}$] were married in [Bracciano$|_{Bracciano}$] ...
>
> On [June 29, 2012$|_{2012-06-29}$], [Holmes$|_{Katie_Holmes}$] filed for divorce from [Cruise$|_{Tom_Cruise}$] after five and a half years of marriage.

Considering Tom Cruise as the query entity and his wife Katie Holmes as the slot filler for the `per:spouse` relation, we normalize the above text to the following form to extract features:

> On _DATE, SLOT_FILLER and QUERY_ENTITY were married in _LOCATION ...
>
> On _DATE, SLOT_FILLER filed for divorce from QUERY_ENTITY after five and a half years of marriage.

Our language model consists of n-grams ($n \leq 5$) like "SLOT_FILLER and QUERY_ENTITY were married", "SLOT_FILLER filed for divorce from" which provides clues for the marriage relation. These n-grams are then used as features with an implementation of a gradient boosted decision trees classifier similar to that described by (Friedman, 2001; Burges, 2010). We also use features provided by the EL system which are based on entity types and categories. We call this "relationship" classifier RELCL. The output of this step is

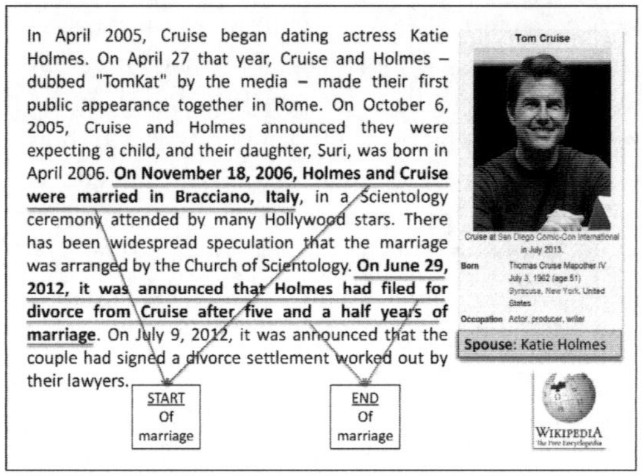

Figure 2: Example of relevant sentences extracted by using query entity and slot-filler names from Wikipedia for the `per:spouse` relation.

a ranked list of sentences which indicate whether there exists a relationship between the query entity and the slot filler.

5.1.3 Learning Algorithm

Our objective is to rank the sentences in a document based on the premise that entities q and z are in the targeted relation r. We tackle this ranking task by using gradient boosted decision trees (GBDT) to learn temporal scope for entity relations. Previous work such as Sil et al. (2011a; 2011b) used SVMs for ranking event preconditions and (Cucerzan, 2012) and (Zhou et al., 2010) employed GBDT for ranking entities. GBDT can achieve high accuracy as they can easily combine features of different scale and missing values. In our experiments, GBDT outperforms both SVMs and MaxEnt models.

We employ the stochastic version of GBDT similar to (Friedman, 2001; Burges, 2010). Basically, the model performs a numerical optimization in the function space by computing a function approximation in a sequence of steps. By building a smaller decision tree at each step, the model computes residuals obtained in the previous step. Note that in the stochastic variant of GBDT, for computing the loss function, the model absorbs several samples instead of using the whole training data. The parameters for our GBDT model were tuned on a development set sampled from our Wikipedia dump independent from the training set. These parameters include the number of regression trees and the shrinkage factor.

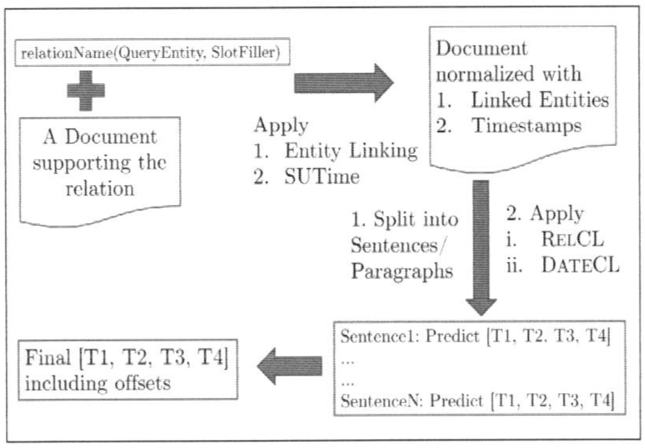

Figure 3: Architecture of the proposed system. Every input document is processed by the (Cucerzan, 2012) entity linking system and the Stanford SUTime system. Temporal information is then extracted automatically using RELCL and DATECL.

5.1.4 Gathering Relevant Sentences

On the unseen test data, we apply our trained model and obtain a score for each new sentence s that contains mentions of entities q and z that are in a targeted relationship by turning s into a feature vector as shown previously. Among all sentences that contain mentions of q and z, we choose the top k with the highest score. The value of k was tuned based on the performance of TSRF on our development set.

5.1.5 Extracting Timestamps

To predict timestamps for each relation, we build another classifier, DATECL similar to that described in the previous section, by using language models for "Start", "End" and "In" predictors of relationship. The "Start" model predicts T1, T2; "End" predicts T3, T4 and "In" predicts T2, T3.

Raw Trigger Features: Similar to previous work by (Sil et al., 2010) on using discriminative words as features, each of these models compose of "Trigger Words" that indicate when a relationship begins or ends. In the current implementation, these triggers are chosen manually from the language model automatically bootstrapped from Wikipedia. Future directions include how to automatically learn these triggers. For example, for the `per:spouse` relation, the triggers for "Start" contain n-grams such as "married since _DATE" and "married SLOT_FILLER on"; the "End" model contains n-grams such as "estranged husband QUERY_ENTITY", "split in _DATE"; the "In" model contains "happily married", "QUERY_ENTITY with his wife" *etc.*. For an input sentence with query entity q and slot-filler z, a first class of raw trigger features consists of cosine-similarity(Text(q, z), Triggers(r)) where $r \in Start, End, In$. Here, Text(q, z) indicates the full sentence as context. We also employ another feature that computes cosine-similarity(Context(q, z), Triggers(r)), which constructs a *mini-sentence* Context(q, z) from the original by choosing windows of three words before and after q and z, and ignoring duplicates.

External Event Triggers: Our system also considers the presence of other events as triggers *e.g.* a "death" event signaled by "SLOT_FILLER died" might imply that a relationship ended on that timestamp. Similarly, a "birth" event can imply that an entity started living in a particular location *e.g.* the `per:born-In`(Obama, Honolulu) relation from the sentence "President Obama was born in Honolulu in 1961" indicates that T1 = 1961-01-01 and T2 = 1961-12-31 for the relation `per:cities_of_residence`(Obama, Honolulu).

At each step, TSRF extracts the top timestamps for predicting "Start", "End" and "In" based on the confidence values of DATECL. Similar to previous work by (Artiles et al., 2011), we aggregate and update the extracted timestamps using the following heuristics:

Step 1: Initialize T= [$-\infty$, $+\infty$, $-\infty$,$+\infty$]
Step 2: Iterate through the classified timestamps
Step 3: For a new T' aggregate :
$$T\&\&T' = [max(t_1, t'_1), min(t_2, t'_2), max(t_3, t'_3), min(t_4, t'_4)]$$
Update only if: $t_1 \leq t_2$; $t_3 \leq t_4$; $t_1 \leq t_4$

This novel two-step classification strategy removes noise introduced by distant supervision training and decides if the extracted (entity, filler, timestamp) tuples belong to the relation under consideration or not. For example, for the `per:spouse` relation between the entities Brad Pitt and Jennifer Aniston, TSRF extracts sentences like "*..On November 22, 2001, Pitt made a guest appearance in the television series Friends, playing a man with a grudge against Rachel Green, played by Jennifer Aniston..*" and "*Pitt met Jennifer Aniston in 1998 and married her in a private wedding ceremony in Malibu on July 29, 2000..*". Note that both sentences contain the query entity and the slot filler. The system automatically rejects the extraction of temporal information from

	S1	S2	S3	S4	S5	S6	S7	**ALL**	StDev
Baseline	24.70	17.40	15.18	17.83	14.75	21.08	23.20	19.10	3.60
TSRF	**31.94**	**36.06**	**32.85**	**40.12**	**33.04**	**31.85**	27.35	**33.15**	3.66
RPI-Blender	31.19	13.07	14.93	26.71	29.04	17.24	**34.68**	23.42	7.98
UNED	26.20	6.88	8.16	15.24	14.47	14.41	19.34	14.79	6.07
CMU-NELL	19.95	7.46	8.47	16.52	13.43	5.65	11.95	11.53	4.77
Abby-Compreno	0.0	2.42	8.56	0.0	13.50	7.91	0.0	5.14	4.99
LDC	69.87	60.22	58.26	72.27	81.10	54.07	91.18	68.84	12.32

Table 3: Results for the TAC-TSF 2013 test set, overall and for individual slots. The slots notation is: S1: org:top members employees, S2: per:city of residence, S3: per:country of residence, S4: per:employee or member of, S5: per:spouse, S6: per:statesorprovince of residence, S7: per:title. The score for the output created by the LDC experts is also shown.

the former even though the sentence contains mentions of both entities. This is because the language model for the marriage relation does not match well this candidate sentence, which is actually focussing on the two entities being in the different relation of co-acting/appearing in the same motion picture. The latter sentence is determined as matching the language model for the marriage relation, and TSRF extracts the temporal scope July 29, 2000 and attaches the START label to it. Most previous systems do not perform this noise removal step, which is a critical component in our distant supervision approach.

6 Experiments

For evaluation, we train our system on the infobox tuples and sentences extracted from the Wikipedia dump of May 2013. We set aside a portion of the dump as our development data. We chose to use the top-relevant n-grams based on the performance on the development data as features. We employ then the TAC evaluation data, which is publicly available through LDC.

We utilize the evaluation metric developed for TAC (Dang and Surdeanu, 2013). In order for a temporal constraint (T1-T4) to be valid, the document must justify both the query relation (which is similar to the regular English slot filling task) and the temporal constraint. Since the time information provided in text may be approximate, the TAC metric measures the similarity of each constraint in the key and system response. Formally, if the date in the gold standard is k_i, while the date hypothesized by the system is r_i, and $d_i = |k_i - r_i|$ is their difference measured in years, then the score for the set of temporal constraints on a slot is computed as:

$$Score(slot) = \frac{1}{4}\sum_{i=1}^{4} \frac{c}{c + d_i}$$

TAC sets the constant c to one year, so that predictions that differ from the gold standard by one year get 50% credit. The absence of a constraint in T1 or T3 is treated as a value of $-\infty$ and the absence of a constraint in T2 or T4 is treated as $+\infty$, which lead to zero-value terms in the scoring sum. Therefore, the overall achievable score has a range between 0 and 1.

We compare TSRF against four other TSF systems: **(i)** RPI-Blender (Artiles et al., 2011), **(ii)** CMU-NELL (Talukdar et al. (2012a; 2012b)), **(iii)** UNED (Garrido et al. (2011; 2012)) and **(iv)** Abby-Compreno (Kozlova et al., 2012). Most of these systems employ distant supervision strategies too. RPI-Blender and UNED obtained the top scores in the 2011 TAC TSF pilot evaluation, and thus, could be considered as the state-of-the-art at the time.

We also compare our system with a reasonable baseline similar to (Ji et al., 2011). This baseline makes the simple assumption that the corresponding relation is valid at the document date. That means that it creates a "within" tuple as follows: $< -\infty, doc\_date, doc\_date, +\infty >$. Hence, this baseline system for a particular relation always predicts T2 = T3 = the date of the document.

Table 3 lists the results obtained by our system on the TAC test set of 201 queries, overall and for each individual slot, in conjunction with the results of the other systems evaluated and the output generated by the LDC human experts. Only two out of the five systems evaluated, TSRF and RPI-Blender, are able to beat the "within" baseline.

TSRF achieves approximately 48% of human performance (LDC) and outperforms all other sys-

	TSF Accuracy	SF F1	SF Prec	SF Recall
LDC	68.8	83.1	97.3	72.5
TSRF	**33.1**	**77.3**	**96.8**	**64.4**
RPI-Blender	23.4	51.8	69.2	41.4
UNED	14.8	46.6	69.9	35.0
CMU-NELL	11.5	32.2	38.5	27.6
Abby-Compreno	5.1	18.5	53.6	11.2

Table 4: Extraction accuracy for slot-filler mentions. TSRF clearly outperforms all systems and comes close to human performance (LDC).

tems in overall score, as well as for all individual relations with the exception of `per:title`, for which RPI-Blender obtains a better score. In fact, TSRF outperforms the next best systems by 10 and 19 points. These two systems obtained the top score in TAC 2011, and outperformed other systems such as Stanford (Surdeanu et al., 2011). TSRF also outperforms CMU-NELL which employs a very large KB of relational facts already extracted from the Web and makes use of the Google N-gram corpus (http://books.google.com/ngrams).

We believe that this large performance difference is due in part to the fact that TSRF uses a language model to clean up the noise introduced by distant supervision before the actual temporal classification step. Also, the learning algorithm employed, GBDT, is highly effective in using the extracted n-grams as features to decide whether the extracted (entity, filler, time) tuples belong to the relation under consideration or not. Finally, Table 4 shows another reason that gives TSRF an edge in obtaining the best score. The employed EL component (Cucerzan, 2012) is a state-of-the-art system for extracting and linking entities, and resolving coreference chains. By using this system, we have been able to extract slot-filler mentions with a precision of 96.8% at 66.4% recall, which is substantially higher than the extraction results of all other systems. Encouragingly, the performance of this component also comes close to that of the LDC annotators, which obtained a precision of 97.3% at 72.5% recall.

It is also important to note that our system exhibits a balanced performance on the relations on which it was tested. As shown in column StDev in Table 3, this system achieves the lowest standard deviation in the performance across the relations tested. It is interesting to note also that TSRF achieves the best performance on the `employee_of` (S4) and `city_of_residence` (S2) relations even though the system development was done on the `spouse` relation (S1) as an encouraging sign that our distant supervision algorithm can be transferred successfully across relations for domain-specific temporal scoping.

7 Conclusion and Future Work

The paper described an automatic temporal scoping system that requires no manual labeling effort. The system uses distant supervision from Wikipedia to obtain a large training set of tuples for training. It uses a novel two-step classification to remove the noise introduced by the distant supervision training. The same algorithm was employed for multiple relations and exhibited similarly high accuracy. Experimentally, the system outperforms by a large margin several other systems that address this relatively less explored problem. Future directions of development include extracting joint slot filler names and temporal information, and leveraging the changes observed over time in Wikipedia for a query entity and a slot filler in a target relation.

References

E. Agichtein and L. Gravano. 2000. Snowball: Extracting relations from large plain-text collections. In *Procs. of the Fifth ACM International Conference on Digital Libraries*.

Javier Artiles, Qi Li, Taylor Cassidy, Suzanne Tamang, and Heng Ji. 2011. CUNY BLENDER TACKBP2011 Temporal Slot Filling System Description. In *TAC*.

Steven Bethard and James H Martin. 2007. Cu-tmp: Temporal relation classification using syntactic and semantic features. In *Proceedings of the 4th International Workshop on Semantic Evaluations*, pages 129–132.

Chris Burges. 2010. From ranknet to lambdarank to lambdamart: An overview. *Learning*, 11:23–581.

Andrew Carlson, Justin Betteridge, Bryan Kisiel, Burr Settles, Estevam R Hruschka Jr, and Tom M Mitchell. 2010. Toward an architecture for never-ending language learning. In *AAAI*.

Nathanael Chambers, Shan Wang, and Dan Jurafsky. 2007. Classifying temporal relations between events. In *Proceedings of the 45th Annual Meeting of the ACL on Interactive Poster and Demonstration Sessions*, pages 173–176.

Angel X Chang and Christopher Manning. 2012. Sutime: A library for recognizing and normalizing time expressions. In *LREC*, pages 3735–3740.

Silviu Cucerzan. 2007. Large-scale named entity disambiguation based on wikipedia data. In *EMNLP-CoNLL*, pages 708–716.

Silviu Cucerzan. 2012. The MSR System for Entity Linking at TAC 2012. In *TAC*.

Hoa Trang Dang and Mihai Surdeanu. 2013. Task description for knowledge-base population at TAC 2013. In *TAC*.

O. Etzioni, M. Cafarella, D. Downey, S. Kok, A. Popescu, T. Shaked, S. Soderland, D. Weld, and A. Yates. 2004. Web-Scale Information Extraction in KnowItAll. In *WWW*, New York City, New York.

R. Fikes and N. Nilsson. 1971. STRIPS: A new approach to the application of theorem proving to problem solving. *Artificial Intelligence*, 2(3/4):189–208.

Jerome H Friedman. 2001. Greedy function approximation: a gradient boosting machine. *Annals of Statistics*, pages 1189–1232.

Guillermo Garrido, Bernardo Cabaleiro, Anselmo Penas, Alvaro Rodrigo, and Damiano Spina. 2011. A distant supervised learning system for the tac-kbp slot filling and temporal slot filling tasks. In *TAC*.

Guillermo Garrido, Anselmo Penas, Bernardo Cabaleiro, and Alvaro Rodrigo. 2012. Temporally anchored relation extraction. In *ACL*.

Heng Ji, Ralph Grishman, and Hoa Trang Dang. 2011. Overview of the tac2011 knowledge base population track. In *TAC*.

Heng Ji, Taylor Cassidy, Qi Li, and Suzanne Tamang. 2013. Tackling representation, annotation and classification challenges for temporal knowledge base population. *Knowledge and Information Systems*, pages 1–36.

Ekaterina Kozlova, Manicheva Maria, Petrova Elena, and Tatiana Popova. 2012. The compreno semantic model as an integral framework for a multilingual lexical database. In *3rd Workshop on Cognitive Aspects of the Lexicon (CogALex-III)*.

Mike Mintz, Steven Bills, Rion Snow, and Daniel Jurafsky. 2009. Distant supervision for relation extraction without labeled data. In *ACL*, pages 1003–1011.

James Pustejovsky and Marc Verhagen. 2009. Semeval-2010 task 13: evaluating events, time expressions, and temporal relations (tempeval-2). In *Proceedings of the Workshop on Semantic Evaluations: Recent Achievements and Future Directions*, pages 112–116.

James Pustejovsky, José M Castano, Robert Ingria, Roser Sauri, Robert J Gaizauskas, Andrea Setzer, Graham Katz, and Dragomir R Radev. 2003. Timeml: Robust specification of event and temporal expressions in text. *New directions in question answering*, 3:28–34.

Avirup Sil and Alexander Yates. 2011a. Extracting STRIPS representations of actions and events. In *RANLP*.

Avirup Sil and Alexander Yates. 2011b. Machine Reading between the Lines: A Simple Evaluation Framework for Extracted Knowledge Bases. In *Workshop on Information Extraction and Knowledge Acquisition (IEKA)*.

Avirup Sil, Fei Huang, and Alexander Yates. 2010. Extracting action and event semantics from web text. In *AAAI Fall Symposium on Common-Sense Knowledge (CSK)*.

Jannik Strötgen and Michael Gertz. 2010. Heideltime: High quality rule-based extraction and normalization of temporal expressions. In *Proceedings of the 5th International Workshop on Semantic Evaluation*, pages 321–324.

Fabian M Suchanek, Gjergji Kasneci, and Gerhard Weikum. 2007. Yago: a core of semantic knowledge. In *WWW*.

Mihai Surdeanu, Sonal Gupta, John Bauer, David McClosky, Angel X Chang, Valentin I Spitkovsky, and Christopher D Manning. 2011. Stanfords distantly-supervised slot-filling system. In *TAC*.

Partha Pratim Talukdar, Derry Wijaya, and Tom Mitchell. 2012a. Acquiring temporal constraints between relations. In *CIKM*.

Partha Pratim Talukdar, Derry Wijaya, and Tom Mitchell. 2012b. Coupled temporal scoping of relational facts. In *WSDM*.

Marc Verhagen, Roser Sauri, Tommaso Caselli, and James Pustejovsky. 2010. Semeval-2010 task 13: Tempeval-2. In *Proceedings of the 5th International Workshop on Semantic Evaluation*, pages 57–62.

Yafang Wang, Mingjie Zhu, Lizhen Qu, Marc Spaniol, and Gerhard Weikum. 2010. Timely yago: harvesting, querying, and visualizing temporal knowledge from wikipedia. In *Proceedings of the 13th International Conference on Extending Database Technology*, pages 697–700. ACM.

Yafang Wang, Bin Yang, Lizhen Qu, Marc Spaniol, and Gerhard Weikum. 2011. Harvesting facts from textual web sources by constrained label propagation. In *CIKM*, pages 837–846.

Daniel S. Weld, Raphael Hoffmann, and Fei Wu. 2009. Using Wikipedia to Bootstrap Open Information Extraction. In *ACM SIGMOD Record*.

Yiping Zhou, Lan Nie, Omid Rouhani-Kalleh, Flavian Vasile, and Scott Gaffney. 2010. Resolving surface forms to wikipedia topics. In *COLING*, pages 1335–1343.

Distributed Word Representation Learning for Cross-Lingual Dependency Parsing

Min Xiao and **Yuhong Guo**
Department of Computer and Information Sciences
Temple University
Philadelphia, PA 19122, USA
{minxiao,yuhong}@temple.edu

Abstract

This paper proposes to learn language-independent word representations to address cross-lingual dependency parsing, which aims to predict the dependency parsing trees for sentences in the target language by training a dependency parser with labeled sentences from a source language. We first combine all sentences from both languages to induce real-valued distributed representation of words under a deep neural network architecture, which is expected to capture semantic similarities of words not only within the same language but also across different languages. We then use the induced interlingual word representation as augmenting features to train a delexicalized dependency parser on labeled sentences in the source language and apply it to the target sentences. To investigate the effectiveness of the proposed technique, extensive experiments are conducted on cross-lingual dependency parsing tasks with nine different languages. The experimental results demonstrate the superior cross-lingual generalizability of the word representation induced by the proposed approach, comparing to alternative comparison methods.

1 Introduction

With the rapid development of linguistic resources and tools in multiple languages, it is very important to develop cross-lingual natural language processing (NLP) systems. Cross-lingual dependency parsing is the task of inferring dependency trees for observed sentences in a target language where there are few or no labeled training sentences by using a dependency parser trained on a large amount of sentences with annotated dependency trees in a source language (Durrett et al., 2012; McDonald et al., 2011; Zhao et al., 2009). Cross-lingual dependency parsing is popularly studied in natural language processing area as it can greatly reduce the expensive manual annotation effort in the target language by exploiting the dependency annotations from a source language (Durrett et al., 2012; McDonald et al., 2011; Täckström et al., 2012).

One fundamental challenge of cross-lingual dependency parsing stems from the word-level representation divergence across languages. Since sentences in different languages are expressed using different vocabularies, if we train a dependency parser on the word-level features of sentences from a source language, it will fail to parse the sentences in a different target language. A variety of work in the literature has attempted to bridge the word-level representation divergence across languages. One intuitive method delexicalizes the dependency parser by replacing the language-specific word-level features with language-independent features such as universal part-of-speech tags (Petrov et al., 2012). With the universal POS tag features, this method provides a possible way to transfer dependency parsing information from the source language to the target language and has demonstrated some good empirical results (McDonald et al., 2011). However, the number of universal POS tags is small, which limits their discriminative capacity as input features for dependency parsing. A few other works hence propose to improve the delexicalized system by learning more effective cross-lingual features such as bilingual word clusters (Täckström et al., 2012) and other interlingual representations (Durrett et al., 2012).

In this paper, we propose to address cross-lingual dependency parsing by learning distributed interlingual word representations using a deep neural network architecture. We first combine all the sentences from two language domains and

Proceedings of the Eighteenth Conference on Computational Language Learning, pages 119–129,
Baltimore, Maryland USA, June 26-27 2014.

build cross language word connections based on Wikitionary, which works as a free bilingual dictionary. Then by exploiting a deep learning architecture, we learn real-valued dense feature vectors for the words in the given sentences as the high-level interlingual representations, which capture semantic similarities across languages. Finally, we use the induced distributed word representation as augmenting features to train a delexicalized dependency parser on the annotated sentences in the source language and applied it on the sentences in the target language. In order to evaluate the proposed cross-lingual learning technique, we conduct extensive experiments on eight cross-lingual dependency parsing tasks with nine different languages. The experimental results demonstrate the efficacy of the proposed approach in transferring dependency parsers across languages, comparing to other methods.

The remainder of the paper is organized as follows. Section 2 reviews related work. Section 3 describes the main approach of cross-lingual word representation learning with deep neural networks and cross-lingual dependency parsing with induced interlingual features. Section 4 presents the empirical study on eight cross language dependency parsing tasks. We then conclude the paper in Section 5.

2 Related Work

Previous works developed in the literature have tackled cross-lingual dependency parsing by using cross-lingual annotation projection methods, multilingual model learning methods, and cross-lingual representation learning methods.

Cross-lingual annotation projection methods use parallel sentences to project the annotations from the source language side to the target language side and then train dependency parsers on the target data with projected annotations (Hwa et al., 2005; Liu et al., 2013; Smith and Eisner, 2009; Zhao et al., 2009). For cross-lingual annotation projection methods, both the word alignment training step and the annotation projection step can introduce errors or noise. Thus much work developed in the literature has focused on designing robust projection algorithms such as graph-based projection with label propagations (Das and Petrov, 2011), improving projection performance by using auxiliary resources such as Wikipedia metadata (Kim and Lee, 2012) or WordNet (Khapra et al., 2010), or boosting projection performance by heuristically modifying or correcting the projected annotations (Hwa et al., 2005; Kim et al., 2010). Some work has also proposed to project the discrete dependency arc instances instead of treebank as the training set (Liu et al., 2013). Moreover, besides cross-lingual dependency parsing, cross-lingual annotation projection methods have also demonstrated success in various other sequence labeling tasks including POS tagging (Das and Petrov, 2011; Yarowsky and Ngai, 2001), relation extraction (Kim et al., 2012), named entity recognition (Kim et al., 2010; Kim and Lee, 2012), constituent syntax parsing (Jiang et al., 2011), and word sense disambiguation (Khapra et al., 2010).

Multilingual model learning methods train cross-lingual dependency parsers with parameter constraints obtained from parallel data (Liu et al., 2013; Ganchev et al., 2009) or linguistic knowledges (Naseem et al., 2010; Naseem et al., 2012). Among these methods, some proposed to train a joint dependency parsing system with parameters shared across the dependency parsing models in individual languages (Liu et al., 2013). Other works used posterior regularization techniques to encode the linguistic constraints in learning dependency parsing models (Ganchev et al., 2009; Naseem et al., 2010; Naseem et al., 2012). The linguistic constraints may either come from manually constructed universal dependency parsing rules (Naseem et al., 2010) or manually specified typological features (Naseem et al., 2012), or be learned from parallel sentences (Ganchev et al., 2009). Besides cross-lingual dependency parsing, multilingual model learning methods have also achieved good empirical results for other multilingual NLP tasks, including named entity recognition (Burkett et al., 2010; Che et al., 2013; Wang and Manning, 2014), syntactic parsing (Burkett et al., 2010), semantic role labeling (Zhuang and Zong, 2010; Kozhevnikov and Titov, 2012), and word sense disambiguation (Guo and Diab, 2010).

Cross-lingual representation learning methods induce language-independent features to bridge the cross-lingual difference in the original word-level representation space and build connections across different languages. They train a dependency parser in the induced representation space by exploiting labeled data from the source language and apply it in the target language (Durrett et al., 2012; Täckström et al., 2012; Zhang et al., 2012). A variety of auxiliary resources have been used to induce interlingual features, including bilingual lexicon (Durrett et al., 2012), and unlabeled parallel sentences (Täckström et al., 2013). Based on different learning mechanisms (whether or not using labeled data) for inducing language-independent features, cross-lingual representation learning methods can be categorized into unsupervised representation learning (Täckström et al., 2013) and supervised representation learning (Durrett et al., 2012). The language-independent features include bilingual word clusters (Täckström et al., 2012), language-independent projection features (Durrett et al., 2012), and automatically induced language-independent POS tags (Zhang et al., 2012). Besides cross-lingual dependency parsing, in the literature cross-lingual representation learning methods have also demonstrated efficacy in different NLP applications such as cross language named entity recognition (Täckström et al., 2012) and cross language semantic role labeling (Titov and Klementiev, 2012). Our work shares similarity with these cross-lingual representation learning methods on inducing new language-independent features, but differs from them in that we learn cross-lingual word embeddings. Though multilingual word embeddings have been employed in the literature, they are developed for other NLP tasks such as cross-lingual sentiment analysis (Klementiev et al., 2012), and machine translation (Zou et al., 2013). Moreover, the method in (Klementiev et al., 2012) requires parallel sentences with observed word-level alignments, and the method in (Zou et al., 2013) first learns language-specific word embeddings in each language separately and then transforms representations from one language to another language with machine translation alignments, while we jointly learn cross-lingual word embeddings in the two languages by only exploiting a small set of bilingual word pairs.

From the perspective of applying deep networks in natural language processing systems, there are a number of works in the literature (Collobert and Weston, 2008; Collobert et al., 2011; Henderson, 2004; Socher et al., 2011; Titov and Henderson, 2010; Turian et al., 2010). Socher et al. (2011) applied recursive autoencoders to address sentence-level sentiment classification problems. Collobert and Weston (2008) and Collobert et al. (2011) employed a deep learning framework for jointly multi-task learning and empirically evaluated it with four NLP tasks, including part-of-speech tagging, chunking, named entity recognition, and semantic role labeling. Henderson (2004) proposed discriminative training methods for learning a neural network statistical parser. Titov and Henderson (2010) extended the incremental sigmoid Belief networks (Titov and Henderson, 2007) to a generative latent variable model for dependency parsing. Turian et al. (2010) employed neural networks to induce word representations for sequence labeling tasks such as named entity recognition.

3 Cross-Lingual Dependency Parsing with Word Representation Learning

In this work, we aim to tackle cross-lingual dependency parsing by learning language-independent distributed word representations with deep neural networks. We first build connections across languages using free bilingual dictionaries. Then we introduce the deep neural network framework for cross-lingual word representation learning and describe how to employ the induced dense word embeddings for cross-lingual dependency parsing.

3.1 Building Cross Language Connections

To induce cross-lingual word representations, we first need to build connections between the source and target languages. In this work, we produce such connections by finding cross-lingual word pairs using the Wikitionary[1], which works as free bilingual dictionaries between language pairs.

Specifically, we first constructed a source language dictionary with all words that appeared in the sentences from the source language domain and translate these words to the target language using the Wikitionary. Then we filtered the produced word-to-word translations by dropping the ones where either the same source language word has multiple different word translations in the target language or the same target language word corresponds to multiple different source language words. We further dropped the word pairs where the translated word in the target language does not appear in the given sentences in the target language domain. After the processing, we have a set of one-to-one bilingual word pairs to build connections between the two language domains. Finally, we built a unified bilingual vocabulary V

[1] http://en.wikitionary.org

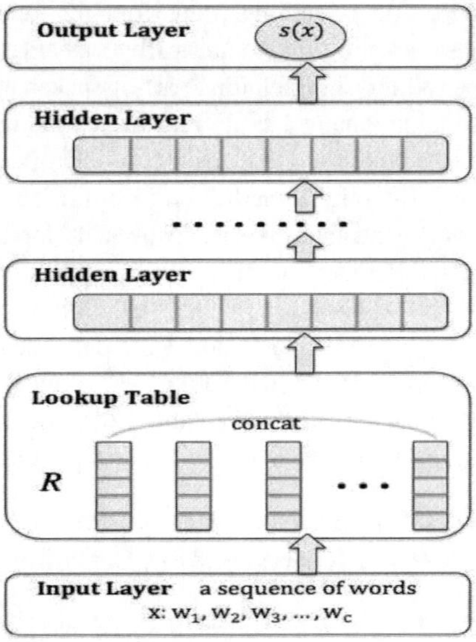

Figure 1: The architecture of the deep neural network for learning cross-lingual word representations. Each word w_i from the training sample $\mathbf{x}$ is mapped to an interlingual representation vector $R(w_i)$ through the embedding matrix R.

with words from all sentences of the two language domains. For each one-to-one bilingual word pair we constructed, we assume the two words have equivalent semantic meaning and map them to the same entry in V. Next we will learn a distributed vector representation for each entry of the bilingual vocabulary V using deep neural networks. By sharing the same representation vectors, the constructed bilingual word pairs will serve as the bridge across languages.

3.2 Interlingual Word Representation Learning with Deep Neural Networks

Given the constructed bilingual vocabulary V with v entries, we will learn a latent word embedding matrix $R \in \mathbb{R}^{k\times v}$ over the sentences in the two language domains by using a deep neural network model. This embedding matrix will map each word w in the vocabulary V into a real valued representation vector $R(w)$ with length k. For each bilingual pair of words that are mapped into the same entry of V, they will be mapped into the same vector in R as well. Following the strategy of (Collobert et al., 2011), we construct a simple two-class classification problem over the given sentences. We use the sub-sentences with fixed window size c constructed from the given sentences in the two language domains as positive samples and construct the negative samples by replacing the middle word of each positive sub-sentence with a random word from V. We then train a deep neural network for this two-class classification problem, while simultaneously learning the latent embedding matrix R.

The deep neural network architecture is given in Figure 1. The bottom layer of the deep architecture is the input layer, which takes a sequence of word tokens, $\mathbf{x} = w_1, w_2, \ldots, w_c$, with a fixed window size c as the input instance. Then we map each word w_i in this sequence to an embedding vector $R(w_i)$ by treating the bilingual embedding matrix R as a look-up table. The embedding vectors of the sequence of words $\mathbf{x}$ will be concatenated into a long vector $R(\mathbf{x}) \in \mathbb{R}^{ck}$ such that

$$R(\mathbf{x}) = [R(w_1); R(w_2); \ldots; R(w_c)]. \quad (1)$$

$R(\mathbf{x})$ will then be used as input for the hidden layer above it. The deep neural network has multiple hidden layers. The first hidden layer applies a nonlinear hyperbolic tangent activation function over the linear transformation of its input vector $R(\mathbf{x})$, such that

$$H_1(\mathbf{x}) = \tanh\left(W_1 \times R(\mathbf{x}) + \mathbf{b}_1\right) \quad (2)$$

where $W_1 \in \mathbb{R}^{h_1\times ck}$ is the weight parameter matrix, $\mathbf{b}_1 \in \mathbb{R}^{h_1}$ is the bias parameter vector, $H_1(\mathbf{x}) \in \mathbb{R}^{h_1}$ is the output vector, and h_1 is the number of hidden units in the first hidden layer. Similarly, each of the other hidden layers takes the previous layer's output as its input and performs a nonlinear transformation to produce an output vector. For example, for the i-th hidden layer, we used $H_{i-1}(\mathbf{x})$ as its input and $H_i(\mathbf{x})$ as its output such that

$$H_i(\mathbf{x}) = \tanh\left(W_i \times H_{i-1}(\mathbf{x}) + \mathbf{b}_i\right) \quad (3)$$

where $W_i \in \mathbb{R}^{h_i\times h_{i-1}}$ is the weight parameter matrix and $\mathbf{b}_i$ is the bias parameter vector for the i-th hidden layer; h_i denotes the number of hidden units of the i-th hidden layer.

Given t hidden layers, the output representation of the last layer will then be used to generate a final score value for the prediction task, such that

$$s(\mathbf{x}) = \theta \times H_t(\mathbf{x}) + u \quad (4)$$

where $\theta \in \mathbb{R}^{h_t}$ is the weight parameter vector and u is the bias parameter for the output layer.

In summary, the model parameters of the deep neural network architecture include the look-up table R, the parameters $\{W_i, \mathbf{b}_i\}_{i=1}^t$ for the hidden layers, and the output layer parameters (θ, u).

3.3 The Training Procedure

The model parameters of the deep network architecture are learned by training a two-class classification model over the the constructed positive and negative samples. Let $D = \{\mathbf{x}_i, \hat{\mathbf{x}}_i\}_{i=1}^N$ denote the constructed training set, where $\mathbf{x}_i$ is a positive sample and $\hat{\mathbf{x}}_i$ is a negative sample constructed by replacing the middle word of $\mathbf{x}_i$ with a random word from V. It is desirable for the model to produce an output score $s(\mathbf{x}_i)$ that is much larger than the score $s(\hat{\mathbf{x}}_i)$ for each pair of training instances. Thus we perform training to maximize the separation margins between the pairs of scores over positive and negative samples under a hinge loss; that is we minimize the following training loss

$$J(D) = \frac{1}{N}\sum_{i=1}^{N} \max(0, 1 - s(\mathbf{x}_i) + s(\hat{\mathbf{x}}_i)) \quad (5)$$

We perform a random initialization over the look-up table and weight model parameters, and set all the bias model parameters to zeros. Then we use a stochastic gradient descent (Bottou, 1991) algorithm to perform optimization.

3.4 Cross-Lingual Dependency Parsing

The training of deep network model above will produce a word embedding matrix R for all words in the two language domains. Moreover, by having each translated bilingual pair of words sharing the same representation vector in R in the training process, the embedding matrix R is expected to capture consistent and comparable semantic meanings across languages, and provide a language-independent and distributed representation for each word in the bilingual dictionary V.

Given R, for each sentence $\mathbf{x} = w_1, w_2, \ldots, w_n$ from the two language domains, we retrieved the representation vector $R(w_i)$ for each word w_i. Moreover, we further delexicalized the sentence by replacing the sequence of language-specific words with a sequence of universal POS tags (Petrov et al., 2012). Finally we train a delexicalized dependency parser on the labeled sentences in the source language based on the universal POS tag features and the learned distributed features. and apply it to perform dependency parsing on the sentences in the target language domain.

4 Experiments

We empirically evaluated the proposed cross-lingual word representation learning for cross-lingual dependency parsing. In this section, we present the experimental setup and the results.

4.1 Dataset

We used the dataset from the CoNLL shared task (Buchholz and Marsi, 2006; Nivre et al., 2007) for cross-lingual dependency parsing. We conducted experiments with the following nine languages: English (EN), Danish (DA), German (DE), Greek (EL), Spanish (ES), Italian (IT), Dutch (NL), Portuguese (PT) and Swedish (SV). For each language, there is a separate training set and a test set. We used English, which usually has more labeled resources, as the source language, while treating the others as target languages. We thus constructed eight cross-lingual dependency parsing tasks (EN2DA, EN2DE, EN2EL, EN2ES, EN2IT, EN2NL, EN2PT, EN2SV), one for each of the eight target languages. For example, the task *EN2DA* means that we used Danish (DA) as the target language while using *English (EN)* as the source language. For each cross language dependency parsing task, we first performed representation learning and then conducted dependency parsing training and test.

In this dataset, each sentence is labeled with gold standard part-of-speech tags. To produce delexicalized cross-lingual dependency parsers, we mapped these language-specific part-of-speech tags into twelve universal POS tags (Petrov et al., 2012): ADJ (adjectives), ADP (prepositions or postpositions), ADV (adverbs), CONJ (conjunctions), DET (determiners), NOUN (nouns), NUM (numerals), PRON (pronouns), PRT (particles), PUNC (punctuation marks), VERB (verbs) and X (for others).

4.2 Representation Learning

For each language pair, we produced a set of one-to-one bilingual word pairs using Wikitionary to build cross language connections. The numbers of bilingual word pairs produced for all the eight language pairs and the numbers of words in each language are given in Table 1.

Table 1: The number of words in each language and the number of selected bilingual word pairs for each of the eight language pairs.

Language Pairs	# Source Words	# Target Words	# Bilingual Word Pairs
English vs Danish	26599	17934	1140
English vs Dutch	26599	27829	2976
English vs German	26599	69336	1905
English vs Greek	26599	13318	869
English vs Italian	26599	13523	2347
English vs Portuguese	26599	27782	2408
English vs Spanish	26599	16465	2910
English vs Swedish	26599	19072	1779

Table 2: The feature templates used for the cross-lingual dependency parsing. dir denotes the direction of the dependency relationship, which has two values $\{left, right\}$. $dist$ denotes the distance between the head word and the dependent word, which has five values {1, 2, 3-5, 6-10, 11+}.

Feature Template	Feature Description
$UPOS(w_h)$	the head word's universal POS tag
$UPOS(w_d)$	the dependent word's universal POS tag
$UPOS(w_h, w_d)$	the universal POS tag pair of the head and dependent word
$R(w_h)$	the head word's distributed representation
$R(w_d)$	the dependent word's distributed representation
$dir\&UPOS$	conjunction features related to the dependency direction
$dist\&UPOS$	conjunction features related to the dependency distance
$dir\&dist\&UPOS$	conjunction features related to the dependency direction and distance

To perform distributed cross-lingual representation learning using the proposed deep network architecture, we first constructed the two-class training dataset from all the sentences (training and test sentences) of the two language domains. This requires the creation of sub-sentences with fixed window size c from the given sentences. We used window size $c = 5$ in the experiments. For example, for a given sentence "I visited New York ." , we can produce a number of sub-sentences, including "<PAD> <S> I visited New", "<S> I visited New York", "I visited New York .", "visited New York . </S>", and "New York . </S> <PAD>", where <PAD> is special token to fill the length requirement. Negative samples are constructed by simply replace the middle word of each sub-sentence with a random word.

With the constructed training data, we then performed training over the deep neural network. We used 3 hidden layers with 100 hidden units in each layer, considering the model capacity and the training effort. The dimension k of the embedding word vectors in R is set as 200.

4.3 Cross-lingual Dependency Parsing

We used the MSTParser (McDonald et al., 2005a; McDonald et al., 2005b) as the basic dependency parsing model. MSTParser uses spanning tree algorithms to seek for the candidate dependency trees and employs an online large margin training optimization algorithm. MSTParser is widely used in the literature for dependency parsing tasks and has demonstrated good empirical results in the CoNLL shared tasks on multilingual dependency parsing (Buchholz and Marsi, 2006; Nivre et al., 2007). For this dependency parsing model, there are a few parameters to be set: the number of maximum iterations for the perceptron training, and the number of best-k dependency tree candidates. We set the number of iterations to be 10 and only considered the best-1 dependency tree candidate.

For the proposed cross-lingual dependency parsing approach, we used both the delexi-

Table 3: Test performance in terms of UAS (unlabeled attachment score) on the eight cross-lingual dependency parsing tasks. Δ denotes the improvements of each method over the *Baseline* method.

Tasks	Baseline	Proj	Δ	Proposed	Δ	X-lingual
EN2DA	36.53	41.25	4.72	42.56	6.03	38.70
EN2DE	46.24	49.15	2.91	49.54	3.30	50.70
EN2EL	61.53	62.36	0.83	62.96	1.43	63.00
EN2ES	52.05	54.54	2.49	55.72	3.67	62.90
EN2IT	56.37	57.71	1.34	59.05	2.68	68.80
EN2NL	61.96	64.41	2.45	65.13	3.17	54.30
EN2PT	68.68	71.47	2.79	72.38	3.70	71.00
EN2SV	57.79	60.99	3.20	61.88	4.09	56.90
Average	55.14	57.74	2.60	58.90	3.51	58.29

calized universal POS tag based features and the language-independent word features produced from the deep learning as input features for the MSTParser. The set of universal POS tag based feature templates is given in Table 2. For each dependency relationship between a head word w_h and a dependent word w_d, a set of features can be produced from the feature templates in Table 2, which can be further augmented by $R(w_h)$ and $R(w_d)$. We compared our proposed approach (*Proposed*) with three other methods, *Baseline, Proj* and *X-lingual*. The *Baseline* method uses a delexicalized MSTParser based only on the universal POS tag features. The *Proj* method is developed in (Durrett et al., 2012), which uses a bilingual dictionary to learn cross-lingual features and then uses them as augmenting features to train a delexicalized MSTParser. The *X-lingual* method uses unlabeled parallel sentences to learn cross-lingual word clusters and used them as augmenting features to train a delexicalized MSTParser (Täckström et al., 2012). All parsers except *X-lingual* are trained on the labeled sentences in the source language domain and tested on the test sentences in the target language domain in the given dataset. The performance is measured using the standard unlabeled attachment score (UAS). The *X-lingual* method uses different auxiliary resources (parallel sentences), and we hence directly cited the results reported in (Täckström et al., 2012) on the same dataset.

4.4 Results and Discussions

We reported the empirical comparison results in terms of unlabeled attachment score (UAS) in Table 3. We can see that the *Baseline* method performs poorly across all the tasks. The average unlabeled attachment score for this approach across all the eight tasks is very low (about 55.14), which suggests that the twelve universal POS tags are far from enough to produce a good cross-lingual dependency parser. Considering the small number of universal POS tags, its limited discriminative capacity as input features for dependency parsing is understandable. To further verify this, we calculated the percentage of sentences in the test data which share the same sequence of universal POS tags with a training sentence in the source language but have different dependency parsing structures. The values for the eight tasks are presented in Table 4. The non-trivial values reported verified the universal POS tags' drawback on lacking discriminative capacity.

Table 4: Statistic differences. For each task, we report the percentage of sentences in the test data from the target language which share the same sequence of universal POS tags with some sentences in the source language but with different dependency trees.

Target Language	Sentence Difference
Danish	0.31%
Dutch	1.81%
German	1.40%
Greek	1.20%
Italian	2.40%
Portuguese	1.04%
Spanish	0.97%
Swedish	2.31%

By *relexicalizing* the delexicalized MSTParser

via augmenting the POS tag sequences with learned interlingual features, both the *Proj* method and the proposed method overcome the drawback of using solely universal POS tags and produce significant improvements over the *Baseline* method across all the tasks. Moreover, the proposed method consistently outperforms both *Baseline* and *Proj* for all the eight tasks. By exploiting only free bilingual dictionaries, the proposed method achieves similar average performance to the *X-lingual* method which requires additional parallel sentences. All these results demonstrated the efficacy of our word representation learning method for cross-lingual dependency parsing.

4.5 Impact of Labeled Training Data in Target Language

In the experiments above, all the labeled sentences for dependency parsing training are from the source language. We wonder how much benefit we can get if there are a small number of labeled sentences in the target language as well. To answer this question, we conducted experiments by using a small number (ℓ_t) of labeled sentences in the target language domain together with the labeled sentences in the source language domain to train cross-lingual dependency parsers. Again the performance of the parsers are evaluated on the test sentences in the target language. We tested a few different ℓ_t values with $\ell_t \in \{500, 1000, 1500\}$. We reported the unlabeled attachment score for all the eight cross-lingual dependency parsing tasks in Figure 2. We can see that the *Baseline* method still performs poorly across the range of different setting for all the eight tasks. The *Proj* method and the proposed method again consistently outperform the baseline method across all the tasks, while the proposed method achieves the best results across all the eight tasks.

4.6 Impact of the Number of Bilingual Word Pairs

For the eight language pairs, we have reported the numbers of words in each language domain and the numbers of selected bilingual word pairs in Table 1. Next we investigated how the number of word pairs affects the performance of the proposed cross-lingual dependency parsing. With the selected full set of bilingual word pairs in Table 1, we random selected $m\%$ of them with $m \in \{50, 75, 100\}$ to conduct experiments. Note when $m = 50$, we only used 435 word pairs for the EN2EL (English vs. Greek) task, which is 1.6% of the number of source words and 3.3% of the number of target words. The results are reported in Figure 3. We can see that by reducing the number of bilingual word pairs, the performance of the proposed cross-lingual dependency parsing method degrades on all tasks. This is reasonable since the word pairs serve as the pivots for learning cross-lingual word embeddings. Nevertheless, by preserving 75% of the selected word pairs, the proposed approach can still outperform the *Proj* method across all the tasks. Even with only 50% of the word pairs, our method still outperforms the *Proj* method on most tasks. These results suggest that the proposed cross-lingual word embedding method only requires a reasonable amount of bilingual word pairs to effectively transfer a dependency parser from the source language to the target language.

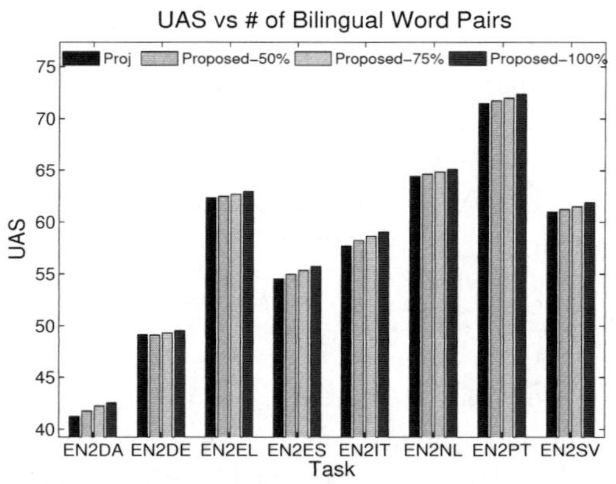

Figure 3: Test performance in terms of UAS (unlabeled attachment score) in the target language with different numbers of bilingual word pairs.

5 Conclusion

In this paper, we proposed to automatically learn language-independent features within a deep neural network architecture to address cross-lingual dependency parsing problems. We first constructed a set of bilingual word pairs with Wiktionary, which serve as the pivots in the bilingual vocabulary for building connections across languages. We then conducted distributed word representation learning by training a constructed auxiliary classifier using deep neural networks, which induced a real-valued embedding vector for each word of the bilingual vocabulary to capture con-

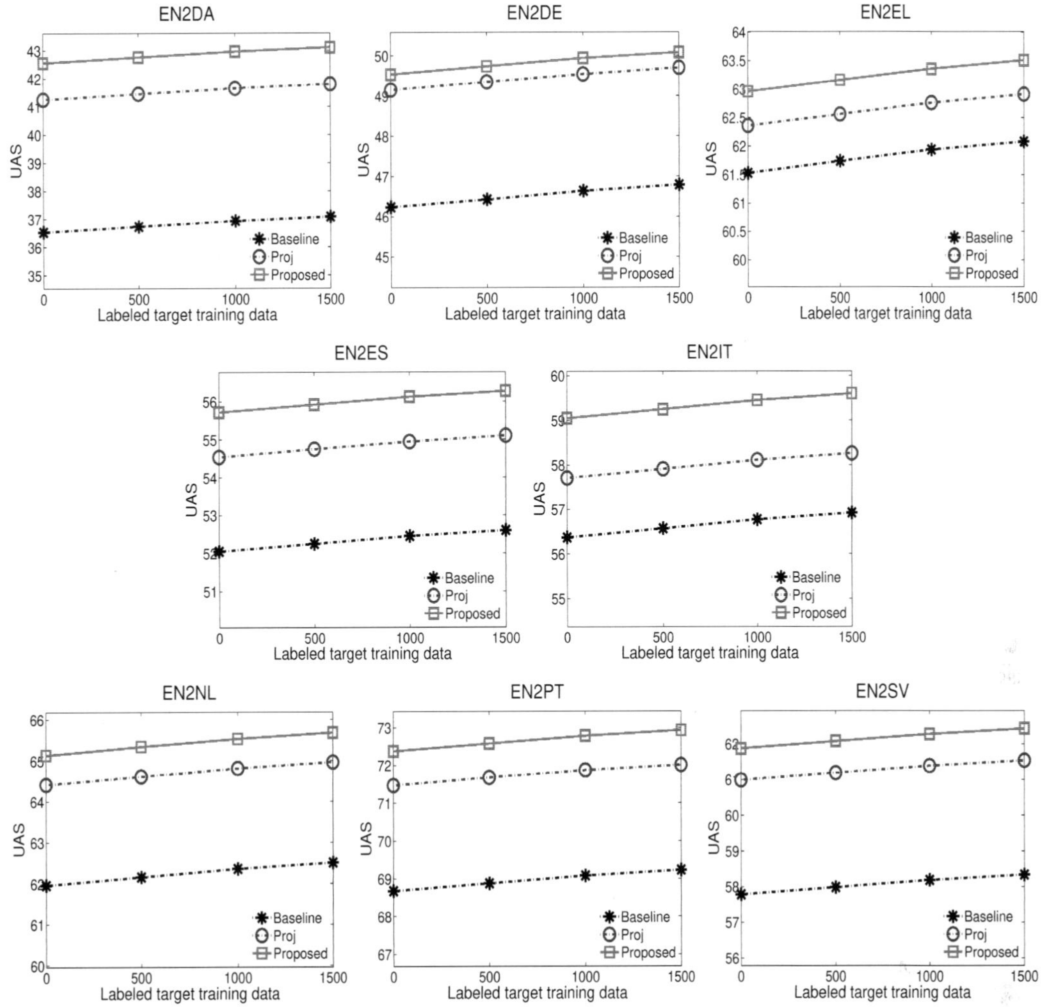

Figure 2: Unlabeled attachment score (UAS) on the test sentences in the target language by using different number of additional labeled training sentences in the target language.

sistent semantic similarities for words in the two language domains. The distributed word embedding vectors were then used to augment the universal POS tags to train cross-lingual dependency parsers. We empirically evaluated the proposed method on eight cross-lingual dependency parsing tasks between eight language pairs. The experimental results demonstrated the effectiveness of the proposed method, comparing to other cross-lingual dependency parsing methods.

References

L. Bottou. 1991. Stochastic gradient learning in neural networks. In *Proceedings of Neuro-Nîmes*.

S. Buchholz and E. Marsi. 2006. Conll-x shared task on multilingual dependency parsing. In *Proceedings of the Conference on Computational Natural Language Learning (CoNLL)*.

D. Burkett, S. Petrov, J. Blitzer, and D. Klein. 2010. Learning better monolingual models with unannotated bilingual text. In *Proceedings of the Conference on Computational Natural Language Learning (CoNLL)*.

W. Che, M. Wang, C. Manning, and T. Liu. 2013. Named entity recognition with bilingual constraints. In *Proceedings of Conference of the North American Chapter of the Association for Computational Linguistics: Human Language Technologies (NAACL)*.

R. Collobert and J. Weston. 2008. A unified architecture for natural language processing: Deep neural networks with multitask learning. In *Proceedings of the International Conference on Machine Learning (ICML)*.

R. Collobert, J. Weston, L. Bottou, M. Karlen, K. Kavukcuoglu, and P. Kuksa. 2011. Natural language processing (almost) from scratch. *Journal of Machine Learning Research (JMLR)*, 12:2493–2537.

D. Das and S. Petrov. 2011. Unsupervised part-of-speech tagging with bilingual graph-based projections. In *Proceedings of the Annual Meeting of the Association for Computational Linguistics: Human Language Technologies (ACL)*.

G. Durrett, A. Pauls, and D. Klein. 2012. Syntactic transfer using a bilingual lexicon. In *Proceedings of the Joint Conference on Empirical Methods in Natural Language Processing and Computational Natural Language Learning (EMNLP-CoNLL)*.

K. Ganchev, J. Gillenwater, and B. Taskar. 2009. Dependency grammar induction via bitext projection constraints. In *Proceedings of the Joint Conference of the Annual Meeting of the ACL and the International Joint Conference on Natural Language Processing of the AFNLP (ACL-IJCNLP)*.

W. Guo and M. Diab. 2010. Combining orthogonal monolingual and multilingual sources of evidence for all words wsd. In *Proceedings of the Annual Meeting of the Association for Computational Linguistics (ACL)*.

J. Henderson. 2004. Discriminative training of a neural network statistical parser. In *Proceedings of the Annual Meeting of the Association for Computational Linguistics (ACL)*.

R. Hwa, P. Resnik, A. Weinberg, C. Cabezas, and O. Kolak. 2005. Bootstrapping parsers via syntactic projection across parallel texts. *Natural Language Engineering*, 11:11–311.

W. Jiang, Q. Liu, and Y. Lü. 2011. Relaxed cross-lingual projection of constituent syntax. In *Proceedings of the Conference on Empirical Methods in Natural Language Processing (EMNLP)*.

M. Khapra, S. Sohoney, A. Kulkarni, and P. Bhattacharyya. 2010. Value for money: Balancing annotation effort, lexicon building and accuracy for multilingual wsd. In *Proceedings of the International Conference on Computational Linguistics (COLING)*.

S. Kim and G. Lee. 2012. A graph-based cross-lingual projection approach for weakly supervised relation extraction. In *Proceedings of the Annual Meeting of the Association for Computational Linguistics (ACL)*.

S. Kim, M. Jeong, J. Lee, and G. Lee. 2010. A cross-lingual annotation projection approach for relation detection. In *Proceedings of the International Conference on Computational Linguistics (COLING)*.

S. Kim, K. Toutanova, and H. Yu. 2012. Multilingual named entity recognition using parallel data and metadata from wikipedia. In *Proceedings of the Annual Meeting of the Association for Computational Linguistics (ACL)*.

A. Klementiev, I. Titov, and B. Bhattarai. 2012. Inducing crosslingual distributed representations of words. In *Proceedings of the International Conference on Computational Linguistics (COLING)*.

M. Kozhevnikov and I. Titov. 2012. Cross-lingual bootstrapping for semantic role labeling. In *Proceedings of the NIPS Workshop on Crosslingual Technologies (XLITE)*.

K. Liu, Y. Lü, W. Jiang, and Q. Liu. 2013. Bilingually-guided monolingual dependency parsing grammar induction. In *Proceedings of the Conference on Annual Meeting of the Association for Computational Linguistics (ACL)*.

R. McDonald, K. Crammer, and F. Pereira. 2005a. Online large-margin training of dependency parsers. In *Proceedings of the Annual Meeting on Association for Computational Linguistics (ACL)*.

R. McDonald, F. Pereira, K. Ribarov, and J. Hajič. 2005b. Non-projective dependency parsing using spanning tree algorithms. In *Proceedings of the Conference on Human Language Technology and Empirical Methods in Natural Language Processing (HLT-EMNLP)*.

R. McDonald, S. Petrov, and K. Hall. 2011. Multi-source transfer of delexicalized dependency parsers. In *Proceedings of the Conference on Empirical Methods in Natural Language Processing (EMNLP)*.

T. Naseem, H. Chen, R. Barzilay, and M. Johnson. 2010. Using universal linguistic knowledge to guide grammar induction. In *Proceedings of the Conference on Empirical Methods in Natural Language Processing (EMNLP)*.

T. Naseem, R. Barzilay, and A. Globerson. 2012. Selective sharing for multilingual dependency parsing. In *Proceedings of the Annual Meeting of the Association for Computational Linguistics (ACL)*.

J. Nivre, J. Hall, S. Kübler, R. McDonald, J. Nilsson, S. Riedel, and D. Yuret. 2007. The conll 2007 shared task on dependency parsing. In *Proceedings of the Joint Conference on Empirical Methods in Natural Language Processing and Computational Natural Language Learning (EMNLP-CoNLL)*.

S. Petrov, D. Das, and R. McDonald. 2012. A universal part-of-speech tagset. In *Proceedings of the International Conference on Language Resources and Evaluation (LREC)*.

D. Smith and J. Eisner. 2009. Parser adaptation and projection with quasi-synchronous grammar features. In *Proceedings of the Conference on Empirical Methods in Natural Language Processing (EMNLP)*.

R. Socher, J. Pennington, E. Huang, A. Ng, and C. Manning. 2011. Semi-supervised recursive autoencoders for predicting sentiment distributions. In *Proceedings of the Conference on Empirical Methods in Natural Language Processing (EMNLP)*.

O. Täckström, R. McDonald, and J. Uszkoreit. 2012. Cross-lingual word clusters for direct transfer of linguistic structure. In *Proceedings of the Conference of the North American Chapter of the Association for Computational Linguistics: Human Language Technologies (NAACL)*.

O. Täckström, R. McDonald, and J. Nivre. 2013. Target language adaptation of discriminative transfer parsers. In *Proceedings of the Conference of the North American Chapter of the Association for Computational Linguistics: Human Language Technologies (NAACL)*.

I. Titov and J. Henderson. 2007. Constituent parsing with incremental sigmoid belief networks. In *Proceedings of the Annual Meeting of the Association for Computational Linguistics (ACL)*.

I. Titov and J. Henderson. 2010. A latent variable model for generative dependency parsing. In *Proceedings of the International Conference on Parsing Technology (IWPT)*.

I. Titov and A. Klementiev. 2012. Crosslingual induction of semantic roles. In *Proceedings of the Annual Meeting of the Association for Computational Linguistics (ACL)*.

J. Turian, L. Ratinov, and Y. Bengio. 2010. Word representations: a simple and general method for semi-supervised learning. In *Proceedings of the Annual Meeting of the Association for Computational Linguistics (ACL)*.

M. Wang and C. Manning. 2014. Cross-lingual pseudo-projected expectation regularization for weakly supervised learning. *Transactions of the Association for Computational Linguistics (TACL)*, 2:55–66.

D. Yarowsky and G. Ngai. 2001. Inducing multilingual pos taggers and np bracketers via robust projection across aligned corpora. In *Proceedings of the Meeting of the North American Chapter of the Association for Computational Linguistics on Language Technologies (NAACL)*.

Y. Zhang, R. Reichart, R. Barzilay, and A. Globerson. 2012. Learning to map into a universal pos tagset. In *Proceedings of the Joint Conference on Empirical Methods in Natural Language Processing and Computational Natural Language Learning (EMNLP-CoNLL)*.

H. Zhao, Y. Song, C. Kit, and G. Zhou. 2009. Cross language dependency parsing using a bilingual lexicon. In *Proceedings of the Joint Conference of the Annual Meeting of the ACL and the International Joint Conference on Natural Language Processing of the AFNLP (ACL-IJCNLP)*.

T. Zhuang and C. Zong. 2010. Joint inference for bilingual semantic role labeling. In *Proceedings of the Conference on Empirical Methods in Natural Language Processing (EMNLP)*.

W. Zou, R. Socher, D. Cer, and C. Manning. 2013. Bilingual word embeddings for phrase-based machine translation. In *Proceedings of the Conference on Empirical Methods in Natural Language Processing (EMNLP)*.

Treebank Translation for Cross-Lingual Parser Induction

Jörg Tiedemann
Dep. of Linguistics and Philology
Uppsala University
jorg.tiedemann@lingfil.uu.se

Željko Agić
Linguistics Department
University of Potsdam
zagic@uni-potsdam.de

Joakim Nivre
Dep. of Linguistics and Philology
Uppsala University
joakim.nivre@lingfil.uu.se

Abstract

Cross-lingual learning has become a popular approach to facilitate the development of resources and tools for low-density languages. Its underlying idea is to make use of existing tools and annotations in resource-rich languages to create similar tools and resources for resource-poor languages. Typically, this is achieved by either projecting annotations across parallel corpora, or by transferring models from one or more source languages to a target language. In this paper, we explore a third strategy by using machine translation to create synthetic training data from the original source-side annotations. Specifically, we apply this technique to dependency parsing, using a cross-lingually unified treebank for adequate evaluation. Our approach draws on annotation projection but avoids the use of noisy source-side annotation of an unrelated parallel corpus and instead relies on manual treebank annotation in combination with statistical machine translation, which makes it possible to train fully lexicalized parsers. We show that this approach significantly outperforms delexicalized transfer parsing.

1 Introduction

The lack of resources and tools is a serious problem for the majority of the world's languages (Bender, 2013). Many applications require robust tools and the development of language-specific resources is expensive and time consuming. Furthermore, many tasks such as data-driven syntactic parsing require strong supervision to achieve reasonable results for real-world applications, since the performance of fully unsupervised methods lags behind by a large margin in comparison with the state of the art. Cross-lingual learning has been proposed as one possible solution to quickly create initial tools for languages that lack the appropriate resources (Ganchev and Das, 2013). By and large, there are two main strategies that have been proposed in the literature: annotation projection and model transfer.

1.1 Previous Cross-Lingual Approaches

Annotation projection relies on the mapping of linguistic annotation across languages using parallel corpora and automatic alignment as basic resources (Yarowsky et al., 2001; Hwa et al., 2005; Täckström et al., 2013a). Tools that exist for the source language are used to annotate the source side of the corpus and projection heuristics are then applied to map the annotation through word alignment onto the corresponding target language text. Target language tools can then be trained on the projected annotation assuming that the mapping is sufficiently correct. Less frequent, but also possible, is the scenario where the source side of the corpus contains manual annotation (Agić et al., 2012). This addresses the problem created by projecting noisy annotations, but it presupposes parallel corpora with manual annotation, which are rarely available, and expensive and time-consuming to produce.

Model transfer instead relies on universal features and model parameters that can be transferred from one language to another. Abstracting away from all language-specific parameters makes it possible to train, e.g., delexicalized parsers that ignore lexical information. This approach has been used with success for a variety of languages, drawing from a harmonized POS tagset (Petrov et al., 2012) that is used as the main source of information. One advantage compared to annotation projection is that no parallel data is required. In addition, training can be performed on gold standard annotation. However, model transfer assumes a common fea-

Proceedings of the Eighteenth Conference on Computational Language Learning, pages 130–140,
Baltimore, Maryland USA, June 26-27 2014.

ture representation across languages (McDonald et al., 2013), which can be a strong bottleneck. Several extensions have been proposed to make the approach more robust. First of all, multiple source languages can be involved to increase the statistical basis for learning (McDonald et al., 2011; Naseem et al., 2012), a strategy that can also be used in the case of annotation projection. Cross-lingual word clusters can be created to obtain additional universal features (Täckström et al., 2012). Techniques for target language adaptation can be used to improve model transfer with multiple sources (Täckström et al., 2013b).

1.2 The Translation Approach

In this paper, we propose a third strategy, based on automatically translating training data to a new language in order to create annotated resources directly from the original source. Recent advances in statistical machine translation (SMT) combined with the ever-growing availability of parallel corpora are now making this a realistic alternative. The relation to annotation projection is obvious as both involve parallel data with one side being annotated. However, the use of direct translation brings two important advantages. First of all, using SMT, we do not accumulate errors from two sources: the tool – e.g., tagger or parser – used to annotate the source language of a bilingual corpus and the noise coming from alignment and projection. Instead, we use the gold standard annotation of the source language which can safely be assumed to be of much higher quality than any automatic annotation obtained by using a tool trained on that data. Moreover, using SMT may help in bypassing domain shift problems, which are common when applying tools trained (and evaluated) on one resource to text from another domain. Secondly, we can assume that SMT will produce output that is much closer to the input than manual translations in parallel texts usually are. Even if this may seem like a short-coming in general, in the case of annotation projection it should rather be an advantage, because it makes it more straightforward and less error-prone to transfer annotation from source to target. Furthermore, the alignment between words and phrases is inherently provided as an output of all common SMT models. Hence, no additional procedures have to be performed on top of the translated corpus. Recent research (Zhao et al., 2009; Durrett et al., 2012) has attempted to address synthetic data creation for syntactic parsing via bilingual lexica. We seek to build on this work by utilizing more advanced translation techniques.

Further in the paper, we first describe the tools and resources used in our experiments (§2). We elaborate on our approach to translating treebanks (§3) and projecting syntactic annotations (§4) for a new language. Finally, we provide empirical evaluation of the suggested approach (§5) and observe a substantial increase in parsing accuracy over the delexicalized parsing baselines.

2 Resources and Tools

In our experiments, we rely on standard resources and tools for both dependency parsing and machine translation without any special enhancements. Since we are primarily trying to provide a proof of concept for the use of SMT-derived synthetic training data in dependency parsing, we believe it is more important to facilitate reproducibility than to tweak system components to obtain maximum accuracy.

We use the Universal Dependency Treebank v1 (McDonald et al., 2013) for annotation projection, parser training and evaluation. It is a collection of data sets with consistent syntactic annotation for six languages: English, French, German, Korean, Spanish, and Swedish.[1] The annotation is based on Stanford Typed Dependencies for English (De Marneffe et al., 2006) but has been adapted and harmonized to allow adequate annotation of typologically different languages. This is the first collection of data sets that allows reliable evaluation of labeled dependency parsing accuracy across multiple languages (McDonald et al., 2013). We use the dedicated training and test sets from the treebank distribution in all our experiments. As argued in (McDonald et al., 2013), most cross-lingual dependency parsing experiments up to theirs relied on heterogeneous treebanks such as the CoNLL datasets for syntactic dependency parsing (Buchholz and Marsi, 2006; Nivre et al., 2007a), making it difficult to address challenges like consistent cross-lingual analysis for downstream applications and reliable cross-lingual evaluation of syntactic parsers. More specifically, none of the previous research could report full labeled parsing accuracies, but rather just unlabeled structural accuracies across different attachment schemes. Following the line of McDonald et al. (2013) regarding the

[1] https://code.google.com/p/uni-dep-tb/

emphasized importance of homogenous data and the assignment of labels, we only report labeled attachment scores (LAS) in all our experiments. As it is likely the first reliable cross-lingual parsing evaluation, we also choose their results as the baseline reference point for comparison with our experiments.

For dependency parsing, we use MaltParser (Nivre et al., 2006a)[2] due to its efficiency in both training and parsing, and we facilitate MaltOptimizer (Ballesteros and Nivre, 2012)[3] to bypass the tedious task of manual feature selection. MaltParser is a transition-based dependency parser that has been evaluated on a number of different languages with competitive results (Nivre et al., 2006b; Nivre et al., 2007b; Hall et al., 2007) and it is widely used for benchmarking and application development. Although more accurate dependency parsers exist for the task of monolingual supervised parsing, it is not clear that these differences carry over to the cross-lingual scenario, where baselines are lower and more complex models are more likely to overfit. The use of a transition-based parser also facilitates comparison with delexicalized transfer parsing, where transition-based parsers are dominant so far (McDonald et al., 2011; McDonald et al., 2013). We leave the exploration of additional parsing approaches for future research.

For machine translation, we select the popular Moses toolbox (Koehn et al., 2007) and the phrase-based translation paradigm as our basic framework. Phrase-based SMT has the advantage of being straightforward and efficient in training and decoding, while maintaining robustness and reliability for many language pairs. More details about the setup and the translation procedures are given in Section 3 below. The most essential ingredient for translation performance is the parallel corpus used for training the translation models. For our experiments we use the freely available and widely used Europarl corpus v7 (Koehn, 2005).[4] It is commonly used for training SMT models and includes parallel data for all languages represented in the Universal Treebank except Korean, which we will, therefore, leave out in our experiments. For tuning we apply the newstest 2012 data provided by the annual workshop on statistical machine translation.[5] For language modeling, we use a combination of

[2]http://www.maltparser.org/

[3]http://nil.fdi.ucm.es/maltoptimizer/

[4]http://www.statmt.org/europarl/

[5]http://www.statmt.org/wmt14

	DE	EN	ES	FR	SV
DE		94 M	94 M	96 M	81 M
EN	2.0 M		103 M	105 M	89 M
ES	1.9 M	2.0 M		104 M	89 M
FR	1.9 M	2.0 M	2.0 M		91 M
SV	1.8 M	1.9 M	1.8 M	1.9 M	
mono	22.9 M	17.1 M	6.3 M	6.3 M	2.3 M

Table 1: Parallel data and monolingual data used for training the SMT models. Lower-left triangle = number of sentence pairs; upper-right triangle = number of tokens (source and target language together); bottom row = number of sentences in monolingual corpora.

Europarl and News data provided from the same source. The statistics of the corpora are given in Table 1.

3 Translating Treebanks

The main contribution of this paper is the empirical study of automatic treebank translation for parser transfer. We compare three different translation approaches in order to investigate the influence of several parameters. All of them are based on automatic word alignment and subsequent extraction of translation equivalents as common in phrase-based SMT. In particular, word alignment is performed using GIZA++ (Och and Ney, 2003) and IBM model 4 as the final model for creating the Viterbi word alignments for all parallel corpora used in our experiments. For the extraction of translation tables, we use the Moses toolkit with its standard settings to extract phrase tables with a maximum of seven tokens per phrase from a symmetrized word alignment. Symmetrization is done using the grow-diag-final-and heuristics (Koehn et al., 2003). We tune phrase-based SMT models using minimum error rate training (Och, 2003) and the development data for each language pair. The language model is a standard 5-gram model estimated from the monolingual data using modified Kneser-Ney smoothing without pruning (applying KenLM tools (Heafield et al., 2013)).

Our first translation approach is based on a very simple word-by-word translation model. For this, we select the most reliable translations of single words from the phrase translation tables extracted from the parallel corpora as described above. We restrict the model to tokens with alphabetic characters only using pre-defined Unicode character sets. The selection of translation alternatives is based on the Dice coefficient, which combines the two essential conditional translation probabilities given in the phrase table. The Dice coefficient is in fact the harmonic mean of these two probabilities and has successfully been used for the extraction of translation equivalents before (Smadja et al., 1996):

$$Dice(s,t) = \frac{2\,p(s,t)}{p(s)+p(t)} = 2\left(\frac{1}{p(s|t)} + \frac{1}{p(t|s)}\right)^{-1}$$

Other association measures would be possible as well but Smadja et al. (1996) argue that the Dice coefficient is more robust with respect to low frequency events than other common metrics such as pointwise mutual information, which can be a serious issue with the unsmoothed probability estimations in standard phrase tables. Our first translation model then applies the final one-to-one correspondences to monotonically translate treebanks word by word. We refer to it as the LOOKUP approach. Note that any bilingual dictionary could have been used to perform the same procedure.

The second translation approach (WORD-BASED MT) is slightly more elaborate but still restricts the translation model to one-to-one word mappings. For this, we extract all single word translation pairs from the phrase tables and apply the standard beam-search decoder implemented in Moses to translate the original treebanks to all target languages. The motivation for this model is to investigate the impact of reordering and language models while still keeping the projection of annotated data as simple as possible. Note that the language model may influence not only the word order but also the lexical choice as we now allow multiple translation options in our phrase table.

The final model implements translation based on the entire phrase table using the standard approach to PHRASE-BASED SMT. We basically run the Moses decoder with default settings and the parameters and models trained on our parallel corpora. Note that it is important for the annotation transfer to keep track of the alignment between phrases and words of the input and output sentences. The Moses decoder provides both, phrase segmentation and word alignment (if the latter is coded into the phrase tables). This will be important as we will see in the annotation projection discussed below.

ORIGINAL					
	DE	EN	ES	FR	SV
	14.0	0.00	7.90	13.3	4.20
WORD-BASED MT					
	DE	EN	ES	FR	SV
DE	–	49.1	62.6	52.8	60.4
EN	43.3	–	27.6	34.8	0.00
ES	54.9	25.1	–	12.3	18.3
FR	68.2	39.6	32.8	–	57.8
SV	34.1	5.20	21.6	33.7	–
PHRASE-BASED MT					
	DE	EN	ES	FR	SV
DE	–	51.5	57.3	58.8	46.8
EN	49.3	–	50.3	61.7	14.6
ES	65.9	66.7	–	62.8	49.0
FR	58.0	53.7	44.7	–	38.2
SV	43.9	43.6	49.6	57.1	–

Table 2: Non-projectivity in synthetic treebanks.

4 Transferring Annotation

The next step in preparing synthetic training data is to project the annotation from the original treebank to the target language. Given the properties of a dependency tree, where every word has exactly one syntactic head and dependency label, the annotation transfer is trivial for the two initial translation models. All annotation can simply be copied using the dictionary LOOKUP in which we enforce a monotonic one-to-one word mapping between source and target language.

In the second approach, we only have to keep track of reordering, which is reported by the decoder when translating with our model. Note that the mapping is strictly one-to-one (bijective) as phrase-based SMT does not allow deletions or insertions at any point. This also ensures that we will always maintain a tree structure even though reordering may have a strong impact on projectivity (see Table 2). An illustration of this type of annotation transfer is shown in the left image of Figure 1.

The third model, full PHRASE-BASED SMT, requires the most attention when transferring annotation across languages. Here we have to rely on the alignment information and projection heuristics similar to the ones presented in related work (Hwa et al., 2005). In their work, Hwa et al. (2005) define a direct projection algorithm that transfers automatic annotation to a target language via word alignment. The algorithm defines a number of

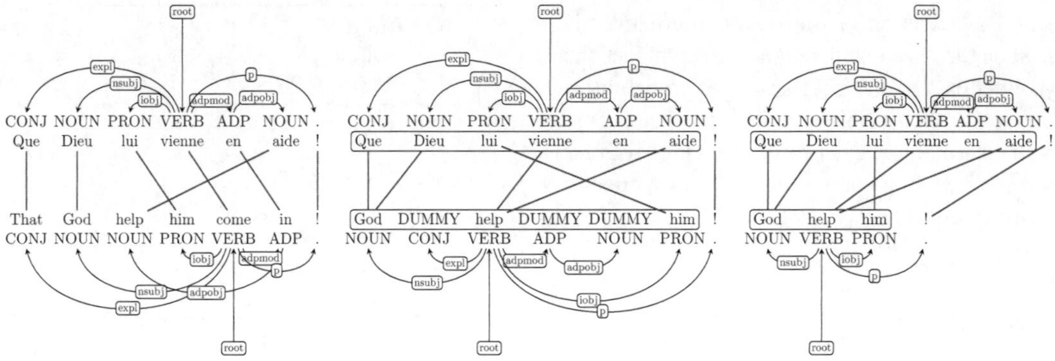

Figure 1: Transferring annotation from French to an English translation with a WORD-BASED translation model (left) and with a PHRASE-BASED translation model (middle and right). Annotation projection using the Direct Projection Algorithm by Hwa et al. (2005) (middle) and our approach (right).

heuristics to handle unaligned, one-to-many, many-to-one and many-to-many alignments. As a side effect, this approach produces several dummy-nodes in the target language to ensure a complete projection of the source language tree (see Hwa et al. (2005) for more details).

In our approach, we try to make use of the additional information provided by the SMT decoder to avoid dummy-nodes and relations that may negatively influence the induced target language parser. Compared to the annotation projection approach of Hwa et al. (2005), the situation in our PHRASE-BASED SMT setting is slightly different. Here, we have two types of alignments that can be considered when relating source and target language items: (i) the alignment between phrases (pairs of consecutive n-grams) and (ii) the phrase-internal word alignment on which phrase extraction is based. The primary information used for annotation transfer is still the latter which has the same properties as described by Hwa et al. (2005) (except that we have truly many-to-many alignments in our data which were not available in their experiments).

Note that words may be unaligned in phrase-based SMT as the phrase extraction algorithm used in Moses includes unaligned adjacent tokens. However, for these unaligned words, we know to which phrase they belong and can also identify the corresponding phrase in the other language using phrase alignment information. This makes it possible to avoid the creation of dummy-nodes altogether and instead to link unaligned words to existing nodes based on the given phrase segmentation.

Similarly, we define heuristics for handling one-to-many, many-to-one and many-to-many alignments that avoid the creation of dummy-nodes. The main procedure is illustrated in Figure 2.

The key feature of this projection algorithm is that ambiguous alignments are handled by attaching words to the nodes that are highest up in the dependency tree (the procedure find_highest() returns the node with minimum distance to the root of the tree). This ensures that we avoid cycles and isolated cliques in the graph. Furthermore, unaligned words are attached to the head of the target phrase they belong to, which seems to be the most appropriate place without further knowledge. The procedures in_trg_phrase() and in_src_phrase() make use of the phrase segmentation used in the translation process.

One complication is the search for the corresponding target head word in cases where the source language head is not aligned or aligned to multiple target language words. Figure 3 shows the head alignment procedure that we define in our projection algorithm. Procedure find_aligned() returns the rightmost word of all words aligned to the given source language word s. Other heuristics or linguistically motivated rules based on POS tags and general language properties would be possible here as well. If s is not aligned, we move up in the dependency tree until we hit ROOT or find an aligned word. If we are at the root position we return ROOT as this does not require further mappings. The effect of this algorithm is illustrated by the right-hand side image in Figure 1.

5 Parsing Across Languages

In this section, we present the results of two experimental batches. First, we establish the base-

```
Input: source tree S, target sentence T,
word alignment A, phrase segmentation P
Output: syntactic heads head[],
word attributes attr[]
treeSize = max_distance_to_root(S) ;
attr = [] ;
head = [] ;
for t ∈ T do
    if is_unaligned_trg(t,A) then
        for t' ∈ in_trg_phrase(t,P) do
            [s_x,...,s_y] = aligned_to(t') ;
            ŝ = find_highest([s_x,...,s_y],S) ;
            t̂ = find_aligned(ŝ,S,T,A) ;
            attr[t] = DUMMY ;
            head[t] = t̂ ;
        end
    else
        [s_x,...,s_y] = aligned_to(t) ;
        s = find_highest([s_x,...,s_y],S) ;
        attr[t] = attr(s) ;
        ŝ = head_of(s,S) ;
        t̂ = find_aligned(ŝ,S,T,A) ;
        if t̂ == t then
            [s_x,...,s_y] = in_src_phrase(s,P) ;
            s* = find_highest([s_x,...,s_y],S) ;
            ŝ = head_of(s*,S) ;
            t̂ = find_aligned(ŝ,S,T,A) ;
            head[t] = t̂ ;
        end
    end
end
```

Figure 2: Annotation projection algorithm.

lines by comparing monolingual supervised parsing to delexicalized transfer parsing following the approach of McDonald et al. (2013). Second, we present the results obtained with parsers trained on target language treebanks produced using machine translation and annotation projection. Here, we also look at delexicalized models trained on translated treebanks to show the effect of machine translation without additional lexical features.

5.1 Baseline Results

First we present the baseline parsing scores. The baselines we explore are: (i) the monolingual baseline, i.e., training and testing using the same language data from the Universal Dependency Treebank and (ii) the delexicalized baseline, i.e., applying delexicalized parsers across languages.

For the monolingual baseline, MaltParser models are trained on the original treebanks with universal POS labels and lexical features but leaving out other language-specific features if they exist in the original treebanks. The delexicalized parsers are trained on universal POS labels only for each language and are then applied to all other languages

```
Input: node s, source tree S with root ROOT,
target sentence T, word alignment A
Output: node t*
if s == ROOT then
    return ROOT ;
end
while is_unaligned_src(s,A) do
    s = head_of(s,S) ;
    if s == ROOT then
        return ROOT ;
    end
end
p = 0 ;
t* = undef ;
for t' ∈ aligned(s,A) do
    if position(t',T) > p then
        t* = t' ;
        p = position(t',T) ;
    end
end
return t* ;
```

Figure 3: Procedure find_aligned().

without modification. For all models, features and options are optimized using MaltOptimizer. The accuracy is given in Table 3 as a set of labeled attachment scores (LAS). We include punctuation in our evaluation. Ignoring punctuation generally leads to slightly higher scores as we have noted in our experiments but we do not report those numbers here. Note also that the columns represent the target languages (used for testing), while the rows denote the source languages (used in training), as in McDonald et al. (2013).

From the table, we can see that the baseline scores are compatible with the ones in the original experiments presented by (McDonald et al., 2013), included in Table 3 for reference. The differences are due to parser selection, as they use a transition-based parser with beam search and perceptron learning along the lines of Zhang and Nivre (2011) whereas we rely on greedy transition-based parsing with linear support vector machines. In the following, we will compare results to our baseline as we have a comparable setup in those experiments. However, most improvements shown below also apply in comparison with (McDonald et al., 2013).

5.2 Translated Treebanks

Now we turn to the experiments on translated treebanks. We consider two setups. First, we look at the effect of translation when training delexicalized parsers. In this way, we can perform a direct comparison to the baseline performance presented

MONOLINGUAL	DE	EN	ES	FR	SV
	72.13	87.50	78.54	77.51	81.28
DELEXICALIZED	DE	EN	ES	FR	SV
DE	62.71	43.20	46.09	46.09	50.64
EN	46.62	77.66	55.65	56.46	**57.68**
ES	44.03	46.73	68.21	**57.91**	53.82
FR	43.91	46.75	**59.65**	67.51	52.01
SV	**50.69**	**49.13**	53.62	51.97	70.22
MCDONALD ET AL. (2013)	DE	EN	ES	FR	SV
DE	64.84	47.09	48.14	49.59	53.57
EN	48.11	78.54	56.86	58.20	**57.04**
ES	45.52	47.87	70.29	**63.65**	53.09
FR	45.96	47.41	**62.56**	73.37	52.25
SV	**52.19**	**49.71**	54.72	54.96	70.90

Table 3: Baselines – labeled attachment score (LAS) for monolingual and delexicalized transfer parsing. Delexicalized transfer parsing results of McDonald et al. (2013) included for reference.

above. The second setup then considers fully lexicalized models trained on translated treebanks. The main advantage of the translation approach is the availability of lexical information and this final setup represents the real power of this approach. In it, we compare lexicalized parsers trained on translated treebanks with their delexicalized counterparts and avoid a direct comparison with the delexicalized baselines as they involve different types of features.

5.3 Delexicalized Parsers

Table 4 presents the scores obtained by training delexicalized parsing models on synthetic data created by our translation approaches presented earlier. Feature models and training options are the same as for the delexicalized source language models when training and testing on the target language data. Note that we exclude the simple dictionary LOOKUP approach here, because this approach leads to identical models as the basic delexicalized models. This is because words are translated one-to-one without any reordering which leads to exactly the same annotation sequences as the source language treebank after projecting POS labels and dependency relations.

From the table, we can see that all but one model improve the scores obtained by delexicalized baseline models. The improvements are quite substantial up to +6.38 LAS. The boost in performance is especially striking for the simpleWORD-BASED translation model considering that the only difference to the baseline model is word order. The impact of the more complex PHRASE-BASED translation model is, however, difficult to judge. In 14 out of 20 models it actually leads to a drop in LAS when applying phrase-based translation instead of single-word translation. This is somewhat surprising but is probably related to the additional ambiguity in annotation projection introduced by many-to-many alignments. The largest drop can be seen for Swedish translated to English, which even falls behind the baseline performance when using the PHRASE-BASED translation model.

WORD-BASED MT	DE	EN	ES	FR	SV
DE	–	48.12 $^{(4.92)}$	50.84 $^{(4.75)}$	52.92 $^{(6.83)}$	55.52 $^{(4.88)}$
EN	49.53 $^{(2.91)}$	–	57.41 $^{(1.76)}$	**58.53** $^{(2.07)}$	**57.82** $^{(0.14)}$
ES	45.48 $^{(1.45)}$	48.46 $^{(1.73)}$	–	58.29 $^{(0.38)}$	55.25 $^{(1.43)}$
FR	46.59 $^{(2.68)}$	47.88 $^{(1.13)}$	**59.72** $^{(0.07)}$	–	52.31 $^{(0.30)}$
SV	**52.16** $^{(1.47)}$	**49.14** $^{(0.01)}$	56.50 $^{(2.88)}$	56.71 $^{(4.74)}$	–
PHRASE-BASED MT	DE	EN	ES	FR	SV
DE	–	45.43 $^{(2.23)}$	47.26 $^{(1.17)}$	49.14 $^{(3.05)}$	53.37 $^{(2.73)}$
EN	49.16 $^{(2.54)}$	–	57.12 $^{(1.47)}$	**58.23** $^{(1.77)}$	**58.23** $^{(0.55)}$
ES	46.75 $^{(2.72)}$	46.82 $^{(0.09)}$	–	58.22 $^{(0.31)}$	54.14 $^{(0.32)}$
FR	48.02 $^{(4.11)}$	**49.06** $^{(2.31)}$	**60.23** $^{(0.58)}$	–	55.24 $^{(3.23)}$
SV	**50.96** $^{(0.27)}$	46.12 $^{-3.01}$	55.95 $^{(2.33)}$	54.71 $^{(2.74)}$	–

Table 4: Translated treebanks: labeled attachment score (LAS) for *delexicalized* parsers trained on synthetic data created by translation. Numbers in superscript show the absolute improvement over our delexicalized baselines.

5.4 Lexicalized Parsers

The final experiment is concerned with lexical parsers trained on translated treebanks. The main objective here is to test the robustness of fully lexicalized models trained on noisy synthetic data created by simple automatic translation engines. Table 5 lists the scores obtained by our models when trained on treebanks translated with our three approaches (dictionary LOOKUP, WORD-BASED MT and full PHRASE-BASED translation). Again, we use the same feature model and training options as for the source language model when training models for the target languages. This time, of course, this refers to the features used by the lexicalized baseline models.

The capacity of the parsing models increases due to the lexical information which is now included. In order to see the effect of lexicalization, we com-

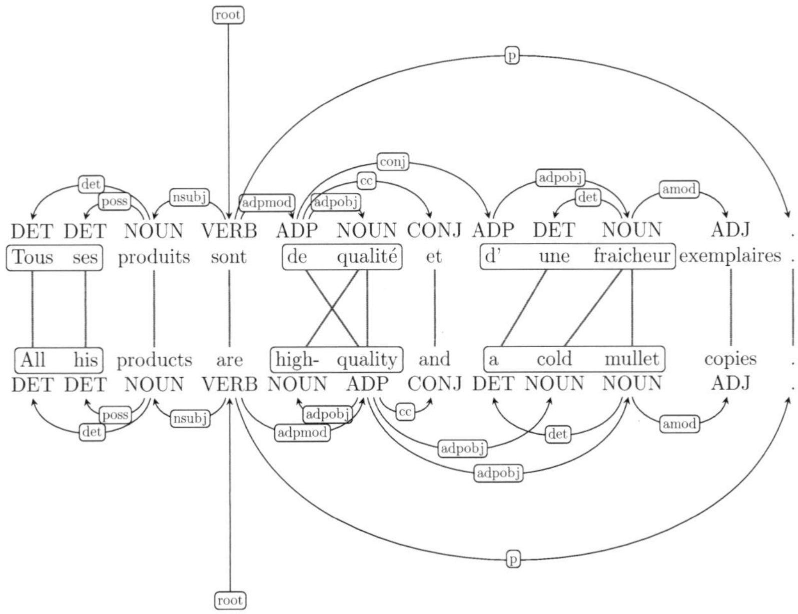

Figure 4: Problematic annotation projection with ambiguous word alignment.

pare the performance now with the corresponding delexicalized models. Note that the LOOKUP approach relates to the delexicalized baseline models without any translation.

As we can see, all models outperform their corresponding delexicalized version (with one exception), which demonstrates the ability of the training procedure to pick up valuable lexical information from the noisy translations. Again, we can see substantial absolute improvements of up to +7.31 LAS showing the effectiveness of the translation approach. Note that this also means that we outperform the delexicalized baselines in all cases by a large margin, even if we should not directly compare these models as they draw on different feature sets. Once again, we can also see that the very simple methods are quite successful. Even the very basic LOOKUP approach leads to significant improvements with one minor exception. Surprisingly, no gain can be seen with the PHRASE-BASED translation approach. The translation quality is certainly better when manually inspecting the data. However, the increased complexity of annotation projection seems to pull down the parsers induced on that kind of data. A question for future work is whether the performance of those models can be improved by better projection algorithms and heuristics that lead to cleaner annotations of otherwise better translations of the original treebanks.

One possible reason for this disappointing result could be the unreliable mapping of POS labels across many-to-many alignments. Figure 4 illustrates a typical case of link ambiguity that leads to erroneous projections. For example, the mapping of the label ADP onto the English word *quality* is due to the left-to-right procedure applied in our projection algorithm and the mapping of the NOUN label to the English adjective *cold* is due to the link to *fraicheur*. How much these errors effect our parsing models trained on the projected treebanks is difficult to estimate and further investigations are required to pinpoint these issues and to find ways of addressing problems that may occur in various contexts.

Nevertheless, the overall results are very positive. The experiments clearly show the potentials of the translation approach. Note that this paper presents the first attempt to study the effect of translation on cross-lingual parser induction. Further optimization of the translation process and the connected annotation projection procedures should lead to further improvements over our basic models.

6 Conclusions and Future Work

In this paper, we have addressed the problem of cross-lingual parser induction by using statistical machine translation to create synthetic training data. Our SMT approach avoids the noisy source-side

LOOKUP					
	DE	EN	ES	FR	SV
DE	–	48.63 $^{(5.43)}$	52.66 $^{(6.57)}$	52.06 $^{(5.97)}$	58.78 $^{(8.14)}$
EN	48.59 $^{(1.97)}$	–	57.79 $^{(2.14)}$	57.80 $^{(1.34)}$	**62.21** $^{(4.53)}$
ES	47.36 $^{(3.33)}$	49.13 $^{(2.40)}$	–	**62.24** $^{(4.33)}$	57.50 $^{(3.68)}$
FR	47.57 $^{(3.66)}$	**54.06** $^{(7.31)}$	**66.31** $^{(6.66)}$	–	57.73 $^{(5.72)}$
SV	**51.88** $^{(1.19)}$	48.84 $^{(0.29)}$	54.74 $^{(1.12)}$	52.95 $^{(0.98)}$	–
WORD-BASED MT					
	DE	EN	ES	FR	SV
DE	–	51.86 $^{(3.74)}$	55.90 $^{(5.06)}$	57.77 $^{(4.85)}$	61.65 $^{(6.13)}$
EN	**53.80** $^{(4.27)}$	–	60.76 $^{(3.35)}$	63.32 $^{(4.79)}$	**62.93** $^{(5.11)}$
ES	49.94 $^{(4.46)}$	49.93 $^{(1.47)}$	–	**65.60** $^{(7.31)}$	59.22 $^{(3.97)}$
FR	52.07 $^{(5.48)}$	**54.44** $^{(6.56)}$	**65.63** $^{(5.91)}$	–	57.67 $^{(5.36)}$
SV	53.18 $^{(1.02)}$	50.91 $^{(1.77)}$	60.82 $^{(4.32)}$	59.14 $^{(2.43)}$	–
PHRASE-BASED MT					
	DE	EN	ES	FR	SV
DE	–	50.89 $^{(5.46)}$	52.54 $^{(5.28)}$	54.99 $^{(5.85)}$	59.46 $^{(6.09)}$
EN	**53.71** $^{(4.55)}$	–	60.70 $^{(3.58)}$	62.89 $^{(4.66)}$	**64.01** $^{(5.78)}$
ES	49.59 $^{(2.84)}$	48.35 $^{(1.53)}$	–	**64.88** $^{(6.66)}$	58.99 $^{(4.85)}$
FR	51.83 $^{(3.81)}$	**53.81** $^{(4.75)}$	**65.55** $^{(5.32)}$	–	59.01 $^{(3.77)}$
SV	53.22 $^{(2.26)}$	49.06 $^{(2.94)}$	58.41 $^{(2.46)}$	58.04 $^{(3.33)}$	–

Table 5: Translated treebanks: labeled attachment score (LAS) for *lexicalized* parsers trained on synthetic data. Numbers in superscript show the absolute improvements over the delexicalized models based on the same translation strategy.

annotations of traditional annotation projection and makes it possible to train fully lexicalized target language models that significantly outperform delexicalized transfer parsers. We have also demonstrated that translation leads to better delexicalized models that can directly be compared with each other as they are based on the same feature space.

We have compared three SMT methods for synthesizing training data: LOOKUP-based translation, WORD-BASED translation and full PHRASE-BASED translation. Our experiments show that even noisy data sets and simple translation strategies can be used to achieve positive results. For all three approaches, we have recorded substantial improvements over the state of the art in labeled cross-lingual parsing (McDonald et al., 2013). According to our results, simple word-by-word translations are often sufficient to create reasonable translations to train lexicalized parsers on. More elaborated phrase-based models together with advanced annotation projection strategies do not necessarily lead to any improvements.

As future work, we want to improve our model by (i) studying the impact of other SMT properties and improve the quality of treebank translation, (ii) implementing more sophisticated methods for annotation projection and (iii) using n-best lists provided by SMT models to introduce additional synthetic data using a single resource. We also aim at (iv) applying our approach to transfer parsing for closely related languages (see Agić et al. (2012) and Zeman and Resnik (2008) for related work), (v) testing it in a multi-source transfer scenario (McDonald et al., 2011) and, finally, (vi) comparing different dependency parsing paradigms within our experimental framework.

Multi-source approaches are especially appealing using the translation approach. However, initial experiments (which we omit in this presentation) revealed that simple concatenation is not sufficient to obtain results that improve upon the single-best translated treebanks. A careful selection of appropriate training examples and their weights given to the training procedure seems to be essential to benefit from different sources.

7 Acknowledgements

This work was supported by the Swedish Research Council (Vetenskapsrådet) through the project on Discourse-Oriented Machine Translation (2012-916).

References

Željko Agić, Danijela Merkler, and Daša Berović. 2012. Slovene-Croatian Treebank Transfer Using Bilingual Lexicon Improves Croatian Dependency Parsing. In *Proceedings of IS-LTC 2012*, pages 5–9.

Miguel Ballesteros and Joakim Nivre. 2012. MaltOptimizer: An Optimization Tool for MaltParser. In *Proceedings of EACL 2012*, pages 58–62.

Emily M. Bender. 2013. *Linguistic Fundamentals for Natural Language Processing: 100 Essentials from Morphology and Syntax*. Morgan & Claypool Publishers.

Sabine Buchholz and Erwin Marsi. 2006. CoNLL-X Shared Task on Multilingual Dependency Parsing. In *Proceedings of CoNLL 2006*, pages 149–164.

Marie-Catherine De Marneffe, Bill MacCartney, and Christopher D. Manning. 2006. Generating Typed Dependency Parses from Phrase Structure Parses. In *Proceedings of LREC 2006*, pages 449–454.

Greg Durrett, Adam Pauls, and Dan Klein. 2012. Syntactic Transfer Using a Bilingual Lexicon. In *Proceedings of EMNLP-CoNLL 2012*, pages 1–11.

Kuzman Ganchev and Dipanjan Das. 2013. Cross-Lingual Discriminative Learning of Sequence Models with Posterior Regularization. In *Proceedings of EMNLP 2013*, pages 1996–2006.

Johan Hall, Jens Nilsson, Joakim Nivre, Gülsen Eryiğit, Beáta Megyesi, Mattias Nilsson, and Markus Saers. 2007. Single Malt or Blended? A Study in Multilingual Parser Optimization. In *Proceedings of the CoNLL Shared Task Session of EMNLP-CoNLL 2007*, pages 933–939.

Kenneth Heafield, Ivan Pouzyrevsky, Jonathan H. Clark, and Philipp Koehn. 2013. Scalable Modified Kneser-Ney Language Model Estimation. In *Proceedings of ACL 2013*, pages 690–696.

Rebecca Hwa, Philip Resnik, Amy Weinberg, Clara Cabezas, and Okan Kolak. 2005. Bootstrapping Parsers via Syntactic Projection across Parallel Texts. *Natural Language Engineering*, 11(3):311–325.

Philipp Koehn, Franz Josef Och, and Daniel Marcu. 2003. Statistical Phrase Based Translation. In *Proceedings of NAACL-HLT 2003*, pages 48–54.

Philipp Koehn, Hieu Hoang, Alexandra Birch, Chris Callison-Burch, Marcello Federico, Nicola Bertoldi, Brooke Cowan, Wade Shen, Christine Moran, Richard Zens, Christopher J. Dyer, Ondřej Bojar, Alexandra Constantin, and Evan Herbst. 2007. Moses: Open Source Toolkit for Statistical Machine Translation. In *Proceedings of ACL 2007*, pages 177–180.

Philipp Koehn. 2005. Europarl: A Parallel Corpus for Statistical Machine Translation. In *Proceedings of MT Summit 2005*, pages 79–86.

Ryan McDonald, Slav Petrov, and Keith Hall. 2011. Multi-Source Transfer of Delexicalized Dependency Parsers. In *Proceedings of EMNLP 2011*, pages 62–72.

Ryan McDonald, Joakim Nivre, Yvonne Quirmbach-Brundage, Yoav Goldberg, Dipanjan Das, Kuzman Ganchev, Keith Hall, Slav Petrov, Hao Zhang, Oscar Täckström, Claudia Bedini, Núria Bertomeu Castelló, and Jungmee Lee. 2013. Universal Dependency Annotation for Multilingual Parsing. In *Proceedings of ACL 2013*, pages 92–97.

Tahira Naseem, Regina Barzilay, and Amir Globerson. 2012. Selective Sharing for Multilingual Dependency Parsing. In *Proceedings of ACL 2012*, pages 629–637.

Joakim Nivre, Johan Hall, and Jens Nilsson. 2006a. MaltParser: A Data-Driven Parser-Generator for Dependency Parsing. In *Proceedings of LREC 2006*, pages 2216–2219.

Joakim Nivre, Johan Hall, Jens Nilsson, Gülsen Eryiğit, and Svetoslav Marinov. 2006b. Labeled Pseudo-Projective Dependency Parsing with Support Vector Machines. In *Proceedings of CoNLL 2006*, pages 221–225.

Joakim Nivre, Johan Hall, Sandra Kübler, Ryan McDonald, Jens Nilsson, Sebastian Riedel, and Deniz Yuret. 2007a. The CoNLL 2007 Shared Task on Dependency Parsing. In *Proceedings of the CoNLL Shared Task Session of EMNLP-CoNLL 2007*, pages 915–932.

Joakim Nivre, Johan Hall, Jens Nilsson, Atanas Chanev, Gülşen Eryiğit, Sandra Kübler, Svetoslav Marinov, and Erwin Marsi. 2007b. MaltParser: A Language-Independent System for Data-Driven Dependency Parsing. *Natural Language Engineering*, 13(2):95–135.

Franz Josef Och and Hermann Ney. 2003. A Systematic Comparison of Various Statistical Alignment Models. *Computational Linguistics*, 29(1):19–52.

Franz Josef Och. 2003. Minimum Error Rate Training in Statistical Machine Translation. In *Proceedings of ACL 2003*, pages 160–167.

Slav Petrov, Dipanjan Das, and Ryan McDonald. 2012. A Universal Part-of-Speech Tagset. In *Proceedings of LREC 2012*, pages 2089–2096.

Frank Smadja, Vasileios Hatzivassiloglou, and Kathleen R. McKeown. 1996. Translating Collocations for Bilingual Lexicons: A Statistical Approach. *Computational Linguistics*, 22(1):1–38.

Oscar Täckström, Ryan McDonald, and Jakob Uszkoreit. 2012. Cross-lingual Word Clusters for Direct Transfer of Linguistic Structure. In *Proceedings of NAACL 2012*, pages 477–487.

Oscar Täckström, Dipanjan Das, Slav Petrov, Ryan McDonald, and Joakim Nivre. 2013a. Token and Type Constraints for Cross-lingual Part-of-speech Tagging. *Transactions of the Association for Computational Linguistics*, 1:1–12.

Oscar Täckström, Ryan McDonald, and Joakim Nivre. 2013b. Target Language Adaptation of Discriminative Transfer Parsers. In *Proceedings of NAACL 2013*, pages 1061–1071.

David Yarowsky, Grace Ngai, and Richard Wicentowski. 2001. Inducing Multilingual Text Analysis Tools via Robust Projection Across Aligned Corpora. In *Proceedings of HLT 2011*, pages 1–8.

Daniel Zeman and Philip Resnik. 2008. Cross-Language Parser Adaptation between Related Languages. In *Proceedings of IJCNLP 2008*, pages 35–42.

Yue Zhang and Joakim Nivre. 2011. Transition-based Dependency Parsing with Rich Non-local Features. In *Proceedings of ACL 2011*, pages 188–193.

Hai Zhao, Yan Song, Chunyu Kit, and Guodong Zhou. 2009. Cross Language Dependency Parsing Using a Bilingual Lexicon. In *Proceedings of ACL-IJCNLP 2009*, pages 55–63.

Weakly-Supervised Bayesian Learning of a CCG Supertagger

Dan Garrette* **Chris Dyer†** **Jason Baldridge‡** **Noah A. Smith†**

*Department of Computer Science, The University of Texas at Austin
†School of Computer Science, Carnegie Mellon University
‡Department of Linguistics, The University of Texas at Austin
*Corresponding author: dhg@cs.utexas.edu

Abstract

We present a Bayesian formulation for weakly-supervised learning of a Combinatory Categorial Grammar (CCG) supertagger with an HMM. We assume supervision in the form of a tag dictionary, and our prior encourages the use of cross-linguistically common category structures as well as transitions between tags that can combine locally according to CCG's combinators. Our prior is theoretically appealing since it is motivated by language-independent, universal properties of the CCG formalism. Empirically, we show that it yields substantial improvements over previous work that used similar biases to initialize an EM-based learner. Additional gains are obtained by further shaping the prior with corpus-specific information that is extracted automatically from raw text and a tag dictionary.

1 Introduction

Unsupervised part-of-speech (POS) induction is a classic problem in NLP. Many proposed solutions are based on Hidden Markov models (HMMs), with various improvements obtainable through: inductive bias in the form of tag dictionaries (Kupiec, 1992; Merialdo, 1994), sparsity constraints (Lee et al., 2010), careful initialization of parameters (Goldberg et al., 2008), feature based representations (Berg-Kirkpatrick et al., 2010; Smith and Eisner, 2005), and priors on model parameters (Johnson, 2007; Goldwater and Griffiths, 2007; Blunsom and Cohn, 2011, *inter alia*).

When tag dictionaries are available, a situation we will call **type-supervision**, POS induction from unlabeled corpora can be relatively successful; however, as the number of possible tags increases, performance drops (Ravi and Knight, 2009). In such cases, there are a large number of possible labels for each token, so picking the right one simply by chance is unlikely; the parameter space tends to be large; and devising good initial parameters is difficult. Therefore, it is unsurprising that the unsupervised (or even weakly-supervised) learning of a Combinatory Categorial Grammar (CCG) supertagger, which labels each word with one of a large (possibly unbounded) number of structured categories called **supertags**, is a considerable challenge.

Despite the apparent complexity of the task, supertag sequences have regularities due to universal properties of the CCG formalism (§2) that can be used to reduce the complexity of the problem; previous work showed promising results by using these regularities to initialize an HMM that is then refined with EM (Baldridge, 2008). Here, we exploit CCG's category structure to motivate a novel prior over HMM parameters for use in Bayesian learning (§3). This prior encourages (i) cross-linguistically common tag types, (ii) tag bigrams that can combine using CCG's combinators, and (iii) sparse transition distributions. We also go beyond the use of these universals to show how additional, *corpus-specific* information can be automatically extracted from a combination of the tag dictionary and raw data, and how that information can be combined with the universal knowledge for integration into the model to improve the prior.

We use a blocked sampling algorithm to sample supertag sequences for the sentences in the training data, proportional to their posterior probability (§4). We experimentally verify that our Bayesian formulation is effective and substantially outperforms the state-of-the-art baseline initialization/EM strategy in several languages (§5). We also evaluate using tag dictionaries that are unpruned and have only partial word coverage, finding even greater improvements in these more realistic scenarios.

Proceedings of the Eighteenth Conference on Computational Language Learning, pages 141–150,
Baltimore, Maryland USA, June 26-27 2014.

2 CCG and Supertagging

CCG (Steedman, 2000; Steedman and Baldridge, 2011) is a grammar formalism in which each lexical token is associated with a structured category, often referred to as a *supertag*. CCG categories are defined by the following recursive definition:

$$C \rightarrow \{\text{S, N, NP, PP, } \ldots\}$$
$$C \rightarrow \{C/C, C\backslash C\}$$

A CCG category can either be an *atomic* category indicating a particular type of basic grammatical phrase (S for a sentence, N for a noun, NP for a noun phrase, etc), or a *complex* category formed from the combination of two categories by one of two *slash* operators. In CCG, complex categories indicate a grammatical relationship between the two operands. For example, the category (S\NP)/NP might describe a transitive verb, looking first to its right (indicated by /) for an object, then to its left (\) for a subject, to produce a sentence. Further, atomic categories may be augmented with *features*, such as S_{dcl}, to restrict the set of atoms with which they may unify. The task of assigning a category to each word in a text is called *supertagging* (Bangalore and Joshi, 1999).

Because they are recursively defined, there is an infinite number of potential CCG categories (though in practice it is limited by the number of actual grammatical contexts). As a result, the number of supertags appearing in a corpus far exceeds the number of POS tags (see Table 1). Since supertags specify the grammatical context of a token, and high frequency words appear in many contexts, CCG grammars tend to have very high lexical ambiguity, with frequent word types associating with a large number of categories. This ambiguity has made type-supervised supertagger learning very difficult because the typical approaches to initializing parameters for EM become much less effective.

Grammar-informed supertagger learning. Baldridge (2008) was successful in extending the standard type-supervised tagger learning to the task of CCG supertagging by setting the initial parameters for EM training of an HMM using two intrinsic properties of the CCG formalism: the tendency for adjacent tags to combine, and the tendency to use less complex tags. These properties are explained in detail in the original work, but we restate the ideas briefly throughout this paper for completeness.

X/Y	Y	$\Rightarrow$	X	$(>)$
Y	$X\backslash Y$	$\Rightarrow$	X	$(<)$
X/Y	Y/Z	$\Rightarrow$	X/Z	$(>\mathbf{B})$
$Y\backslash Z$	$X\backslash Y$	$\Rightarrow$	$X\backslash Z$	$(<\mathbf{B})$
Y/Z	$X\backslash Y$	$\Rightarrow$	X/Z	$(<\mathbf{B}_\times)$

Figure 1: Combination rules used by CCGBank.

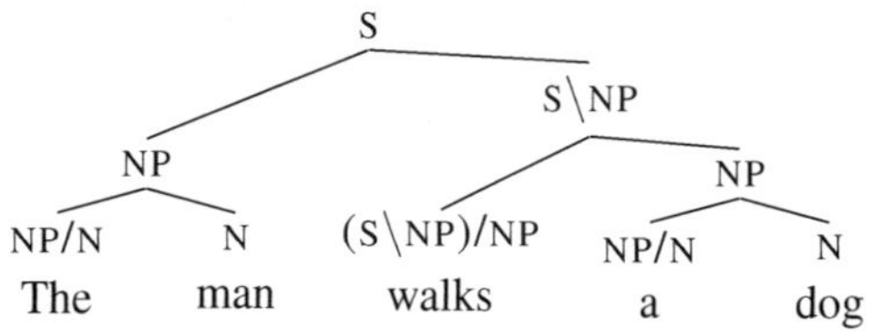

Figure 2: CCG parse for "The man walks a dog."

Tag combinability. A CCG parse of a sentence is derived by recursively combining the categories of sub-phrases. Category combination is performed using only a small set of generic rules (see Figure 1). In the tree in Figure 2, we can see that *a* and *dog* can combine via Forward Application ($>$), with NP/N and N combining to produce NP.

The associativity engendered by CCG's composition rules means that most adjacent lexical categories may be combined. In the Figure 2 tree, we can see that instead of combining (walks·(a·dog)), we could have combined ((walks·a)·dog) since (S\NP)/NP and NP/N can combine using $>\mathbf{B}$.

3 Model

In this section we define the generative process we use to model a corpus of sentences. We begin by generating the model parameters: for each supertag type $\mathbf{t}$ in the tag set T, the transition probabilities to the next state ($\pi_{\mathbf{t}}$) and the emission probabilities ($\phi_{\mathbf{t}}$) are generated by draws from Dirichlet distributions parameterized with per-tag mean distributions ($\pi^0_{\mathbf{t}}$ and $\phi^0_{\mathbf{t}}$, respectively) and concentration parameters (α_π and α_ϕ). By setting α_π close to zero, we can encode our prior expectation that transition distributions should be relatively peaked (i.e., that each tag type should be followed by relatively few tag types). The prior means, discussed below, encode both linguistic intuitions about expected tag-tag transition behavior and automatically-extracted corpus information. Given these parameters, we next generate the sentences of the corpus. This process is summarized as follows:

Parameters:

$$\phi_{\mathbf{t}} \sim \text{Dirichlet}(\alpha_\phi, \phi^0_{\mathbf{t}}) \quad \forall \mathbf{t} \in T$$

$$\pi_{\mathbf{t}} \sim \text{Dirichlet}(\alpha_\pi, \pi^0_{\mathbf{t}}) \quad \forall \mathbf{t} \in T$$

Sentence:

$$y_1 \sim \text{Categorical}(\pi_{\langle \mathrm{S} \rangle})$$

$$\text{for } i \in \{1, 2, \ldots\}, \text{until } y_i = \langle \mathrm{E} \rangle$$

$$x_i \mid y_i \sim \text{Categorical}(\phi_{y_i})$$

$$y_{i+1} \mid y_i \sim \text{Categorical}(\pi_{y_i})$$

This model can be understood as a Bayesian HMM (Goldwater and Griffiths, 2007). We next discuss how the prior distributions are constructed to build in additional inductive bias.

3.1 Transition Prior Means ($\pi^0_{\mathbf{t}}$)

We use the prior mean for each tag's transition distribution to build in two kinds of bias. First, we want to favor linguistically probable tags. Second, we want to favor transitions that result in a tag pair that combines according to CCG's combinators. For simplicity, we will define $\pi^0_{\mathbf{t}}$ as a mixture of two components, the first, $P_\pi(\mathbf{u})$ is an (unconditional) distribution over category types $\mathbf{u}$ that favors cross-linguistically probable categories. The second component, $P_\pi(\mathbf{u} \mid \mathbf{t})$, conditions on the previous tag type, $\mathbf{t}$, and assigns higher probability to pairs of tags that can be combined. That is, the probability of transitioning from $\mathbf{t}$ to $\mathbf{u}$ in the Dirichlet mean distribution is given by[1]

$$\pi^0_{\mathbf{t}}(\mathbf{u}) = \lambda \cdot P_\pi(\mathbf{u}) + (1 - \lambda) \cdot P_\pi(\mathbf{u} \mid \mathbf{t}).$$

We discuss the two mixture components in turn.

3.1.1 Unigram Category Generator ($P_\pi(\mathbf{u})$)

In this section, we define a CCG category generator that generates cross-linguistically likely category types. Baldridge's approach estimated the likelihood of a category using the inverse number of sub-categories: $P_{\text{CPLX}}(\mathbf{u}) \propto 1/\mathit{complexity}(\mathbf{u})$. We propose an improvement, P_{G}, expressed as a probabilistic grammar:[2]

$\mathrm{C} \rightarrow a$	$p_{term} \cdot p_{atom}(a)$
$\mathrm{C} \rightarrow \mathrm{A}/\mathrm{A}$	$\overline{p}_{term} \cdot p_{fw} \cdot p_{mod} \cdot P_{\text{G}}(\mathrm{A})$
$\mathrm{C} \rightarrow \mathrm{A}/\mathrm{B},\ \mathrm{A}{\neq}\mathrm{B}$	$\overline{p}_{term} \cdot p_{fw} \cdot \overline{p}_{mod} \cdot P_{\text{G}}(\mathrm{A}) \cdot P_{\text{G}}(\mathrm{B})$
$\mathrm{C} \rightarrow \mathrm{A}\backslash\mathrm{A}$	$\overline{p}_{term} \cdot \overline{p}_{fw} \cdot p_{mod} \cdot P_{\text{G}}(\mathrm{A})$
$\mathrm{C} \rightarrow \mathrm{A}\backslash\mathrm{B},\ \mathrm{A}{\neq}\mathrm{B}$	$\overline{p}_{term} \cdot \overline{p}_{fw} \cdot \overline{p}_{mod} \cdot P_{\text{G}}(\mathrm{A}) \cdot P_{\text{G}}(\mathrm{B})$

where A, B, C are categories and a is an atomic category (and terminal): $a \in \{\mathrm{S}, \mathrm{N}, \mathrm{NP}, ...\}$.[3]

We have designed this grammar to capture several important CCG characteristics. In particular we encode four main ideas, each captured through a different parameter of the grammar and discussed in greater detail below:

1. Simpler categories are more likely: e.g. N/N is *a priori* more likely than (N/N)/(N/N).
2. Some atoms are more likely than others: e.g. NP is more likely than S, much more than NP_{nb}.
3. Modifiers are more likely: e.g. (S\NP)/(S\NP) is more likely than (S\NP)/(NP\NP).
4. Operators occur with different frequencies.

The first idea subsumes the complexity measure used by Baldridge, but accomplishes the goal naturally by letting the probabilities decrease as the category grows. The rate of decay is governed by the p_{term} parameter: the marginal probability of generating a terminal (atomic) category in each expansion. A higher p_{term} means a stronger emphasis on simplicity. The probability distribution over categories is guaranteed to be proper so long as $p_{term} > \frac{1}{2}$ since the probability of the depth of a tree will decrease geometrically (Chi, 1999).

The second idea is a natural extension of the complexity concept and is particularly relevant when features are used. The original complexity measure treated all atoms uniformly, but e.g. we would expect NP_{expl}/N to be less likely than NP/N since it contains the more specialized, and thus rarer, atom NP_{expl}. We define the distribution $p_{atom}(a)$ as the prior over atomic categories.

Due to our weak, type-only supervision, we have to estimate p_{atom} from just the tag dictionary and raw corpus, without frequency data. Our goal is to estimate the number of each atom in the supertags that should appear on the raw corpus tokens. Since we don't know what the correct supertags are, we first estimate counts of supertags, from which we can extract estimated atom counts. Our strategy is to uniformly distribute each raw corpus token's counts over all of its possible supertags, as specified in the tag dictionary. Word types not appearing in the tag dictionary are ig-

[1]Following Baldridge (2008), we fix $\lambda = 0.5$ for our experiments.

[2]For readability, we use the notation $\overline{p} = (1 - p)$.

[3]While very similar to standard probabilistic context-free grammars seen in NLP work, this grammar is not context-free because modifier categories must have matching operands. However, this is not a problem for our approach since the grammar is unambiguous, defines a proper probability distribution, and is only used for modeling the relative likelihoods of categories (not parsing categories).

nored for the purposes of these estimates. Assuming that $C(w)$ is the number of times that word type w is seen in the raw corpus, $atoms(a,t)$ is the number of times atom a appears in $\mathbf{t}$, $\text{TD}(w)$ is the set of tags associated with w, and $\text{TD}(\mathbf{t})$ is the set of word types associated with $\mathbf{t}$:

$$C_{supertag}(\mathbf{t}) = \sum_{w \in \text{TD}(\mathbf{t})} (C(w)+\delta)/|\text{TD}(w)|$$
$$C_{atom}(a) = \sum_{\mathbf{t} \in T} atoms(a,\mathbf{t}) \cdot C_{supertag}(\mathbf{t})$$
$$p_{atom}(a) \propto C_{atom}(a) + \delta$$

Adding δ smooths the estimates.

Using the raw corpus and tag dictionary data to set p_{atom} allows us to move beyond Baldridge's work in another direction: it provides us with a natural way to combine CCG's universal assumptions with corpus-specific data.

The third and fourth ideas pertain only to complex categories. If the category is complex, then we consider two additional parameters. The parameter p_{fw} is the marginal probability that the complex category's operator specifies a forward argument. The parameter p_{mod} gives the amount of marginal probability mass that is allocated for modifier categories. Note that it is not necessary for p_{mod} to be greater than $\frac{1}{2}$ to achieve the desired result of making modifier categories more likely than non-modifier categories: the number of potential modifiers make up only a tiny fraction of the space of possible categories, so allocating more than that mass as p_{mod} will result in a category grammar that gives disproportionate weight to modifiers, increasing the likelihood of any particular modifier from what it would otherwise be.

3.1.2 Bigram Category Generator ($P_\pi(\mathbf{u} \mid \mathbf{t})$)

While the above processes encode important properties of the distribution over categories, the internal structure of categories is not the full story: cross-linguistically, the categories of adjacent tokens are much more likely to be combinable via some CCG rule. This is the second component of our mixture model.

Baldridge derives this bias by allocating the majority of the transition probability mass from each tag $\mathbf{t}$ to tags that can follow $\mathbf{t}$ according to some combination rule. Let $\kappa(\mathbf{t},\mathbf{u})$ be an indicator of whether $\mathbf{t}$ connects to $\mathbf{u}$; for $\sigma \in [0,1]$:[4]

$$P_\kappa(\mathbf{u} \mid \mathbf{t}) = \begin{cases} \sigma \cdot \text{uniform}(\mathbf{u}) & \text{if } \kappa(\mathbf{t},\mathbf{u}) \\ (1-\sigma) \cdot \text{uniform}(\mathbf{u}) & \text{otherwise} \end{cases}$$

[4]Again, following Baldridge (2008), we fix $\sigma = 0.95$ for our experiments.

There are a few additional considerations that must be made in defining κ, however. In assuming the special tags $\langle\text{S}\rangle$ and $\langle\text{E}\rangle$ for the start and end of the sentence, respectively, we can define $\kappa(\langle\text{S}\rangle,\mathbf{u}) = 1$ when $\mathbf{u}$ seeks no left-side arguments (since there are no tags to the left with which to combine) and $\kappa(\mathbf{t},\langle\text{E}\rangle) = 1$ when $\mathbf{t}$ seeks no right-side arguments. So $\kappa(\langle\text{S}\rangle, \text{NP/N}) = 1$, but $\kappa(\langle\text{S}\rangle, \text{S}\backslash\text{NP}) = 0$. If atoms have *features* associated, then the atoms are allowed to unify if the features match, or if at least one of them does not have a feature. So $\kappa(\text{NP}_{nb}, \text{S}\backslash\text{NP}) = 1$, but $\kappa(\text{NP}_{nb}, \text{S}\backslash\text{NP}_{conj}) = 0$. In defining κ, it is also important to ignore possible arguments on the wrong side of the combination since they can be consumed without affecting the connection between the two. To achieve this for $\kappa(\mathbf{t},\mathbf{u})$, it is assumed that it is possible to consume all preceding arguments of $\mathbf{t}$ and all following arguments of $\mathbf{u}$. So $\kappa(\text{NP}, (\text{S}\backslash\text{NP})/\text{NP}) = 1$. This helps to ensure the associativity discussed earlier. Finally, the atom NP is allowed to unify with N if N is the argument. So $\kappa(\text{N}, \text{S}\backslash\text{NP}) = 1$, but $\kappa(\text{NP/N}, \text{NP}) = 0$. This is due to the fact that CCGBank assumes that N can be rewritten as NP.

Type-supervised initialization. As above, we want to improve upon Baldridge's ideas by encoding not just universal CCG knowledge, but also automatically-induced corpus-specific information where possible. To that end, we can define a conditional distribution $P_{tr}(\mathbf{u} \mid \mathbf{t})$ based on statistics from the raw corpus and tag dictionary. We use the same approach as we did above for setting p_{atom} (and the definition of $\phi^0_{\mathbf{t}}$ below): we estimate by evenly distributing raw corpus counts over the tag dictionary entries. Assume that $C(w_1,w_2)$ is the (δ-smoothed) count of times word type w_1 was directly followed by w_2 in the raw corpus, and ignoring any words not found in the tag dictionary:

$$C(\mathbf{t},\mathbf{u}) = \delta + \sum_{w_1 \in \text{TD}(\mathbf{t}),\, w_2 \in \text{TD}(\mathbf{u})} \frac{C(w_1,w_2)}{|\text{TD}(w_1)| \cdot |\text{TD}(w_2)|}$$

$$P_{tr}(\mathbf{u} \mid \mathbf{t}) = C(\mathbf{t},\mathbf{u}) / \textstyle\sum_{\mathbf{u}'} C(\mathbf{t},\mathbf{u}')$$

Then the alternative definition of the compatibility distribution is as follows:

$$P^{tr}_\kappa(\mathbf{u} \mid \mathbf{t}) = \begin{cases} \sigma \cdot P_{tr}(\mathbf{u} \mid \mathbf{t}) & \text{if } \kappa(\mathbf{t},\mathbf{u}) \\ (1-\sigma) \cdot P_{tr}(\mathbf{u} \mid \mathbf{t}) & \text{otherwise} \end{cases}$$

Our experiments compare performance when $\pi^0_{\mathbf{t}}$ is set using $P_\pi(\mathbf{u}) = P_{\text{CPLX}}$ (experiment 3) versus our category grammar P_{G} (4–6), and using $P_\pi(\mathbf{u} \mid \mathbf{t}) = P_\kappa$ as the compatibility distribution (3–4) versus P^{tr}_κ (5–6).

3.2 Emission Prior Means ($\phi^0_{\mathbf{t}}$)

For each supertag type $\mathbf{t}$, $\phi^0_{\mathbf{t}}$ is the mean distribution over words it emits. While Baldridge's approach used a uniform emission initialization, treating all words as equally likely, we can, again, induce token-level corpus-specific information:[5] To set $\phi^0_{\mathbf{t}}$, we use a variant and simplification of the procedure introduced by Garrette and Baldridge (2012) that takes advantage of our prior over categories P_{G}.

Assuming that $C(w)$ is the count of word type w in the raw corpus, $\text{TD}(w)$ is the set of supertags associated with word type w in the tag dictionary, and $\text{TD}(\mathbf{t})$ is the set of *known* word types associated with supertag $\mathbf{t}$, the count of word/tag pairs for known words (words appearing in the tag dictionary) is estimated by uniformly distributing a word's (δ-smoothed) raw counts over its tag dictionary entries:

$$C_{known}(\mathbf{t}, w) = \begin{cases} \frac{C(w)+\delta}{|\text{TD}(w)|} & \text{if } \mathbf{t} \in \text{TD}(w) \\ 0 & \text{otherwise} \end{cases}$$

For *unknown* words, we first use the idea of tag "openness" to estimate the likelihood of a particular tag t applying to an unknown word: if a tag applies to many word types, it is likely to apply to some new word type.

$$P(\text{unk} \mid \mathbf{t}) \propto |\text{known words } w \text{ s.t. } \mathbf{t} \in \text{TD}(w)|$$

Then, we apply Bayes' rule to get $P(\mathbf{t} \mid \text{unk})$, and use that to estimate word/tag counts for unknown words:

$$P(\mathbf{t} \mid \text{unk}) \propto P(\text{unk} \mid \mathbf{t}) \cdot P_{\text{G}}(\mathbf{t})$$

$$C_{\text{unk}}(\mathbf{t}, w) = C(w) \cdot P(\mathbf{t} \mid \text{unk})$$

Thus, with the estimated counts for all words:

$$P_{em}(w \mid \mathbf{t}) = \frac{C_{known}(\mathbf{t}, w) + C_{unk}(\mathbf{t}, w)}{\sum_{w'} C_{known}(\mathbf{t}, w') + C_{unk}(\mathbf{t}, w')}$$

We perform experiments comparing performance when $\phi^0_{\mathbf{t}}$ is uniform (3–5) and when $\phi^0_{\mathbf{t}}(w) = P_{em}(w \mid \mathbf{t})$ (6).

[5] Again, without gold tag frequencies.

4 Posterior Inference

We wish to find the most likely supertag of each word, given the model we just described and a corpus of training data. Since there is exact inference with these models is intractable, we resort to Gibbs sampling to find an approximate solution. At a high level, we alternate between resampling model parameters $(\phi_{\mathbf{t}}, \pi_{\mathbf{t}})$ given the current tag sequence and resampling tag sequences given the current model parameters and observed word sequences. It is possible to sample a new tagging from the posterior distribution over tag sequences for a sentence, given the sentence and the HMM parameters using the forward-filter backward-sample (FFBS) algorithm (Carter and Kohn, 1996). To efficiently sample new HMM parameters, we exploit Dirichlet-multinomial conjugacy. By repeating these alternating steps and accumulating the number of times each supertag is used in each position, we obtain an approximation of the required posterior quantities.

Our inference procedure takes as input the transition prior means $\pi^0_{\mathbf{t}}$, the emission prior means $\phi^0_{\mathbf{t}}$, and concentration parameters α_π and α_ϕ, along with the raw corpus and tag dictionary. The set of supertags associated with a word w will be known as $\text{TD}(w)$. We will refer to the set of word types included in the tag dictionary as "known" words and others as "unknown" words. For simplicity, we will assume that $\text{TD}(w)$, for any unknown word w, is the full set of CCG categories. During sampling, we always restrict the possible tag choices for a word w to the categories found in $\text{TD}(w)$. We refer to the sequence of word tokens as $\mathbf{x}$ and tags as $\mathbf{y}$.

We initialize the sampler by setting $\pi_{\mathbf{t}} = \pi^0_{\mathbf{t}}$ and $\phi_{\mathbf{t}} = \phi^0_{\mathbf{t}}$ and then sampling tagging sequences using FFBS.

To sample a tagging for a sentence $\mathbf{x}$, the strategy is to inductively compute, for each token x_i starting with $i = 0$ and going "forward", the probability of generating $x_0, x_1, \ldots, x_i$ via any tag sequence that ends with $y_i = \mathbf{u}$:

$$p(y_i = \mathbf{u} \mid x_{0:i}) = \phi_{\mathbf{u}}(x_i) \cdot \sum_{\mathbf{t} \in T} \pi_{\mathbf{t}}(\mathbf{u}) \cdot p(y_{i-1} = \mathbf{t} \mid x_{0:i-1})$$

We then pass through the sequence again, this time "backward" starting at $i = |\mathbf{x}| - 1$ and sampling

$$y_i \mid y_{i+1} \sim p(y_i = \mathbf{t} \mid x_{0:i}) \cdot \pi_{\mathbf{t}}(y_{i+1}).$$

Corpus		num. tags	raw tokens	TD tokens	TD entries	ambiguity type	ambiguity token	dev tokens	test tokens
English	CCGBank POS	50	158k	735k	45k	3.75	13.11	—	—
	CCGBank	1,171			65k	56.98	296.18	128k	127k
Chinese	CTB-CCG	829	99k	439k	60k	96.58	323.37	59k	85k
Italian	CCG-TUT	955	6k	27k	9k	178.88	426.13	5k	5k

Table 1: Statistics for the various corpora used. CCGBank is English, CCG-CTB is Chinese, and TUT is Italian. The number of tags includes only those tags found in the tag dictionary (TD). Ambiguity rates are the average number of entries in the unpruned tag dictionary for each word in the raw corpus. English POS statistics are shown only for comparison; only CCG experiments were run.

The block-sampling approach of choosing new tags for a sentence all at once is particularly beneficial given the sequential nature of the model of the HMM. In an HMM, a token's adjacent tags tend to hold onto its current tag due to the relationships between the three. Resampling all tags at once allows for more drastic changes at each iteration, providing better opportunities for mixing during inference. The FFBS approach has the additional advantage that, by resampling the distributions only once per iteration, we are able to resample all sentences in parallel. This is not strictly true of all HMM problems with FFBS, but because our data is divided by sentence, and each sentence has a known start and end tag, the tags chosen during the sampling of one sentence cannot affect the sampling of another sentence in the same iteration.

Once we have sampled tags for the entire corpus, we resample π and ϕ. The newly-sampled tags $\mathbf{y}$ are used to compute $C(w, \mathbf{t})$, the count of tokens with word type w and tag $\mathbf{t}$, and $C(\mathbf{t}, \mathbf{u})$, the number of times tag $\mathbf{t}$ is directly followed by tag $\mathbf{u}$. We then sample, for each $\mathbf{t} \in T$ where T is the full set of valid CCG categories:

$$\pi_{\mathbf{t}} \sim \text{Dir}\left(\langle \alpha_\pi \cdot \pi^0_{\mathbf{t}}(\mathbf{u}) + C(\mathbf{t}, \mathbf{u})\rangle_{\mathbf{u}\in T}\right)$$
$$\phi_{\mathbf{t}} \sim \text{Dir}\left(\langle \alpha_\phi \cdot \phi^0_{\mathbf{t}}(w) + C(w, \mathbf{t})\rangle_{w\in V}\right)$$

It is important to note that this method of resampling allows the draws to incorporate both the data, in the form of counts, and the prior mean, which includes all of our carefully-constructed biases derived from both the intrinsic, universal CCG properties as well as the information we induced from the raw corpus and tag dictionary.

With the distributions resampled, we can continue the procedure by resampling tags as above, and then resampling distributions again, until a maximum number of iterations is reached.

5 Experiments[6]

To evaluate our approach, we used CCGBank (Hockenmaier and Steedman, 2007), which is a transformation of the English Penn Treebank (Marcus et al., 1993); the CTB-CCG (Tse and Curran, 2010) transformation of the Penn Chinese Treebank (Xue et al., 2005); and the CCG-TUT corpus (Bos et al., 2009), built from the TUT corpus of Italian text (Bosco et al., 2000). Statistics on the size and ambiguity of these datasets are shown in Table 1.

For CCGBank, sections 00–15 were used for extracting the tag dictionary, 16–18 for the raw corpus, 19–21 for development data, and 22–24 for test data. For TUT, the first 150 sentences of each of the CIVIL_LAW and NEWSPAPER sections were used for raw data, the next sentences 150–249 of each was used for development, and the sentences 250–349 were used for test; the remaining data, 457 sentences from CIVIL_LAW and 548 from NEWSPAPER, plus the much smaller 132-sentence JRC_ACQUIS data, was used for the tag dictionary. For CTB-CCG, sections 00–11 were used for the tag dictionary, 20–24 for raw, 25–27 for dev, and 28–31 for test.

Because we are interested in showing the relative gains that our ideas provide over Baldridge (2008), we reimplemented the initialization procedure from that paper, allowing us to evaluate all approaches consistently. For each dataset, we ran a series of experiments in which we made further changes from the original work. We first ran a baseline experiment with uniform transition and emission initialization of EM (indicated as "1." in Table 2) followed by our reimplementation of the initialization procedure by Baldridge (2). We then

[6]All code and experimental scripts are available at http://www.github.com/dhgarrette/2014-ccg-supertagging

Corpus		English				Chinese				Italian			
TD cutoff		0.1	0.01	0.001	no	0.1	0.01	0.001	no	0.1	0.01	0.001	no
1. uniform	EM	77	62	47	38	64	39	30	26	51	32	30	30
2. init (Baldridge)	EM	78	67	55	41	66	43	33	28	**54**	36	33	32
3. init	Bayes	74	68	56	42	65	56	47	37	52	46	40	40
4. P_G	Bayes	74	70	59	42	64	57	47	36	52	40	39	40
5. P_G, P_κ^{tr}	Bayes	75	72	61	50	66	58	49	44	52	44	41	43
6. P_G, P_κ^{tr}, P_{em}	Bayes	**80**	**80**	**73**	**51**	**69**	**62**	**56**	**49**	53	**47**	**45**	**46**

Table 2: Experimental results: test-set per-token supertag accuracies. "TD cutoff" indicates the level of tag dictionary pruning; see text. (1) is uniform EM initialization. (2) is a reimplementation of (Baldridge, 2008). (3) is Bayesian formulation using only the ideas from Baldridge: P_{CPLX}, P_κ, and uniform emissions. (4–6) are our enhancements to the prior: using our category grammar in P_G instead of P_{CPLX}, using P_κ^{tr} instead of P_κ, and using P_{em} instead of uniform.

experimented with the Bayesian formulation, first using the same information used by Baldridge, and then adding our enhancements: using our category grammar in P_G, using P_κ^{tr} as the transition compatability distribution, and using P_{em} as $\phi_t^0(w)$.

For each dataset, we ran experiments using four different levels of tag dictionary pruning. Pruning is the process of artificially removing noise from the tag dictionary by using token-level annotation counts to discard low-probability tags; for each word, for cutoff x, any tag with probability less than x is excluded. Tag dictionary pruning is a standard procedure in type-supervised training, but because it requires information that does not truly conform to the type-supervised scenario, we felt that it was critical to demonstrate the performance of our approach under situations of less pruning, *including* no artificial pruning at all.

We emphasize that unlike in most previous work, we use *incomplete* tag dictionaries. Most previous work makes the unrealistic assumption that the tag dictionary contains an entry for every word that appears in either the training *or testing* data. This is a poor approximation of a real tagging system, which will never have complete lexical knowledge about the test data. Even work that only assumes complete knowledge of the tagging possibilities for the lexical items in the training corpus is problematic (Baldridge, 2008; Ravi et al., 2010). This still makes learning unrealistically easy since it dramatically reduces the ambiguity of words that would have been unseen, and, in the case of CCG, introduces additional tags that would not have otherwise been known. To ensure that our experiments are more realistic, we draw our tag dictionary entries from data that is totally disjoint from both the raw and test corpora. During learning, any unknown words (words not appearing in the tag dictionary) are unconstrained so that they may take *any* tag, and are, thus, maximally ambiguous.

We only performed minimal parameter tuning, choosing instead to stay consistent with Baldridge (2008) and simply pick reasonable-seeming values for any additional parameters. Any tuning that was performed was done with simple hill-climbing on the development data of English CCGBank. All parameters were held consistent across experiments, including across languages. For EM, we used 50 iterations; for FFBS we used 100 burn-in iterations and 200 sampling iterations.[7] For all experiments, we used $\sigma = 0.95$ for $P_\kappa^{(tr)}$ and $\lambda = 0.5$ for π_t^0 to be consistent with previous work, $\alpha_\pi = 3000$, $\alpha_\phi = 7000$, $p_{term} = 0.6$, $p_{fw} = 0.5$, $p_{mod} = 0.8$, and $\delta = 1000$ for p_{atom}. Test data was run only once, for the final figures.

The final results reported were achieved by using the following training sequence: initialize parameters according to the scenario, train an HMM using EM or FFBS starting with that set of parameters, tag the raw corpus with the trained HMM, add-0.1 smooth counts from the now-tagged raw corpus, and train a maximum entropy Markov model (MEMM) from this "auto-supervised" data.[8]

Results are shown in Table 2. Most notably, the contributions described in this paper improve results in nearly every experimental scenario. We can see immediate, often sizable, gains in most

[7] Final counts are averaged across the sampling iterations.

[8] Auto-supervised training of an MEMM increases accuracy by 1–3% on average (Garrette and Baldridge, 2013). We use the OpenNLP MEMM implementation with its standard set of features: `http://opennlp.apache.org`

cases simply by using the Bayesian formulation. Further gains are seen from adding each of the other various contributions of this paper. Perhaps most interestingly, the gains are only minimal with maximum pruning, but the gains increase as the pruning becomes less aggressive — as the scenarios become more realistic. This indicates that our improvements make the overall procedure more robust.

Error Analysis Like POS-taggers, the learned supertagger frequently confuses nouns (N) and their modifiers (N/N), but the most frequent error made by the English (6) experiment was (((S\NP)\(S\NP))/N) instead of (NP_{nb}/N). However, these are both determiner types, indicating an interesting problem for the supertagger: it often predicts an object type-raised determiner instead of the vanilla NP/N, but in many contexts, both categories are equally valid. (In fact, for parsers that use type-raising as a rule, this distinction in lexical categories does not exist.)

6 Related Work

Ravi et al. (2010) also improved upon the work by Baldridge (2008) by using integer linear programming to find a minimal model of supertag transitions, thereby generating a better starting point for EM than the grammatical constraints alone could provide. This approach is complementary to the work presented here, and because we have shown that our work yields gains under tag dictionaries of various levels of cleanliness, it is probable that employing minimization to set the base distribution for sampling could lead to still higher gains.

On the Bayesian side, Van Gael et al. (2009) used a non-parametric, *infinite* HMM for truly unsupervised POS-tagger learning (Van Gael et al., 2008; Beal et al., 2001). While their model is not restricted to the standard set of POS tags, and may learn a more fine-grained set of labels, the induced labels are arbitrary and not grounded in any grammatical formalism.

Bisk and Hockenmaier (2013) developed an approach to CCG grammar induction that does not use a tag dictionary. Like ours, their procedure learns from general properties of the CCG formalism. However, while our work is intended to produce categories that match those used in a particular training corpus, however complex they might be, their work produces categories in a simplified form of CCG in which N and S are the only atoms and no atoms have features. Additionally, they assume that their training corpus is annotated with POS tags, whereas we assume truly raw text.

Finally, we find the task of weakly-supervised supertagger learning to be particularly relevant given the recent surge in popularity of CCG. An array of NLP applications have begun using CCG, including semantic parsing (Zettlemoyer and Collins, 2005) and machine translation (Weese et al., 2012). As CCG finds more applications, and as these applications move to lower-resource domains and languages, there will be increased need for the ability to learn without full supervision.

7 Conclusion and Future Work

Standard strategies for type-supervised HMM estimation are less effective as the number of categories increases. In contrast to POS tag sets, CCG supertags, while quite numerous, have structural clues that can simplify the learning problem. Baldridge (2008) used this formalism-specific structure to inform an initialization procedure for EM. In this work, we have shown that CCG structure can instead be used to motivate an effective *prior distribution* over the parameters of an HMM supertagging model, allowing our work to outperform Baldridge's previously state-of-the-art approach, and to do so in a principled manner that lends itself better to future extensions such as incorporation in more complex models.

This work also improves on Baldridge's simple "complexity" measure, developing instead a probabilistic category grammar over supertags that allows our prior to capture a wider variety of interesting and useful properties of the CCG formalism.

Finally, we were able to achieve further gains by augmenting the universal CCG knowledge with corpus-specific information that could be automatically extracted from the weak supervision that is available: the raw corpus and the tag dictionary. This allows us to combine the cross-linguistic properties of the CCG formalism with corpus- or language-specific information in the data into a single, unified Bayesian prior.

Our model uses a relatively large number of parameters, e.g., p_{term}, p_{fw}, p_{mod}, p_{atom}, in the prior. Here, we fixed each to a single value (i.e., a "fully Bayesian" approach). Future work might explore sensitivity to these choices, or empirical Bayesian or maximum *a posteriori* inference for their values (Johnson and Goldwater, 2009).

In this work, as in most type-supervised work, the tag dictionary was automatically extracted from an existing tagged corpus. However, a tag dictionary could instead be automatically induced via multi-lingual transfer (Das and Petrov, 2011) or generalized from human-provided information (Garrette and Baldridge, 2013; Garrette et al., 2013). Again, since the approach presented here has been shown to be somewhat robust to tag dictionary noise, it is likely that the model would perform well even when using an automatically-induced tag dictionary.

Acknowledgements

This work was supported by the U.S. Department of Defense through the U.S. Army Research Office (grant number W911NF-10-1-0533). Experiments were run on the UTCS Mastodon Cluster, provided by NSF grant EIA-0303609.

References

Jason Baldridge. 2008. Weakly supervised supertagging with grammar-informed initialization. In *Proceedings of COLING*.

Srinivas Bangalore and Aravind K. Joshi. 1999. Supertagging: An approach to almost parsing. *Computational Linguistics*, 25(2).

Matthew J. Beal, Zoubin Ghahramani, and Carl Edward Rasmussen. 2001. The innite hidden Markov model. In *NIPS*.

Taylor Berg-Kirkpatrick, Alexandre Bouchard-Côté, John DeNero, and Dan Klein. 2010. Painless unsupervised learning with features. In *Proceedings of NAACL*.

Yonatan Bisk and Julia Hockenmaier. 2013. An HDP model for inducing combinatory categorial grammars. *Transactions of the Association for Computational Linguistics*, 1.

Phil Blunsom and Trevor Cohn. 2011. A hierarchical Pitman-Yor process HMM for unsupervised part of speech induction. In *Proceedings of ACL*.

Johan Bos, Cristina Bosco, and Alessandro Mazzei. 2009. Converting a dependency treebank to a categorial grammar treebank for Italian. In M. Passarotti, Adam Przepiórkowski, S. Raynaud, and Frank Van Eynde, editors, *Proceedings of the Eighth International Workshop on Treebanks and Linguistic Theories (TLT8)*.

Cristina Bosco, Vincenzo Lombardo, Daniela Vassallo, and Leonardo Lesmo. 2000. Building a treebank for Italian: a data-driven annotation schema. In *Proceedings of LREC*.

Christopher K. Carter and Robert Kohn. 1996. On Gibbs sampling for state space models. *Biometrika*, 81(3):341–553.

Zhiyi Chi. 1999. Statistical properties of probabilistic context-free grammars. *Computational Linguistics*, 25(1).

Dipanjan Das and Slav Petrov. 2011. Unsupervised part-of-speech tagging with bilingual graph-based projections. In *Proceedings of ACL-HLT*.

Dan Garrette and Jason Baldridge. 2012. Type-supervised hidden Markov models for part-of-speech tagging with incomplete tag dictionaries. In *Proceedings of EMNLP*.

Dan Garrette and Jason Baldridge. 2013. Learning a part-of-speech tagger from two hours of annotation. In *Proceedings of NAACL*.

Dan Garrette, Jason Mielens, and Jason Baldridge. 2013. Real-world semi-supervised learning of POS-taggers for low-resource languages. In *Proceedings of ACL*.

Yoav Goldberg, Meni Adler, and Michael Elhadad. 2008. EM can find pretty good HMM POS-taggers (when given a good start). In *Proceedings of ACL*.

Sharon Goldwater and Thomas L. Griffiths. 2007. A fully Bayesian approach to unsupervised part-of-speech tagging. In *Proceedings of ACL*.

Julia Hockenmaier and Mark Steedman. 2007. CCG-bank: A corpus of CCG derivations and dependency structures extracted from the Penn Treebank. *Computational Linguistics*, 33(3).

Mark Johnson and Sharon Goldwater. 2009. Improving nonparameteric Bayesian inference: Experiments on unsupervised word segmentation with adaptor grammars. In *Proceedings of NAACL*.

Mark Johnson. 2007. Why doesn't EM find good HMM POS-taggers? In *Proceedings of EMNLP-CoNLL*.

Julian Kupiec. 1992. Robust part-of-speech tagging using a hidden Markov model. *Computer Speech & Language*, 6(3).

Yoong Keok Lee, Aria Haghighi, and Regina Barzilay. 2010. Simple type-level unsupervised pos tagging. In *Proceedings of EMNLP*.

Mitchell P. Marcus, Beatrice Santorini, and Mary Ann Marcinkiewicz. 1993. Building a large annotated corpus of English: The Penn Treebank. *Computational Linguistics*, 19(2).

Bernard Merialdo. 1994. Tagging English text with a probabilistic model. *Computational Linguistics*, 20(2).

Sujith Ravi and Kevin Knight. 2009. Minimized models for unsupervised part-of-speech tagging. In *Proceedings of ACL-AFNLP*.

Sujith Ravi, Jason Baldridge, and Kevin Knight. 2010. Minimized models and grammar-informed initialization for supertagging with highly ambiguous lexicons. In *Proceedings of ACL*, pages 495–503.

Noah A. Smith and Jason Eisner. 2005. Contrastive estimation: Training log-linear models on unlabeled data. In *Proceedings of ACL*.

Mark Steedman and Jason Baldridge. 2011. Combinatory categorial grammar. In Robert Borsley and Kersti Borjars, editors, *Non-Transformational Syntax: Formal and Explicit Models of Grammar*. Wiley-Blackwell.

Mark Steedman. 2000. *The Syntactic Process*. MIT Press.

Daniel Tse and James R. Curran. 2010. Chinese CCGbank: Extracting CCG derivations from the Penn Chinese treebank. In *Proceedings of COLING*.

Jurgen Van Gael, Yunus Saatci, Yee Whye Teh, and Zoubin Ghahramani. 2008. Beam sampling for the infinite hidden Markov model. In *Proceedings of ICML*.

Jurgen Van Gael, Andreas Vlachos, and Zoubin Ghahramani. 2009. The infinite HMM for unsupervised PoS tagging. In *Proceedings of EMNLP*.

Jonathan Weese, Chris Callison-Burch, and Adam Lopez. 2012. Using categorial grammar to label translation rules. In *Proceedings of WMT*.

Nianwen Xue, Fei Xia, Fu-Dong Chiou, and Martha Palmer. 2005. The Penn Chinese TreeBank: Phrase structure annotation of a large corpus. *Natural Language Engineering*, 11(2):207–238.

Luke S. Zettlemoyer and Michael Collins. 2005. Learning to map sentences to logical form: Structured classification with probabilistic categorial grammars. In *Proceedings of UAI*.

Factored Markov Translation with Robust Modeling

Yang Feng[†] **Trevor Cohn**[‡] **Xinkai Du**

[†] Information Sciences Institue
Computer Science Department
University of Southern California

[‡] Computing and Information Systems
The University of Melbourne
VIC 3010 Australia

{yangfeng145, xinkaid}@gmail.com t.cohn@unimelb.edu.au

Abstract

Phrase-based translation models usually memorize local translation literally and make independent assumption between phrases which makes it neither generalize well on unseen data nor model sentence-level effects between phrases. In this paper we present a new method to model correlations between phrases as a Markov model and meanwhile employ a robust smoothing strategy to provide better generalization. This method defines a recursive estimation process and backs off in parallel paths to infer richer structures. Our evaluation shows an 1.1–3.2% BLEU improvement over competitive baselines for Chinese-English and Arabic-English translation.

1 Introduction

Phrase-based methods to machine translation (Koehn et al., 2003; Koehn et al., 2007) have drastically improved beyond word-based approaches, primarily by using phrase-pairs as translation units, which can memorize local lexical context and reordering patterns. However, this literal memorization mechanism makes it generalize poorly to unseen data. Moreover, phrase-based models make an independent assumption, stating that the application of phrases in a derivation is independent to each other which conflicts with the underlying truth that the translation decisions of phrases should be dependent on context.

There are some work aiming to solve the two problems. Feng and Cohn (2013) propose a word-based Markov model to integrate translation and reordering into one model and use the sophisticated hierarchical Pitman-Yor process which backs off from larger to smaller context to provide dynamic adaptive smoothing. This model shows good generalization to unseen data while it uses words as the translation unit which cannot handle multiple-to-multiple links in real word alignments. Durrani et al. (2011) and Durrani et al. (2013) propose an operation sequence model (OSM) which models correlations between minimal translation units (MTUs) and evaluates probabilities with modified Kneser-Ney smoothing. On one hand the use of MTUs can help retain the multiple-to-multiple alignments, on the other hand its definition of operations where source words and target words are bundled into one operation makes it subjected to sparsity. The common feature of the above two methods is they both back off in one fixed path by dropping least recent events first which precludes some useful structures. For the segment pairs <bǎ tā kǎolǜ jìnqù, take it into account> in Figure 1, the more common structure is <bǎ ... kǎolǜ jìnqù, take ... into account>. If we always drop the least recent events first, then we can only learn the pattern <... tā kǎolǜ jìnqù, ... it into account>.

On these grounds, we propose a method with new definition of correlations and more robust probability modeling. This method defines a Markov model over correlations between minimal phrases where each is decomposed into three factors (*source, target* and *jump*). In the meantime it employs a fancier smoothing strategy for the Markov model which backs off by dropping multiple conditioning factors in parallel in order to learn richer structures. Both the uses of factors and parallel backoff give rise to robust modeling against sparsity. In addition, modeling bilingual information and reorderings into one model instead of adding them to the linear model as separate features allows for using more sophisticated estimation methods rather than get a loose weight for each feature from tuning algorithms.

We compare the performance of our model with that of the phrase-based model and the hierarchical phrase-based model on the Chinese-English and Arabic-English NIST test sets, and get an im-

Proceedings of the Eighteenth Conference on Computational Language Learning, pages 151–159, Baltimore, Maryland USA, June 26-27 2014.

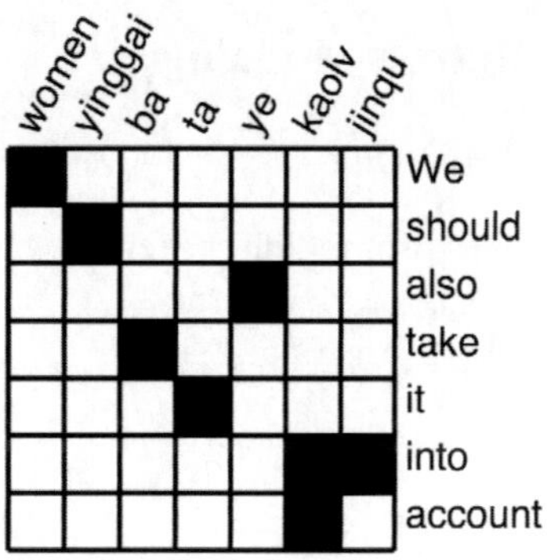

Figure 1: Example Chinese-English sentence pair with word alignments shown as filled grid squares.

provement up to 3.2 BLEU points absolute.[1]

2 Modelling

Our model is phrase-based and works like a phrase-based decoder by generating target translation left to right using phrase-pairs while jumping around the source sentence. For each derivation, we can easily get its minimal phrase (*MPs*) sequence where MPs are ordered according to the order of their target side. Then this sequence of events is modeled as a Markov model and the log probability under this Markov model is included as an additional feature into the linear SMT model (Och, 2003).

A MP denotes a phrase which cannot contain other phrases. For example, in the sentence pair in Figure 1, <*bǎ tā* , take it> is a phrase but not a minimal phrase, as it contains smaller phrases of <*bǎ* , take> and <*tā* , it>. MPs are a complex event representation for sequence modelling, and using these naively would be a poor choice because few bigrams and trigrams will be seen often enough for reliable estimation. In order to reason more effectively from sparse data, we consider more generalized representations by decomposing MPs into their component events: the source phrase (*source* $\bar{f}$), the target phrase (*target* $\bar{e}$) and the jump distance from the preceding MP (*jump* j), where the jump distance is counted in MPs, not in words. For sparsity reasons, we do not use the jump distance directly but instead group it into 12 buckets:

$$\{\text{insert}, \leq -5, -4, -3, -2, -1, 0, 1, 2, 3, 4, \geq 5\},$$

where the jump factor is denoted as insert when the source side is NULL. For the sentence pair in Figure 1, the MP sequence is shown in Figure 2.

To evaluate the Markov model, we condition each MP on the previous $k-1$ MPs and model each of the three factors separately based on a chain rule decomposition. Given a source sentence $\boldsymbol{f}$ and a target translation $\boldsymbol{e}$, the joint probability is defined as

$$p(\bar{\boldsymbol{e}}_1^I, \boldsymbol{j}_1^I, \bar{\boldsymbol{f}}_1^I) = \prod_{i=1}^{I} p(\bar{e}_i | \bar{f}_{i-k+1}^{i}, j_{i-k+1}^{i}, \bar{e}_{i-k+1}^{i-1}) \times \prod_{i=1}^{I} p(\bar{f}_i | \bar{f}_{i-k+1}^{i-1}, j_{i-k+1}^{i}, \bar{e}_{i-k+1}^{i-1}) \times \prod_{i=1}^{I} p(j_i | \bar{f}_{i-k+1}^{i-1}, j_{i-k+1}^{i-1}, \bar{e}_{i-k+1}^{i-1}) \quad (1)$$

where $\bar{f}_i$, $\bar{e}_i$ and j_i are the factors of MP_i, $\bar{\boldsymbol{f}}_1^I = (\bar{f}_1, \bar{f}_2, \ldots, \bar{f}_I)$ is the sequence of source MPs, $\bar{\boldsymbol{e}}_1^I = (\bar{e}_1, \bar{e}_2, \ldots, \bar{e}_I)$ is the sequence of target MPs, and $\boldsymbol{j}_1^I = (j_1, j_2, \ldots, j_I)$ is the vector of jump distance between MP_{i-1} and MP_i, or `insert` for MPs with null source sides.[2] To evaluate each of the k-gram models, we use modified Keneser-Ney smoothing to back off from larger context to smaller context recursively.

In summary, adding the Markov model into the decoder involves two passes: 1) training a model over the MP sequences extracted from a word aligned parallel corpus; and 2) calculating the probability of the Markov model for each translation hypothesis during decoding. This Markov model is combined with a standard phrase-based model[3] (Koehn et al., 2007) and used as an additional feature in the linear model.

In what follows, we will describe how to estatimate the k-gram Markov model, focusing on backoff (§2.1) and smoothing (§2.2).

2.1 Parallel Backoff

Backoff is a technique used in language model — when estimating a higher-order gram, instead of using the raw occurrence count, only a portion is used and the remainder is computed using a lower-order model in which one of the context factors

[1] We will contribute the code to Moses.

[2] Note that factors at indices $0, -1, \ldots, -(k-1)$ are set to a sentinel value to denote the start of sentence.

[3] The phrase-based model considers larger phrase-pairs than just MPs, while our Markov model consider only MPs. As each phrase-pair is composed of a sequence of MPs under fixed word alignment, by keeping the word alignment for each phrase, a decoder derivation unambiguously specifies the MP sequence for scoring under our Markov model.

index	*sentence pair*							*minimal phrase sequence*		
	wǒmén	yīnggāi	bǎ	tā	yě	kǎolǜ jìnqù		*jump*	*source*	*target*
1	We						T_1	1	wǒmén	We
2		should					T_2	1	yīnggāi	should
3					also		T_3	3	yě	also
4			take				T_4	-2	bǎ	take
5				it			T_5	1	tā	it
6						into account	T_6	2	kǎolǜ jìnqù	into account

Figure 2: The minimal phrase sequence $T_1, ..., T_6$ extracted from the sentence pair in Figure 1.

step	3-gram $\bar{e}_3 \vert \bar{f}_3, j_3, \bar{e}_2, \bar{f}_2, j_2, \bar{e}_1, \bar{f}_1, j_1$
0	into account | kǎolǜ jìnqù, 2, it, tā, 1, take, bǎ, -2
	↓ 1
1	into account | kǎolǜ jìnqù, 2, it, tā, –, take, bǎ, -2
	↓ tā
2	into account | kǎolǜ jìnqù, 2, it, –, –, take, bǎ, -2
	↓ it
3	into account | kǎolǜ jìnqù, 2, –, –, –, take, bǎ, -2
	↓ -2
4	into account | kǎolǜ jìnqù, 2, –, –, –, take, bǎ, –
	↓ bǎ
5	into account | kǎolǜ jìnqù, 2, –, –, –, take, –, –
	↓ take
6	into account | kǎolǜ jìnqù, 2, –, –, –, –, –, –
	↓ 2
7	into account | kǎolǜ jìnqù, –, –, –, –, –, –, –
	↓ kǎolǜ jìnqù
8	into account | –, –, –, –, –, –, –, –

Figure 3: One backoff path for the 3-gram in Equation 2. The symbols besides each arrow mean the current factor to drop; "–" is a placeholder for factors which can take any value.

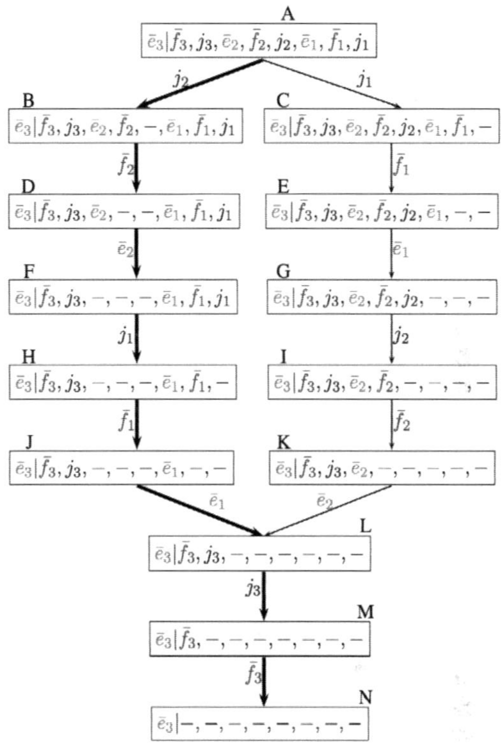

Figure 4: The backoff graph for the 3-gram model of the target factor. The symbol beside each arrow is the factor to drop.

is dropped. Here the probabilities of the lower-order which is used to construct the higher-order is called the *backoff probability* of the higher-order gram. Different from standard language models which drop the least recent words first, we employ a different backoff strategy which considers all possible backoff paths. Taking as an example the 3-gram $T_4T_5T_6$ in Figure 2, when estimating the probability of the target factor

$$\text{p(into account} \mid \text{kǎolǜ jìnqù, 2, it, tā, 1, take, bǎ, -2)}\ , \quad (2)$$

we consider two backoff paths: path_1 drops the factors in the order *-2, bǎ, take, 1, tā, it, 2, kǎolǜ jìnqù*; path_2 uses order *1, tā, it, -2, bǎ, take, 2, kǎolǜ jìnqù*. Figure 3 shows the backoff process for path_2. In this example with two backoff paths, the backoff probability g is estimated as

$$g(\text{into acc.}|\boldsymbol{c}) = \frac{1}{2}\,p(\text{into acc.}|\boldsymbol{c}') + \frac{1}{2}\,p(\text{into acc.}|\boldsymbol{c}'')\ ,$$

where $\boldsymbol{c} =<$ kǎolǜ jìnqù, 2, it, tā, 1, take, bǎ, -2 $>$, $\boldsymbol{c}' =<$ kǎolǜ jìnqù, 2, it, tā, 1, take, bǎ, – $>$ and $\boldsymbol{c}'' =<$ kǎolǜ jìnqù, 2, it, tā, –, take, bǎ, -2 $>$.

Formally, we use the notion of backoff graph to define the recursive backoff process of a k-gram and denote as nodes the k-gram and the lower-order grams generated by the backoff. Once one node occurs in the training data fewer than τ times, then estimates are calculated by backing off to the nodes in the next lower level where one factor is dropped (denoted using the placeholder – in Figure 4). One node can have one or several candidate backoff nodes. In the latter case, the backoff probability is defined as the *average* of the probabilities of the backoff nodes in the next lower level.

We define the backoff process for the 3-gram model predicting the target factor, $\bar{e}_3$, as illustrated in Figure 4. The top level is the full 3-gram, from which we derive two backoff paths by dropping factors from contextual events, one at a time. Formally, the backoff strategy is to drop the previous two MPs one by one while for each MP the dropping routine is first the jump factor, then the source factor and final the target factor. Each step on the path corresponds to dropping an individual contextual factor from the context. The paths converge when only the third MP left, then the backoff proceeds by dropping the jump action, j_3, then finally the source phrase, $\bar{f}_3$. The paths B-D-F-H-J and C-E-G-I-K show all the possible orderings (corresponding to $\boldsymbol{c}''$ and $\boldsymbol{c}'$, respectively) for dropping the two previous MPs. The example backoff in Figure 3 corresponds the path A-B-D-F-H-J-L-M-N in Figure 4, shown as heavier lines. When generizing to the k-gram for target $p(\bar{e}_k|\bar{f}_1^k, j_1^k, \bar{e}_1^{k-1})$, the backoff strategy is to first drop the previous k-1 MPs one by one (for each MP, still drops in the order of jump, source and target), then the *kth* jump factor and finally the *kth* source factor. According to the strategy, the top node has k-1 nodes to back off to and for the node $\bar{e}_k|\bar{f}_2^k, j_2^k, \bar{e}_2^{k-1}$ where only the factors of MP_1 are dropped, there are k-2 nodes to back off to.

2.2 Probability Estimation

We adopt the technique used in factor language models (Bilmes and Kirchhoff, 2003; Kirchhoff et al., 2007) to estimate the probability of a k-gram $p(\bar{e}_i|\boldsymbol{c})$ where $\boldsymbol{c} = \bar{f}_{i-k+1}^i, j_{i-k+1}^i, \bar{e}_{i-k+1}^{-1}$. According to the definition of backoff, only when the count of the k-gram exceeds some given threshold, its maximum-likelihood estimate, $p_{ML}(\bar{e}_k|\boldsymbol{c}) = \frac{N(\bar{e}_k,\boldsymbol{c})}{N(\boldsymbol{c})}$ is used, where $N(\cdot)$ is the count of an event and/or context. Otherwise, only a portion of $p_{ML}(\bar{e}_k|\boldsymbol{c})$ is used and the remainder is constructed from a lower-level (by dropping a factor). In order to ensure valid probability estimates, i.e. sums to unity, probability mass needs to be "stolen" from the higher level and given to the lower level. Hence, the whole definition is

$$p(\bar{e}_i|\boldsymbol{c}) = \begin{cases} d_{N(\bar{e}_i,\boldsymbol{c})} p_{ml}(\bar{e}_i|\boldsymbol{c}) & \text{if } N(\bar{e}_i,\boldsymbol{c}) > \tau_k \\ \alpha(\boldsymbol{c}) g(\bar{e}_i,\boldsymbol{c}) & \text{otherwise} \end{cases} \tag{3}$$

where $d_{N(\bar{e}_i,\boldsymbol{c})}$ is a discount parameter which reserves probability from the maximum-likelihood estimate for backoff smoothing at the next lower-level, and we estimate $d_{N(\bar{e}_i,\boldsymbol{c})}$ using modified Kneser-Ney smoothing (Kneser and Ney, 1995; Chen and Goodman, 1996); τ_k is the threshold for the count of the k-gram, $\alpha(\boldsymbol{c})$ is the backoff weight used to make sure the entire distribution still sums to unity,

$$\alpha(\boldsymbol{c}) = \frac{1 - \sum_{\bar{e}:N(\bar{e},\boldsymbol{c})>\tau_k} d_{N(\bar{e},\boldsymbol{c})} p_{ML}(\bar{e}|\boldsymbol{c})}{\sum_{\bar{e}:N(\bar{e},\boldsymbol{c})\leq\tau_k} g(\bar{e},\boldsymbol{c})},$$

and $g(\bar{e}_i,\boldsymbol{c})$ is the backoff probability which we estimate by averaging over the nodes in the next lower level,

$$g(\bar{e}_i,\boldsymbol{c}) = \frac{1}{\phi} \sum_{\boldsymbol{c}'} p(\bar{e}_i|\boldsymbol{c}'),$$

where ϕ is the number of nodes to back off, $\boldsymbol{c}'$ is the lower-level context after dropping one factor from $\boldsymbol{c}$.

The k-gram for the source and jump factors are estimated in the same way, using the same backoff semantics.[4] Note (3) is applied independently to each of the three models, so the use of backoff may differ in each case.

3 Discussion

As a part of the backoff process our method can introduce gaps in estimating rule probabilities; these backoff patterns often bear close resemblance to SCFG productions in the hierarchical phrase-based model (Chiang, 2007). For example, in step 0 in Figure 3, as all the jump factors are present, this encodes the full ordering of the MPs and gives rise to the aligned MP pairs shown in Figure 5 (a). Note that an $X_{\boxed{1}}$ placeholder is included to ensure the jump distance from the previous MP to the MP <*bǎ, take*> is *-2*. The approximate SCFG production for the MP pairs is <bǎ tā $X_{\boxed{1}}$ kǎolǜ jìnqù, $X_{\boxed{1}}$ take it into account>.

[4]Although there are fewer final steps, L-M-N in Fig. 4, as we assume the MP is generated in the order jump, source phrase then target phrase in a chain rule decomposition.

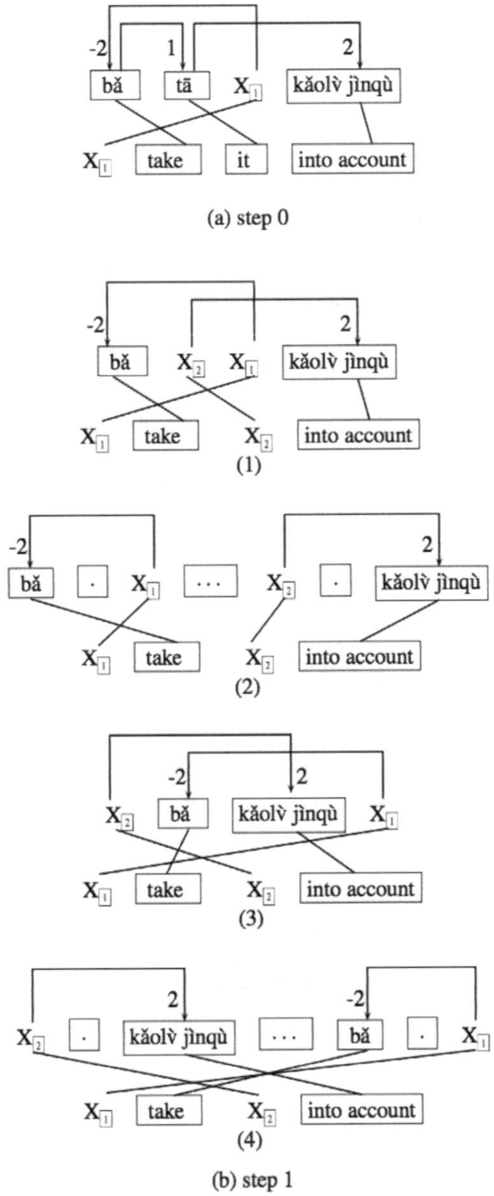

Figure 5: Approximate SCFG patterns for step 0, 3 of Figure 3. X is a non-terminal which can only be rewritten by one MP. $\boxed{\cdot}$ and $\boxed{\cdots}$ denote gaps introduced by the left-to-right decoding algorithm and $\boxed{\cdot}$ can only cover one MP while $\boxed{\cdots}$ can cover zero or more MPs.

In step 1, as the jump factor *1* is dropped, we do not know the orientation between bǎ and tā. However several jump distances are known: from $X_{\boxed{1}}$ to *bǎ* is distance *-2* and *tā* to *kǎolǜ jìnqù* is 2. In this case, the source side can be

bǎ tā $X_{\boxed{1}}$ *kǎolǜ jìnqù*,

bǎ $\boxed{\cdot}$ $X_{\boxed{1}}$ $\boxed{\cdots}$ *tā* $\boxed{\cdot}$ *kǎolǜ jìnqù*,

tā bǎ kǎolǜ jìnqù $X_{\boxed{1}}$,

tā $\boxed{\cdot}$ *kǎolǜ jìnqù* $\boxed{\cdots}$ bǎ $\boxed{\cdot}$ $X_{\boxed{1}}$,

where X and $\boxed{\cdot}$ can only hold one MP while $\boxed{\cdots}$ can cover zero or more MPs. In step 3 after dropping *tā* and *it*, we introduce a gap $X_{\boxed{2}}$ as shown in Figure 5 (b).

From above, we can see that our model has two kinds of gaps: 1) in the source due to the left-to-right target ordering (such as the $\boxed{\cdot}$ in step 3); and 2) in the target, arising from backoff (such as the $X_{\boxed{2}}$ in step 3). Accordingly our model supports rules than cannot be represented by a 2-SCFG (e.g., step 3 in Figure 5 requires a 4-SCFG). In contrast, the hierarchical phrase-based model allows only 2-SCFG as each production can rewrite as a maximum of two nonterminals. On the other hand, our approach does not enforce a valid hierarchically nested derivation which is the case for Chiang's approach.

4 Related Work

The method introduced in this paper uses factors defined in the same manner as in Feng and Cohn (2013), but the two methods are quite different. That method (Feng and Cohn, 2013) is word-based and under the frame of Bayesian model while this method is MP-based and uses a simpler Kneser-Ney smoothing method. Durrani et al. (2013) also present a Markov model based on MPs (they call minimal translation units) and further define operation sequence over MPs which are taken as the events in the Markov model. For the probability estimation, they use Kneser-Ney smoothing with a single backoff path. Different from operation sequence, our method gives a neat definition of factors which uses jump distance directly and avoids the bundle of source words and target words like in their method, and hence mitigates sparsity. Moreover, the use of parallel backoff infers richer structures and provides robust modeling.

There are several other work focusing on modeling bilingual information into a Markov model. Crego et al. (2011) develop a bilingual language model which incorporates words in the source and target languages to predict the next unit, and use it as a feature in a translation system. This line of work was extended by Le et al. (2012) who develop a novel estimation algorithm based around discriminative projection into continuous spaces. Neither work includes the jump distance, and nor do they consider dynamic strategies for estimating k-gram probabilities.

Galley and Manning (2010) propose a method to introduce discontinuous phrases into the phrase-based model. It makes use of the decoding mechanism of the phrase-based model which jumps over the source words and hence can hold discontinuous phrases naturally. However, their method doesn't touch the correlations between phrases and probability modeling which are the key points we focus on.

5 Experiments

We design experiments to first compare our method with the phrase-based model (PB), the operation sequence model (OSM) and the hierarchical phrase-based model (HPB), then we present several experiments to test:

1. how each of the factors in our model and parallel backoff affect overall performance;
2. how the language model order affects the relative gains, in order to test if we are just learning a high order LM, or something more useful;
3. how the Markov model interplay with the distortion and lexical reordering models of Moses, and are they complemenatary;
4. whether using MPs as translation units is better in our approach than the simpler tactic of using only word pairs.

5.1 Data Setup

We consider two language pairs: Chinese-English and Arabic-English. The Chinese-English parallel training data is made up of the non-UN portions and non-HK Hansards portions of the NIST training corpora, distributed by the LDC, having 1,658k sentence pairs with 40m and 44m Chinese and English words. We used the NIST 02 test set as the development set and evaluated performance on the test sets from NIST 03 and 05.

For the Arabic-English task, the training data comprises several LDC corpora,[5] including 276k sentence pairs and 8.21m and 8.97m words in Arabic and English, respectively. We evaluated on the NIST test sets from 2003 and 2005, and the NIST 02 test set was used for parameter tuning.

On both cases, we used the factor language model module (Kirchhoff et al., 2007) of the SRILM toolkit (Stolcke, 2002) to train a Markov model with the order $= 3$ over the MP sequences.[6] The threshold count of backoff for all nodes was $\tau = 2$.

We aligned the training data sets by first using GIZA++ toolkit (Och and Ney, 2003) to produce word alignments on both directions and then combining them with the *diag-final-and* heuristic. All experiments used a 5-gram language model which was trained on the Xinhua portion of the GIGAWORD corpus using the SRILM toolkit. Translation performance was evaluated using BLEU (Papineni et al., 2002) with case-insensitive $n \leq 4$-grams. We used minimum error rate training (Och, 2003) to tune the feature weights to maximize the BLEU score on the development set.

We used *Moses* for PB and *Moses-chart* for HPB with the configuration as follows. For both, max-phrase-length=*7*, ttable-limit[7]=*20*, stack-size=*50* and max-pop-limit=*500*; For Moses, search-algorithm=*1* and distortion-limit=*6*; For Moses-chart, search-algorithm=*3* and max-char-span[8]=*20* for Moses-chart. We used both the distortion model and the lexical reordering model for Moses (denoted as *Moses-l*) except in §5.5 we only used the distortion model (denoted as *Moses-d*). We implemented the OSM according to Durrani et al. (2013) and used the same configuration with *Moses-l*. For *our method* we used the same configuration as *Moses-l* but adding an additional feature of the Markov model over MPs.

5.2 Performance Comparison

We first give the results of performance comparison. Here we add another system (denoted as *Moses-l+trgLM*): *Moses-l* together with the target language model trained on the training data set, using the same configuration with *Moses-l*. This system is used to test whether our model gains improvement just for using additional information on the training set. We use the open tool of Clark et al. (2011) to control for optimizer stability and test statistical significance.

The results are shown in Tables 1 and 2. The two language pairs we used are quite different: Chinese has a much bigger word order difference c.f. English than does Arabic. The results show that our system can outperform the baseline

[5] LDC2004E72, LDC2004T17, LDC2004T18, LDC2006T02

[6] We only employed MPs with the length ≤ 3. If a MP had more than 3 words on either side, we omitted the alignment links to the first target word of this MP and extracted MPs according to the new alignment.

[7] The maximum number of lexical rules for each source span.

[8] The maximum span on the source a rule can cover.

System	NIST 02 (dev)	NIST 03	NIST 05
Moses-l	36.0	32.8	32.0
Moses-chart	36.9	33.6	32.6
Moses-l+trgLM	36.4	33.9	32.9
OSM	36.6	34.0	33.1
our model	37.9	36.0	35.1

Table 1: BLEU % scores on the Chinese-English data set.

System	NIST 02 (dev)	NIST 03	NIST 05
Moses-l	60.4	52.0	52.8
Moses-chart	60.7	51.8	52.4
Moses-l+trgLM	60.8	52.6	53.3
OSM	61.1	52.9	53.4
our model	62.2	53.6	53.9

Table 2: BLEU % scores on the Arabic-English data set.

systems significantly (with $p < 0.005$) on both language pairs, nevertheless, the improvement on Chinese-English is bigger. The big improvement over *Moses-l+trgLM* proves that the better performance of our model does not solely comes from the use of the training data. And the gain over OSM means our definition of factors gives a better handling to sparsity. We also notice that HPB does not give a higher BLEU score on Arabic-English than PB. The main difference between HPB and PB is that HPB employs gapped rules, so this result suggests that gaps are detrimental for Arabic-English translation. In §5.3, we experimentally validate this claim with our Markov model.

5.3 Impact of Factors and Parallel Backoff

We now seek to test the contribution of target, jump, source factors, as well as the parallel backoff technique in terms of BLEU score. We performed experiments on both Chinese-English and Arabic-English to test whether the contribution was related to language pairs. We designed the experiments as follows. We first trained a 3-gram Markov model only over target factors, $p(\bar{\boldsymbol{e}}_1^I|\bar{\boldsymbol{f}}_1^I) = \prod_{i=1}^I p(\bar{e}_i|\bar{e}_{i-2}^{i-1})$, denoted *+t*. Then we added the jump factor (*+t+j*), such that we now considering both target and jump events, $p(\bar{\boldsymbol{e}}_1^I, \bar{\boldsymbol{j}}_1^I|\bar{\boldsymbol{f}}_1^I) = \prod_{i=1}^I p(\bar{e}_i|\bar{j}_{i-2}^i, \bar{e}_{i-2}^{i-1})p(\bar{j}_i|\bar{j}_{i-2}^{i-1}, \bar{e}_{i-2}^{i-1})$. Next we added the source factor (*+t+j+s*) such that now all three factors are included from Equation 1. For the above three Markov models we used simple least-recent backoff (akin to a standard language model), and consequently these methods cannot represent gaps in the target. Finally, we trained another Markov model by introducing parallel backoff to the third one as described in §2.1. Each of the four Markov model approaches are implemented as adding an additional feature, respectively, into the *Moses-l* baseline.

System	Chinese-English		Arabic-English	
	NIST 02	NIST 03	NIST 02	NIST 03
Moses-l	36.0	32.8	60.4	52.0
+t	36.3	33.8	60.9	52.4
+t+j	37.1	34.7	62.1	53.4
+t+j+s	37.6	34.8	62.5	53.9
+t+j+s+p	37.9	36.0	62.2	53.6

Table 3: The impact of factors and parallel backoff. Key: *t–target, j–jump, s–source, p–parallel backoff.*

System	2gram	3gram	4gram	5gram	6gram
Moses-l	27.2	32.4	33.0	32.8	33.2
our method	31.6	34.0	35.8	36.0	36.2

Table 4: The impact of the order of the standard language models.

The results are shown in Table 3. Observe that adding each factor results in near uniform performance improvements on both language pairs. The jump factor gives big improvements of about 1% BLEU in both language pairs. However when using parallel backoff, the performance improves greatly for Chinese-English but degrades slightly on Arabic-English. The reason may be parallel backoff is used to encode common structures to capture the different word ordering between Chinese and English while for Arabic-English there are fewer consistent reordering patterns. This is also consistent with the results in Table 1 and 2 where HPB gets a little bit lower BLEU scores.

5.4 Impact of LM order

Our system resembles a language model in common use in SMT systems, in that it uses a Markov model over target words, among other factors. This raises the question of whether its improvements are due to it functioning as a target language model. Our experiments use order $k = 3$ over MP sequences and each MP can have at most 3 words. Therefore the model could in principle memorize 9-grams, although usually MPs are much smaller. To test whether our improvements are from using a higher-order language model or other reasons, we evaluate our system and the baseline system with a range of LMs of different order. If we can get consistent improvements over the baseline for

System	NIST 02 (dev)	NIST 03
Moses-d	35.1	31.3
Moses-l	36.0	32.8
Moses-d+M	36.4	34.8
Moses-l+M	37.9	36.0

Table 5: Comparison between our Markov model (denoted as *M*) and the lexical reordering model of Moses.

System	NIST 02 (dev)	NIST 03
Moses-l	36.0	32.8
Moses-l+word	36.9	34.0
Moses-l+MP	37.6	34.8

Table 6: Comparison between the MP-based Markov model and the word-based Markov model.

both small and large n, this suggests it's not the long context that plays the key role but is other information we have learned (e.g., jumps or rich structures).

Table 4 shows the results of using standard language models with orders $2-6$ in *Moses-l* and our method. We can see that language model order is very important. When we increase the order from 2 to 4, the BLEU scores for both systems increases drastically, but levels off for 4-gram and larger. Note that our system outperforms *Moses-l* by 4.4, 1.6, 2.8, 3.2 and 3.0 BLEU points, respectively. The large gain for 2-grams is likely due to the model behaving like a LM, however the fact that consistent gains are still realized for higher k suggests that the approach brings considerable complementary information, i.e., it is doing much more than simply language modelling.

5.5 Comparison with Lexical Reordering

Our Markov model learns a joint model of jump, source and target factors and this is similar to the lexical reordering model of Moses (Koehn et al., 2007), which learns general orientations of pairs of adjacent phrases (classed as monotone, swap or other). Our method is more complex, by learning explicit jump distances, while also using broader context. Here we compare the two methods, and test whether our approach is complementary by realizing gains over the lexicalized reordering baseline. We test this hypothesis by comparing the results of Moses with its simple distortion model (*Moses-d*), then with both simple distortion and lexicalized reordering (*Moses-l*), and then with our Markov model (denoted as *Moses-d+M* or *Moses-l+M*, for both baselines respectively).

The results are shown in Table 5. Comparing the results of *Moses-l* and *Moses-d*, we can see that the lexical reordering model outperforms the distortion model by a margin of 1.5% BLEU. Comparing *Moses-d+M* with *Moses-l*, our Markov model provides further improvements of 2.0% BLEU. Our approach does much more than model reordering, so it is unlikely that this improvement is solely due to being better a model of distortion. This is underscored by the final result in Table 5, for combining lexicalized distortion with our model (*Moses-l+M*) which gives the highest BLEU score, yielding another 1.2% increase.

5.6 Comparison with Word-based Markov

Our approach uses minimal phrases as its basic unit of translation, in order to preserve the many-to-many links found from the word alignments. However we now seek to assess the impact of the choice of these basic units, considering instead a simpler word-based setting which retains only 1-to-1 links in a Markov model. To do this, we processed target words left-to-right and for target words with multiple links, we only retained the link which had the highest lexical translation probability. Then we trained a 3-gram word-based Markov model which backs off by dropping the factors of the least recent word pairs in the order of first jump then source then target. This model was included as a feature in the *Moses-l* baseline (denoted as *Moses-l+word*), which we compared to a system using a MP-based Markov model backing off in the same way (denoted as *Moses-l+MP*).

According to the results in Table 6, using MPs leads to better performance. Surprisingly even the word based method outperforms the baseline. This points to inadequate phrase-pair features in the baseline, which can be more robustly estimated using a Markov decomposition. In addition to allowing for advanced smoothing, the Markov model can be considered to tile phrases over one another (each k-gram overlaps $k-1$ others) rather than enforcing a single segmentation as is done in the PB and HPB approaches. Fox (2002) states that phrases tend to move as a whole during reordering, i.e., breaking MPs into words opens the possibility of making more reordering errors. We could easily use larger phrase pairs as the basic unit, such as the phrases used during decoding. However, doing this involves a hard segmentation and would exacerbate issues of data sparsity.

6 Conclusions

In this paper we try to give a solution to the problems in phrase-based models, including weak generalization to unseen data and negligence of correlations between phrases. Our solution is to define a Markov model over minimal phrases so as to model translation conditioned on context and meanwhile use a fancy smoothing technique to learn richer structures such that can be applied to unseen data. Our method further decomposes each minimal phrase into three factors and operates in the unit of factors in the backoff process to provide a more robust modeling.

In our experiments, we prove that our definition of factored Markov model provides complementary information to lexicalized reordering and high order language models and the use of parallel backoff infers richer structures even those out of the reach of 2-SCFG and hence brings big performance improvements. Overall our approach gives significant improvements over strong baselines, giving consistent improvements of between 1.1 and 3.2 BLEU points on large scale Chinese-English and Arabic-English evaluations.

7 Acknowledges

The first author is supported by DARPA BOLT, contract HR0011-12-C-0014. The second author is the recipient of an Australian Research Council Future Fellowship (project number FT130101105). Thank the anonymous reviews for their insightful comments.

References

Jeff Bilmes and Katrin Kirchhoff. 2003. Factored language models and generalized parallel backoff. In *Proc. of HLT-NAACL*.

Stanley F. Chen and Joshua Goodman. 1996. An empirical study of smoothing techniques for language modeling. In *Proc. of ACL*, pages 310–318.

David Chiang. 2007. Hierarchical phrase-based translation. *Computational Linguistics*, 33:201–228.

Jonathan H. Clark, Chris Dyer, Alon Lavie, and Noah A. Smith. 2011. Better hypothesis testing for statistical machine translation: Controlling for optimizer instability. In *Proc. of ACL-HLT*, pages 176–181.

Josep Maria Crego, François Yvon, and José B. Mariño. 2011. Ncode: an open source bilingual n-gram smt toolkit. *Prague Bull. Math. Linguistics*, 96:49–58.

Nadir Durrani, Helmut Schmid, and Alexander Fraser. 2011. A joint sequence translation model with integrated reordering. In *Proc. of ACL-HLT*, pages 1045–1054, June.

Nadir Durrani, Alexander Fraser, and Helmut Schmid. 2013. Model with minimal translation units, but decode with phrases. In *Proc. of NAACL*, pages 1–11.

Yang Feng and Trevor Cohn. 2013. A markov model of machine translation using non-parametric bayesian inference. In *Proc. of ACL*, pages 333–342.

Heidi Fox. 2002. Phrasal cohesion and statistical machine translation. In *Proc. of EMNLP*, pages 304–311, July.

Michel Galley and Christopher D. Manning. 2010. Accurate non-hierarchical phrase-based translation. In *Proc. of NAACL*, pages 966–974.

Katrin Kirchhoff, Jeff Bilmes, and Kevin Duh. 2007. Factored language models tutorial.

Reinhard Kneser and Hermann Ney. 1995. Improved backing-off for m-gram language modeling. In *In Proceedings of the IEEE International Conference on Acoustics, Speech and Signal Processing*, volume 1, pages 181–184.

Philipp Koehn, Franz J. Och, and Daniel Marcu. 2003. Statistical phrase-based translation. In *Proc. of HLT-NAACL*, pages 127–133.

Philipp Koehn, Hieu Hoang, Alexandra Birch Mayne, Christopher Callison-Burch, Marcello Federico, Nicola Bertoldi, Brooke Cowan, Wade Shen, Christine Moran, Richard Zens, Chris Dyer, Ondrej Bojar, Alexandra Constantin, and Evan Herbst. 2007. Moses: Open source toolkit for statistical machine translation. In *Proc. of ACL, Demonstration Session*.

Hai-Son Le, Alexandre Allauzen, and François Yvon. 2012. Continuous space translation models with neural networks. In *Proc. of NAACL*, pages 39–48.

Frans J. Och and Hermann Ney. 2003. A systematic comparison of various statistical alignment models. *Computational Linguistics*, 29:19–51.

Frans J. Och. 2003. Minimum error rate training in statistical machine translation. In *Proc. of ACL*, pages 160–167.

Kishore Papineni, Salim Roukos, Todd Ward, and Wei-Jing Zhu. 2002. Bleu: a method for automatic evaluation of machine translation. In *Proceedings of ACL*, pages 311–318.

Andreas Stolcke. 2002. Srilm-an extensible language modeling toolkit. In *Proc. of ICSLP*.

Hallucinating Phrase Translations for Low Resource MT

Ann Irvine
Center for Language and Speech Processing
Johns Hopkins University

Chris Callison-Burch
Computer and Information Science Dept.
University of Pennsylvania

Abstract

We demonstrate that "hallucinating" phrasal translations can significantly improve the quality of machine translation in low resource conditions. Our hallucinated phrase tables consist of entries *composed* from multiple unigram translations drawn from the baseline phrase table and from translations that are induced from monolingual corpora. The hallucinated phrase table is very noisy. Its translations are low precision but high recall. We counter this by introducing 30 new feature functions (including a variety of monolingually-estimated features) and by aggressively pruning the phrase table. Our analysis evaluates the intrinsic quality of our hallucinated phrase pairs as well as their impact in end-to-end Spanish-English and Hindi-English MT.

1 Introduction

In this work, we augment the translation model for a low-resource phrase-based SMT system by automatically expanding its phrase table. We "hallucinate" new phrase table entries by composing the unigram translations from the baseline system's phrase table and translations learned from comparable monolingual corpora. The composition process yields a very large number of new phrase pair translations, which are high recall but low precision. We filter the phrase table using a new set of feature functions estimated from monolingual corpora. We evaluate the hallucinated phrase pairs intrinsically as well as in end-to-end machine translation. The augmented phrase table provides more coverage than the original phrase table, while being high quality enough to improve translation performance.

We propose a four-part approach to hallucinating and using new phrase pair translations:

1. Learn potential translations for out-of-vocabulary (OOV) words from comparable monolingual corpora
2. "Hallucinate" a large, noisy set of phrase translations by composing unigram translations from the baseline model and from the monolingually-induced bilingual dictionary
3. Use comparable monolingual corpora to score, rank, and prune the huge number of hallucinated translations
4. Augment the baseline phrase table with hallucinated translations and new feature functions estimated from monolingual corpora

We define an algorithm for generating *loosely compositional* phrase pairs, which we use to hallucinate new translations. In oracle experiments, we show that such loosely compositional phrase pairs contribute substantially to the performance of end-to-end SMT, beyond that of component unigram translations. In our non-oracle experiments, we show that adding a judiciously pruned set of automatically hallucinated phrase pairs to an end-to-end baseline SMT model results in a significant improvement in translation quality for both Spanish-English and Hindi-English.

2 Motivation

Translation models learned over small amounts of parallel data suffer from the problem of *low coverage*. That is, they do not include translations for many words and phrases. Unknown

Proceedings of the Eighteenth Conference on Computational Language Learning, pages 160–170,
Baltimore, Maryland USA, June 26-27 2014.

words, or out-of-vocabulary (OOV) words, have been the focus of previous work on integrating bilingual lexicon induction and machine translation (Daumé and Jagarlamudi, 2011; Irvine and Callison-Burch, 2013a; Razmara et al., 2013). Bilingual lexicon induction is the task of learning translations from monolingual texts, and typical approaches compare projected distributional signatures of words in the source language with distributional signatures representing target language words (Rapp, 1995; Schafer and Yarowsky, 2002; Koehn and Knight, 2002; Haghighi et al., 2008). If the source and target language each contain, for example, $100,000$ words, the number of pairwise comparisons is about 10 billion, which is significant but computationally feasible.

In contrast to unigrams, the difficulty in inducing a comprehensive set of *phrase* translations is that the number of both source and target phrases is immense. For example, there are about 83 million unique phrases up to length three in the English Wikipedia. Pairwise comparisons of two sets of 100 million phrases corresponds to 1 x 10^{16}. Thus, even if we limit the task to short phrases, the number of pairwise phrase comparisons necessary to do an exhaustive search is infeasible. However, multi-word translation units have been shown to improve the quality of SMT dramatically (Koehn et al., 2003). Phrase translations allow translation models to memorize local context-dependent translations and reordering patterns.

3 Approach

Rather than compare *all* source language phrases with *all* target language phrases, our approach efficiently proposes a smaller set of hypothesis phrase translations for each source language phrase. Our method builds upon the notion that many phrase translations can be composed from the translations of its component words and subphrases. For example Spanish *la bruja verde* translates into English as *the green witch*. Each Spanish word corresponds to exactly one English word. The phrase pair could be memorized and translated as a unit, or the English translation could be composed from the translations of each Spanish unigram.

Zens et al. (2012) found that only 2% of phrase pairs in German-English, Czech-English, Spanish-English, and French-English phrase tables consist of multi-word source and target phrases and are non-compositional. That is, for these languages, the vast majority of phrase pairs in a given phrase table could be composed from smaller units. Our approach takes advantage of the fact that many phrases can be translated compositionally.

We describe our approach in three parts. In Section 3.1, we begin by inducing translations for unknown unigrams. Then, in 3.2, we introduce our algorithm for composing phrase translations. In order to achieve a high recall in our set of hypothesis translations, we define compositionality more loosely than is typical. Finally, in 3.3, we use comparable corpora to prune the large set of hypothesis translations for each source phrase.

3.1 Unigram Translations

In any low resource setting, many word translations are likely to be unknown. Therefore, before moving to phrases, we use a bilingual lexicon induction technique to identify translations for unigrams. Specifically, because we assume a setting where we have some small amount of parallel data, we follow our prior work on supervised bilingual lexicon induction (Irvine and Callison-Burch, 2013b). We take examples of good translation pairs from our word aligned training data (described in Section 4) and use random word pairs as negative supervision. We use this supervision to learn a log-linear classifier that predicts whether a given word pair is a translation or not. We pair and score all source language unigrams in our tuning and test sets with target language unigrams that appear in our comparable corpora. Then, for each source language unigram, we use the log-linear model scores to rerank candidate target language unigram translations. As in our prior work, we include the following word pair features in our log-linear classifier: contextual similarity, temporal similarity, topic similarity, frequency similarity, and orthographic similarity.

3.2 Loosely Compositional Translations

We propose a novel technique for *loosely composing* phrasal translations from an existing dictionary of unigram translations and stop word lists. Given a source language phrase, our approach considers all *combinations* and all *permutations* of all unigram translations for each source phrase content word. We ignore stop words in the input source phrase and allow any number of stop words anywhere in the output target phrase. In order to make the enumeration efficient, we precompute an inverted index that maps sorted target

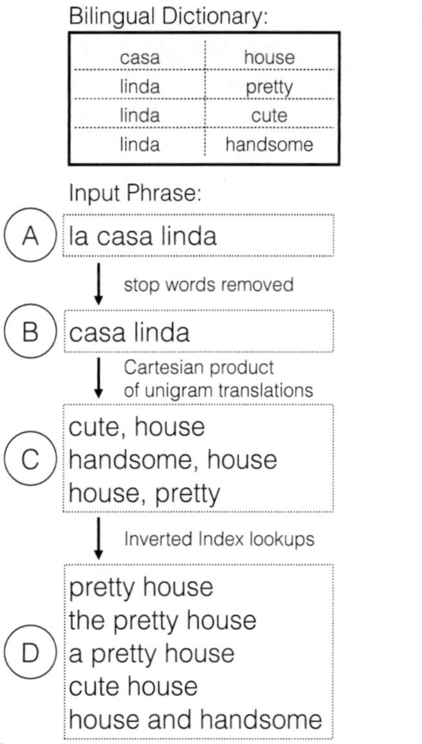

Figure 1: Example of loosely composed translations for the Spanish input in A, *la casa linda*. In B, we remove the stop word *la*. Then, in C, we enumerate the cartesian product of all unigram translations in the bilingual dictionary and sort the words within each alphabetically. Finally, we look up each list of words in C in the inverted index, and corresponding target phrases are enumerated in D. The inverted index contains all phrasal combinations and permutations of the word lists in C which also appear monolingually with some frequency and with, optionally, any number of stop words.

Input: A set of source language phrases of interest, **S**, each consisting of a sequence of words $s_1^m, s_2^m, ...s_i^m$; A list of all target language phrases, $targetPhrases$; Source and target stop word lists, $Stop_{src}$ and $Stop_{trg}$; Set of unigram translations, $\mathbf{t}_{s_i^m}$, for all source language words $s_i^m \notin Stop_{src}$; monolingual target language phrase frequencies, $Freq_T$; Monolingual frequency threshold θ_{Freq_T}

Output: $\forall\ S^m \in \mathbf{S}$, a set of candidate phrase translations, $T_1^m, T_2^m, ...T_k^m$

Construct TargetInvertedIndex:
for $T \in targetPhrases$ **do**
  if $Freq_T(T) \geqslant \theta_{Freq_T}$ **then**
    $T' \leftarrow$words $t_j \in T$ if $t_j \notin Stop_{trg}$
    $T'_{sorted} \leftarrow$ sorted(T')
    append T to TargetInvertedIndex$[T'_{sorted}]$
  end
end

for $S^m \in \mathbf{S}$ **do**
  $S' \leftarrow$words $s_i^m \in S^m$ if $s_i^m \notin Stop_{src}$
  Combs$_{S'} \leftarrow \mathbf{t}_{s'_1} \times \mathbf{t}_{s'_2} \times ... \times \mathbf{t}_{s'_k}$
  $T \leftarrow [\,]$
  for $c_{s'} \in Combs_{S'}$ **do**
    $c_{s'_{sorted}} \leftarrow$ sorted$(c_{s'})$
    $T \leftarrow T+$TargetInvertedIndex$(c_{s'_{sorted}})$
  end
  $T^m = T$
end

Algorithm 1: Computing a set of candidate compositional phrase translations for each source phrase in the set S. An inverted index of target phrases is constructed that maps sorted lists of content words to phrases that contain those content words, as well as optionally any stop words, and have a frequency of at least θ_{Freq_T}. Then, for a given source phrase S^m, stop words are removed from the phrase. Next, the cartesian product of all unigram translations is computed. Each element in the product is sorted and any corresponding phrases in the inverted index are added to the output.

language content words to sets of phrases containing those words in any order along with, optionally, any number of stop words. Our algorithm for composing candidate phrase translations is given in Algorithm 1, and an example translation is composed in Figure 1. Although in our experiments we compose translations for source phrases up to length three, the algorithm is generally applicable to any set of source phrases of interest.

Algorithm 1 yields a set of target language translations for any source language phrase for which all content unigrams have at least one known translation. For most phrases, the resulting set of hypothesis translations is very large and the majority are incorrect. In an initial pruning step, we add a monolingual frequency cutoff to the composition algorithm and only add target phrases that have a frequency of at least θ_{Freq_T} to the inverted index. Doing so eliminates improbable target language constructions early on, for example *house handsome her* or *cute a house*.

3.3 Pruning Phrase Pairs Using Scores Derived from Comparable Corpora

We further prune the large, noisy set of hypothesized phrase translations before augmenting a seed translation model. To do so, we use a supervised setup very similar to that used for inducing unigram translations; we estimate a variety of signals that indicate translation equivalence, including temporal, topical, contextual, and string similarity. As we showed in Klementiev et al. (2012), such signals are effective for identifying phrase translations as well as unigram translations. We add ngram length, alignment, and unigram translation features to the set, listed in Appendix A.

We learn a log-linear model for combining the features into a single score for predicting the quality of a given phrase pair. We extract training data from the seed translation model. We rank hypothesis translations for each source phrase using classification scores and keep the top-k. We found that using a score threshold sometimes improves precision. However, as experiments below show, the recall of the set of phrase pairs is more important, and we did not observe improvements in translation quality when we used a score threshold.

4 Experimental Setup

In all of our experiments, we assume that we have access to only a small parallel corpus. For our Spanish experiments, we randomly sample $2,000$ sentence pairs (about $57,000$ Spanish words) from the Spanish-English Europarl v5 parallel corpus (Koehn, 2005). For Hindi, we use the parallel corpora released by Post et al. (2012). Again, we randomly sample $2,000$ sentence pairs from the training corpus (about $39,000$ Hindi words). We expect that this amount of parallel text could be compiled for a single text domain and any pair of modern languages. Additionally, we use approximately $2,500$ and $1,000$ single-reference parallel sentences each for tuning and testing our Spanish and Hindi models, respectively. Spanish tuning and test sets are newswire articles taken from the 2010 WMT shared task (Callison-Burch et al., 2010).[1] We use the Hindi development and testing splits released by Post et al. (2012).

4.1 Unigram Translations

Of the $16,269$ unique unigrams in the source side of our Spanish MT tuning and test sets, 73% are OOV with respect to our training corpus. 21% of unigram tokens are OOV. For Hindi, 61% of the $8,137$ unique unigrams in the tuning and test sets are OOV with respect to our training corpus, and 18% of unigram tokens are OOV. However, because automatic word alignments estimated over the small parallel training corpora are noisy, we use bilingual lexicon induction to induce translations for *all* unigrams. We use the Wikipedia and online news web crawls datasets that we released in Irvine and Callison-Burch (2013b) to estimate similarity scores. Together, the two datasets contain about 900 million words of Spanish data and about 50 million words of Hindi data. For both languages, we limit the set of hypothesis target unigram translations to those that appear at least 10 times in our comparable corpora.

We use $3,000$ high probability word translation pairs extracted from each parallel corpus as positive supervision and $9,000$ random word pairs as negative supervision. We use Vowpal Wabbit[2] for learning. The top-5 induced translations for each source language word are used as both a baseline set of new translations (Section 6.3) and for composing phrase translations.

4.2 Composing and Pruning Phrase Translations

There are about 183 and 66 thousand unique bigrams and trigrams in the Spanish and Hindi tuning and test sets, respectively. However, many of these phrases do not demand new hypothesis translations. We do not translate those which contain numbers or punctuation. Additionally, for Spanish, we exclude names, which are typically translated identically between Spanish and English.[3] We exclude phrases which are sequences of stop words only. Additionally, we exclude phrases that appear more than 100 times in the small training corpus because our seed phrase table likely already contains high quality translations for them. Finally, we exclude phrases that appear fewer than 20 times in our comparable corpora as our features are unreliable when estimated over so few tokens. We hypothesize translations for the approximately 15 and 6 thousand Spanish and Hindi phrases, respectively, which meet these criteria. Our approach for inducing translations straightforwardly generalizes to any set of source phrases.

In defining loosely compositional phrase translations, we use both the induced unigram dictionary (Section 3.1) and the dictionary extracted from the word aligned parallel corpus. We expand these dictionaries further by mapping unigrams to their five-character word prefixes. We use monolingual corpora of Wikipedia articles[4] to construct stop word lists, containing the most frequent 300 words in each language, and indexes of monolingual phrase frequencies. There are about 83 million unique phrases up to length three in the English Wikipedia. However, we ignore target phrases that appear fewer than three times, reducing this set to 10 million English phrases. On

[1] *news-test2008* plus *news-syscomb2009* for tuning and *newstest2009* for testing.

[2] `http://hunch.net/~vw/`, version 6.1.4. with standard learning parameters

[3] Our names list comes from page titles of Spanish Wikipedia pages about people. We iterate through years, beginning with 1AD, and extract names from Wikipedia 'born in' category pages, e.g. '2013 births,' or 'Nacidos en 2013.'

[4] All inter-lingually linked source language and English articles.

average, our Spanish model yields $7,986$ English translations for each Spanish bigram, and $9,231$ for each trigram, or less than 0.1% of all possible candidate English phrases. Our Hindi model yields even fewer candidate English phrases, 826 for each bigram and $1,113$ for each trigram, on average.

We use the same comparable corpora used for bilingual lexicon induction to estimate features over hypothesis phrase translations. The full feature set is listed in Appendix A. We extract supervision from the seed translation models by first identifying phrase pairs with multi-word source strings, that appear at least three times in the training corpus, and that are composeable using baseline model unigram translations and induced dictionaries. Then, for each language pair, we use the $3,000$ that have the highest $p(f|e)$ scores as positive supervision. We randomly sample $9,000$ compositional phrase pairs from those not in each phrase table as negative supervision. Again, we use Vowpal Wabbit for learning a log linear model to score any phrase pair.

4.3 Machine Translation

We use GIZA++ to word align each training corpus. We use the Moses SMT framework (Koehn et al., 2007) and the standard phrase-based MT feature set, including phrase and lexical translation probabilities and a lexicalized reordering model. When we augment our models with new translations, we use the average reordering scores over all bilingually estimated phrase pairs. We tune all models using batch MIRA (Cherry and Foster, 2012). We average results over three tuning runs and use approximate randomization to measure statistical significance (Clark et al., 2011).

For Spanish, we use a 5-gram language model trained on the English side of the complete Europarl corpus and for Hindi a 5-gram language model trained on the English side of the complete training corpus released by Post et al. (2012). We train our language models using SRILM with Kneser-Ney smoothing. Our baseline models use a phrase limit of three, and we augment them with translations of phrases up to length three in our experiments.

5 Oracle Experiment

Before moving to the results of our proposed approach for composing phrase translations, we present an oracle experiment to answer these research questions: Would a low resource translation model benefit from composing its unigram translations into phrases? Would this be further improved by adding unigram translations that are learned from monolingual texts? We answer these questions by starting with our low-resource Spanish-English and Hindi-English baselines and augmenting each with (1) phrasal translations composed from baseline model unigram translations, and (2) phrasal translations composed of a mix of baseline model unigram translations and the monolingually-induced unigrams.

Figure 2 illustrates how our hallucinated phrase-table entries can result in improved translation quality for Spanish to English translation. Since the baseline model is trained from such a small amount of data, it typically translates individual words instead of phrases. In our augmented system, we compose a translation of *was no one* from *habia nadie,* since *habia* translates as *was* in the baseline model, *nadie* translates as *one,* and *no* is a stop word. We are able to monolingually-induce translations for the OOVs *centros* and *electorales* before composing the phrase translation *polling stations* for *centros electorales*.

In our oracle experiments, composed translations are only added to the phrase table if they are contained in the reference. This eliminates the huge number of noisy translations that our compositional algorithm generates. We augment baseline models with translations for the same sets of source language phrases described in Section 4. We use GIZA++ to word align our tuning and test sets[5] and use a standard phrase pair extraction heuristic[6] to identify oracle phrase translations. We add oracle translations to each baseline model *without* bilingually estimated translation scores[7] because such scores are not available for our automatically induced translations. Instead, we score the oracle phrase pairs using the 30 new phrase table features described in Section 3.3.

Table 1 shows the results of our oracle experiments. Augmenting the baselines with the subset of oracle translations which are *composed* given the unigram translations in the baseline models themselves (i.e. in the small training sets) yields

[5]For both languages, we learn an alignment over our tuning and test sets and complete parallel training sets.

[6]grow-diag-final

[7]We use an indicator feature for distinguishing new composed translations from bilingually extracted phrase pairs.

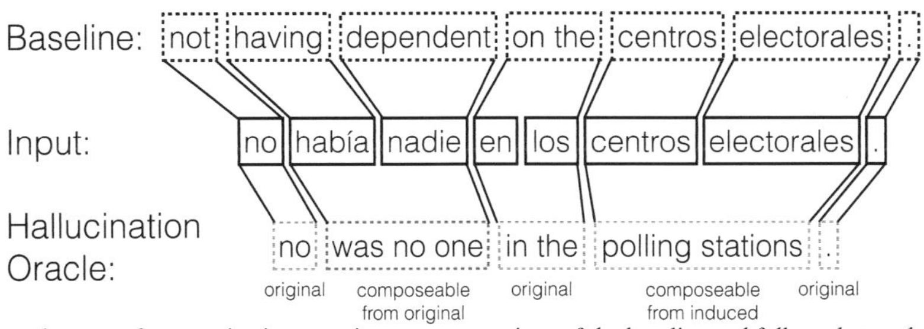

Figure 2: Example output from motivating experiment: a comparison of the baseline and full oracle translations of Spanish *no había nadie en los centros electorales*, which translates correctly as *there was nobody at the voting offices*. The full oracle is augmented with translations composed from the seed model as well as induced unigram translations. The phrase *was no one* is composeable from *había nadie* given the seed model. In contrast, the phrase *polling stations* is composeable from *centros electorales* using induced translations. For each translation, the phrase segmentations used by the decoder are highlighted.

Experiment	BLEU Baseline Features	BLEU Monolingually Estimated Feats.
Spanish		
Low Resource Baseline	13.47	13.35
+ Composeable Oracle from Initial Model	14.90	15.18
+ Composeable Oracle w/ Induced Unigram Trans.	15.47	15.94
Hindi		
Low Resource Baseline	8.49	8.26
+ Composeable Oracle from Initial Model	9.12	9.54
+ Composeable Oracle w/ Induced Unigram Trans.	10.09	10.19

Table 1: Motivating Experiment: BLEU results using the baseline SMT model and composeable oracle translations with and without induced unigram translations.

a BLEU score improvement of about 1.4 points for Spanish and about 0.6 for Hindi. This finding itself is noteworthy, and we investigated the reason for it. A representative example of a compositional oracle translation that was added to the Spanish model is *para evitarlos*, which translates as *to prevent them*. In the training corpus, *para* translates far more frequently as *for* than *to*. Thus, it is useful for the translation model to know that, in the context of *evitarlos*, *para* should translate as *to* and not *for*. Additionally, *evitarlos* was observed only translating as the unigram *prevent*. The small model fails to align the adjoined clitic *los* with its translation *them*. However, our loose definition of compositionality allows the English stop word *them* to appear anywhere in the target translation.

In the first result, composeable translations do not include those that contain new, induced word translations. Using the baseline model *and* induced unigram translations to compose phrase translations results in a 2 and 1.6 BLEU point gain for Spanish and Hindi, respectively.

The second column of Table 1 shows the results of augmenting the baseline models with the same oracle phrase pairs as well as the new features estimated over *all* phrase pairs. Although the features do not improve the performance of the baseline models, this diverse set of scores improves performance dramatically when new, oracle phrase pairs are added. Adding all oracle translations and the new feature set results in a total gain of about 2.6 BLEU points for Spanish and about 1.9 for Hindi. These gains are the maximum that we could hope to achieve by augmenting models with our hallucinated translations and new feature set.

6 Experimental Results

6.1 Unigram Translations

Table 2 shows examples of top ranked translations for several Spanish words. Although performance is generally quite good, we do observe some instances of false cognates, for example the top ranked translation for *aburridos*, which translates correctly as *bored*, is *burritos*. Using automatic word alignments as a reference, we find that 44% of Spanish tuning set unigrams have a correct translation in their top-10 ranked lists and 62% in the top-100. For Hindi, 31% of tuning set unigrams have a correct translation in their top-10 ranked lists and 43% in the top-100.

6.2 Hallucinated Phrase Pairs

Before moving to end-to-end SMT experiments, we evaluate the goodness of the hallucinated and pruned phrase pairs themselves. In order to do so, we use the same set of oracle phrase translations described in Section 5.

Table 3 shows the top three English translations for several Spanish phrases along with their model scores. Common, loose translations of some phrases are scored higher than less common but literal translations. For example, *very obvi-*

Spanish	abdominal	abejorro	abril	aburridos	accionista	aceite	actriz
	abdominal	**bumblebees**	**april**	burritos	actionists	adulterated	**actress**
Top 5	abdomen	bombus	march	**boredom**	actionist	iooc	actor
English	bowel	xylocopa	june	agatean	telmex	olive	award
Translations	appendicitis	ilyitch	july	burrito	**shareholder**	milliliters	american
	acute	bumble	december	poof	antagonists	canola	singer

Table 2: Top five induced translations for several source words. Correct translations are bolded. *aceite* translates as *oil.*

Spanish	English	Score
ambos partidos	**two parties**	5.72
	both parties	5.31
	and parties	3.16
había apoyado	were supported	4.80
	were members	4.52
	had supported	4.39
ministro neerlandès	finnish minister	4.76
	finnish ministry	2.77
	dutch minister	1.31
unas cuantas semanas	over a week	4.30
	a few weeks	3.72
	few weeks	3.22
muy evidentes	**very obvious**	1.88
	very evident	1.87
	obviously very	1.84

Table 3: Top three compositional translations for several source phrases and their model scores. Correct translations are bolded.

ous scores higher than *very evident* as a translation of Spanish *muy evidentes*. Similarly, *dutch minister* is scored higher than *netherlands minister* as a translation for *ministro neerlandès*.

We use model scores to rerank candidate translations for each source phrase and keep the top-k translations. Figure 3 shows the precision and type-based recall (the percent of source phrases for which at least one correct translation is generated) as we vary k for each language pair. At $k = 1$, precision and recall are about 27% for Spanish and about 25% for Hindi.[8] At $k = 200$, recall increases to 57% for Spanish and precision drops to 2%. For Hindi, recall increases to 40% and precision drops to 1%.

Moving from $k = 1$ to $k = 200$, precision drops at about the same rate for the two source languages. However, recall increases less for Hindi than for Spanish. We attribute this to two things. First, Hindi and English are less related than Spanish and English, and fewer phrases are translated compositionally. Our oracle experiments showed that there is less to gain in composing phrase translations for Hindi than for Spanish. Second, the accuracy of our induced unigram translations is lower for Hindi than it is for Spanish. Without accurate unigram translations, we are unable to compose high quality phrase translations.

[8]Since we are computing type-based recall, and at k=1, we produce exactly one translation for each source phrase, precision and recall are the same.

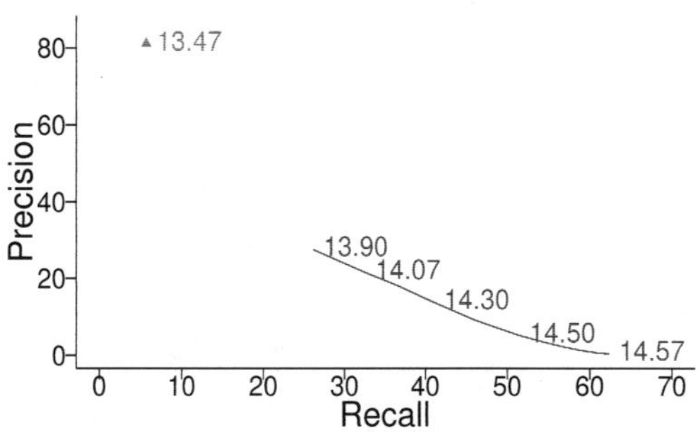

(a) Spanish

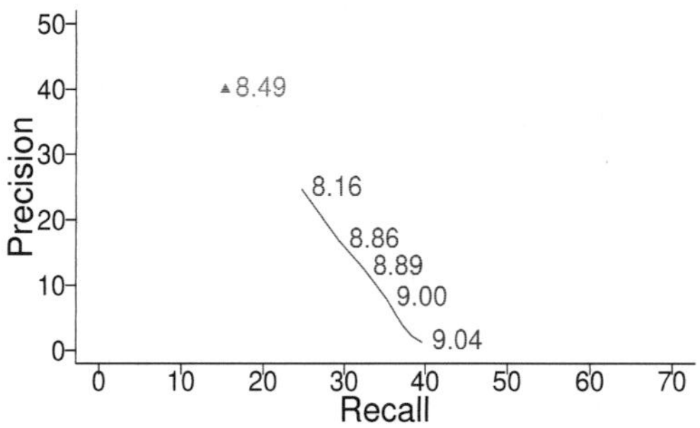

(b) Hindi

Figure 3: Precision Recall curve with BLEU scores for the top-k scored hallucinated translations. k varies from 1 to 200. Baseline model performance is shown with a red triangle.

Because we hallucinate translations for source phrases that appear in the training data up to 100 times, our baseline models include some of the oracle phrase translations. Not surprisingly, the bilingually extracted phrase pairs have relatively high precision (81% and 40% for Spanish and Hindi, respectively) and low recall (6% and 15% for Spanish and Hindi, respectively).

6.3 End-to-End Translation

Table 4 shows end-to-end translation BLEU score results (Papineni et al., 2002). Our first baseline SMT models are trained using only 2,000 parallel sentences and no new translation model features. Our Spanish baseline achieves a BLEU score of 13.47 and our Hindi baseline a BLEU score of 8.49. When we add the 30 new feature functions estimated over comparable monolingual corpora, performance is slightly lower, 13.35 for

Experiment	BLEU	
	Spanish	Hindi
Baseline	13.47	**8.49**
+ Mono. Scores	13.35	8.26
+ Mono. Scores & OOV Trans	**14.01**	8.31
+ Phrase Trans, k=1	13.90	8.16
+ Phrase Trans, k=2	14.07	8.86*
+ Phrase Trans, k=5	14.30*	8.89*
+ Phrase Trans, k=25	14.50*	9.00*
+ Phrase Trans, k=200	**14.57***	**9.04***

Table 4: Experimental results. First, the baseline models are augmented with monolingual phrase table features and then also with the top-5 induced translations for all OOV unigrams. Then, we append the top-k hallucinated phrase translations to the third baseline models. BLEU scores are averaged over three tuning runs. We measure the statistical significance of each +Phrase Trans model in comparison with the highest performing (bolded) baseline for each language; * indicates statistical significance with $p < 0.01$.

Spanish and 8.26 for Hindi. Our third baselines augment the second with unigram translations for all OOV tuning and test set source words using the bilingual lexicon induction techniques described in Section 3.1. We append the top-5 translations for each,[9] score both the original and the new phrase pairs with the new feature set, and retune. With these additional unigram translations, performance increases to 14.01 for Spanish and 8.31 for Hindi.

We append the top-k composed translations for the source phrases described in Section 4 to the third baseline models. Both original and new phrase pairs are scored using the new feature set. BLEU score results are shown at different values of k along the precision-recall plots for each language pair in Figure 3 as well as in Table 4. We would expect that higher precision and higher recall would benefit end-to-end SMT. As usual, a tradeoff exists between precision and recall, however, in this case, improvements in recall outweigh the risk of a lower precision. As k increases, precision decreases but both recall and BLEU scores increase. For both Spanish and Hindi, BLEU score gains start to taper off at k values over 25.

In additional experiments, we found that **without** the new features the same sets of hallucinated phrase pairs hurt performance slightly in comparison with the baseline augmented with unigram translations, and results don't change as we vary k.[10] Thus, the translation models are able to effectively use the higher recall sets of new phrase pairs because we also augmented the models with 30 new feature functions, which help them distinguish good from bad translations.

7 Discussion

Our results showed that including a high recall set of "hallucinated" translations in our augmented phrase table successfully improved the quality of our machine translations. The algorithm that we proposed for hypothesizing translations is flexible, and in future work we plan to modify it slightly to output even more candidate translations. For example, we could retrieve target phrases which contain at least one source word translation instead of all. Alternatively, we could identify candidates using entirely different information, for example the monolingual frequency of a source and target word, instead of unigram translations. This type of inverted index may improve recall in the set of hypothesis phrase translations at the cost of generating a much bigger set for reranking.

Our new phrase table features were informative in distinguishing correct from incorrect phrase translations, and they allowed us to make use of noisy but high recall supplemental phrase pairs. This is a critical result for research on identifying phrase translations from non-parallel text. We also believe that using fairly strong target (English) language models contributed to our models' ability to discriminate between good and bad hallucinated phrase pairs. We leave research on the influence of the language model in our setting to future work.

In this work, we experimented with two language pairs, Spanish-English and Hindi-English. While Spanish and English are very closely related, Hindi and English are less related. Our oracle experiments showed potential for composing phrase translations for both language pairs, and, indeed, in our experiments using hallucinated phrase translations we saw significant translation quality gains for both. We expect that improving the quality of induced unigram translations will yield even more performance gains.

The vast majority of prior work on low resource MT has focused on Spanish-English (Haghighi et al., 2008; Klementiev et al., 2012; Ravi and Knight, 2011; Dou and Knight, 2012; Ravi, 2013; Dou and Knight, 2013). Although such experiments serve as important proofs of concept, we found it important to also experiment with a more

[9]The same set used for composing phrase translations.

[10]For all values of k between 1 and 100, without the new features, BLEU scores are about 13.70 for Spanish

truly low resource language pair. The success of our approach that we have seen for Spanish and Hindi suggests that it is worth pursuing such directions for other even less related and resourced language pairs. In addition to language pair, text genre and the degree of looseness or literalness of given parallel corpora may also affect the amount of phrase translation compositionality.

8 Related Work

Phrase-based SMT models estimated over very large parallel corpora are expensive to store and process. Prior work has reduced the size of SMT phrase tables in order to improve efficiency without the loss of translation quality (He et al., 2009; Johnson et al., 2007; Zens et al., 2012). Typically, the goal of pruning is to identify and remove phrase pairs which are likely to be inaccurate, using either the scores and counts of a given pair itself or those relative to other phrase pairs. Our work, in contrast, focuses on low resource settings, where training data is limited and provides incomplete and unreliable scored phrase pairs. We begin by dramatically *increasing* the size of our SMT phrase table in order to expand its coverage and then use non-parallel data to rescore and filter the table.

In the decipherment task, translation models are learned from comparable corpora without any parallel text (Ravi and Knight, 2011; Dou and Knight, 2012; Ravi, 2013). In contrast, we begin with a small amount of parallel data and take a very different approach to learning translation models. In our prior work (Irvine and Callison-Burch, 2013b), we showed how effective even small amounts of bilingual data can be for learning translations from monolingual texts.

Garera and Yarowsky (2008) pivot through bilingual dictionaries in several language pairs to compose translations for compound words. Zhang and Zong (2013) construct a set of new, additional phrase pairs for the task of domain adaptation for machine translation. That work uses two dictionaries to bootstrap a set of phrase pair translations: one probabilistic dictionary extracted from 2 million words of bitext and one manually created new-domain dictionary of 140, 000 word translations. Our approach to the construction of new phrase pairs is somewhat similar to Zhang and Zong (2013), but we don't rely on a very large manually generated dictionary. Additionally, we focus on the low resource language pair setting, where a large training corpus is not available.

Deng et al. (2008) work in a standard SMT setting but use a discriminative framework for extracting phrase pairs from parallel corpora. That approach yields a phrase table with higher precision and recall than the table extracted by standard world alignment based heuristics (Och and Ney, 2003; Koehn et al., 2003). The discriminative model combines features from word alignments and bilingual training data as well as information theoretic features estimated over monolingual data into a single log-linear model and then the phrase pairs are filtered using a threshold on model scores. The phrase pairs that it extracts are limited to those that appear in pairs of sentences in the parallel training data. Our work takes a similar approach to that of Deng et al. (2008), however, unlike that work, we *hallucinate* phrase pairs that did *not* appear in training data in order to augment the original, bilingually extracted phrase table.

Other prior work has used comparable corpora to extract parallel sentences and phrases (Munteanu and Marcu, 2006; Smith et al., 2010). Such efforts are orthogonal to our approach. We use parallel corpora, when available, and hallucinates phrase translations without assuming any parallel text in our comparable corpora.

9 Conclusions

We showed that "hallucinating" phrasal translations can significantly improve machine translation performance in low resource conditions. Our hallucinated translations are *composed* from unigram translations. The translations are low precision but high recall. We countered this by introducing new feature functions and pruning aggressively.

10 Acknowledgements

This material is based on research sponsored by DARPA under contract HR0011-09-1-0044 and by the Johns Hopkins University Human Language Technology Center of Excellence. The views and conclusions contained in this publication are those of the authors and should not be interpreted as representing official policies or endorsements of DARPA or the U.S. Government.

References

Chris Callison-Burch, Philipp Koehn, Christof Monz, Kay Peterson, Mark Przybocki, and Omar Zaidan. 2010. Findings of the 2010 joint workshop on statistical machine translation and metrics for machine translation. In *Proceedings of the Workshop on Statistical Machine Translation (WMT)*.

Colin Cherry and George Foster. 2012. Batch tuning strategies for statistical machine translation. In *Proceedings of the Conference of the North American Chapter of the Association for Computational Linguistics (NAACL)*.

Jonathan H. Clark, Chris Dyer, Alon Lavie, and Noah A. Smith. 2011. Better hypothesis testing for statistical machine translation: controlling for optimizer instability. In *Proceedings of the Conference of the Association for Computational Linguistics (ACL)*.

Hal Daumé, III and Jagadeesh Jagarlamudi. 2011. Domain adaptation for machine translation by mining unseen words. In *Proceedings of the Conference of the Association for Computational Linguistics (ACL)*.

Yonggang Deng, Jia Xu, and Yuqing Gao. 2008. Phrase table training for precision and recall: What makes a good phrase and a good phrase pair? In *Proceedings of the Conference of the Association for Computational Linguistics (ACL)*.

Qing Dou and Kevin Knight. 2012. Large scale decipherment for out-of-domain machine translation. In *Proceedings of the Joint Conference on Empirical Methods in Natural Language Processing and Computational Natural Language Learning (EMNLP/CoNLL)*.

Qing Dou and Kevin Knight. 2013. Dependency-based decipherment for resource-limited machine translation. In *Proceedings of the Conference on Empirical Methods in Natural Language Processing (EMNLP)*.

Nikesh Garera and David Yarowsky. 2008. Translating compounds by learning component gloss translation models via multiple languages. In *Proceedings of the International Joint Conference on Natural Language Processing (IJCNLP)*.

Aria Haghighi, Percy Liang, Taylor Berg-Kirkpatrick, and Dan Klein. 2008. Learning bilingual lexicons from monolingual corpora. In *Proceedings of the Conference of the Association for Computational Linguistics (ACL)*.

Zhongjun He, Yao Meng, and Hao Yu. 2009. Discarding monotone composed rule for hierarchical phrase-based statistical machine translation. In *Proceedings of the 3rd International Universal Communication Symposium*.

Ann Irvine and Chris Callison-Burch. 2013a. Combining bilingual and comparable corpora for low resource machine translation. In *Proceedings of the Workshop on Statistical Machine Translation (WMT)*.

Ann Irvine and Chris Callison-Burch. 2013b. Supervised bilingual lexicon induction with multiple monolingual signals. In *Proceedings of the Conference of the North American Chapter of the Association for Computational Linguistics (NAACL)*.

Howard Johnson, Joel Martin, George Foster, and Roland Kuhn. 2007. Improving translation quality by discarding most of the phrasetable. In *Proceedings of the Joint Conference on Empirical Methods in Natural Language Processing and Computational Natural Language Learning (EMNLP/CoNLL)*.

Alex Klementiev, Ann Irvine, Chris Callison-Burch, and David Yarowsky. 2012. Toward statistical machine translation without parallel corpora. In *Proceedings of the Conference of the European Association for Computational Linguistics (EACL)*.

Philipp Koehn and Kevin Knight. 2002. Learning a translation lexicon from monolingual corpora. In *ACL Workshop on Unsupervised Lexical Acquisition*.

Philipp Koehn, Franz Joseph Och, and Daniel Marcu. 2003. Statistical phrase-based translation. In *Proceedings of the Conference of the North American Chapter of the Association for Computational Linguistics (NAACL)*.

Philipp Koehn, Hieu Hoang, Alexandra Birch, Chris Callison-Burch, Marcello Federico, Nicola Bertoldi, Brooke Cowan, Wade Shen, Christine Moran, Richard Zens, Chris Dyer, Ondrej Bojar, Alexandra Constantin, and Evan Herbst. 2007. Moses: Open source toolkit for statistical machine translation. In *Proceedings of the Conference of the Association for Computational Linguistics (ACL)*.

Philipp Koehn. 2005. Europarl: A parallel corpus for statistical machine translation. In *Proceedings of the Machine Translation Summit*.

Prasanth Kolachina, Nicola Cancedda, Marc Dymetman, and Sriram Venkatapathy. 2012. Prediction of learning curves in machine translation. In *Proceedings of the Conference of the Association for Computational Linguistics (ACL)*.

Dragos Munteanu and Daniel Marcu. 2006. Extracting parallel sub-sentential fragments from non-parallel corpora. In *Proceedings of the Conference of the Association for Computational Linguistics (ACL)*.

Franz Josef Och and Hermann Ney. 2003. A systematic comparison of various statistical alignment models. *Computational Linguistics*, 29(1):19–51, March.

Kishore Papineni, Salim Roukos, Todd Ward, and Wei-Jing Zhu. 2002. Bleu: a method for automatic evaluation of machine translation. In *Proceedings of the Conference of the Association for Computational Linguistics (ACL)*.

Matt Post, Chris Callison-Burch, and Miles Osborne. 2012. Constructing parallel corpora for six indian languages via crowdsourcing. In *Proceedings of the Workshop on Statistical Machine Translation (WMT)*.

Reinhard Rapp. 1995. Identifying word translations in non-parallel texts. In *Proceedings of the Conference of the Association for Computational Linguistics (ACL)*.

Sujith Ravi and Kevin Knight. 2011. Deciphering foreign language. In *Proceedings of the Conference of the Association for Computational Linguistics (ACL)*.

Sujith Ravi. 2013. Scalable decipherment for machine translation via hash sampling. In *Proceedings of the Conference of the Association for Computational Linguistics (ACL)*.

Majid Razmara, Maryam Siahbani, Reza Haffari, and Anoop Sarkar. 2013. Graph propagation for paraphrasing out-of-vocabulary words in statistical machine translation. In *Proceedings of the Conference of the Association for Computational Linguistics (ACL)*.

Charles Schafer and David Yarowsky. 2002. Inducing translation lexicons via diverse similarity measures and bridge languages. In *Proceedings of the Conference on Natural Language Learning (CoNLL)*.

Jason R. Smith, Chris Quirk, and Kristina Toutanova. 2010. Extracting parallel sentences from comparable corpora using document level alignment. In *Proceedings of the Conference of the North American Chapter of the Association for Computational Linguistics (NAACL)*.

Richard Zens, Daisy Stanton, and Peng Xu. 2012. A systematic comparison of phrase table pruning techniques. In *Proceedings of the Joint Conference on Empirical Methods in Natural Language Processing and Computational Natural Language Learning (EMNLP/CoNLL)*.

Jiajun Zhang and Chengqing Zong. 2013. Learning a phrase-based translation model from monolingual data with application to domain adaptation. In *Proceedings of the Conference of the Association for Computational Linguistics (ACL)*.

Appendix A: Phrase pair filtering features

The first ten features are similar to those described by Irvine and Callison-Burch (2013b). Stop words are defined as the most frequent 300 words in each language's Wikipedia, and content words are all non-stop words.

- Web crawl phrasal context similarity score
- Web crawl lexical context similarity score, averaged over aligned unigrams
- Web crawl phrasal temporal similarity score
- Web crawl lexical temporal similarity score, averaged over aligned unigrams
- Wikipedia phrasal context similarity score
- Wikipedia lexical context similarity score, averaged over aligned unigrams
- Wikipedia phrasal topic similarity score
- Wikipedia lexical topic similarity score, averaged over aligned unigrams
- Normalized edit distance, averaged over aligned unigrams
- Absolute value of difference between the logs of the source and target phrase Wikipedia monolingual frequencies
- Log target phrase Wikipedia monolingual frequency
- Log source phrase Wikipedia monolingual frequency
- Indicator: source phrase is longer
- Indicator: target phrase is longer
- Indicator: source and target phrases same length
- Number of source content words higher than target
- Number of target content words higher than source
- Number of source and target content words same
- Number of source stop words higher than target
- Number of target stop words higher than source
- Number of source and target stop words same
- Percent of source words aligned to at least one target word
- Percent of target words aligned to at least one source word
- Percent of source content words aligned to at least one target word
- Percent of target content words aligned to at least one source word
- Percent of aligned word pairs aligned in bilingual training data
- Percent of aligned word pairs in induced dictionary
- Percent of aligned word pairs in stemmed induced dictionary

Linguistic Regularities in Sparse and Explicit Word Representations

Omer Levy* and **Yoav Goldberg**
Computer Science Department
Bar-Ilan University
Ramat-Gan, Israel
{omerlevy,yoav.goldberg}@gmail.com

Abstract

Recent work has shown that neural-embedded word representations capture many relational similarities, which can be recovered by means of vector arithmetic in the embedded space. We show that Mikolov et al.'s method of first adding and subtracting word vectors, and then searching for a word similar to the result, is equivalent to searching for a word that maximizes a linear combination of three pairwise word similarities. Based on this observation, we suggest an improved method of recovering relational similarities, improving the state-of-the-art results on two recent word-analogy datasets. Moreover, we demonstrate that analogy recovery is not restricted to neural word embeddings, and that a similar amount of relational similarities can be recovered from traditional distributional word representations.

1 Introduction

Deep learning methods for language processing owe much of their success to neural network language models, in which words are represented as dense real-valued vectors in $\mathbb{R}^d$. Such representations are referred to as distributed word representations or *word embeddings*, as they embed an entire vocabulary into a relatively low-dimensional linear space, whose dimensions are latent continuous features. The embedded word vectors are trained over large collections of text using variants of neural networks (Bengio et al., 2003; Collobert and Weston, 2008; Mnih and Hinton, 2008; Mikolov et al., 2011; Mikolov et al., 2013b). The word embeddings are designed to capture what Turney (2006) calls *attributional similarities* between vocabulary items: words that appear in similar contexts will be close to each other in the projected space. The effect is grouping of words that share semantic ("dog cat cow", "eat devour") or syntactic ("cars hats days", "emptied carried danced") properties, and are shown to be effective as features for various NLP tasks (Turian et al., 2010; Collobert et al., 2011; Socher et al., 2011; Al-Rfou et al., 2013). We refer to such word representations as *neural embeddings* or just *embeddings*.

Recently, Mikolov et al. (2013c) demonstrated that the embeddings created by a recursive neural network (RNN) encode not only attributional similarities between words, but also similarities between *pairs of words*. Such similarities are referred to as *linguistic regularities* by Mikolov et al. and as *relational similarities* by Turney (2006). They capture, for example, the *gender* relation exhibited by the pairs "man:woman", "king:queen", the *language-spoken-in* relation in "france:french", "mexico:spanish" and the *past-tense* relation in "capture:captured", "go:went". Remarkably, Mikolov et al. showed that such relations are reflected in vector offsets between word pairs ($apples - apple \approx cars - car$), and that by using simple vector arithmetic one could apply the relation and solve analogy questions of the form "a is to a^* as b is to —" in which the nature of the relation is hidden. Perhaps the most famous example is that the embedded representation of the word *queen* can be roughly recovered from the representations of *king*, *man* and *woman*:

$$queen \approx king - man + woman$$

The recovery of relational similarities using vector arithmetic on RNN-embedded vectors was evaluated on many relations, achieving state-of-the-art results in relational similarity identification tasks

* Supported by the European Community's Seventh Framework Programme (FP7/2007-2013) under grant agreement no. 287923 (EXCITEMENT).

Proceedings of the Eighteenth Conference on Computational Language Learning, pages 171–180,
Baltimore, Maryland USA, June 26-27 2014.

(Mikolov et al., 2013c; Zhila et al., 2013). It was later demonstrated that relational similarities can be recovered in a similar fashion also from embeddings trained with different architectures (Mikolov et al., 2013a; Mikolov et al., 2013b).

This fascinating result raises a question: to what extent are the relational semantic properties a result of the *embedding* process? Experiments in (Mikolov et al., 2013c) show that the RNN-based embeddings are superior to other dense representations, but how crucial is it for a representation to be dense and low-dimensional at all?

An alternative approach to representing words as vectors is the distributional similarity representation, or *bag of contexts*. In this representation, each word is associated with a very high-dimensional but sparse vector capturing the contexts in which the word occurs. We call such vector representations *explicit*, as each dimension directly corresponds to a particular context. These explicit vector-space representations have been extensively studied in the NLP literature (see (Turney and Pantel, 2010; Baroni and Lenci, 2010) and the references therein), and are known to exhibit a large extent of attributional similarity (Pereira et al., 1993; Lin, 1998; Lin and Pantel, 2001; Sahlgren, 2006; Kotlerman et al., 2010).

In this study, we show that similarly to the neural embedding space, the explicit vector space also encodes a vast amount of relational similarity which can be recovered in a similar fashion, suggesting the explicit vector space representation as a competitive baseline for further work on neural embeddings. Moreover, this result implies that the neural embedding process is not discovering novel patterns, but rather is doing a remarkable job at preserving the patterns inherent in the word-context co-occurrence matrix.

A key insight of this work is that the vector arithmetic method can be decomposed into a linear combination of three pairwise similarities (Section 3). While mathematically equivalent, we find that thinking about the method in terms of the decomposed formulation is much less puzzling, and provides a better intuition on why we would expect the method to perform well on the analogy recovery task. Furthermore, the decomposed form leads us to suggest a modified optimization objective (Section 6), which outperforms the state-of-the-art at recovering relational similarities under both representations.

2 Explicit Vector Space Representation

We adopt the traditional word representation used in the distributional similarity literature (Turney and Pantel, 2010). Each word is associated with a sparse vector capturing the contexts in which it occurs. We call this representation *explicit*, as each dimension corresponds to a particular context.

For a vocabulary V and a set of contexts C, the result is a $|V|\times|C|$ sparse matrix S in which S_{ij} corresponds to the strength of the association between word i and context j. The association strength between a word $w \in V$ and a context $c \in C$ can take many forms. We chose to use the popular *positive pointwise mutual information* (PPMI) metric:

$$S_{ij} = PPMI(w_i, c_j)$$

$$PPMI(w,c) = \begin{cases} 0 & PMI(w,c) < 0 \\ PMI(w,c) & otherwise \end{cases}$$

$$PMI(w,c) = \log \frac{P(w,c)}{P(w)P(c)} = \log \frac{freq(w,c)|corpus|}{freq(w)freq(c)}$$

where $|corpus|$ is the number of items in the corpus, $freq(w,c)$ is the number of times word w appeared in context c in the corpus, and $freq(w)$, $freq(c)$ are the corpus frequencies of the word and the context respectively.

The use of PMI in distributional similarity models was introduced by Church and Hanks (1990) and widely adopted (Dagan et al., 1994; Turney, 2001). The PPMI variant dates back to at least (Niwa and Nitta, 1994), and was demonstrated to perform very well in Bullinaria and Levy (2007).

In this work, we take the linear contexts in which words appear. We consider each word surrounding the target word w in a window of 2 to each side as a context, distinguishing between different sequential positions. For example, in the sentence `a b c d e` the contexts of the word `c` are $\texttt{a}^{-2}$, $\texttt{b}^{-1}$, $\texttt{d}^{+1}$ and $\texttt{e}^{+2}$. Each vector's dimenstion is thus $|C| \approx 4\,|V|$. Empirically, the number of non-zero dimensions for vocabulary items in our corpus ranges between 3 (for some rare tokens) and 474,234 (for the word "and"), with a mean of 1595 and a median of 415.

Another popular choice of context is the syntactic relations the word participates in (Lin, 1998; Padó and Lapata, 2007; Levy and Goldberg, 2014). In this paper, we chose the sequential context as it is compatible with the information available to the state-of-the-art neural embedding method we are comparing against.

3 Analogies and Vector Arithmetic

Mikolov et al. demonstrated that vector space representations encode various relational similarities, which can be recovered using vector arithmetic and used to solve word-analogy tasks.

3.1 Analogy Questions

In a word-analogy task we are given two pairs of words that share a relation (e.g. "man:woman", "king:queen"). The identity of the fourth word ("queen") is hidden, and we need to infer it based on the other three (e.g. answering the question: "*man* is to *woman* as *king* is to — ?"). In the rest of this paper, we will refer to the four words as a:a^*, b:b^*. Note that the type of the relation is not explicitly provided in the question, and solving the question correctly (by a human) involves first inferring the relation, and then applying it to the third word (b).

3.2 Vector Arithmetic

Mikolov et al. showed that relations between words are reflected to a large extent in the offsets between their vector embeddings ($queen - king \approx woman - man$), and thus the vector of the hidden word b^* will be similar to the vector $b - a + a^*$, suggesting that the analogy question can be solved by optimizing:

$$\arg\max_{b^* \in V} (sim(b^*, b - a + a^*))$$

where V is the vocabulary excluding the question words b, a and a^*, and sim is a similarity measure. Specifically, they used the cosine similarity measure, defined as:

$$\cos(u, v) = \frac{u \cdot v}{\|u\| \|v\|}$$

resulting in:

$$\arg\max_{b^* \in V} (\cos(b^*, b - a + a^*)) \tag{1}$$

Since cosine is inverse to the angle, high cosine similarity (close to 1) means that the vectors share a very similar direction. Note that this metric normalizes (and thus ignores) the vectors' lengths, unlike the Euclidean distance between them. For reasons that will be clear later, we refer to (1) as the 3CosAdd method.

An alternative to 3CosAdd is to require that the *direction* of transformation be conserved:

$$\arg\max_{b^* \in V} (\cos(b^* - b, a^* - a)) \tag{2}$$

This basically means that $b^* - b$ shares the same direction with $a^* - a$, ignoring the distances. We refer to this method as PairDirection. Though it was not mentioned in the paper, Mikolov et al. (2013c) used PairDirection for solving the semantic analogies of the SemEval task, and 3CosAdd for solving the syntactic analogies.[1]

3.3 Reinterpreting Vector Arithmetic

In Mikolov et al.'s experiments, all word-vectors were normalized to unit length. Under such normalization, the $\arg\max$ in (1) is mathematically equivalent to (derived using basic algebra):

$$\arg\max_{b^* \in V} (\cos(b^*, b) - \cos(b^*, a) + \cos(b^*, a^*)) \tag{3}$$

This means that solving analogy questions with vector arithmetic is mathematically equivalent to seeking a word (b^*) which is similar to b and a^* but is different from a. Relational similarity is thus expressed as a sum of attributional similarities. While (1) and (3) are equal, we find the intuition as to why (3) ought to find analogies clearer.

4 Empirical Setup

We derive explicit and neural-embedded vector representations, and compare their capacities to recover relational similarities using objectives 3CosAdd (eq. 3) and PairDirection (eq. 2).

Underlying Corpus and Preprocessing Previous reported results on the word analogy tasks using vector arithmetics were obtained using proprietary corpora. To make our experiments reproducible, we selected an open and widely accessible corpus – the English Wikipedia. We extracted all sentences from article bodies (excluding titles, infoboxes, captions, etc) and filtered non-alphanumeric tokens, allowing mid-token symbols as apostrophes, hyphens, commas, and periods. All the text was lowercased. Duplicates and sentences with less than 5 tokens were then removed. Overall, we retained a corpus of about 1.5 billion tokens, in 77.5 million sentences.

Word Representations To create contexts for both embedding and sparse representation, we used a window of two tokens to each side (5-grams, in total), ignoring words that appeared less

[1]This was confirmed both by our independent trials and by corresponding with the authors.

than 100 times in the corpus. The filtered vocabulary contained 189,533 terms.[2]

The explicit vector representations were created as described in Section 2. The neural embeddings were created using the `word2vec` software[3] accompanying (Mikolov et al., 2013b). We embedded the vocabulary into a 600 dimensional space, using the state-of-the-art skip-gram architecture, the negative-training approach with 15 negative samples (NEG-15), and sub-sampling of frequent words with a parameter of 10^{-5}. The parameter settings follow (Mikolov et al., 2013b).

4.1 Evaluation Conditions

We evaluate the different word representations using the three datasets used in previous work. Two of them (MSR and GOOGLE) contain analogy questions, while the third (SEMEVAL) requires ranking of candidate word pairs according to their relational similarity to a set of supplied word pairs.

Open Vocabulary The open vocabulary datasets (MSR and GOOGLE) present questions of the form "a is to a^* as b is to b^*", where b^* is hidden, and must be guessed from the entire vocabulary. Performance on these datasets is measured by micro-averaged accuracy.

The **MSR** dataset[4] (Mikolov et al., 2013c) contains 8000 analogy questions. The relations portrayed by these questions are morpho-syntactic, and can be categorized according to parts of speech – adjectives, nouns and verbs. Adjective relations include comparative and superlative (*good* is to *best* as *smart* is to *smartest*). Noun relations include single and plural, possessive and non-possessive (*dog* is to *dog's* as *cat* is to *cat's*). Verb relations are tense modifications (*work* is to *worked* as *accept* is to *accepted*).

The **GOOGLE** dataset[5] (Mikolov et al., 2013a) contains 19544 questions. It covers 14 relation types, 7 of which are semantic in nature and 7 are morpho-syntactic (enumerated in Section 8). The dataset was created by manually constructing example word-pairs of each relation, and providing all the pairs of word-pairs (within each relation type) as analogy questions.

[2]Initial experiments with different window-sizes and cut-offs showed similar trends.

[3]`http://code.google.com/p/word2vec`

[4]`research.microsoft.com/en-us/projects/rnn/`

[5]`code.google.com/p/word2vec/source/browse/trunk/questions-words.txt`

Out-of-vocabulary words[6] were removed from both test sets.

Closed Vocabulary The SEMEVAL dataset contains the collection of 79 semantic relations that appeared in SemEval 2012 Task 2: Measuring Relation Similarity (Jurgens et al., 2012). Each relation is exemplified by a few (usually 3) characteristic word-pairs. Given a set of several dozen target word pairs, which supposedly have the same relation, the task is to rank the target pairs according to the degree in which this relation holds. This can be cast as an analogy question in the following manner: For example, take the *Recipient:Instrument* relation with the prototypical word pairs *king*:*crown* and *police*:*badge*. To measure the degree that a target word pair *wife*:*ring* has the same relation, we form the two analogy questions "*king* is to *crown* as *wife* is to *ring*" and "*police* is to *badge* as *wife* is to *ring*". We calculate the score of each analogy, and average the results. Note that as opposed to the first two test sets, this one does not require searching the entire vocabulary for the most suitable word in the corpus, but rather to rank a list of existing word pairs.

Following previous work, performance on SEMEVAL was measured using accuracy, macro-averaged across all the relations.

5 Preliminary Results

Our first experiment uses 3COSADD (method (3) in Section 3) to measure the prevalence of linguistic regularities within each representation.

Representation	MSR	GOOGLE	SEMEVAL
Embedding	53.98%	62.70%	38.49%
Explicit	29.04%	45.05%	38.54%

Table 1: Performance of **3COSADD** on different tasks with the explicit and neural embedding representations.

The results in Table 1 show that a large amount of relational similarities can be recovered with both representations. In fact, both representations achieve the same accuracy on the SEMEVAL task. However, there is a large performance gap in favor of the neural embedding in the open-vocabulary MSR and GOOGLE tasks.

Next, we run the same experiment with PAIRDIRECTION (method (2) in Section 3).

[6]i.e. words that appeared in English Wikipedia less than 100 times. This removed 882 instances from the MSR dataset and 286 instances from GOOGLE.

Representation	MSR	GOOGLE	SEMEVAL
Embedding	9.26%	14.51%	44.77%
Explicit	0.66%	0.75%	45.19%

Table 2: Performance of **PAIRDIRECTION** on different tasks with the explicit and neural embedding representations.

The results in Table 2 show that the PAIRDIRECTION method is better than 3COSADD on the restricted-vocabulary SEMEVAL task (accuracy jumps from 38% to 45%), but fails at the open-vocabulary questions in GOOGLE and MSR. When the method does work, the numbers for the explicit and embedded representations are again comparable to one another.

Why is PAIRDIRECTION performing so well on the SEMEVAL task, yet so poorly on the others? Recall that the PAIRDIRECTION objective focuses on the similarity of $b^* - b$ and $a^* - a$, but does not take into account the spatial distances between the individual vectors. Relying on direction alone, while ignoring spatial distance, is problematic when considering the entire vocabulary as candidates (as is required in the MSR and GOOGLE tasks). We are likely to find candidates b^* that have the same relation to b as reflected by $a - a^*$ but are not necessarily similar to b. As a concrete example, in *man:woman, king:?*, we are likely to recover feminine entities, but not necessarily royal ones. The SEMEVAL test set, on the other hand, already provides related (and therefore geometrically close) candidates, leaving mainly the direction to reason about.

6 Refining the Objective Function

The 3COSADD objective, as expressed in (3), reveals a "balancing act" between two attractors and one repeller, i.e. two terms that we wish to maximize and one that needs to be minimized:

$$\arg\max_{b^* \in V} (\cos(b^*, b) - \cos(b^*, a) + \cos(b^*, a^*))$$

A known property of such linear objectives is that they exhibit a "soft-or" behavior and allow one sufficiently large term to dominate the expression. This behavior is problematic in our setup, because each term reflects a different aspect of similarity, and the different aspects have different scales. For example, *king* is more royal than it is masculine, and will therefore overshadow the gender aspect of the analogy. It is especially true in the case of explicit vector representations, as each aspect of the similarity is manifested by a different set of features with varying sizes and weights.

A case in point is the analogy question "*London* is to *England* as *Baghdad* is to — ?", which we answer using:

$$\arg\max_{x \in V} (\cos(x, en) - \cos(x, lo) + \cos(x, ba))$$

We seek a word (*Iraq*) which is similar to *England* (both are countries), is similar to *Baghdad* (similar geography/culture) and is dissimilar to *London* (different geography/culture). Maximizing the sum yields an incorrect answer (under both representations): *Mosul*, a large Iraqi city. Looking at the computed similarities in the explicit vector representation, we see that both *Mosul* and *Iraq* are very close to *Baghdad*, and are quite far from *England* and *London*:

(EXP)	↑ England	↓ London	↑ Baghdad	Sum
Mosul	0.031	0.031	0.244	0.244
Iraq	0.049	0.038	0.206	0.217

The same trends appear in the neural embedding vectors, though with different similarity scores:

(EMB)	↑ England	↓ London	↑ Baghdad	Sum
Mosul	0.130	0.141	0.755	0.748
Iraq	0.153	0.130	0.631	0.655

While *Iraq* is much more similar to *England* than *Mosul* is (both being countries), both similarities (0.049 and 0.031 in explicit, 0.130 and 0.153 in embedded) are small and the sums are dominated by the geographic and cultural aspect of the analogy: *Mosul* and *Iraq*'s similarity to *Baghdad* (0.24 and 0.20 in explicit, 0.75 and 0.63 in embedded).

To achieve better balance among the different aspects of similarity, we propose switching from an additive to a multiplicative combination:

$$\arg\max_{b^* \in V} \frac{\cos(b^*, b)\cos(b^*, a^*)}{\cos(b^*, a) + \varepsilon} \quad (4)$$

($\varepsilon = 0.001$ is used to prevent division by zero)

This is equivalent to taking the logarithm of each term before summation, thus amplifying the differences between small quantities and reducing the differences between larger ones. Using this objective, *Iraq* is scored higher than *Mosul* (0.259 vs 0.236, 0.736 vs 0.691). We refer to objective (4) as 3COSMUL.[7]

[7] 3COSMUL requires that all similarities be non-negative, which trivially holds for explicit representations. With embeddings, we transform cosine similarities to $[0, 1]$ using $(x+1)/2$ before calculating (4).

7 Main Results

We repeated the experiments, this time using the 3CosMul method. Table 3 presents the results, showing that the multiplicative objective recovers more relational similarities in both representations. The improvements achieved in the explicit representation are especially dramatic, with an absolute increase of over 20% correctly identified relations in the MSR and Google datasets.

Objective	Representation	MSR	Google
3CosAdd	Embedding	53.98%	62.70%
	Explicit	29.04%	45.05%
3CosMul	Embedding	**59.09%**	66.72%
	Explicit	56.83%	**68.24%**

Table 3: Comparison of **3CosAdd** and **3CosMul**.

3CosMul outperforms the state-of-the-art (3CosAdd) on these two datasets. Moreover, the results illustrate that a comparable amount of relational similarities can be recovered with both representations. This suggests that the linguistic regularities apparent in neural embeddings are not a consequence of the embedding process, but rather are well preserved by it.

On SemEval, 3CosMul preformed on par with 3CosAdd , recovering a similar amount of analogies with both explicit and neural representations (38.37% and 38.67%, respectively).

8 Error Analysis

With 3CosMul, both the explicit vectors and the neural embeddings recover similar amounts of analogies, but are these the same patterns, or perhaps different types of relational similarities?

8.1 Agreement between Representations

Considering the open-vocabulary tasks (MSR and Google), we count the number of times both representations guessed correctly, both guessed incorrectly, and when one representations leads to the right answer while the other does not (Table 4). While there is a large amount of agreement between the representations, there is also a non-negligible amount of cases in which they complement each other. If we were to run in an oracle setup, in which an answer is considered correct if it is correct in either representation, we would have achieved an accuracy of 71.9% on the MSR dataset and 77.8% on Google.

	Both Correct	Both Wrong	Embedding Correct	Explicit Correct
MSR	43.97%	28.06%	15.12%	12.85%
Google	57.12%	22.17%	9.59%	11.12%
ALL	53.58%	23.76%	11.08%	11.59%

Table 4: Agreement between the representations on open-vocabulary tasks.

	Relation	Embedding	Explicit
Google	capital-common-countries	90.51%	**99.41%**
	capital-world	77.61%	**92.73%**
	city-in-state	56.95%	**64.69%**
	currency	**14.55%**	10.53%
	family (gender inflections)	**76.48%**	60.08%
	gram1-adjective-to-adverb	**24.29%**	14.01%
	gram2-opposite	**37.07%**	28.94%
	gram3-comparative	**86.11%**	77.85%
	gram4-superlative	56.72%	**63.45%**
	gram5-present-participle	63.35%	**65.06%**
	gram6-nationality-adjective	89.37%	**90.56%**
	gram7-past-tense	**65.83%**	48.85%
	gram8-plural (nouns)	72.15%	**76.05%**
	gram9-plural-verbs	**71.15%**	55.75%
MSR	adjectives	45.88%	**56.46%**
	nouns	56.96%	**63.07%**
	verbs	**69.90%**	52.97%

Table 5: Breakdown of relational similarities in each representation by relation type, using 3CosMul.

8.2 Breakdown by Relation Type

Table 5 presents the amount of analogies discovered in each representation, broken down by relation type. Some trends emerge: the explicit representation is superior in some of the more semantic tasks, especially geography related ones, as well as the ones superlatives and nouns. The neural embedding, however, has the upper hand on most verb inflections, comparatives, and family (gender) relations. Some relations (currency, adjectives-to-adverbs, opposites) pose a challenge to both representations, though are somewhat better handled by the embedded representations. Finally, the nationality-adjectives and present-participles are equally handled by both representations.

8.3 Default-Behavior Errors

The most common error pattern under both representations is that of a "default behavior", in which one central representative word is provided as an answer to many questions of the same type. For example, the word "Fresno" is returned 82 times as an incorrect answer in the *city-in-state* relation in the embedded representation, and the word "daughter" is returned 47 times as an incorrect answer in the *family* relation in the explicit represen-

Relation	Word	Emb	Exp
gram7-past-tense	who	0	138
city-in-state	fresno	82	24
gram6-nationality-adjective	slovak	39	39
gram6-nationality-adjective	argentine	37	39
gram6-nationality-adjective	belarusian	37	39
gram8-plural (nouns)	colour	36	35
gram3-comparative	higher	34	35
city-in-state	smith	1	61
gram7-past-tense	and	0	49
gram1-adjective-to-adverb	be	0	47
family (gender inflections)	daughter	8	47
city-in-state	illinois	3	40
currency	currency	5	40
gram1-adjective-to-adverb	and	0	39
gram7-past-tense	enhance	39	20

Table 6: Common default-behavior errors under both representations. Emb / Exp: the number of time the word was returned as an incorrect answer for the given relation under the embedded or explicit representation.

tation. Loosely, "Fresno" is identified by the embedded representation as a prototypical location, while "daughter" is identified by the explicit representation as a prototypical female. Under a definition in which a default behavior error is one in which the same incorrect answer is returned for a particular relation 10 or more times, such errors account for 49% of the errors in the explicit representation, and for 39% of the errors in the embedded representation.

Table 6 lists the 15 most common default errors under both representations. In most default errors the category of the default word is closely related to the analogy question, sharing the category of either the correct answer, or (as in the case of "Fresno") the question word. Notable exceptions are the words "who", "and", "be" and "smith" that are returned as default answers in the explicit representation, and which are very far from the intended relation. It seems that in the explicit representation, some very frequent function words act as "hubs" and confuse the model. In fact, the performance gap between the representations in the *past-tense* and *plural-verb* relations can be attributed specifically to such function-word errors: 23.4% of the mistakes in past-tense relation are due to the explicit representation's default answer of "who" or "and", while 19% of the mistakes in the plural-verb relations are due to default answers of "is/and/that/who".

8.4 Verb-inflection Errors

A correct solution to the morphological analogy task requires recovering both the correct inflection (requiring syntactic similarity) and the correct base word (requiring semantic similarity). We observe that linguistically, the morphological distinctions and similarities tend to rely on a few common word forms (for example, the "walk:walking" relation is characterized by modals such as "will" appearing before "walk" and never before "walking", and *be* verbs appearing before walking and never before "walk"), while the support for the semantic relations is spread out over many more items. We hypothesize that the morphological distinctions in verbs are much harder to capture than the semantics. Indeed, under both representations, errors in which the selected word has a correct form with an incorrect inflection are over ten times more likely than errors in which the selected word has the correct inflection but an incorrect base form.

9 Interpreting Relational Similarities

The ability to capture relational similarities by performing vector (or similarity) arithmetic is remarkable. In this section, we try and provide intuition as to why it works.

Consider the word "*king*"; it has several aspects, high-level properties that it implies, such as royalty or (male) gender, and its attributional similarity with another word is based on a mixture of those aspects; e.g. *king* is related to *queen* on the royalty and the human axes, and shares the gender and the human aspect with *man*. Relational similarities can be viewed as a composition of attributional similarities, each one reflecting a different aspect. In "*man* is to *woman* as *king* is to *queen*", the two main aspects are gender and royalty. Solving the analogy question involves identifying the relevant aspects, and trying to change one of them while preserving the other.

How are concepts such as gender, royalty, or "cityness" represented in the vector space? While the neural embeddings are mostly opaque, one of the appealing properties of explicit vector representations is our ability to read and understand the vectors' features. For example, *king* is represented in our explicit vector space by 51,409 contexts, of which the top 3 are tut^{+1}, jeongjo^{+1}, adulyadej^{+2} – all names of monarchs. The explicit representation allows us to glimpse at the way different aspects are represented. To do so, we choose a representative pair of words that share an aspect, intersect their vectors, and inspect the highest scoring

Aspect	Examples	Top Features
Female	$woman \odot queen$	estrid^{+1} ketevan^{+1} adeliza^{+1} nzinga^{+1} gunnhild^{+1} impregnate^{-2} hippolyta^{+1}
Royalty	$queen \odot king$	savang^{+1} uncrowned^{-1} pmare^{+1} sisowath^{+1} nzinga^{+1} tupou^{+1} uvea^{+2} majesty^{-1}
Currency	$yen \odot ruble$	devalue^{-2} banknote^{+1} denominated^{+1} billion^{-1} banknotes^{+1} pegged^{+2} coin^{+1}
Country	$germany \odot australia$	emigrates^{-2} 1943-45^{+2} pentathletes^{-2} emigrated^{-2} emigrate^{-2} hong-kong^{-1}
Capital	$berlin \odot canberra$	hotshots^{-1} embassy^{-2} 1925-26^{+2} consulate-general^{+2} meetups^{-2} nunciature^{-2}
Superlative	$sweetest \odot tallest$	freshest^{+2} asia's^{-1} cleveland's^{-2} smartest^{+1} world's^{-1} city's^{-1} america's^{-1}
Height	$taller \odot tallest$	regnans^{-2} skyscraper^{+1} skyscrapers^{+1} 6'4^{+2} windsor's^{-1} smokestacks^{+1} burj^{+2}

Table 7: The top features of each aspect, recovered by pointwise multiplication of words that share that aspect. The result of pointwise multiplication is an "aspect vector" in which the features common to both words, characterizing the relation, receive the highest scores. The feature scores (not shown) correspond to the weight the feature contributes to the cosine similarity between the vectors. The superscript marks the position of the feature relative to the target word.

features in the intersection. Table 7 presents the top (most influential) features of each aspect.

Many of these features are names of people or places, which appear rarely in our corpus (e.g. Adeliza, a historical queen, and Nzinga, a royal family) but are nonetheless highly indicative of the shared concept. The prevalence of rare words stems from PMI, which gives them more weight, and from the fact that words like *woman* and *queen* are closely related (a queen is a woman), and thus have many features in common. Ordering the features of $woman \odot queen$ by prevalence reveals female pronouns ("she", "her") and a long list of common feminine names, reflecting the expected aspect shared by *woman* and *queen*. Word pairs that share more specific aspects, such as capital cities or countries, show features that are characteristic of their shared aspect (e.g. capital cities have *embassies* and *meetups*, while immigration is associated with countries). It is also interesting to observe how the relatively syntactic "superlativity" aspect is captured with many regional possessives ("america's", "asia's", "world's").

10 Related Work

Relational similarity (and answering analogy questions) was previously tackled using explicit representations. Previous approaches use task-specific information, by either relying on a $(word\text{-}pair, connectives)$ matrix rather than the standard $(word, context)$ matrix (Turney and Littman, 2005; Turney, 2006), or by treating analogy detection as a supervised learning task (Baroni and Lenci, 2009; Jurgens et al., 2012; Turney, 2013). In contrast, the vector arithmetic approach followed here is unsupervised, and works on a generic single-word representation. Even though the training process is oblivious to the task of analogy detection, the resulting representation is able to detect them quite accurately. Turney (2012) assumes a similar setting but with two types of word similarities, and combines them with products and ratios (similar to 3CosMul) to recover a variety of semantic relations, including analogies.

Arithmetic combination of explicit word vectors is extensively studied in the context of compositional semantics (Mitchell and Lapata, 2010), where a phrase composed of two or more words is represented by a single vector, computed by a function of its component word vectors. Blacoe and Lapata (2012) compare different arithmetic functions across multiple representations (including embeddings) on a range of compositionality benchmarks. To the best of our knowledge such methods of word vector arithmetic have not been explored for recovering relational similarities in explicit representations.

11 Discussion

Mikolov et al. showed how an unsupervised neural network can represent words in a space that "naturally" encodes relational similarities in the form of vector offsets. This study shows that finding analogies through vector arithmetic is actually a form of balancing word similarities, and that, contrary to the recent findings of Baroni et al. (2014), under certain conditions traditional word similarities induced by explicit representations can perform just as well as neural embeddings on this task.

Learning to represent words is a fascinating and important challenge with implications to most current NLP efforts, and neural embeddings in particular are a promising research direction. We believe that to improve these representations we should understand how they work, and hope that the methods and insights provided in this work will help to deepen our grasp of current and future investigations of word representations.

References

Rami Al-Rfou, Bryan Perozzi, and Steven Skiena. 2013. Polyglot: Distributed word representations for multilingual nlp. In *Proc. of CoNLL 2013*.

Marco Baroni and Alessandro Lenci. 2009. One distributional memory, many semantic spaces. In *Proceedings of the Workshop on Geometrical Models of Natural Language Semantics*, pages 1–8, Athens, Greece, March. Association for Computational Linguistics.

Marco Baroni and Alessandro Lenci. 2010. Distributional memory: A general framework for corpus-based semantics. *Computational Linguistics*, 36(4):673–721.

Marco Baroni, Georgiana Dinu, and Germán Kruszewski. 2014. Dont count, predict! a systematic comparison of context-counting vs. context-predicting semantic vectors. In *Proceedings of the 52nd Annual Meeting of the Association for Computational Linguistics (Volume 1: Long Papers)*, Baltimore, Maryland, USA, June. Association for Computational Linguistics.

Yoshua Bengio, Réjean Ducharme, Pascal Vincent, and Christian Jauvin. 2003. A neural probabilistic language model. *Journal of Machine Learning Research*, 3:1137–1155.

William Blacoe and Mirella Lapata. 2012. A comparison of vector-based representations for semantic composition. In *Proceedings of the 2012 Joint Conference on Empirical Methods in Natural Language Processing and Computational Natural Language Learning*, pages 546–556, Jeju Island, Korea, July. Association for Computational Linguistics.

John A. Bullinaria and Joseph P. Levy. 2007. Extracting semantic representations from word cooccurrence statistics: A computational study. *Behavior Research Methods*, 39(3):510–526.

Kenneth Ward Church and Patrick Hanks. 1990. Word association norms, mutual information, and lexicography. *Computational linguistics*, 16(1):22–29.

Ronan Collobert and Jason Weston. 2008. A unified architecture for natural language processing: Deep neural networks with multitask learning. In *Proceedings of the 25th International Conference on Machine Learning*, pages 160–167.

Ronan Collobert, Jason Weston, Léon Bottou, Michael Karlen, Koray Kavukcuoglu, and Pavel Kuksa. 2011. Natural language processing (almost) from scratch. *The Journal of Machine Learning Research*, 12:2493–2537.

Ido Dagan, Fernando Pereira, and Lillian Lee. 1994. Similarity-based estimation of word cooccurrence probabilities. In *Proceedings of the 32nd annual meeting on Association for Computational Linguistics*, pages 272–278. Association for Computational Linguistics.

David A Jurgens, Peter D Turney, Saif M Mohammad, and Keith J Holyoak. 2012. Semeval-2012 task 2: Measuring degrees of relational similarity. In *Proceedings of the First Joint Conference on Lexical and Computational Semantics*, pages 356–364. Association for Computational Linguistics.

Lili Kotlerman, Ido Dagan, Idan Szpektor, and Maayan Zhitomirsky-Geffet. 2010. Directional distributional similarity for lexical inference. *Natural Language Engineering*, 16(4):359–389.

Omer Levy and Yoav Goldberg. 2014. Dependency-based word embeddings. In *Proceedings of the 52nd Annual Meeting of the Association for Computational Linguistics (Volume 2: Short Papers)*, Baltimore, Maryland, USA, June. Association for Computational Linguistics.

Dekang Lin and Patrick Pantel. 2001. Dirt: discovery of inference rules from text. In *KDD*, pages 323–328.

Dekang Lin. 1998. Automatic retrieval and clustering of similar words. In *Proceedings of the 36th Annual Meeting of the Association for Computational Linguistics and 17th International Conference on Computational Linguistics - Volume 2*, ACL '98, pages 768–774, Stroudsburg, PA, USA. Association for Computational Linguistics.

Tomas Mikolov, Stefan Kombrink, Lukas Burget, JH Cernocky, and Sanjeev Khudanpur. 2011. Extensions of recurrent neural network language model. In *Acoustics, Speech and Signal Processing (ICASSP), 2011 IEEE International Conference on*, pages 5528–5531. IEEE.

Tomas Mikolov, Kai Chen, Greg Corrado, and Jeffrey Dean. 2013a. Efficient estimation of word representations in vector space. *CoRR*, abs/1301.3781.

Tomas Mikolov, Ilya Sutskever, Kai Chen, Gregory S. Corrado, and Jeffrey Dean. 2013b. Distributed representations of words and phrases and their compositionality. In *Advances in Neural Information Processing Systems 26: 27th Annual Conference on Neural Information Processing Systems 2013. Proceedings of a meeting held December 5-8, 2013, Lake Tahoe, Nevada, United States*, pages 3111–3119.

Tomas Mikolov, Wen-tau Yih, and Geoffrey Zweig. 2013c. Linguistic regularities in continuous space word representations. In *Proceedings of the 2013 Conference of the North American Chapter of the Association for Computational Linguistics: Human Language Technologies*, pages 746–751, Atlanta, Georgia, June. Association for Computational Linguistics.

Jeff Mitchell and Mirella Lapata. 2010. Composition in distributional models of semantics. *Cognitive Science*, 34(8):1388–1439.

Andriy Mnih and Geoffrey E Hinton. 2008. A scalable hierarchical distributed language model. In *Advances in Neural Information Processing Systems*, pages 1081–1088.

Yoshiki Niwa and Yoshihiko Nitta. 1994. Co-occurrence vectors from corpora vs. distance vectors from dictionaries. In *Proceedings of the 15th conference on Computational linguistics-Volume 1*, pages 304–309. Association for Computational Linguistics.

Sebastian Padó and Mirella Lapata. 2007. Dependency-based construction of semantic space models. *Computational Linguistics*, 33(2):161–199.

Fernando Pereira, Naftali Tishby, and Lillian Lee. 1993. Distributional clustering of english words. In *Proceedings of the 31st annual meeting on Association for Computational Linguistics*, pages 183–190. Association for Computational Linguistics.

Magnus Sahlgren. 2006. *The Word-Space Model: Using distributional analysis to represent syntagmatic and paradigmatic relations between words in high-dimensional vector spaces*. Ph.D. thesis, Stockholm.

Richard Socher, Jeffrey Pennington, Eric H Huang, Andrew Y Ng, and Christopher D Manning. 2011. Semi-supervised recursive autoencoders for predicting sentiment distributions. In *Proceedings of the Conference on Empirical Methods in Natural Language Processing*, pages 151–161. Association for Computational Linguistics.

Joseph Turian, Lev Ratinov, and Yoshua Bengio. 2010. Word representations: a simple and general method for semi-supervised learning. In *Proceedings of the 48th Annual Meeting of the Association for Computational Linguistics*, pages 384–394. Association for Computational Linguistics.

Peter D. Turney and Michael L. Littman. 2005. Corpus-based learning of analogies and semantic relations. *Machine Learning*, 60(1-3):251–278.

Peter D. Turney and Patrick Pantel. 2010. From frequency to meaning: Vector space models of semantics. *Journal of Artificial Intelligence Research*, 37(1):141–188.

Peter D. Turney. 2001. Mining the web for synonyms: Pmi-ir versus lsa on toefl. In *Proceedings of the 12th European Conference on Machine Learning*, pages 491–502. Springer-Verlag.

Peter D. Turney. 2006. Similarity of semantic relations. *Computational Linguistics*, 32(3):379–416.

Peter D. Turney. 2012. Domain and function: A dual-space model of semantic relations and compositions. *Journal of Artificial Intelligence Research*, 44:533–585.

Peter D. Turney. 2013. Distributional semantics beyond words: Supervised learning of analogy and paraphrase. *CoRR*, abs/1310.5042.

Alisa Zhila, Wen-tau Yih, Christopher Meek, Geoffrey Zweig, and Tomas Mikolov. 2013. Combining heterogeneous models for measuring relational similarity. In *Proceedings of the 2013 Conference of the North American Chapter of the Association for Computational Linguistics: Human Language Technologies*, pages 1000–1009, Atlanta, Georgia, June. Association for Computational Linguistics.

Probabilistic Modeling of Joint-context in Distributional Similarity

Oren Melamud[§], **Ido Dagan**[§], **Jacob Goldberger**[◇], **Idan Szpektor**[†], **Deniz Yuret**[‡]
§ Computer Science Department, Bar-Ilan University
◇ Faculty of Engineering, Bar-Ilan University
† Yahoo! Research Israel
‡ Koç University
{melamuo,dagan,goldbej}@{cs,cs,eng}.biu.ac.il
idan@yahoo-inc.com, dyuret@ku.edu.tr

Abstract

Most traditional distributional similarity models fail to capture syntagmatic patterns that group together multiple word features within the same joint context. In this work we introduce a novel generic distributional similarity scheme under which the power of probabilistic models can be leveraged to effectively model joint contexts. Based on this scheme, we implement a concrete model which utilizes probabilistic n-gram language models. Our evaluations suggest that this model is particularly well-suited for measuring similarity for verbs, which are known to exhibit richer syntagmatic patterns, while maintaining comparable or better performance with respect to competitive baselines for nouns. Following this, we propose our scheme as a framework for future semantic similarity models leveraging the substantial body of work that exists in probabilistic language modeling.

1 Introduction

The Distributional Hypothesis is commonly phrased as "words which are similar in meaning occur in similar contexts" (Rubenstein and Goodenough, 1965). Distributional similarity models following this hypothesis vary in two major aspects, namely the representation of the context and the respective computational model. Probably the most prominent class of distributional similarity models represents context as a vector of word features and computes similarity using feature vector arithmetics (Lund and Burgess, 1996; Turney et al., 2010). To construct the feature vectors, the context of each target word token[1], which is commonly a word window around it, is first broken into a set of individual independent words. Then the weights of the entries in the word feature vector capture the degree of association between the target word type and each of the individual word features, *independently* of one another.

Despite its popularity, it was suggested that the word feature vector approach misses valuable information, which is embedded in the colocation and inter-relations of words (e.g. word order) within the same context (Ruiz-Casado et al., 2005). Following this motivation, Ruiz-Casado et al. (2005) proposed an alternative *composite-feature* model, later adopted in (Agirre et al., 2009). This model adopts a richer context representation by considering entire word window contexts as features, while keeping the same computational vector-based model. Although showing interesting potential, this approach suffers from a very high-dimensional feature space resulting in data sparseness problems. Therefore, it requires exceptionally large learning corpora to consider large windows effectively.

A parallel line of work adopted richer context representations as well, with a different computational model. These works utilized neural networks to learn low dimensional continuous vector representations for word types, which were found useful for measuring semantic similarity (Collobert and Weston, 2008; Mikolov et al., 2013). These vectors are trained by optimizing the prediction of target words given their observed contexts (or variants of this objective). Most of these models consider each observed context as a joint set of context words within a word window.

In this work we follow the motivation in the previous works above to exploit richer *joint-context* representations for modeling distributional similarity. Under this approach the set of features in the context of each target word token is considered to jointly reflect on the meaning of the target word type. To further facilitate this type of mod-

[1] We use *word type* to denote an entry in the vocabulary, and *word token* for a particular occurrence of a word type.

Proceedings of the Eighteenth Conference on Computational Language Learning, pages 181–190,
Baltimore, Maryland USA, June 26-27 2014.

eling we propose a novel probabilistic computational scheme for distributional similarity, which leverages the power of probabilistic models and addresses the data sparseness challenge associated with large joint-contexts. Our scheme is based on the following probabilistic corollary to the distributional hypothesis:

"words are similar in meaning if they are *likely* to occur in the same contexts" (1)

To realize this corollary, our distributional similarity scheme assigns high similarity scores to word pairs a and b, for which a is likely in the contexts that are observed for b and vice versa. The scheme is generic in the sense that various underlying probabilistic models can be used to provide the estimates for the likelihood of a target word given a context. This allows concrete semantic similarity models based on this scheme to leverage the capabilities of probabilistic models, such as established language models, which typically address the modeling of joint-contexts.

We hypothesize that an underlying model that could capture syntagmatic patterns in large word contexts, yet is flexible enough to deal with data sparseness, is desired. It is generally accepted that the semantics of verbs in particular are correlated with their syntagmatic properties (Levin, 1993; Hanks, 2013). This provides grounds to expect that such model has the potential to excel for verbs. To capture syntagmatic patterns, we choose in this work standard n-gram language models as the basis for a concrete model implementing our scheme. This choice is inspired by recent work on learning syntactic categories (Yatbaz et al., 2012), which successfully utilized such language models to represent word window contexts of target words. However, we note that other richer types of language models, such as class-based (Brown et al., 1992) or hybrid (Tan et al., 2012), can be seamlessly integrated into our scheme.

Our evaluations suggest that our model is indeed particularly advantageous for measuring semantic similarity for verbs, while maintaining comparable or better performance with respect to competitive baselines for nouns.

2 Background

In this section we provide additional details regarding previous works that we later use as baselines in our evaluations.

To implement the composite-feature approach, Ruiz-Casado et al. (2005) used a Web search engine to compare entire window contexts of target word types. For example, a single feature that could be retrieved this way for the target word *like* is "Children ___ cookies and milk". They showed good results on detecting synonyms in the 80 multiple-choice questions TOEFL test. Agirre et al. (2009) constructed composite-feature vectors using an exceptionally large 1.6 Teraword learning corpus. They found that this approach outperforms the traditional independent feature vector approach on a subset of the WordSim353 test-set (Finkelstein et al., 2001), which is designed to test the more restricted relation of semantic similarity (to be distinguished from looser semantic relatedness). We are not aware of additional works following this approach, of using entire word windows as features.

Neural networks have been used to train language models that are based on low dimensional continuous vector representations for word types, also called *word embeddings* (Bengio et al., 2003; Mikolov et al., 2010). Although originally designed to improve language models, later works have shown that such word embeddings are useful in various other NLP tasks, including measuring semantic similarity with vector arithmetics (Collobert and Weston, 2008; Mikolov et al., 2013). Specifically, the recent work by Mikolov et al. (2013) introduced the *CBOW* and *Skip-gram* models, achieving state-of-the-art results in detecting semantic analogies. The CBOW model is trained to predict a target word given the set of context words in a word window around it, where this context is considered *jointly* as a bag-of-words. The Skip-gram model is trained to predict each of the context words independently given the target word.

3 Probabilistic Distributional Similarity

3.1 Motivation

In this section we briefly demonstrate the benefits of considering joint-contexts of words. As an illustrative example, we note that the target words *like* and *surround* may share many individual word features such as "school" and "campus" in the sentences "Mary's son *likes* the school campus" and "The forest *surrounds* the school campus". This potentially implies that individual features may not be sufficient to accurately reflect the difference between such words. Alternatively, we could use the following composite features to model the context of these words, "Mary's son ___ the school campus" and "The forest ___ the school campus". This would discriminate better between *like* and *surround*. However, in this case sentences such as "Mary's son *likes* the school campus" and "John's son *loves* the school campus" will not provide any evidence to the similarity between *like* and *love*, since "Mary's son ___ the school campus" is a different feature than "John's son ___ the school campus".

In the remainder of this section we propose a modeling scheme and then a concrete model, which can predict that *like* and *love* are likely to occur in each other's joint-contexts, whereas *like* and *surround* are not, and then assign similarity scores accordingly.

3.2 The probabilistic similarity scheme

We now present a computational scheme that realizes our proposed corollary (1) to the distributional hypothesis and facilitates robust probabilistic modeling of joint contexts. First, we slightly rephrase this corollary as follows: "words a and b are similar in meaning if word b is likely in the contexts of a and vice versa". We denote the probability of an occurrence of a target word b given a joint-context c by $p(b|c)$. For example, p(love|"Mary's son _ the school campus") is the probability of the word *love* to be the filler of the 'place-holder' in the given joint-context "Mary's son _ the school campus". Similarly, we denote $p(c|a)$ as the probability of a joint-context c given a word a, which fills its place-holder. We now propose $p^{sim}(b|a)$ to reflect how likely b is in the joint-contexts of a. We define this measure as:

$$p^{sim}(b|a) = \sum_{c} p(c|a) \cdot p(b|c) \qquad (2)$$

where c goes over all possible joint-contexts in the language.

To implement this measure we need to find an efficient estimate for $p^{sim}(b|a)$. The most straight forward strategy is to compute simple corpus count ratio estimates for $p(b|c)$ and $p(c|a)$, denoted $p_{\#}(b|c) = \frac{count(b,c)}{count(*,c)}$ and $p_{\#}(c|a) = \frac{count(a,c)}{count(a,*)}$. However, when considering large joint-contexts for c, this approach becomes similar to the composite-feature approach since it is based on co-occurrence counts of target words with large joint-contexts. Therefore, we expect in this case to encounter the data sparseness problems mentioned in Section 1, where semantically similar word type pairs that share only few or no identical joint-contexts yield very low $p^{sim}(b|a)$ estimates.

To address the data sparseness challenge and adopt more advanced context modeling, we aim to use a more robust underlying probabilistic model θ for our scheme and denote the probabilities estimated by this model by $p_\theta(b|c)$ and $p_\theta(c|a)$. We note that contrary to the count ratio model, given a robust model θ, such as a language model, $p_\theta(b|c)$ and $p_\theta(c|a)$ can be positive even if the target words b and a were not observed with the joint-context c in the learning corpus.

While using $p_\theta(b|c)$ and $p_\theta(c|a)$ to estimate the value of $p^{sim}(b|a)$ addresses the sparseness challenge, it introduces a computational challenge. This is because estimating $p^{sim}(b|a)$ would require computing the sum over all of the joint-contexts in the learning corpus regardless of whether they were actually observed with either word type a or b. For that reason we choose a middle ground approach, estimating $p(b|c)$ with θ, while using a count ratio estimate for $p(c|a)$, as follows. We denote the collection of all joint-contexts observed for the target word a in the learning corpus by C_a, where $|C_a|= count(a,*)$. For example, C_{like} = {c_1="Mary's son ___ the school campus", c_2="John's daughter ___ to read poetry",...}. We note that this collection is a multiset, where the same joint-context can appear more than once.

We now approximate $p^{sim}(b|a)$ from Equation (2) as follows:

$$\begin{aligned}\hat{p}_\theta^{sim}(b|a) = \sum_{c} p_{\#}(c|a) \cdot p_\theta(b|c) = \\ \frac{1}{|C_a|} \cdot \sum_{c \in C_a} p_\theta(b|c)\end{aligned} \qquad (3)$$

We note that this formulation still addresses sparseness of data by using a robust model, such as a language model, to estimate $p_\theta(b|c)$. At the same time it requires our model to sum only over the joint-contexts in the collection C_a, since contexts not observed for a yield $p_{\#}(c|a) = 0$. Even so, since the size of these context collections grows linearly with the corpus size, considering all observed contexts may still present a scalability challenge. Nevertheless, we expect our approximation $\hat{p}_\theta^{sim}(b|a)$ to converge with a reasonable sample size from a's joint-contexts. Therefore, in order to bound computational complexity, we limit the size of the context collections used to train our model to a maximum of N by randomly sampling N entries from larger collections. In all our experiments we use $N = 10,000$. Higher values of N yielded negligible performances differences. Overall we see that our model estimates $\hat{p}_\theta^{sim}(b|a)$ as the average probability predicted for b in (a large sample of) the contexts observed for a.

Finally, we define our similarity measure for target word types a and b:

$$sim_\theta(a,b) = \sqrt{\hat{p}_\theta^{sim}(b|a) \cdot \hat{p}_\theta^{sim}(a|b)} \quad (4)$$

As intended, this similarity measure promotes word pairs in which both b is likely in the contexts of a and vice versa. Next, we describe a model which implements this scheme with an n-gram language model as a concrete choice for θ.

3.3 Probabilistic similarity using language models

In this work we focus on the word window context representation, which is the most common. We define a word window of order k around a target word as a window with up to k words to each side of the target word, not crossing sentence boundaries. The word window does not include the target word itself, but rather a 'place-holder' for it.

Since word windows are sequences of words, probabilistic language models are a natural choice of a model θ for estimating $p_\theta(b|c)$. Language models assign likelihood estimates to sequences of words using approximation strategies. In this work we choose n-gram language models, aiming to capture syntagmatic properties of the word contexts, which are sensitive to word order. To approximate the probability of long sequences of words, n-gram language models compute the product of the estimated probability of each word in the sequence conditioned on at most the $n-1$ words preceding it. Furthermore, they use 'discounting' methods to improve the estimates of conditional probabilities when learning data is sparse. Specifically, in this work we use the Kneser-Ney n-gram model (Kneser and Ney, 1995).

We compute $p_\theta(b|c)$ as follows:

$$p_\theta(b|c) = \frac{p_\theta(b,c)}{p_\theta(c)} \quad (5)$$

where $p_\theta(b,c)$ is the probability of the word sequence comprising the word window c, in which the word b fills the place-holder. For instance, for c = "I drive my ___ to work every" and b = *car*, $p_\theta(b,c)$ is the estimated language model probability of "I drive my car to work every". $p_\theta(c)$ is the marginal probability of $p_\theta(*,c)$ over all possible words in the vocabulary. [2]

4 Experimental Settings

Although sometimes used interchangeably, it is common to distinguish between semantic *similarity* and semantic *relatedness* (Budanitsky and Hirst, 2001; Agirre et al., 2009). Semantic similarity is used to describe 'likeness' relations, such as the relations between synonyms, hypernym-hyponyms, and co-hyponyms. Semantic relatedness refers to a broader range of relations including also meronymy and various other associative relations as in 'pencil-paper' or 'penguin-Antarctica'. In this work we focus on semantic similarity and evaluate all compared methods on several semantic similarity tasks.

Following previous works (Lin, 1998; Riedl and Biemann, 2013) we use Wordnet to construct large scale gold standards for semantic similarity evaluations. We perform the evaluations separately for nouns and verbs to test our hypothesis that our model is particularly well-suited for verbs. To further evaluate our results on verbs we use the verb similarity test-set released by (Yang and Powers, 2006), which contains pairs of verbs associated with semantic similarity scores based on human judgements.

4.1 Compared methods

We compare our model with a traditional feature vector model, the composite-feature model (Agirre et al., 2009), and the recent state-of-the-art word embedding models, CBOW and Skip-gram (Mikolov et al., 2013), all trained on the same learning corpus and evaluated on equal grounds.

We denote the traditional feature vector baseline by IFV^{W-k}, where *IFV* stands for *"Independent-Feature Vector"* and k is the order of the context word window considered. Similarly, we

[2]Computing $p_\theta(c)$ by summing over all possible place-holder filler words, as we did in this work, is computationally intensive. However, this can be done more efficiently by implementing customized versions of (at least some) n-gram language models with little computational overhead, e.g. by counting the learning corpus occurrences of n-gram templates, in which one of the elements matches any word.

denote the composite-feature vector baseline by CFV^{W-k}, where *CFV* stands for *"Composite-Feature Vector"*. This baseline constructs traditional-like feature vectors, but considers entire word windows around target word tokens as single features. In both of these baselines we use Cosine as the vector similarity measure, and positive pointwise mutual information (PPMI) for the feature vector weights. PPMI is a well-known variant of pointwise mutual information (Church and Hanks, 1990), and the combination of Cosine with PPMI was shown to perform particularly well in (Bullinaria and Levy, 2007).

We denote Mikolov's CBOW and Skip-gram baseline models by $CBOW^{W-k}$ and $SKIP^{W-k}$ respectively, where k denotes again the order of the window used to train these models. We used Mikolov's word2vec utility[3] with standard parameters (600 dimensions, negative sampling 15) to learn the word embeddings, and Cosine as the vector similarity measure between them.

As the underlying probabilistic language model for our method we use the Berkeley implementation[4] (Pauls and Klein, 2011) of the Kneser-Ney n-gram model with the default discount parameters. We denote our model PDS^{W-k}, where *PDS* stands for *"Probabilistic Distributional Similarity"*, and k is the order of the context word window. In order to avoid giving our model an unfair advantage of tuning the order of the language model n as an additional parameter, we use a fixed $n = k + 1$. This means that the conditional probabilities that our n-gram model learns consider a scope of up to half the size of the window, which is the distance in words between the target word and either end of the window. We note that this is the smallest reasonable value for n, as smaller values effectively mean that there will be context words within the window that are more than n words away from the target word, and therefore will not be considered by our model.

As learning corpus we used the first CD of the freely available Reuters RCV1 dataset (Rose et al., 2002). This learning corpus contains approximately 100M words, which is comparable in size to the British National Corpus (BNC) (Aston, 1997). We first applied part-of-speech tagging and lemmatization to all words. Then we represented each word w in the corpus as the pair $[pos(w), lemma(w)]$, where $pos(w)$ is a coarse-grained part-of-speech category and $lemma(w)$ is the lemmatized form of w. Finally, we converted every pair $[pos(w), lemma(w)]$ that occurs less than 100 times in the learning corpus to the pair $[pos(w), ?]$, which represents all rare words of the same part-of-speech tag. Ignoring rare words is a common practice used in order to clean up the corpus and reduce the vocabulary size (Gorman and Curran, 2006; Collobert and Weston, 2008).

The above procedure resulted in a word vocabulary of 27K words. From this vocabulary we constructed a *target verb set* with over 2.5K verbs by selecting all verbs that exist in Wordnet (Fellbaum, 2010). We repeated this procedure to create a *target noun set* with over 9K nouns. We used our learning corpus for all compared methods and had them assign a semantic similarity score for every pair of verbs and every pair of nouns in these target sets. These scores were later used in all of our evaluations.

4.2 Wordnet evaluation

There is a shortage of large scale test-sets for semantic similarity. Popular test-sets such as WordSim353 and the TOEFL synonyms test contain only 353 and 80 test items respectively, and therefore make it difficult to obtain statistically significant results. To automatically construct larger-scale test-sets for semantic similarity, we sampled large target word subsets from our corpus and used Wordnet as a gold standard for their semantically similar words, following related previous evaluations (Lin, 1998; Riedl and Biemann, 2013). We constructed two test-sets for our primary evaluation, one for verb similarity and another for noun similarity.

To perform the verb similarity evaluation, we randomly sampled 1,000 verbs from the target verb set, where the probability of each verb to be sampled is set to be proportional to its frequency in the learning corpus. Next, for each sampled verb a we constructed a Wordnet-based gold standard set of semantically similar words. In this set each verb a' is annotated as a 'synonym' of a if at least one of the senses of a' is a synonym of any of the senses of a. In addition, each verb a' is annotated as a 'semantic neighbor' of a if at least one of the senses of a' is a synonym, co-hyponym, or a direct hypernym/hyponym of any of the senses of a. We note that by definition all verbs annotated as

[3]http://code.google.com/p/word2vec

[4]http://code.google.com/p/berkeleylm/

synonyms of a are annotated as semantic neighbors as well. Next, per each verb a and an evaluated method, we generated a ranked list of all other verbs, which was induced according to the similarity scores of this method.

Finally, we evaluated the compared methods on two tasks, 'synonym detection' and 'semantic neighbor detection'. In the synonym detection task we evaluated the methods' ability to retrieve as much verbs annotated in our gold standard as 'synonyms', in the top-n entries of their ranked lists. Similarly, we evaluated all methods on the 'semantic neighbors' task. The synonym detection task is designed to evaluate the ability of the compared methods to identify a more restrictive interpretation of semantic similarity, while the semantic neighbor detection task does the same for a somewhat broader interpretation.

We repeated the above procedure for sampling 1,000 target nouns, constructing the noun Wordnet-based gold standards and evaluating on the two semantic similarity tasks.

4.3 VerbSim evaluation

The publicly available VerbSim test-set contains 130 verb pairs, each annotated with an average of 6 human judgements of semantic similarity (Yang and Powers, 2006). We extracted a 107 pairs subset of this dataset for which all verbs are in our learning corpus. We followed works such as (Yang and Powers, 2007; Agirre et al., 2009) and compared the Spearman correlations between the verb-pair similarity scores assigned by the compared methods and the manually annotated scores in this dataset.

5 Results

For each method and verb a in our 1,000 tested verbs, we used the Wordnet gold standard to compute the precision at top-1, top-5 and top-10 of the ranked list generated by this method for a. We then computed mean precision values averaged over all verbs for each of the compared methods, denoted as P@1, P@5 and P@10. The detailed report of P@10 results is omitted for brevity, as they behave very similarly to P@5. We varied the context window order used by all methods to test its effect on the results. We measured the same metrics for nouns.

The results of our Wordnet-based 1,000 verbs evaluation are presented in the upper part of Figure 1. The results show significant improvement of our method over all baselines, with a margin between 2 to 3 points on the synonyms detection task and 5 to 7 points on the semantic neighbors detection task. Our best performing configurations are PDS^{W-3} and PDS^{W-4}, outperforming all other baselines on both tasks and in all precision categories. This difference is statistically significant at $p < 0.001$ using a paired t-test in all cases except for the P@1 in the synonyms detection task. Within the baselines, the composite feature vector (CFV) performs somewhat better than the independent feature vector (IFV) baseline, and both methods perform best around window order of two, with gradual decline for larger windows. The word embedding baselines, CBOW and SKIP, perform comparably to the feature vector baselines and to one another, with best performance achieved around window order of four.

When gradually increasing the context window order within the range of up to 4 words, our PDS model shows improvement. This is in contrast to the feature vector baselines, whose performance declines for context window orders larger than 2. This suggests that our approach is able to take advantage of larger contexts in comparison to standard feature vector models. The decline in performance for the independent feature vector baseline (IFV) may be related to the fact that independent features farther away from the target word are generally more loosely related to it. This seems consistent with previous works, where narrow windows of the order of two words performed well (Bullinaria and Levy, 2007; Agirre et al., 2009; Bruni et al., 2012) and in particular so when evaluating semantic similarity rather than relatedness. On the other hand, the decline in performance for the composite feature vector baseline (CFV) may be attributed to the data sparseness phenomenon associated with larger windows. The performance of the word embedding baselines (CBOW and SKIP) starts declining very mildly only for window orders larger than 4. This might be attributed to the fact that these models assign lower weights to context words the farther away they are from the center of the window.

The results of our Wordnet-based 1,000 nouns evaluation are presented in the lower part of Figure 1. These results are partly consistent with the results achieved for verbs, but with a couple of notable differences. First, though our model still

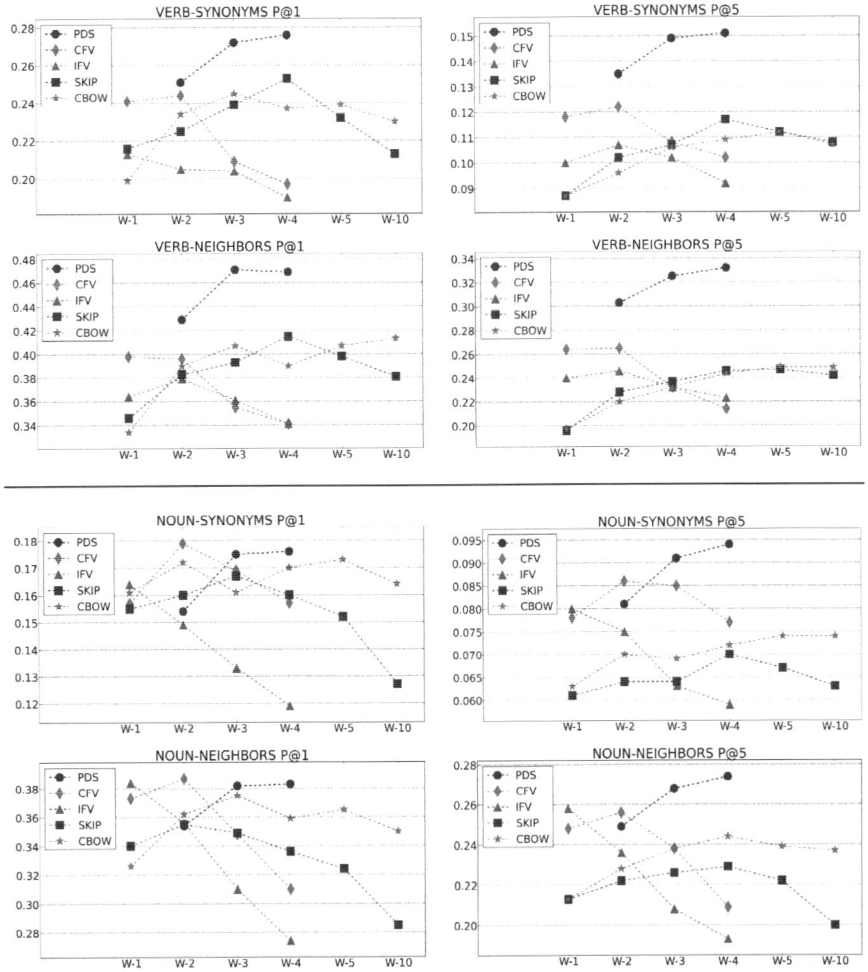

Figure 1: Mean precision scores as a function of window order, obtained against the Wordnet-based gold standard, on both the verb and noun test-sets with both the synonyms and semantic neighbor detection tasks. "P@n" stands for precision in the top-n words of the ranked lists. Note that the Y-axis scale varies between graphs.

outperforms or performs comparably to all other baselines, in this case the advantage of our model over the feature vector baselines is much more moderate and not statistically significant. Second, the word embedding baselines generally perform worst (with CBOW performing a little better than SKIP), and our model outperforms them in both P@5 and P@10 with a margin of around 2 points for the synonyms detection task and 3-4 points for the neighbor detection task, with statistical significance at $p < 0.001$.

Next, to reconfirm the particular applicability of our model to verb similarity as apparent from the Wordnet evaluation, we performed the VerbSim evaluation and present the results in Table 1. We compared the Spearman correlation obtained for the top-performing window order of each of the evaluated methods in the Wordnet verbs evaluation. We present two sets of results. The 'all scores' results follow the standard evaluation procedure, considering all similarity scores produced by each method. In the 'top-100 scores' results, for each method we converted to zero the scores that it assigned to word pairs, where neither of the words is in the top-100 most similar words of the other. Then we performed the evaluation with these revised scores. This procedure focuses on evaluating the quality of the methods' top-100 ranked word lists. The results show that our method outperforms all baselines by a nice mar-

Method	All scores	top-100 scores
PDS W-4	**0.616**	**0.625**
CFV W-2	0.477	0.497
IFV W-2	0.467	0.546
SKIP W-4	0.469	0.512
CBOW W-5	0.528	0.469

Table 1: Spearman correlation values obtained for the VerbSim evaluation. Each method was evaluated with the optimal window order found in the Wordnet verbs evaluation.

gin of more than 8 points with the score of 0.616 and 0.625 for the 'all scores' and 'top-100 scores' evaluations respectively. Though not statistically significant, due to the small test-set size, these results support the ones from the Wordnet evaluation, suggesting that our model performs better than the baselines on measuring verb similarity.

In summary, our results suggest that in lack of a robust context modeling scheme it is hard for distributional similarity models to effectively leverage larger word window contexts for measuring semantic similarity. It appears that this is somewhat less of a concern when it comes to noun similarity, as the simple feature vector models reach near-optimal performance with small word windows of order 2, but it is an important factor for verb similarity. In his recent book, Hanks (2013) claims that contrary to nouns, computational models that are to capture the meanings of verbs must consider their syntagmatic patterns in text. Our particularly good results on verb similarity suggest that our modeling approach is able to capture such information in larger context windows. We further conjecture that the reason the word embedding baselines did not do as well as our model on verb similarity might be due to their particular choice of joint-context formulation, which is not sensitive to word order. However, these conjectures should be further validated with additional evaluations in future work.

6 Future Directions

In this paper we investigated the potential for improving distributional similarity models by modeling jointly the occurrence of several features under the same context. We evaluated several previous works with different context modeling approaches and suggest that the type of the underlying context modeling may have significant effect on the performance of the semantic model. Furthermore, we introduced a generic probabilistic distributional similarity approach, which can leverage the power of established probabilistic language models to effectively model joint-contexts for the purpose of measuring semantic similarity. Our concrete model utilizing n-gram language models outperforms several competitive baselines on semantic similarity tasks, and appears to be particularly well-suited for verbs. In the remainder of this section we describe some potential future directions that can be pursued.

First, the performance of our generic scheme is largely inherited from the nature of its underlying language model. Therefore, we see much potential in exploring the use of other types of language models, such as class-based (Brown et al., 1992), syntax-based (Pauls and Klein, 2012) or hybrid (Tan et al., 2012). Furthermore, a similar approach to ours could be attempted in word embedding models. For instance, our syntagmatic joint-context modeling approach could be investigated by word embedding models to generate better embeddings for verbs.

Another direction relates to the well known tendency of many words, and particularly verbs, to assume different meanings (or senses) under different contexts. To address this phenomenon context sensitive similarity and inference models have been proposed (Dinu and Lapata, 2010; Melamud et al., 2013). Similarly to many semantic similarity models, our current model aggregates information from all observed contexts of a target word type regardless of its different senses. However, we believe that our approach is well suited to address context sensitive similarity with proper enhancements, as it considers joint-contexts that can more accurately disambiguate the meaning of target words. As an example, it is possible to consider the likelihood of word b to occur in a subset of the contexts observed for word a, which is biased towards a particular sense of a.

Finally, we note that our model is not a classic vector space model and therefore common vector composition approaches (Mitchell and Lapata, 2008) cannot be directly applied to it. Instead, other methods, such as similarity of compositions (Turney, 2012), should be investigated to extend our approach for measuring similarity between phrases.

Acknowledgments

This work was partially supported by the Israeli Ministry of Science and Technology grant 3-8705, the Israel Science Foundation grant 880/12, the European Community's Seventh Framework Programme (FP7/2007-2013) under grant agreement no. 287923 (EXCITEMENT) and the Scientific and Technical Research Council of Turkey (TÜBİTAK, Grant Number 112E277).

References

Eneko Agirre, Enrique Alfonseca, Keith Hall, Jana Kravalova, Marius Paşca, and Aitor Soroa. 2009. A study on similarity and relatedness using distributional and wordnet-based approaches. In *Proceedings of NAACL*. Association for Computational Linguistics.

Guy Aston. 1997. The BNC Handbook Exploring the British National Corpus with SARA Guy Aston and Lou Burnard.

Yoshua Bengio, Rjean Ducharme, Pascal Vincent, and Christian Jauvin. 2003. A neural probabilistic language model. *Journal of Machine Learning Research*, 3:1137–1155.

Peter F. Brown, Peter V. Desouza, Robert L. Mercer, Vincent J. Della Pietra, and Jenifer C. Lai. 1992. Class-based n-gram models of natural language. *Computational linguistics*, 18(4):467–479.

Elia Bruni, Gemma Boleda, Marco Baroni, and Nam-Khanh Tran. 2012. Distributional semantics in technicolor. In *Proceedings of ACL*.

Alexander Budanitsky and Graeme Hirst. 2001. Semantic distance in wordnet: An experimental, application-oriented evaluation of five measures. In *Workshop on WordNet and Other Lexical Resources*.

John A. Bullinaria and Joseph P. Levy. 2007. Extracting semantic representations from word co-occurrence statistics: A computational study. *Behavior Research Methods*, 39(3):510–526.

Kenneth W. Church and Patrick Hanks. 1990. Word association norms, mutual information, and lexicography. *Computational Linguistics*, 16(1):22–29.

Ronan Collobert and Jason Weston. 2008. A unified architecture for natural language processing: Deep neural networks with multitask learning. In *Proceedings of the 25th international conference on Machine learning*, pages 160–167. ACM.

Georgiana Dinu and Mirella Lapata. 2010. Measuring distributional similarity in context. In *Proceedings of EMNLP*.

Christiane Fellbaum. 2010. *WordNet*. Springer.

Lev Finkelstein, Evgeniy Gabrilovich, Yossi Matias, Ehud Rivlin, Zach Solan, Gadi Wolfman, and Eytan Ruppin. 2001. Placing search in context: The concept revisited. In *Proceedings of the 10th international conference on World Wide Web*. ACM.

James Gorman and James R. Curran. 2006. Scaling distributional similarity to large corpora. In *Proceedings of ACL*.

Patrick Hanks. 2013. *Lexical Analysis: Norms and Exploitations*. Mit Press.

Reinhard Kneser and Hermann Ney. 1995. Improved backing-off for m-gram language modeling. In *International Conference on Acoustics, Speech, and Signal Processing*. IEEE.

Beth Levin. 1993. *English verb classes and alternations: A preliminary investigation*. University of Chicago press.

Dekang Lin. 1998. Automatic retrieval and clustering of similar words. In *Proceedings of COLING-ACL*.

Kevin Lund and Curt Burgess. 1996. Producing high-dimensional semantic spaces from lexical co-occurrence. *Behavior Research Methods, Instruments, & Computers*.

Oren Melamud, Jonathan Berant, Ido Dagan, Jacob Goldberger, and Idan Szpektor. 2013. A two level model for context sensitive inference rules. In *Proceedings of ACL*.

Tomas Mikolov, Martin Karafiát, Lukas Burget, Jan Cernockỳ, and Sanjeev Khudanpur. 2010. Recurrent neural network based language model. In *INTERSPEECH*.

Tomas Mikolov, Kai Chen, Greg Corrado, and Jeffrey Dean. 2013. Efficient estimation of word representations in vector space. *arXiv preprint arXiv:1301.3781*.

Jeff Mitchell and Mirella Lapata. 2008. Vector-based models of semantic composition. In *Proceedings of ACL*.

Adam Pauls and Dan Klein. 2011. Faster and Smaller N-Gram Language Models. In *Proceedings of ACL*.

Adam Pauls and Dan Klein. 2012. Large-scale syntactic language modeling with treelets. In *Proceedings of ACL*.

Martin Riedl and Chris Biemann. 2013. Scaling to large^3 data: An efficient and effective method to compute distributional thesauri. In *Proceedings of EMNLP*.

Tony Rose, Mark Stevenson, and Miles Whitehead. 2002. The Reuters Corpus Volume 1-from Yesterday's News to Tomorrow's Language Resources. In *LREC*.

Herbert Rubenstein and John B. Goodenough. 1965. Contextual correlates of synonymy. *Communications of the ACM.*

Maria Ruiz-Casado, Enrique Alfonseca, and Pablo Castells. 2005. Using context-window overlapping in synonym discovery and ontology extension. *Proceedings of RANLP.*

Ming Tan, Wenli Zhou, Lei Zheng, and Shaojun Wang. 2012. A scalable distributed syntactic, semantic, and lexical language model. *Computational Linguistics*, 38(3):631–671.

Peter D. Turney, Patrick Pantel, et al. 2010. From frequency to meaning: Vector space models of semantics. *Journal of artificial intelligence research.*

Peter D. Turney. 2012. Domain and function: A dual-space model of semantic relations and compositions. *Journal of Artificial Intelligence Researc*, 44(1):533–585, May.

Dongqiang Yang and David M. W. Powers. 2006. Verb similarity on the taxonomy of wordnet. In *the 3rd International WordNet Conference (GWC-06).*

Dongqiang Yang and David M. W. Powers. 2007. An empirical investigation into grammatically constrained contexts in predicting distributional similarity. In *Australasian Language Technology Workshop 2007*, pages 117–124.

Mehmet Ali Yatbaz, Enis Sert, and Deniz Yuret. 2012. Learning syntactic categories using paradigmatic representations of word context. In *Proceedings of EMNLP.*

A Rudimentary Lexicon and Semantics Help Bootstrap Phoneme Acquisition

Abdellah Fourtassi **Emmanuel Dupoux**

Laboratoire de Sciences Cognitives et Psycholinguistique, ENS/EHESS/CNRS, Paris
{abdellah.fourtassi, emmanuel.dupoux}@gmail.com

Abstract

Infants spontaneously discover the relevant phonemes of their language without any direct supervision. This acquisition is puzzling because it seems to require the availability of high levels of linguistic structures (lexicon, semantics), that logically suppose the infants having a set of phonemes already. We show how this circularity can be broken by testing, in real-size language corpora, a scenario whereby infants would learn approximate representations at all levels, and then refine them in a mutually constraining way. We start with corpora of spontaneous speech that have been encoded in a varying number of detailed context-dependent allophones. We derive, in an unsupervised way, an approximate lexicon and a rudimentary semantic representation. Despite the fact that all these representations are poor approximations of the ground truth, they help reorganize the fine grained categories into phoneme-like categories with a high degree of accuracy.

One of the most fascinating facts about human infants is the speed at which they acquire their native language. During the first year alone, i.e., before they are able to speak, infants achieve impressive landmarks regarding three key language components. First, they tune in on the phonemic categories of their language (Werker and Tees, 1984). Second, they learn to segment the continuous speech stream into discrete units (Jusczyk and Aslin, 1995). Third, they start to recognize frequent words (Ngon et al., 2013), as well as the semantics of many of them (Bergelson and Swingley, 2012).

Even though these landmarks have been documented in detail over the past 40 years of research, little is still known about the mechanisms that are operative in infant's brain to achieve such a result. Current work in early language acquisition has proposed two competing but incomplete hypotheses that purports to account for this stunning development path. The bottom-up hypothesis holds that infants converge onto the linguistic units of their language through a statistical analysis over of their input. In contrast, the top-down hypothesis emphasizes the role of higher levels of linguistic structure in learning the lower level units.

1 A chicken-and-egg problem

1.1 Bottom-up is not enough

Several studies have documented the fact that infants become attuned to the native sounds of their language, starting at 6 months of age (see Gervain & Mehler, 2010 for a review). Some researchers have claimed that such an early attunement is due to a statistical learning mechanism that only takes into account the distributional properties of the sounds present in the native input (Maye et al., 2002). Unsupervised clustering algorithms running on simplified input have, indeed, provided a proof of principle for bottom-up learning of phonemic categories from speech (see for instance Vallabha et al., 2007).

It is clear, however, that distributional learning cannot account for the entire developmental pattern. In fact, phoneme tokens in real speech exhibit high acoustic variability and result in phonemic categories with a high degree of overlap (Hillenbrand et al., 1995). When purely bottom up clustering algorithms are tested on realistic input, they ended up in either a too large number of subphonemic units (Varadarajan et al., 2008) or a too small number of coarse grained categories (Feldman et al., 2013a).

Proceedings of the Eighteenth Conference on Computational Language Learning, pages 191–200,
Baltimore, Maryland USA, June 26-27 2014. ©2014 Association for Computational Linguistics

1.2 The top-down hypothesis

Inspection of the developmental data shows that infants do not wait to have completed the acquisition of their native phonemes to start to learn words. In fact, lexical and phonological acquisition largely overlap. Infant can recognize highly frequent word forms like their own names, by as early as 4 months of age (Mandel et al., 1995). Vice versa, the refinement of phonemic categories does not stop at 12 months. The sensitivity to phonetic contrasts has been reported to continue at 3 years of age (Nittrouer, 1996) and beyond (Hazan and Barrett, 2000), on par with the development of the lexicon.

Some researchers have therefore suggested that there might be a learning synergy which allows infants to base some of their acquisition not only on bottom up information, but also on statistics over lexical items or even on the basis of word meaning (Feldman et al., 2013a; Feldman et al., 2013b; Yeung and Werker, 2009)

These experiments and computational models, however, have focused on simplified input or/and used already segmented words. It remains to be shown whether the said top-down strategies scale up when real size corpora and more realistic representations are used. There are indeed indications that, in the absence of a proper phonological representation, lexical learning becomes very difficult. For example, word segmentation algorithms that work on the basis of phoneme-like units tend to degrade quickly if phonemes are replaced by contextual allophones (Boruta et al., 2011) or with the output of phone recognizers (Jansen et al., 2013; Ludusan et al., 2014).

In brief, we are facing a chicken-and-egg problem: lexical and semantic information could help to learn the phonemes, but phonemes are needed to acquire lexical information.

1.3 Breaking the circularity: An incremental discovery procedure

Here, we explore the idea that instead of learning adult-like hierarchically organized representations in a sequential fashion (phonemes, words, semantics), infants learn approximate, provisional linguistic representations in parallel. These approximate representations are subsequently used to improve each other.

More precisely, we make four assumptions. First, we assume that infants start by paying attention to fine grained variation in the acoustic input, thus constructing perceptual phonetic categories that are not phonemes, but segments encoding fine grained phonetic details (Werker and Curtin, 2005; Pierrehumbert, 2003). Second, we assume that these units enable infants to segment proto-words from continuous speech and store them in this detailed format. Importantly, this proto-lexicon will not be adult-like: it will contain badly segmented word forms, and store several alternant forms for the same word. Ngon et al. (2013) have shown that 11 month old infants recognize frequent sound sequences that do not necessarily map to adult words. Third, we assume that infants can use this imperfect lexicon to acquire some semantic representation. As shown in Shukla et al. (2011), infants can simultaneously segment words and associate them with a visual referent. Fourth, we assume that as their exposure to language develops, infants reorganize these initial categories along the relevant dimensions of their native language based on cues from all these representations.

The aim of this work is to provide a proof of principle for this general scenario, using real size corpora in two typologically different languages, and state-of-the-art learning algorithms.

The paper is organized as follows. We begin by describing how we generated the input and how we modeled different levels of representation. Then, we explain how information from the higher levels (word forms and semantics) can be used to refine the learning of the lower level (phonetic categories). Next, we present the results of our simulations and discuss the potential implications for the language learning process.

2 Modeling the representations

Here, we describe how we model different levels of representation (phonetic categories, lexicon and semantics) starting from raw speech in English and Japanese.

2.1 Corpus

We use two speech corpora: the Buckeye Speech corpus (Pitt et al., 2007), which contains 40 hours of spontaneous conversations in American English, and the 40 hours core of the Corpus of Spontaneous Japanese (Maekawa et al., 2000), which contains spontaneous conversations and public speeches in different fields, ranging from engineering to humanities. Following Boruta (2012), we use an inventory of 25 phonemes for transcribing Japanese, and for English, we use the set of 45 phonemes in the phonemic transcription of Pitt et al. (2007).

2.2 Phonetic categories

Here, we describe how we model the perceptual phonetic categories infants learn in a first step before converging on the functional categories (phonemes). We make the assumption that these initial categories correspond to fine grained *allophones*, i.e., different systematic realizations of phonemes, depending on context. Allophonic variation can range from categorical effects due to phonological rules to gradient effects due to coarticulation, i.e, the phenomenon whereby adjacent sounds affect the physical realization of a given phoneme. An example of a rather categorical allophonic rule is given by /r/ devoicing in French:

$$/\text{r}/ \rightarrow \begin{cases} [\chi]\ / & \text{before a voiceless obstruent} \\ [\text{ʁ}] & \text{elsewhere} \end{cases}$$

Figure 1: Allophonic variation of French /r/

The phoneme /r/ surfaces as voiced ([ʁ]) before a voiced obstruent like in [kanaʁ ʒon] ("canard jaune", yellow duck) and as voiceless ([χ]) before a voiceless obstruent as in [kanaχ puχpʁ] ("canard pourpre", purple duck). The challenge facing the leaner is, therefore, to distinguish pairs of segments that are in an allophonic relationship ([ʁ], [χ]) from pairs that are two distinct phonemes and can carry a meaning difference ([ʁ],[l]).

Previous work has generated allophonic variation artificially (Martin et al., 2013). Here, we follow Fourtassi et al. (2014b) in using a linguistically and statistically controlled method, starting from audio recordings and using a standard Hidden Markov Models (HMM) phone recognizer to generate them, as follows.

We convert the raw speech waveform into successive 10ms frames containing a vector of Mel Frequency Cepstrum Coefficients (MFCC). We use 12 MFC coefficients (plus the energy) computed over a 25ms window, to which we add the first and second order derivatives, yielding 39 dimensions per frame.

The HMM training starts with one three-state model per phoneme. Each state is modeled by a mixture of 17 diagonal Gaussians. After training, each phoneme model is cloned into context-dependent triphone models, for each context in which the phoneme actually occurs (for example, the phoneme /ɑ/ occurs in the context [d–ɑ–g] as in the word /dɑg/ ("dog"). The triphone models cloned from the phonemes are then retrained, but, this time, only on the relevant subset of the data, corresponding to the given triphone context. Finally, these detailed models are clustered back into inventories of various sizes (from 2 to 20 times the size of the phonemic inventory) and retrained. Clustering is done state by state using a phonetic feature-based decision tree, and results in tying together the HMM states of linguistically similar triphones so as to maximize the likelihood of the data. The HMM were built using the HMM Toolkit (HTK: Young et al., 2006).

2.3 The proto-lexicon

Finding word boundaries in the continuous sequence of phones is part of the problem infants have to solve without direct supervision. We model this segmentation using a state-of-the-art unsupervised word segmentation model based on the Adaptor Grammar framework (Johnson et al., 2007). The input consists of a phonetic transcription of the corpus, with boundaries between words eliminated (we vary this transcription to correspond to different inventories with different granularity in the allophonic representation as explained above). The model tries to reconstruct the boundaries based on a Pitman-Yor process (Pitman and Yor, 1997), which uses a language-general statistical learning process to find a compact representation of the input. The algorithm stores high frequency chunks and re-uses them to parse novel utterances. We use a grammar which learns a hierarchy of three levels of chunking and use the intermediate level to correspond to the lexical level. This grammar was shown by Fourtassi et al. (2013) to avoid both over-segmentation and under-segmentation.

2.4 The proto-semantics

It has been shown that infants can keep track of co-occurrence statistics (see Lany and Saffran (2013) for a review). This ability can be used to develop a sense of semantic similarity as suggested by Harris (1954). The intuition behind the *distributional hypothesis* is that words that are similar in meaning occur in similar contexts. In order to model the acquisition of this semantic similarity from a transcribed and segmented corpus, we use one of the simplest and most commonly used distributional semantic models, Latent Semantic Analysis (LSA: Landauer & Dumais, 1997). The LSA algorithm takes as input a matrix consisting of rows representing word types and columns representing contexts in which tokens of the word type occur. A context is defined as a fixed number of utterances. Singular value decomposition (a kind of matrix factorization) is used to extract a more compact representation. The cosine of the angle between vectors in the resulting space is used to measure the semantic similarity between words. Two words have a high semantic similarity if they have similar distributions, i.e., if they co-occur in most contexts. The model parameters, namely the dimension of the semantic space and the number of utterances to be taken as defining the context of a given word form, are set in an unsupervised way to optimize the latent structure of the semantic model (Fourtassi and Dupoux, 2013). Thus, we use 20 utterances as a semantic window and set the semantic space to 100 dimensions.

3 Method

Here we explore whether the approximate high level representations, built bottom-up and without supervision, still contain useful information one can use to refine the phonetic categories into phoneme-like units. To this end, we extract potential cues from the lexical and the semantic information, and test their performance in discriminating allophonic contrasts from non-allophonic (phonemic) contrasts.

3.1 Top down cues

3.1.1 Lexical cue

The top down information from the lexicon is based on the insight of Martin et al. (2013). It rests on the idea that true lexical minimal pairs are not very frequent in human languages, as compared to minimal pairs due to mere phonological processes (figure 1). The latter creates alternants of the same lexical item since adjacent sounds condition the realization of the first and final phoneme. Therefore, finding a minimal pair of words differing in the first or last segment (as in [kanaχ] and [kanaʁ]) is good evidence that these two phones ([ʁ], [χ]) are allophones of one another. Conversely, if a pair of phones is not forming any minimal pair, it is classified as non-allophonic (phonemic).

However, this binary strategy clearly gives rise to false alarms in the (albeit relatively rare) case of true minimal pairs like [kanaχ] ("duck") and [kanal] ("canal"), where ([χ], [l]) will be mistakenly labeled as allophonic. In order to mitigate the problem of false alarms, we use Boruta's continuous version (Boruta, 2011) and we define the lexical cue of a pair of phones $Lex(x, y)$ as the number of lexical minimal pairs that vary on the first segment (xA, yA) or the last segment (Ax, Ay). The higher this number, the more the pair of phones is likely to be considered as allophonic.

The lexical cue is consistent with experimental findings. For example Feldman et al. (2013b) showed that 8 month-old infants pay attention to word level information, and demonstrated that they do not discriminate between sound contrasts that occur in minimal pairs (as suggested by our cue), and, conversely, discriminate contrasts that occur in non-minimal pairs.

3.1.2 Semantic cue

The semantic cue is based on the intuition that true minimal pairs ([kanaχ] and [kanal]) are associated with different events, whereas alternants of the same word ([kanaχ] and [kanal]) are expected to co-occur with similar events.

We operationalize the semantic cue associated with a pair of phones $Sem(x, y)$ as the average semantic similarity between all the lexical minimal pairs generated by this pair of phones. The higher the average semantic similarity, the more the learner is prone to classify them as allophonic. We take as a measure of the semantic similarity, the cosine of the angle between word vectors of the pairs that vary on the final segment $cos(\widehat{Ax, Ay})$ or the first segment $cos(\widehat{xA, yA})$.

This strategy is similar in principle to the phenomenon of *acquired distinctiveness*, according to which, pairing two target stimuli with distinct events enhances their perceptual differentiation, and *acquired equivalence*, whereby pairing two target stimuli with the same event, impairs their subsequent differentiation (Lawrence, 1949). In the same vein, Yeung and Werker (2009) tested 9 month-olds english learning infants in a task that consists in discriminating two non-native phonetic categories. They found that infants succeeded only when the categories co-occurred with two distinct visual cues.

	Segmentation						Lexicon					
	English			Japanese			English			Japanese		
Allo./phon.	F	P	R	F	P	R	F	P	R	F	P	R
2	0.61	0.57	0.65	0.45	0.44	0.47	0.29	0.42	0.22	0.23	0.54	0.15
4	0.52	0.46	0.59	0.38	0.34	0.43	0.22	0.37	0.15	0.16	0.50	0.10
10	0.51	0.45	0.59	0.34	0.30	0.38	0.21	0.34	0.16	0.16	0.41	0.10
20	0.42	0.38	0.47	0.28	0.26	0.32	0.21	0.29	0.17	0.16	0.32	0.10

Table 1 : Scores of the segmentation and the resulting lexicon, as a function of the average number of allophones per phoneme. P=Precison, R=Recall and F=F-score.

3.1.3 Combined cue

Finally, we consider the combination of both cues in one single cue where the contextual information (semantics) is used as a weighing scheme of the lexical information, as follows:

$$Comb(x,y) = \sum_{(Ax,Ay)\in L^2} cos(\widehat{Ax,Ay}) + \sum_{(xA,yA)\in L^2} cos(\widehat{xA,yA}) \quad (1)$$

where $\{Ax \in L\}$ is the set of words in the lexicon L that end in the phone x, and $\{(Ax, Ay) \in L^2\}$ is the set of phonological minimal pairs in $L \times L$ that vary on the final segment.

The lexical cue is incremented by one, for every minimal pair. The combined cue is, instead, incremented by one, times the cosine of the angle between the word vectors of this pair. When the words have similar distributions, the angle goes to zero and the cosine goes to 1, and when the words have orthogonal distributions, the angle goes to 90° and the cosine goes to 0.

The semantic information here would basically enable us to avoid false alarms generated by potential true minimal pairs like the above-mentioned example of ([kanaχ] and [kanal]). Such a pair will probably score high as far as the lexical cue is concerned, but it will score low on the semantic level. Thus, by taking the combination, the model will be less prone to mistakenly classify ([χ], [l]) as allophones.

3.2 Task

For each corpus we list all possible pairs of allophones. Some of these pairs are allophones of the same phoneme (allophonic pair) and others are allophones of different phonemes (non-allophonic pairs). The task is a same-different classification, whereby each of these pairs is given a score from the cue that is being tested. A good cue gives higher scores to allophonic pairs.

Only pairs of phones that generate at least one lexical minimal pair are considered. Phonetic variation that does not cause lexical variation is "invisible" to top down strategies, and is, therefore, more probably clustered through purely bottom up strategies (Fourtassi et al., 2014b)

3.3 Evaluation

We use the same evaluation procedure as Martin et al. (2013). This is carried out by computing the associated ROC curve (varying the z-score threshold and computing the resulting proportions of misses and false alarms). We then derive the Area Under the Curve (AUC), which also corresponds to the probability that given two pairs of phones, one allophonic, one not, they are correctly classified on the basis of the score. A value of 0.5 represents chance and a value of 1 represents perfect performance.

In order to lessen the potential influence of the structure of the corpus (mainly the order of the utterances) on the results, we use a statistical resampling scheme. The corpus is divided into small blocks of 20 utterances each (the semantic window). In each run, we draw randomly with replacement from this set of blocks a sample of the same size as the original corpus. This sample is then used to retrain the acoustic models and generate a phonetic inventory that we used to re-transcribe the corpus and re-compute the cues. We report scores averaged over 5 such runs.

4 Results and discussion

4.1 Segmentation

We first explore how phonetic variation influences the quality of the segmentation and the resulting lexicon. For the evaluation, we use the same measures as Brent (1999) and Goldwater et al. (2009), namely Segmentation Precision (P), Recall (R) and F-score (F). Segmentation precision is defined as the number of correct word tokens found, out of all tokens posited. Recall is the number of correct word tokens found, out of all tokens in the ideal segmentation. The F-score is defined as the harmonic mean of Precision and Recall:

$$F = \frac{2 * P * R}{P + R}$$

We define similar measures for word types (lexicon). Table 1 shows the scores as a function of the number of allophones per phonemes. For both corpora, the segmentation performance decreases as we increase the number of allophones. As for the lexicon, the recall scores show that only 15 to 22% of the 'words' found by the algorithm in the English corpus are real words; in Japanese, this number is even lower (between 10 and 15%). This pattern can be attributed in part to the fact that increasing the number of allophones increases the number of word forms, which occur therefore with less frequency, making the statistical learning harder. Table 2 shows the average number of word forms per word as a function of the average number of allophones per phoneme, in the case of ideal segmentation.

Allo./Phon.	W. forms/Word	
	English	Japanese
2	1.56	1.20
4	2.03	1.64
10	2.69	2.11
20	3.47	2.83

Table 2 : Average number of word-forms per word as a function of the average number of allophones per phoneme.

Another effect seen in Table 1 is the lower overall performance of Japanese compared to English. This difference was shown by Fourtassi et al. (2013) to be linked to the intrinsic segmentation ambiguity of Japanese, caused by the fact that Japanese words contain more syllables compared to English.

4.2 Allophonic vs phonemic status of sound contrasts

Here we test the performance of the cues described above, in discriminating between allophonic contrasts from phonemic ones. We vary the number of allophones per phoneme, on the one hand (Figure 2a), and the amount of data available to the learner, on the other hand, in the case of two allophones per phonemes (Figure 2b). In both situations, we compare the case wherein the lexical and semantic cues are computed on the output of the unsupervised segmentation (right), to the control case where these cues are computed on the ideally segmented speech (left).

We see that the overall accuracy of the cues is quite high, even in the case of bad word segmentation and very small amount of data.

The lexical cue is robust to extreme variation and to the scarcity of data. Indeed, it does not seem to vary monotonically neither with the number of allophones, nor with the size of the corpus. The associated f-score generally remains above the value of 0.7 (chance level is 0.5). The semantics, on the other hand, gets better as the variability decreases and as the amount of data increases. This is a natural consequence of the fact that the semantic structure is more accurate with more data and with word forms consistent enough to sustain a reasonable co-occurrence statistics.

The comparison with the ideal segmentation, shows, interestingly, that the semantics is more robust to segmentation errors than the lexical cue. In fact, while the lexical strategy performs, overall, better than the semantics under the ideal segmentation, the patterns reverses as we move to a a more realistic (unsupervised) segmentation.

These results suggest that both lexical and semantic strategies can be crucial to learning the phonemic status of phonetic categories since they provide non-redundant information. This finding is summarized by the combined cue which resists to both variation and segmentation errors, overall, better than each of the cues taken alone.

From a developmental point of view, this shows that infants can, in principle, benefit from higher level linguistic structures to refine their phonetic categories, even if these structures are rudimentary. Previous studies about top down strategies have mainly emphasized the role of word forms; the results of this work show that the semantics can be at least as useful. Note that the notion of semantics used here is weaker than the classic notion of referential semantics as in a word-concept matching. The latter might, indeed, not be fully operative at the early stages of the child development, since it requires some advanced conceptual abilities (like forming symbolic representations and understanding a speaker's referential

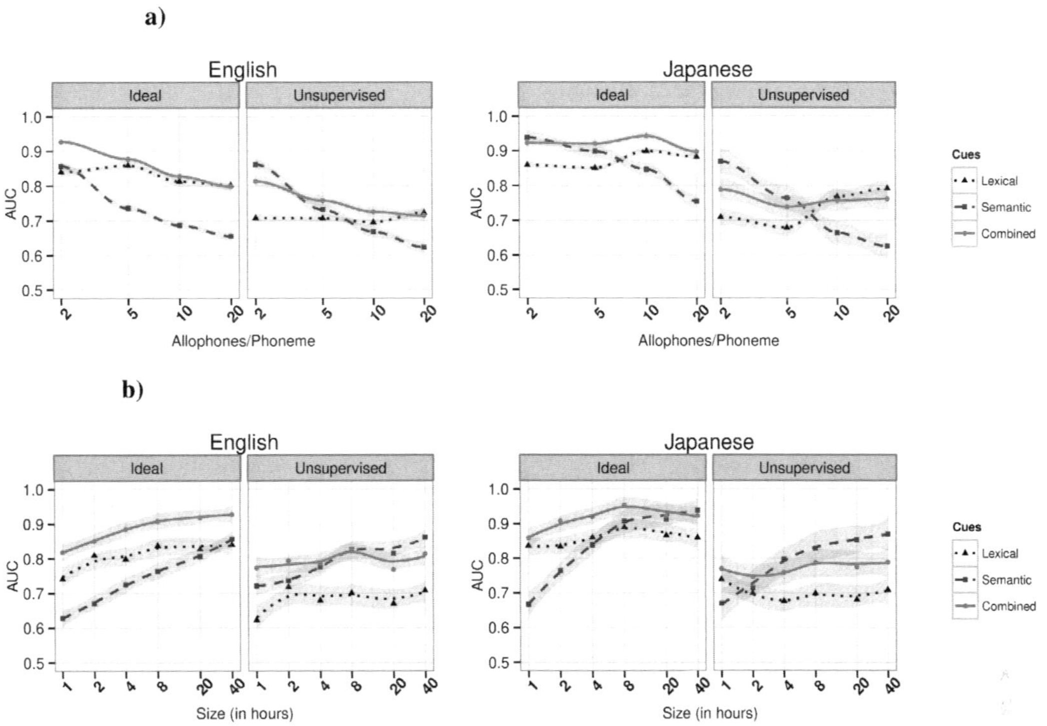

Figure 2: Same-different scores (AUC) for different cues as a function of the average number of allophones per phoneme (a), and as a function of the size of the corpus, in the case of two allophones per phonemes (b). The scores are shown for both ideal and unsupervised word segmentation in English and Japanese. The points show the mean scores over 5 runs. The lines are smoothed interpolations (local regressions) through the means. The grey band shows a 95% confidence interval.

intentions) (Waxman and Gelman, 2009). What we call the "semantics" of a word in this study, is the general context provided by the co-occurrence with other words. Infants have been shown to have a powerful mechanism for tracking co-occurrence relationships both in the speech and the visual domain (Lany and Saffran, 2013) . Our experiments demonstrate that a similar mechanism could be enough to develop a sense of semantic similarity that can successfully be used to refine phonetic categories.

5 General discussion and future work

Phonemes are abstract categories that form the basis for words in the lexicon. There is a traditional view that they should be defined by their ability to contrast word meanings (Trubetzkoy, 1939). Their full acquisition, therefore, requires lexical and semantic top-down information. However, since the quality of the semantic representations depends on the quality of the phonemic representations that are used to build the lexicon, we face a chicken-and-egg problem. In this paper, we proposed a way to break the circularity by building approximate representation at all the levels.

The infants' initial attunement to language-specific categories was represented in a way that mirrors the linguistic and statistical properties of the speech closely. We showed that this detailed (proto-phonemic) inventory enabled word segmentation from continuous transcribed speech, but, as expected, resulted in a low quality lexicon. The poorly segmented corpus was then used to derive a semantic similarity matrix between pairs of words, based on their co-occurrence statistics. The results showed that information from the derived lexicon and semantics, albeit very rudimentary, help discriminate between allophonic and phonemic contrasts, with a high degree of accuracy. Thus, this works strongly support the claim that the lexicon and semantics play a role in the refinement of the phonemic inventory (Feldman et al., 2013a; Frank et al., 2014), and, interestingly, that this role remains functional under more realistic assumptions (unsupervised word segmentation, and bottom-up inferred semantics). We also found that lexical and semantic information were not redundant and could be usefully combined, the former being more resistant to the scarcity of data and variation, and the latter being more resistant to segmentation errors.

That being said, this work relies on the assumption that infants start with initial perceptual categories (allophones), but we did not show how such categories could be constructed from raw speech. More work is needed to explore the robustness of the model when these units are learned in an unsupervised fashion (Lee and Glass, 2012; Huijbregts et al., 2011; Jansen and Church, 2011; Varadarajan et al., 2008).

This work could be seen as a proof of principle for an iterative learning algorithm, whereby phonemes emerge from the interaction of low level perceptual categories, word forms, and the semantics (see Werker and Curtin (2005) for a similar theoretical proposition). The algorithm has yet to be implemented, but it has to address at least two major issues: First, the fact that some sound pairs are not captured by top down cues because they do not surface as minimal word forms. For instance, in English, /h/ and /ŋ/ occur in different syllable positions and therefore, cannot appear in any minimal pair. Second, even if we have enough information about how phonetic categories are organized in the perceptual space, we still need to know how many categories are relevant in a particular language (i.e., where to stop the categorization process).

For the first problem, Fourtassi et al. (2014b) showed that the gap could, in principle, be filled by bottom-up information (like acoustic similarity). As for the second problem, a possible direction could be found in the notion of *Self-Consistency*. In fact, (Fourtassi et al., 2014a) proposed that an optimal level of clustering is also a level that globally optimizes the predictive power of the lexicon. Too detailed allophones result in too many synonyms. Too broad classes result in too many homophones. Somewhere in the middle, the optimal number of phonemes optimizes how lexical items predict each other. Future work will address these issues in more detail in order to propose a complete phoneme learning algorithm.

Acknowledgments

This work was supported in part by the European Research Council (ERC-2011-AdG-295810 BOOTPHON), the Agence Nationale pour la Recherche (ANR-10-LABX-0087 IEC, ANR-10-IDEX-0001-02 PSL*), the Fondation de France, the Ecole de Neurosciences de Paris, and the Région Ile de France (DIM cerveau et pensée).

References

Elika Bergelson and Daniel Swingley. 2012. At 6 to 9 months, human infants know the meanings of many common nouns. *Proceedings of the National Academy of Sciences*, 109(9).

Luc Boruta, Sharon Peperkamp, Benoît Crabbé, and Emmanuel Dupoux. 2011. Testing the robustness of online word segmentation: Effects of linguistic diversity and phonetic variation. In *Proceedings of CMCL*, pages 1–9. Association for Computational Linguistics.

Luc Boruta. 2011. Combining Indicators of Allophony. In *Proceedings ACL-SRW*, pages 88–93.

Luc Boruta. 2012. *Indicateurs d'allophonie et de phonémicité*. Doctoral dissertation, Université Paris-Diderot - Paris VII.

M. Brent. 1999. An efficient, probabilistically sound algorithm for segmentation and word discovery. *Machine Learning*, 34:71–105.

N. Feldman, T. Griffiths, S. Goldwater, and J. Morgan. 2013a. A role for the developing lexicon in phonetic category acquisition. *Psychological Review*, 120(4):751–778.

N. Feldman, B. Myers, K. White, T. Griffiths, and J. Morgan. 2013b. Word-level information influences phonetic learning in adults and infants. *Cognition*, 127:427–438.

Abdellah Fourtassi and Emmanuel Dupoux. 2013. A corpus-based evaluation method for distributional semantic models. In *51st Annual Meeting of the Association for Computational Linguistics Proceedings of the Student Research Workshop*, pages 165–171, Sofia, Bulgaria. Association for Computational Linguistics.

Abdellah Fourtassi, Benjamin Börschinger, Mark Johnson, and Emmanuel Dupoux. 2013. WhyisEnglishsoeasytosegment? In *Proceedings of CMCL*, pages 1–10. Association for Computational Linguistics.

Abdellah Fourtassi, Ewan Dunbar, and Emmanuel Dupoux. 2014a. Self-consistency as an inductive bias in early language acquisition. In *Proceedings of the 36th annual meeting of the Cognitive Science Society*.

Abdellah Fourtassi, Thomas Schatz, Balakrishnan Varadarajan, and Emmanuel Dupoux. 2014b. Exploring the Relative Role of Bottom-up and Top-down Information in Phoneme Learning. In *Proceedings of the 52nd Annual Meeting of the Association for Computational Linguistics*.

Stella Frank, Naomi Feldman, and Sharon Goldwater. 2014. Weak semantic context helps phonetic learning in a model of infant language acquisition. In *Proceedings of the 52nd Annual Meeting of the Association of Computational Linguistics*.

Judit Gervain and Jacques Mehler. 2010. Speech perception and language acquisition in the first year of life. *Annual Review of Psychology*, 61:191–218.

Sharon Goldwater, Thomas L. Griffiths, and Mark Johnson. 2009. A Bayesian framework for word segmentation: Exploring the effects of context. *Cognition*, 112(1):21–54.

Zellig Harris. 1954. Distributional structure. *Word*, 10(23):146–162.

Valerie Hazan and Sarah Barrett. 2000. The development of phonemic categorization in children aged 6 to12. *Journal of Phonetics*, 28:377–396.

James Hillenbrand, Laura A. Getty, Michael J. Clark, and Kimberlee Wheeler. 1995. Acoustic characteristics of american english vowels. *Journal of the Acoustical Society of America*, 97:3099–3109.

M. Huijbregts, M. McLaren, and D. van Leeuwen. 2011. Unsupervised acoustic sub-word unit detection for query-by-example spoken term detection. In *Proceedings of ICASSP*, pages 4436–4439.

A. Jansen and K. Church. 2011. Towards unsupervised training of speaker independent acoustic models. In *Proceedings of INTERSPEECH*, pages 1693–1696.

Aren Jansen, Emmanuel Dupoux, Sharon Goldwater, Mark Johnson, Sanjeev Khudanpur, Kenneth Church, Naomi Feldman, Hynek Hermansky, Florian Metze, Richard Rose, Mike Seltzer, Pascal Clark, Ian McGraw, Balakrishnan Varadarajan, Erin Bennett, Benjamin Borschinger, Justin Chiu, Ewan Dunbar, Abdallah Fourtassi, David Harwath, Chia ying Lee, Keith Levin, Atta Norouzian, Vijay Peddinti, Rachel Richardson, Thomas Schatz, and Samuel Thomas. 2013. A summary of the 2012 jhu clsp workshop on zero resource speech technologies and models of early language acquisition. In *Proceedings of ICASSP*.

Mark Johnson, Thomas L. Griffiths, and Sharon Goldwater. 2007. Adaptor Grammars: A framework for specifying compositional nonparametric Bayesian models. In B. Schölkopf, J. Platt, and T. Hoffman, editors, *Advances in Neural Information Processing Systems 19*, pages 641–648. MIT Press, Cambridge, MA.

Peter W Jusczyk and Richard N Aslin. 1995. Infants' detection of the sound patterns of words in fluent speech. *Cognitive psychology*, 29(1):1–23.

Thomas K Landauer and Susan T Dumais. 1997. A solution to Plato's problem: The Latent Semantic Analysis theory of acquisition, induction and representation of knowledge. *Psychological Review*, 104(2):211–240.

J. Lany and J. Saffran. 2013. Statistical learning mechanisms in infancy. In J. Rubenstein and P. Rakic, editors, *Comprehensive Developmental Neuroscience: Neural Circuit Development and Function in the Brain*, volume 3, pages 231–248. Elsevier, Amsterdam.

D.H. Lawrence. 1949. Acquired distinctiveness of cues: I. transfer between discriminations on the basis of familiarity with the stimulus. *Journal of Experimental Psychology*, 39(6):770–784.

C. Lee and J. Glass. 2012. A nonparametric bayesian approach to acoustic model discovery. In *Proceedings of the 50th Annual Meeting of the Association for Computational Linguistics: Long Papers-Volume 1*, pages 40–49.

Bogdan Ludusan, Maarten Versteegh, Aren Jansen, Guillaume Gravier, Xuan-Nga Cao, Mark Johnson, and Emmanuel Dupoux. 2014. Bridging the gap between speech technology and natural language processing: an evaluation toolbox for term discovery systems. In *Proceedings of LREC*.

Kikuo Maekawa, Hanae Koiso, Sadaoki Furui, and Hitoshi Isahara. 2000. Spontaneous speech corpus of japanese. In *LREC*, pages 947–952, Athens, Greece.

D.R. Mandel, P.W. Jusczyk, and D.B. Pisoni. 1995. Infants' recognition of the sound patterns of their own names. *Psychological Science*, 6(5):314–317.

Andrew Martin, Sharon Peperkamp, and Emmanuel Dupoux. 2013. Learning phonemes with a protolexicon. *Cognitive Science*, 37(1):103–124.

J. Maye, J. F. Werker, and L. Gerken. 2002. Infant sensitivity to distributional information can affect phonetic discrimination. *Cognition*, 82:B101–B111.

C. Ngon, A. Martin, E. Dupoux, D. Cabrol, M. Duthat, and S. Peperkamp. 2013. (non)words, (non)words, (non)words: evidence for a protolexicon during the first year of life. *Developmental Science*, 16(1):24–34.

S. Nittrouer. 1996. Discriminability and perceptual weighting of some acoustic cues to speech perception by 3-year-olds. *Journal of Speech and Hearing Research*, 39:278–297.

J. B. Pierrehumbert. 2003. Phonetic diversity, statistical learning, and acquisition of phonology. *Language and Speech*, 46(2-3):115–154.

J. Pitman and M. Yor. 1997. The two-parameter Poisson-Dirichlet distribution derived from a stable subordinator. *Annals of Probability*, 25:855–900.

M. A. Pitt, L. Dilley, K. Johnson, S. Kiesling, W. Raymond, E. Hume, and Fosler-Lussier. 2007. Buckeye corpus of conversational speech.

M Shukla, K White, and R Aslin. 2011. Prosody guides the rapid mapping of auditory word forms onto visual objects in 6-mo-old infants. *Proceedings of the National Academy of Sciences*, 108(15):6038–6043.

N. S. Trubetzkoy. 1939. *Grundzüge der Phonologie (Principles of phonology).* Vandenhoeck & Ruprecht, Göttingen, Germany.

G. K. Vallabha, J. L. McClelland, F. Pons, J. F. Werker, and S. Amano. 2007. Unsupervised learning of vowel categories from infant-directed speech. *Proceedings of the National Academy of Sciences*, 104(33):13273.

Balakrishnan Varadarajan, Sanjeev Khudanpur, and Emmanuel Dupoux. 2008. Unsupervised learning of acoustic sub-word units. In *Proceedings of ACL-08: HLT, Short Papers*, pages 165–168. Association for Computational Linguistics.

Sandra R. Waxman and Susan A. Gelman. 2009. Early word-learning entails reference, not merely associations. *Trends in Cognitive Sciences*, 13(6):258–263.

J. F. Werker and S. Curtin. 2005. PRIMIR: A developmental framework of infant speech processing. *Language Learning and Development*, 1(2):197–234.

Janet F. Werker and Richard C. Tees. 1984. Cross-language speech perception: Evidence for perceptual reorganization during the first year of life. *Infant Behavior and Development*, 7(1):49 – 63.

H Yeung and J Werker. 2009. Learning words' sounds before learning how words sound: 9-month-olds use distinct objects as cues to categorize speech information. *Cognition*, 113:234–243.

Steve J. Young, D. Kershaw, J. Odell, D. Ollason, V. Valtchev, and P. Woodland. 2006. *The HTK Book Version 3.4.* Cambridge University Press.

Author Index

Association for Computational Linguistics
209 N. Eighth Street
Stroudsburg, Pennsylvania 18360

International Conference on Historic Ships 2020

Online
2 - 3 December 2020

The Royal Institution of
Naval Architects